PEOPLE OF CHANCE

* * * * * * * * * * * * * * * * *

People of Chance

Gambling in American Society
from Jamestown to Las Vegas

* * * * * * * * * * * * * * * * *

JOHN M. FINDLAY

New York   Oxford
Oxford University Press
1986

Oxford University Press

Oxford   New York   Toronto
Delhi   Bombay   Calcutta   Madras   Karachi
Petaling Jaya   Singapore   Hong Kong   Tokyo
Nairobi   Dar es Salaam   Cape Town
Melbourne   Auckland

and associated companies in
Beirut   Berlin   Ibadan   Nicosia

Published by Oxford University Press, Inc.,
200 Madison Avenue, New York, New York 10016

Library of Congress Cataloging-in-Publication Data
Findlay, John M., 1955–
People of chance.
Bibliography: p.   Includes index.
1. Gambling—United States—History.
2. Gambling—Nevada—Las Vegas—History.   I. Title.
HV6715.F56   1986   306′.482′0973   85-21605
ISBN 0-19-503740-5

Printing (last digit): 9 8 7 6 5 4 3 2 1

Printed in the United States of America

Acknowledgments

I gratefully acknowledge the contributions of many individuals who gave their time and interest to my work.

Gunther Barth served as an inspiration from the project's beginning as a dissertation at the University of California, Berkeley. He edited and encouraged tirelessly, pushed continuously for greater insight, disciplined my way of thinking, and supported the project in ways too numerous to recount. I will always be thankful for his instruction, his advice, and his humanity.

A number of teachers, friends, and colleagues read all or part of the manuscript and commented constructively. The work benefited greatly from the close scrutiny of Jim Kettner, who offered his suggestions cheerfully and unhaltingly and made sure that his door was always open. Gene Moehring helped to ensure that the chapters on Las Vegas got off on the right foot, and the remarks of Bill Rorabaugh helped to polish the prose at a later stage. I gained from discussions with Mike Allen, Dave Bowman, and Ken McCreedy, who turned their critical eyes upon Chapter 2. Robert Dawidoff, Carolyn Grattan, James Leiby, Carol McKibben, and David Smith all offered suggestions and encouragement after reviewing the work.

Jim Bard, Colin Busby, and Larry Kobori gave employment at a critical point, introduced me to the study of Nevada, made their office supplies and equipment freely available, and brought me into contact with a supportive group of co-workers at Basin Research Associates, Inc. One of those friends, Melody Tannam, mapped Las Vegas for the book.

I am grateful for the assistance provided by the staffs at the Bancroft, Doe, and branch libraries at the University of California, Berkeley; the Special Collections at the University of Nevada, Las Vegas, and the University of Nevada, Reno; the Reno office of the Nevada Historical Society; the Las Vegas News Bureau; the libraries at Louisiana State University; the New Orleans Public Library; and the Mississippi Department of Archives and History. John Harkins, archivist for Memphis and Shelby County, Tennessee, furnished me with interesting data and reviewed the chapter on the Mississippi River frontier. Gordon Cotton, director of the Old Court House Museum in Vicksburg, Mississippi, gave me an education in both local history and southern hospitality.

I am indebted to Sheldon Meyer at Oxford University Press for betting on the manuscript and to Melissa Spielman and Pamela Nicely for their careful attention to its conversion into a book.

Relatives and friends gave unstinting aid and comfort. My parents offered loving encouragement at all times and made sure that I appreciated the rewards of learning. Lou and Jean Carter's reading of the manuscript was but one token of their support. Susan Findlay and Dan Radin helped with the typing. My siblings, my close friends, and my son, Geoffrey David, helped to place the whole matter into perspective. And my wife Linda, who participated in all phases of the process, demonstrated through her support, patience, and love that sure things truly do exist in this world.

Contents

Illustrations follow page 78.

PEOPLE OF CHANCE

Introduction

Las Vegas, Nevada, during the mid-twentieth century attested the growth of American society, its direction, and its distinctiveness. The gambling resort epitomized the restless, commercial, and middle-class orientations that made Americans a singular people. In one tourist district modeled after yesteryear and another devoted to the future, its styles evinced the borrowing as well as the innovation that had shaped American culture over the centuries, and its games typified the confident pursuit of fortune that had been the essence of so many American lives. Las Vegas gambling confirmed an insight of Alexis de Tocqueville who, one hundred years prior to the legalization of casino gaming in Nevada, had speculated on the character of the citizens of the young republic: ("Those who live in the midst of democratic fluctuations have always before their eyes the image of chance; and they end by liking all undertakings in which chance plays a part."[1])

A social history of gambling, focusing on the development of modern casino styles, indicates that the far western location of Las Vegas as index to national culture was not incidental. The qualities that identified Americans as a people of chance stood out most boldly on western frontiers where gambling tended to flourish and where distinctly American betting games emerged for the first time. The affinity between gambling and frontiers has been forceful from the time that lotteries funded the first permanent English settlement in North America to the years when Las Vegas casi-

3

nos, embodying Southern California culture, emerged as stunning new landmarks of United States civilization.

From the seventeenth century through the twentieth, both gambling and westering thrived on high expectations, risk taking, opportunism, and movement, and both activities helped to shape a distinctive culture. Like bettors, pioneers have repeatedly grasped the chance to get something for nothing—to claim free land, to pick up nuggets of gold, to speculate on western real estate. Like bettors, frontiersmen have cherished risks in order to get ahead and establish identity. Like bettors, migrants to new territories have sought to begin again in a setting that made all participants equal at the start. And whenever frontier society minimized risk or engendered inequality, curtailed enterprise or submerged individuality, Westerners could still turn to gambling to recreate those vanishing ideals on a different scale, in the same fashion that Easterners regarded the frontier as an arena to test their luck anew. Both groups were just as likely to lose at gaming as they were to see their expectations fade in the gamble of life, but in a historical perspective, the dogged pursuit of success, on the frontier or at betting tables, looms larger than success or failure itself. For a people of chance, participation in migrating and gambling counted for more than winning or losing; the game mattered more than the outcome.

Because they thrived on risk taking, western societies have been the scene of change for betting practices throughout American history. As a cultural form, American gambling moved from West to East, just as modern casino gaming appeared in Las Vegas and then reached out for Atlantic City. New types of public, commercial gambling flourished throughout the country because they reinforced values and practices that were central throughout the society, but they emerged first in frontier settings where the entrepreneurial, individualistic outlook of the people found its least diluted expression.

Westering Americans embraced virtually all forms of chance taking. They adopted and modified Old World betting practices, imparted the flavor of their distinctive societies to the games, and popularized them throughout American civilization. By the time that Frederick Jackson Turner assessed the closing of the frontier in 1893, Westerners had cultivated a native-born tradition of gambling. Then, tourists and people resettling in the Far West—the two streams of travelers who comprised the westward migration during the twentieth century—continued to shape new American ways of betting by patronizing Las Vegas casinos and building the desert resort into the nation's gaming capital. Like other westbound people, they developed unprecedented forms of gambling that Easterners ultimately accepted.

In the twentieth century, as the Far West became an increasingly fertile source of new styles and values for the entire nation, western styles of gambling became typical. Prior to 1900, however, the frontier beginnings of American styles of gambling stood out distinctly because most cultural change emanated from eastern centers of civilization. Frontier people devoted more attention to getting ahead quickly than to creating new cultural forms. Too engrossed in material pursuits and too dispersed throughout newly settled lands, they contributed little to the cultural enrichment of the United States before the twentieth century.[2] Migrants often developed expedients to tide them over until eastern civilization could be reproduced, but seldom did these devices persist as vital parts of regional, let alone national, culture.

The culture of gambling, however, was different. It thrived in the relatively fluid society on the frontier, amid footloose and acquisitive men, and continued to flourish in the urban Far West where the ambience of frontier life endured into the twentieth century. Successive Wests in the United States, populated by those engaged in resettling and pursuing fortune, provided the most productive milieu for the cultivation of novel and distinctly American betting practices. To explain such characteristically American phenomena as quarter-horse races, riverboat gamblers, or Las Vegas casinos, it is essential to understand their western origins.

In tracing the development of American gambling, the colonial and early national frontiers provide a context in which to examine the legacy of English gaming practices in North America. In the process of migrating to the wilderness of the New World, English colonists and citizens of the early republic developed a hybrid culture of gambling that illustrated the differences between their comparatively open and dispersed society and the more hierarchical and commercial civilization of Britain. Quarter-horse racing, an informal, rowdy, and backwoodsy deviation from more genteel forms of thoroughbred racing, exemplified the distinctions between gaming in America and England. So did one prominent backcountry sportsman, Andrew Jackson, who typified the adventurousness that set early American gambling apart from Britain's aristocratic styles.

In the colonies and the young republic, frontier conditions encouraged the Americanization of horse racing and lottery contests, but in the years after 1800 the West's influence on casino games, that form of public and commercial gambling that culminated in twentieth-century Las Vegas establishments, became much more pronounced. Western society did not continue to reshape substantially betting on horses and lotteries because these and related forms of gambling generally required more resources, stability, and organization than frontier people possessed. Casino games, on the other hand, run as legitimate businesses and permitted by law or convention, were ideally suited to frontier shaping. Their speed and relative portability catered to the preferences of a fluid and impatient society, and their design provided opportunities for a class of gaming operators whose livelihood remained suspect in eastern eyes. Professional gamblers thrived in the West because, rather than pay much heed to the established custom of more settled places, they changed the nature of games to suit the styles of western customers, and thus contributed to the modification of American styles of betting.

In the United States, many commercial casino games were initially played on a large scale during the early nineteenth century. In the frontier society of the lower Mississippi River Valley, a mixture of Spanish, French, Southern, and pioneer influences, compounded with the perpetual fluidity of life along the river, comprised a most fertile field for the sprouting of these new American modes of betting. First in river towns between New Orleans and St. Louis, and then aboard a multitude of steamboats, a class of professional gamblers cultivated gaming as a business venture. These entrepreneurs demonstrated that new forms of betting emerged most quickly when they were played for profit in frontier settings.

Developments on colonial and nineteenth-century frontiers illustrated Americans' longstanding ambivalence toward gambling. Because of the risky and transient nature of life on the frontier, gambling in the open gained an acceptance that it lacked in settled places. People back East certainly bet, too, but never quite so publicly or adventurously as Westerners. In fact, reckless gaming became so synonymous with frontier settings that when successive waves of Westerners set out to bring their societies into line with eastern standards, they frequently turned first against gambling. English colonists and southern gentlemen encumbered the activity with restriction and ritual. Later on, the people of Vicksburg, Mississippi, and residents of other emerging settlements sought respectability by lynching professional gamblers, so closely did some of them identify wide-open betting with the instability and disorder of the frontier.

The purging of professional gamblers from the old Southwest prevented them neither from introducing organized gambling to syndicates in eastern cities nor from transporting the business to the Far West during the last half of the century. Gambling flourished again on the mining frontier, the most speculative of all American Wests, taking particularly strong root in the golden city of San Francisco and the Silver State of Nevada.

Since the mid-nineteenth century, California has been the American source of new forms of casino gaming. The flux and hazard that typified frontier living never really diminished there as much as in earlier western societies aspiring to be yet another East. Continued migration perpetuated in California the westering mentality, the fondness for risk and change, well into the twentieth century. Restless and ambitious individuals who accepted chance taking as a way of life populated the Pacific Coast. They continued their lives' gamble with the Gold Rush, and then branched out to speculate on mining stocks, land, railroads, and scenery. As site of a pattern of economic growth that erased the memory of boom and bust with another boom, and as destination for migrants bearing high expectations to a land of promise, the state fostered an acquisitive, impatient outlook that heightened the urge to gamble.

As the ultimate American West and as the modern fountain of new gambling practices, California passed through two cultural phases. Before 1900 the state, like other frontier areas, was a cultural backwater of eastern civilization. Californians looked to the East for social standards and national approval. Their dependence on more established centers of culture was symbolized by the transcontinental railroad, which fettered the state to eastern ways of life and business, and made San Francisco the center of Atlantic Coast civilization in the West.

During the twentieth century, in a remarkably short span of time, California developed from outpost of eastern civilization into cultural pacesetter for the country. It seemed as if the depleted, westbound wave of culture, now broken upon the shores of the Pacific, gave way quickly to a strong undertow that swept aspects of a new California civilization eastward to the other states of the union. The metropolis of this indigenous culture was not San Francisco but Los Angeles, with its character determined not by emulation of eastern standards but by the unique adaptation of the growing and affluent population to new styles and technologies sustaining unprecedented ways of life.

A new far western culture burst into bloom when Californians, now less concerned with eastern precedents, turned eagerly to embrace forward-looking changes that promised to realize the vision of the good life that had attracted so many Americans to the Pacific Coast. By accepting cultural advances so wholeheartedly, residents of the Golden State created a new kind of society, a civilization for a postindustrial age, that foreshadowed the nation's tomorrow. As the seat of futuristic change, Los Angeles, once heralded by Mexicans as the preeminent settlement in Alta California before the discovery of gold directed a flood of newcomers to San Francisco, at long last became the leading city in the state. It simultaneously assumed the lead in generating new fashions of betting.

The Golden State's shaping of American gambling paralleled its cultural development. Gold Rush Californians, living the epitome of the nation's westering experience, initially seized upon betting as an integral part of frontier society. They cherished the risks and the thrills offered by "gambling saloons" such as those clustered at the city center of young San Francisco, where Argonauts heading to and from the mines stopped to try their luck. Nothing better summarized the restlessness and adventure of the first far western mining frontier than the play at these early clubs, where crowds gathered nightly to challenge fate at games more public and commercial than ever before. When Californians departed for other strikes on the Pacific slope, they took their characteristic brands of speculation with them, proving time and again that they "were essentially a gambling people."[3]

Early Californians lived intimately with gaming until eastern standards overwhelmed them. Then, although they continued to recognize chance as a necessary ingredient of their lives, they increasingly distinguished between respectable and unrespectable forms of risk taking. They naturally continued to share in both kinds of adventure, but the state slowly outlawed public and commercial gambling and drove away illicit operators. To enjoy the styles of betting that they had cultivated, Californians either resorted more and more to illegal clubs or traveled beyond the boundaries of the state.

The urge to gamble remained strong in the Far West, and by the midtwentieth century Californians found it most convenient to satisfy this urge across the state line in Las Vegas, a city shaped extensively by the tastes of the Los Angeles residents who made up the majority of its visitors. Californians had finally isolated gambling from their daily lives by moving it to Nevada, but not before they remade the practice to suit emerging styles. As gambling resort and as residential city, modern Las Vegas assumed a prominent place on the eastbound cultural frontier that originated in Southern California. On Nevada soil suited for the cultivation of legal and open gambling, Las Vegas became a place where the outlines of the new California civilization blossomed for all the country to see.

As with cars, movies, and tract homes, Southern Californians popularized and commercialized, mass-produced and mass-consumed gambling in the casinos of southern Nevada, and so included the practice in the novel culture they transmitted to the rest of the nation. In Las Vegas, the California style of gambling dramatized the character of Pacific Coast civilization in the postindustrializing age. Casino betting provided players with a condensed dose of the chance, change, and anticipation that exemplified life in a golden land of opportunity, and offered a streamlined version of the cultural forms taking shape in Southern California. It was promoted to average Americans not only in the same fashion as films and suburban living and automobility, but also as a related kind of experience.

In Las Vegas visitors encountered a bit of Hollywood and a bit of Disneyland, a bit of Beverly Hills and a bit of the Sunset Strip. The resort city catered to Southern California's fondness for glamour and fantasy, affluence and movement. Moreover, casinos ensured that, like cars, movies, and tract homes, gambling was available to everyman. In short, gambling in southern Nevada distilled for vacationers from across the land those aspects of Southern California culture that made the Far West a pacesetter for American society.

At the same time that Las Vegas illuminated the direction of rapid cultural change, it also registered the tribute that such change demanded. If Southern California's outpost in Nevada presaged the future, it became increasingly clear after midcentury that the future had its limits, that the westering process perhaps had an end after all. Again, legal casino gaming only condensed and highlighted in Las Vegas the senses of constraint and malaise present in the Los Angeles basin. Along the Las Vegas Strip and in the downtown Casino Center, the gambling business tended to be dominated by rigid formulas that standardized the design of hotels and casinos and maximized the volume of players, suggesting that postindustrial developments yet required greater imagination.

As the future came to be packaged like a gambling vacation, residents of Los Angeles and Las Vegas experienced doubts about the prospect of tomorrow. In both places simple growth and perpetual mobility were partially responsible for a strained sense of community, but tensions stemmed as well from the novel styles of living that shaped both cities. In the desert metropolis, gambling served to intensify the rootless and atomistic character of society. Those urbanites who styled themselves Las Vegans nurtured an individualistic ethos for city living, enshrined the privacy of autos and single-family houses as essential for the good life, and turned inward from the risks of the gambling capital. They thus built a hometown that could protect them from the bettor and the tourist, but their responses to the proximity of gambling, and to the boomtown conditions, increased the fragmentation of community rather than reducing it. The future that Las Vegas represented was hardly a sure thing.

Like Americans on earlier frontiers, residents of Las Vegas proved ambivalent about betting, but more than previous Westerners, they found themselves living with gambling and its trappings. At first they tried to limit the prevalence of betting by subordinating it to the idea of the last frontier, a theme chosen to characterize life in the Silver State and promote Nevada to tourists. But during and after the Second World War, Las Vegans reoriented themselves quickly from old West to ultimate West, from Nevada to California, and appealed much more successfully to tourists from the Pacific slope and around the nation. Accepting gambling and its social consequences as facts of life, they built an urban resort, with gaming as its central feature, that expressed the growing influence of the Far West on American culture. Both as last frontier and as new frontier, Las Vegas capsulized the relationship between gambling and the American West.

The restless and shifting populations of Las Vegas and Los Angeles lived in a fashion that recalled the western societies that had remade American gaming prior to the twentieth century. The two cities marked the culmination of the frontier. Both exemplified the relatively loosely knit social order that had always set West apart from East; both reflected the characteristic mentality of westering people. These twentieth-century communities demonstrated that as social process and as set of attitudes, the frontier concept retains historical usefulness.

As a focus for social history, gambling limits the range of frontier people that receive discussion. Betting belonged primarily within the sphere of men rather than women for most of American history. It depended heavily on the influences of various ethnic groups; many changes were advanced by those with greater exposure to European or Latin American precedents. The cultural progress of gaming took place primarily on relatively "cosmopolitan" frontiers, backcountries that maintained strong ties to centers of civilization, rather than on "insular" frontiers, which were more remote from the parent culture.[4] The closer ties between these "gamblers' frontiers" and the East helped to explain why new developments in forms of gambling were transmitted eastward with the same efficiency that eastern culture was transmitted westward.

Similarly, as the background for the gambling to be analyzed, the frontier experience recommends an anthropological view of American gaming. The following chapters regard gambling not as an aspect of abnormal psychology, although for some people betting is a destructive addiction, but rather as a practice within the usual range of human behavior. From the perspective of social history, the kinds of gambling that culminated in twentieth-century Las Vegas, functioning as representative and often accepted practices in American culture, helped to shape the movement, identity, and outlook of a people of chance.

1

Adventurers

The Colonial and Early National Frontiers

As the new year of 1612 dawned over London, the officers of the Virginia Company fretted about their plantation in the New World. Reports from Jamestown continued to betray the glorious hopes once raised for North American settlement. The company, after sinking hundreds of men and thousands of pounds into that death trap in the wilderness, had realized nary a dividend on its investment. Far from achieving self-sufficiency, the colony still depended utterly on a tenuous lifeline across the Atlantic that supplied provisions and replacements for dying settlers. Desperately seeking funds to keep the project going, the leaders of the debt-ridden company also searched for an explanation of the predicament. They might have held themselves to account for poor planning, inadequate financing, and unrealistic expectations, but they tended to assign most of the responsibility for failure to the colonists in Jamestown.

While the company had only itself to blame for the low caliber of men that it had sent to the Chesapeake, it was justified in pointing out the shortcomings of the early settlers. As with the unsuccessful experiment at Sagadahoc on the coast of Maine in 1607–1608, the initial English population in Virginia proved largely unfit for colonizing the New World. Misled by expectations of a life of ease in North America, and demoralized by the strangeness and deadliness of the place, the colonists did less than was necessary to survive. Captain John Smith recalled that many were "devoted to pure idlenesse" at the beginning, and Gabriel Archer, upon arriving at Jamestown in mid-1609, decided that "Idleness and other vices" were primarily responsible for the inability of the colony to sustain itself.[1]

Among the vices naturally associated with idleness was gambling. The frontier settlement earned a reputation for gaming that endured at least into the 1630s and 1640s, when Englishmen living along the James River reportedly wagered their indentured servants in gambling contests. The vice came to be particularly condemned, however, during the first fifteen years of Jamestown, when it appeared to contribute to the failure of the plantation. The Lawes Divine, Morall and Martiall, codified between 1610 and 1612, provided specific and serious penalties for the most threatening kinds of betting, and foreshadowed the other antigambling ordinances that soon followed.[2]

At the same time that company officials tried to check gaming and other idle practices in Virginia in an effort to secure returns on their investment, they resorted to the gambling spirit of Englishmen in order to provide a sounder financial footing for the American plantation. The third charter of the Virginia Company of London, granted by the Crown in 1612, not only extended the boundaries of the colony to include Bermuda and encouraged additional investment by making the firm a full-fledged joint-stock company, but also permitted the privilege of holding lotteries to raise money for the colonial venture.

Lotteries had long been familiar to Europeans on the Continent, but to Englishmen they remained novelties as late as 1612. Queen Elizabeth authorized the first official raffle in 1566 in order to finance harbor improvements, but Britons' unfamiliarity with the method of gaming limited the success of early lotteries. When James I allowed the Virginia Company to conduct the contests, it was still among the very first such authorizations in English history. Yet, this new mode of raising capital was quite appropriate for planting a settlement in the New World. Participants in both speculations were aptly termed "adventurers," and for both the colonists in Jamestown and the ticketholders in England, prospects for success were not very good.[3]

Anxious to restore credibility to their sagging enterprise, the officers of the Virginia Company wasted no time in staging lotteries. Between 1612 and 1615 they conducted four raffles in London. Three were standing lotteries in which all tickets were sold before prizes were awarded; the other, a running lottery, offered instant gratification as a participant learned of his fate immediately upon purchasing a ticket. From the outset, problems plagued the contests, or "schemes," and compelled the company to struggle to make its privilege profitable. A lack of interest or trust among Londoners forced postponements of the drawings in the three standing lotteries, and sponsors heard complaints about the high price of tickets. After a couple of delays, the completion of the First Great Standing Lottery, in which a London tailor won the grand prize of "foure thousand crownes in fayre plate, which was sent to his house in very stately manner," reaffirmed the honorable intentions of the company, but regardless of all efforts interest in the schemes continued to lag. Despite other inducements offered to prospective adventurers, enthusiasm in the city steadily diminished. In 1615 the company sent running lotteries to the smaller towns and counties of England, and for the next five years the traveling contests enjoyed some success.[4]

The company toiled to overcome the lethargic response to its ventures. It enlisted the support of the Privy Council, the mayor of London, town aldermen, and county officials. It appealed to livery companies and implored churches to purchase tickets. The Virginia Company also beckoned to the English gentry, a relatively new source of capital for overseas expansion.[5]

Knights had begun to subscribe increasingly to colonizing projects after 1600 and formed a substantial portion of the backers of the Virginia plantation. Now they were asked to participate in lotteries as well. The gentry were not typical adventurers, however. They invested not so much to improve their fortunes by winning prizes, making money, or settling in the New World, but rather to enhance their status by following the example of great noblemen and government leaders already committed to financing overseas colonies.[6] Knights' motives in subscribing to the Virginia Company and its lotteries exemplified the attitude toward gambling that set aristocrats apart from adventurers. Gentlemen invested more to establish rank than to experience the thrill of chance or the pleasure of winning.

Officers of the Virginia Company, in many cases gentry themselves, touted their lotteries in a fashion that appealed to the interests of knights. They paid less attention to the limited prospect of profit than to the honor and dignity of British empire. Such a promotional emphasis pleased gentlemen who had subscribed less for personal fortune than to demonstrate noble commitment to a national undertaking. At all times the company identified both the colony and the lottery with the greater glory of the country by promising that "so worthie an enterprise" would enhance "the Christian truth, the honor of our nation, & benefite of English people."[7] A ballad composed in 1612 to encourage participation appealed to people of every social position to enter the patriotic contest:

> Let no man thinke that he shall loose,
>   though he no Prize poscesse:
> His substaunce to Virginia goes,
>   which God, no doubt will blesse:
> And in short time send from that land,
>   much rich commoditie;
> So shall we thinke all well bestowd,
>   upon this Lotterie.

> Heere profite doth with pleasure joyne,
> and bids each chearefull heart,
> To this high praysed enterprise,
> performe a Christian part. . . .[8]

The colonists at Jamestown exported far too little "rich commoditie" to vindicate the company's promises about the progress of the plantation, however, and the lotteries generated far less "profite" and "pleasure" than were needed. All the revenues raised by the schemes went immediately to meet the debts of the Virginia Company and restock the settlement in the New World. Living hand to mouth, the proprietors became dependent on the lottery as their only reliable source of capital for replenishing company coffers. In 1621 John Smith described the raffles as "the real and substantiall food, by which Virginia hath been nourished," referring to the men and provisions that had been shipped to the Chesapeake with funds raised through lotteries.[9] The contests had kept both company and colony afloat during the second decade of the seventeenth century.

No doubt because the proprietors relied so heavily on the lottery, they made the device a "general nuisance to the kingdom."[10] Since 1612 the Virginia Company's schemes had attracted plenty of unfavorable criticism. Charges of fraud and mismanagement sullied the reputation of the firm, and concern about the disruptive impact of the raffles on the lower classes added to the dissatisfaction. Even within the company the lottery came under attack. Although most shareholders had to admit that the company possessed no means of support besides the contests, some doubted that lotteries were suitable for furthering such a lofty project as a plantation in the New World. Spaniards had felt similarly since 1612 as they kept close watch over English settlement in territory they claimed. If it had to be maintained by such "a generall kynde of begging" as a lottery, Spanish observers surmised, the plantation in Virginia was surely doomed to failure.[11]

Critics of the lotteries accelerated their attack in 1620 and 1621. In the midst of a nationwide economic slump, townspeople complained about interruptions to trade and industry and worried about agitating "the Common sort." Parliament, unhappy that it had never approved the privilege granted to the proprietors, asserted that all Englishmen had been "drayned" for the benefit of a private company. In *A Plain Pathway to Plantations* (1624), Richard Eburne questioned the manner in which revenues from the lotteries had been spent and recalled that the raffles had "robbed the country of her money wonderfully."[12] Finally, at the request of the House of Commons, the Crown banned any additional lotteries on March 8, 1621. King James I explained that he had never wholeheartedly approved of the schemes, but granted the privilege because of the company's predicament. Now that the Virginia plantation needed lotteries more than before, however, the royal proclamation depicted them as a growing "inconuenience, to the hinderance of multitudes of Our Subjects."[13]

His Majesty's prohibition demonstrated to the proprietors of Virginia how deeply they had come to rely on lotteries. The "soddaine suppressing" of the contests nudged the company over the brink of collapse.[14] Much of its assets had been converted to silver plate to be paid out as prizes for winning tickets, and now the plate had to be sold at a loss in order to cover ever-mounting debts. The company had also lost its only dependable source of revenue, and so began its headlong slide into bankruptcy. As enemies picked the firm apart between 1622 and 1624, the Virginia lotteries, with their alleged frauds, mismanagement, and misappropriation of Englishmen's money, were mentioned repeatedly as additional reasons to dismember the joint-stock concern.[15] Having lost both its financial underpinnings and the good will of Englishmen, the company was dissolved in 1624, and the Virginia venture was placed upon a different footing.

In several ways the lotteries typified the English experience in Virginia during the early seventeenth century. They embodied the hope as well as the despair, the promotion as well as the criticism that surrounded colonization. They also illustrated the failure of both the company and the settlers between 1607 and 1624 to create a self-supporting plantation in the New World. Although the raffles did help to sustain the colony so that it narrowly avoided the fates of Roanoke and Sagadahoc, the story of the lotteries, for the most part, constituted an all too familiar chapter in the unsteady course of early English settlement in the Chesapeake region.

In a broader perspective, the risk taking inherent in the lotteries, and the gaming so common in Jamestown, paralleled the chance undertaken in the larger enterprise of the movement across the Atlantic and into a new continent. Setting precedents for Europeans and Americans who followed, the early colonists in Virginia were among the very first to take the gamble that came to be known as the westward migration of English-speaking people in North America. The lottery, accompanying pioneers to the initial American frontier, symbolized the gambling spirit that has characterized the American West. Whether seventeenth-century colonizers for the Virginia Company or twentieth-century vacationers in Las Vegas casinos, westering peoples have been adventurers.

The English colonies comprised the first in a series of American Wests where the affinity between gambling and the frontier stood out boldly. The experience of migration has continually likened the pioneer to the bettor. On the frontier as well as at gaming tables, Westerners found opportunities to get something for nothing, and held high expectations about prospects for success. In both cases, win or lose, the direct exposure to chance and change tested people's character and made the risk taking worthwhile for its own sake.

The adventurous outlook of westward migrants made the frontier an ideal breeding ground for distinctly American forms of gambling, and the footloose and dispersed nature of western settlement encouraged new gaming practices. As a result of the frontier's shaping, new American styles of betting emerged and ultimately came to be accepted by Easterners.

Native-born gambling was cultivated not simply on the frontier, moreover, but in a series of Wests that shaped the new styles differently. Each indigenous betting practice evolved during a specific time as well as in a distinct setting, and consequently reflected the dynamic culture of the frontier on which it appeared. Emerging forms of gambling provided a measure of the changing character of successive western societies and an index to the relationship between the East and the West.

Styles of gambling that developed on the British imperial frontier in North America during the seventeenth and eighteenth centuries illuminated the divergence of colonial culture from the mainstream of English civilization. The difference had been foreshadowed by participants in the early colonization of Virginia. On one shore of the Atlantic, adventurers strove to gain a foothold on the new continent; on the other side, gentlemen speculated in order to enhance their genteel status. In England, thoroughbred racing suited noble tastes, while in the American backcountry quarter-horse racing developed to meet the needs of the common man on the frontier. In the mother country, large-scale lotteries financed national government, while in the colonies local lotteries helped to build a new society. This dichotomy between East and West contributed to the emergence of a distinctive style of gaming that persisted in America over the next two hundred years.

As the first in a series of Wests, the English colonies cultivated new forms of betting that typified the adventurousness of migration into an unknown continent. They also expressed an uncertainty toward the practice of gambling that stood the test of time as well. Americans' ambivalence toward gambling could be traced back to late Tudor and Stuart England. In fact, one could have detected it in the Crown's authorization of the Virginia lotteries in 1612 and its prohibition of the same nine years later.

People have felt uncertain about gaming throughout the ages, but this ambivalence gained significance in the English world of the late sixteenth and seventeenth centuries as it was absorbed by a larger debate over the proper nature of leisure and recreation. The two sides of the argument, which can with simplification be labeled puritanism and "Merrie England," became clearest on the western shores of the Atlantic during the first century of English settlement in North America. There, differences were expressed geographically as entire colonies came to be established along the guidelines of one side or the other. The wilderness served as a stage upon which colonists rehearsed competing scripts of English attitudes toward gambling and recreation. The founders of New England and Pennsylvania viewed the New World as an opportunity to recast society entirely, incorporating puritan attitudes toward gaming and play. The other colonies, led by Virginia, mostly tried to adopt traditional English attitudes toward gaming and recreation.

Conventional notions of gambling in Tudor-Stuart Britain illustrated the nature of leisure in a prevalently agricultural society, dominated by aristocrats but increasingly capitalistic as well. With that sense of time peculiar to preindustrial cultures in European civilization, popular recreations followed the rhythms of the rich calendar of holidays as well as the seasons of agrarian life. The discipline of industrialism had not yet strictly separated time for play from time for work; limitations on recreation derived instead from the hierarchical nature of society. Statutes limited gaming among commoners to the twelve days of Christmas, thereby reserving the practice to the monied classes for the rest of the year, but like most anti-gambling laws these proved virtually impossible to enforce. Lawmakers also sought to minimize the undesired side effects of gaming, such as military unpreparedness, rioting, fighting, and other disorders, but they did not really attack gambling itself. The Englishman's right to enjoy "lawful recreations" was never much in dispute, save among Puritans.[16] The Stuart kings acted often to protect customary forms of popular recreation and preserve the conventional balance between work and play.

Within this traditional context of recreation, gambling flourished between 1580 and 1640. The apparent increase in gaming mirrored the growth of a mercantile society. A rising tide of affluence permitted more Englishmen to participate in games generally dominated by the monied strata of society. Perhaps even more significant were new notions of making money. While Puritans may have derived a more ascetic message from the imperatives of capitalism, most Englishmen felt encouraged to gamble by "the growing legitimacy of using capital to accrue profit and the increasingly speculative nature of many purely economic transactions."[17] The trend toward heavier play became particularly notable among nobility, which, partly in an effort to live conspicuously, gambled more deeply, or at least more visibly, than ever before. Aristocrats joined in "gambling orgies" at the Stuart court, thus identifying themselves with the increasingly unpopular Crown and helping to provoke the disfavor of Puritans and country squires.[18]

The picture of peers of the realm dissipating in the royal household doubtless nettled the English revolutionaries of the mid-seventeenth century. The saints addressed the situation when they took power from the king, but controls imposed on gambling during the Interregnum merely served to popularize the practice after the Restoration. The courts of Charles II and James II set an unbridled pace for the rest of the country as Englishmen resumed betting where they had left off at the outbreak of revolution. Abundant gambling earned for the period a reputation of license and "exceptional depravity."[19] Courtiers viewed gambling as evidence of proper breeding and adopted the genteel sport of cockfighting as the most preferred game. Encouraged by the aristocracy, the passion spread to all layers of society. Even women joined the wagering crowds at court, much to the dismay of social critics inclined to defend female "Honour": "when the Fair one can't the Debt defray,/ In Sterling Coin, does Sterling Beauty pay."[20]

A voice of reason during the age helped to mediate between gamblers and their critics. In *The Compleat Gamester* (1674), Charles Cotton argued that people needed recreation and suggested that each individual ought to pursue that pastime most enjoyable to him, "for what to one is most pleasant, to another is most offensive." Cotton found gambling as useful as any other recreation, but warned that it presented pitfalls for the unwary. One was immoderation. A bettor invited perpetual dissatisfaction by playing too hungrily, for he could never win enough and would always lose too much. Moreover, excessive gambling brought the "disreputation of being a gamester"; "if you lose not your estate, you will certainly lose your credit and good name, than which there is nothing more valuable." Professional gamesters, or cardsharps and cheaters, comprised another evil. Those "rooks," "wolves," and "rogues" endangered all that was honorable about gambling by turning the innocent pastime into a profession that profited from deceit and depravity.[21]

Increasing concern about professional gamblers resulted in part from the swelling ranks of sharpers and cheaters, but it also grew out of a larger effort to regularize sport. As bettors during the seventeenth century staked more and more money on horse races, cockfights, and card games, they sought to protect their wagers from irregular play and uncertain procedure by developing firm guidelines. One historian notes that the "regulation of games grew up not from noble motives of 'fair play,' but to protect the financial investments of gamblers."[22] The increase in gaming thus heightened the importance of rules. An expanding body of regulations came to govern the turf, and a series of works such as Cotton's *Compleat Gamester* and Edmond Hoyle's *Short Treatise on the Game of Whist* (1742) taught readers how to play betting games properly and to detect cheating. This regularizing of games stemmed in turn from the even broader process of "the commercialisation of leisure" in England.[23] More widespread and heavier betting was in fact the first step by which sport became a business, but the organizing impetus of capitalism could be detected in all the forms of leisure—theater, literature, horse racing—that characterized Merrie England. The rise of professional "gamesters," or sharps and cheats, accompanied the rise of a mercantile society that transformed virtually all traditional recreations in the late seventeenth and eighteenth centuries.

The regularization and commercialization of gaming did not console Puritans; nor were they satisfied with royal edicts intended to curb the unwanted side effects of gambling without condemning the practice itself. They contended that gaming was not only sinful in itself but also served as "a doore and a window" into all sorts of ungodly behavior.[24] Moreover, while most Englishmen naturally followed the nobility in deriving encouragement to gamble from the emerging economic culture, Puritans incorporated the ideas of capitalism into a more self-denying, and hence more self-righteous, mode of thinking. Their perspective came to be identified with the "urban bourgeoisie."[25]

The saints associated diversions that involved betting with both pagan ungodliness and idleness. In England Puritans objected to popular recreations like gaming because they violated Sabbatarian principles. Sins like gambling were doubly condemned because they profaned the Lord's day. Puritans held that an introspective abstinence from both play and work would constitute the best method of eliminating ungodly diversions on the Sabbath. In the saints' distinctive mixture of capitalism and Calvinism, the obverse of keeping Sundays sacred, of course, was to work intently the other six days of the week. Puritans wanted to abandon all rural festivals as well as the paganlike Saints' days and holidays that appeared on traditional Catholic calendars. They held May-games in especially strong contempt, not only for their yearly idleness but also for the drunkenness and bastardy that called to mind the saturnalia and bacchanalia of ancient Rome.[26] Similarly, the Puritans' aversion to celebrating Christmas was no doubt stiffened by the gambling that with lawful sanction flourished during the Yuletide.[27]

A minority in England, Puritans had little success in implementing their ideas about gaming and recreation. Without much hope of transforming English society, they turned to the New World where they saw a wilderness in which a model society might be erected without hindrance from tradition. The American frontier constituted the best environment, they believed, for achieving ideals that could hardly be realized clearly in England. Indeed, the Puritans' lack of success in changing the homeland may help to explain why in such New England towns as Plymouth and Boston, colonists proved so vigilant at protecting their exemplary settlements in the New World.

The puritan indictment of traditional recreations was transported across the Atlantic and served with a vengeance at Ma-re Mount.[28] Thomas Morton's company threatened the saints as a rival claimant to territory in New England, as a provider of arms to local Indians, and as a superior competitor in the fur trade, but the renegade plantation also offended puritan notions of leisure and recreation. In 1627 Morton and his young, lonely male followers proclaimed a yearly holiday on the first of May, erected a maypole to celebrate the founding of Ma-re Mount, and asked neighboring Indians, especially the women, to join the festivities. In sum, Morton's corps of adventurers proposed to resurrect the traditional English festivities of May Day, replete with all sorts of promiscuous revel, in North America. By transplanting a pagan celebration to the pristine New World, and by inviting heathen natives, who were known to the saints as unrepentant gamblers, Morton and his followers challenged all puritan strictures on play.

The holy experiments at Plymouth and Massachusetts Bay could not tolerate Morton and Ma-re Mount in their midst. The Pilgrims, led by Miles
Standish, took the first action by imprisoning Thomas Morton and extradit-
ing him to England in 1628. Morton, an Anglican lawyer with good connections, quickly disposed of the groundless charges against him and
returned to New England to torment the Puritans once more. This time the
"grizzly saints" of Massachusetts Bay, led by John Endecott, burned Ma-re
Mount to the ground, confiscated the renegades' corn and pelts, arrested
Morton again, and shipped him back to England. Having broken no law,
Thomas Morton once again escaped punishment and returned to New
England, but his effort to reproduce in the New World "Revels, & merrie-
ment after the old English custome" was finished.[29] The suppression of Ma-
re Mount preserved for at least a short while the predominance of puritan
attitudes toward play in New England.

Saintly opposition to popular English recreations also took shape in statutes enacted in the New World against gambling. The leaders of Massachusetts Bay Colony promulgated laws that discouraged gaming through minor
punishments. The regulations first prohibited ownership of betting imple-
ments like cards and dice and forbade participation in public games, then
banned gambling in private homes and outlawed horse racing in towns or
on commonly used roads. Lawmakers gave many reasons for the ordinances—to prevent "much waste of Wine and Beer," to forestall "the
corup[t]ing of youth with other sad consequences," and to prevent "hazard" to the "Limbs and Lives" of racehorse riders—that indicated concern
about the disruptive side effects of gambling.[30] However, two overriding
arguments against sinfulness stood out as the bases for outlawing gaming.
One hinged on the problem of idleness, the other on the profaning of God.

Puritans viewed idleness as a vice because it signified the "misspence of
pretious time." "Every man's Eternity in another world," warned Increase
Mather, "will be according to his improvement of time here."[31] In com-
pliance with inflexible Sabbatarianism, Puritans devoted the six weekdays
to individuals' "particular Callings," and Sundays to worship and abstinence from play and work. Gaming simply had no place within this
crowded week. Moreover, the aversion to idleness assumed even more
importance in early New England because of the primitive and unfamiliar
environment. Idleness endangered physical as well as spiritual survival in
frontier lands, as settlers in Jamestown had already discovered.[32]

As the wilderness began to recede, as second and third generations
replaced the first Puritan settlers, and as Massachusetts Bay grew more prosperous during the later seventeenth century, the colonists apparently
became less concerned about idleness. Opponents of gaming, however,
still had another, more enduring line of reasoning. Gambling, they argued,
was akin to taking the Lord's name in vain; both were appeals to God to
pass judgment on insignificant events. Perry Miller explained that for Puritans any game of chance "prostituted divine providence to unworthy ends.

Lotteries are appeals to providence, said Increase Mather, and so they 'may not be used in trivial matters.' God determines the cast of the dice or the shuffle of the cards, and we are not to implicate His providence in frivolity."[33] Like swearing, gambling debased the Lord by dragging Him into the petty vices of men.

As strong as these arguments must have appeared to seventeenth-century colonists in New England, they were not always effective. By 1670 gambling had increased markedly in Massachusetts, particularly among the lower classes.[34] The growth of gaming, a consequence of increasing social diversity after the first generation, came to be regarded as a sign of declension. Quakers experienced a like fate as they tried to found the colony of Pennsylvania with similar regulations against gaming. Basing their restrictions upon Sabbatarian ideals, an aversion to idleness, an attachment to the godly life, and an apprehensiveness about the disruptive effects of gaming on society, the followers of William Penn tried to prohibit betting between 1682 and 1740 through a series of "blue laws." The statutes proved somewhat successful among the relatively homogeneous settlers of the early colony, but as the population grew more diverse after 1715, gambling became more common. The Friends were also thwarted by the continuing opposition of English monarchs and Privy Councils to saintly limitations on gaming. The Crown objected not only to the colony's ban of lotteries, which interfered with the sale of English tickets in Pennsylvania, but also to Quaker laws against traditional pastimes like cockfights, card games, and stage plays, which all the King's subjects had a right to enjoy.[35]

Both Puritans and Quakers had perceived the wilderness of seventeenth-century North America as untainted soil in which to cultivate model societies rooted in religious principles. Settling in the New World, they hoped to leave behind the aristocratic traditions that plagued England and establish instead more lofty guidelines for conducting life. The saintly colonizers did not initially reckon with the disruptive forces, from both within and without, that undermined the purity of new societies. Infections like Morton of Ma-re Mount could easily be cured in the early years of settlement, but as time passed the immunity of Massachusetts and Pennsylvania to gambling diminished in the face of growth and diversity inside the colonies as well as royal protests from across the Atlantic.

Although doomed to decline, however, these holy experiments succeeded for much of the seventeenth and eighteenth centuries in upholding saintly attitudes toward leisure and recreation and preserving sanctions against such practices as gambling and cockfighting. The degree to which these colonies challenged conventional patterns of play can be measured by contrasting them with early Virginia, Maryland, New York, and South Carolina, where settlers generally adhered to traditional notions of popular recreation.[36] In the seventeenth century, Virginians led the way in transplanting traditional English pastimes to the New World in an effort to preserve aristocratic culture. Though gaming in the Old Dominion underwent significant changes in adjusting to the western frontier of the British empire, it drew its inspiration from the types of play that characterized preindustrial, stratified, land-based society in Tudor-Stuart England.

The founders of Virginia initially placed gambling on the same legal footing as in England. Betting supposedly remained a "gentleman's privilege," except during the Christmas season when commoners could wager in private homes or in their master's household with his consent. This restriction no doubt fell short of banning year-round play among the lower orders, but it did reiterate the elite's customary leadership in matters of gaming. Among the gentlemen of Virginia, gambling became "the favorite vice" and horse racing the preferred vehicle for wagering.[37] Without the refinements of English society, however, colonists on the imperial frontier adopted a type of racing more fitted to the wilderness of the New World. Early Virginia sportsmen held informal road sprints rather than organized meets at regular tracks, and nobody kept or bred horses strictly for the turf during the seventeenth century.[38]

The cultural significance of racing to Virginians served as a measure of the impact of the pioneer experience in England's imperial West. The importance of the sport emerged clearly during the last three decades of the seventeenth century as participants increasingly settled in court grievances over race results. Justices of the peace took very seriously the cases brought before them and generally upheld wagers as binding contracts so long as they had been negotiated fairly and with due regard for the well-being of all society.[39] The verdict of a York County trial in 1674 illustrated the meaning of the gaming sport not only by punishing a tailor for matching his mount against a planter's, "it being contrary to Law for a Labourer to make a race, being a sport only for Gentlemen," but also by sentencing the planter "to be putt in the stocks and there sitt the space of one houre," for the crime of arranging to fix the race with the tailor.[40] The integrity of both the gentry class and the gentry sport depended upon excluding the lower orders as well as upon eliminating outright cheating in a contest on which a great deal of money, or rather a great many pounds of tobacco, had been wagered.

Like Englishmen, Virginia planters wanted to regulate racing more closely as all aspects of recreation came to be commercialized, but the notable increase in court cases pertaining to bets on horses suggests another factor at work. Such inordinate litigiousness was the hallmark of an insecure gentry forming on the imperial frontier. While a self-assured aristocracy dominated gaming and society in England, a new and uncertain gentry had begun to prevail in Virginia.[41] This class regarded horse racing as its exclusive domain in the late seventeenth and early eighteenth century, and regarded racing events as chances to stake individual honor. Every match seemed to reiterate to planters the personal daring and enterprise—the adventurousness—that characterized their penetration of a new continent. Moreover, the rituals of racing and gambling provided a common ground for fractious planters striving to bring order to the colony.

The sport underlined the shared values of individualism, competitiveness, and acquisitiveness, and at the same time provided a peaceful outlet for aggression between members of the elite.[42] Isolated on the outskirts of empire and distant from English conventions of status, the leading planters of Virginia remade horse racing to suit both their own uncertain image and conditions on the colonial frontier.

The notable absence of cockfighting may also be attributed to the frontier circumstances of seventeenth-century Virginia. Widely popular in Restoration England, this particular kind of contest apparently became common in the southern colonies only after 1725. One historian has reasoned that the early colonists did not share the Englishman's thirst for blood sports because as members of pioneer cultures they regularly hunted instead.[43] In addition, for an elite striving to set itself apart, cockfights may have occasioned too much promiscuous intermixture of social rank. In England a few cockpits catered primarily to the upper orders of society, but most brought diverse types together. In 1663 Samuel Pepys attended a cockfight where members of the audience ranged "from Parliament man . . . to the poorest 'prentices," betting and cursing with each other.[44] The planters of Virginia, concerned for the moment with establishing status, may not have welcomed cockfights to the colony if the contests served to blur social distinctions. They behaved more as adventurers striving to find order in the wilderness than as aristocrats secure in their social position.

During the mid-eighteenth century, the growing appeal of cockfights reflected changes in elite attitudes and pioneer conditions. The Virginia gentry apparently felt more confident of its social position and incorporated different kinds of gambling into its expressions of status. Presiding over diverse audiences at such contests as cockfights and horse races, and dominating the betting that accompanied all sporting events, the great tidewater planters ever more surely asserted their authority among all layers of society.

Philip Vickers Fithian, a plantation tutor during the early 1770s, recorded the prevalence of betting among the elite and attested Virginians' proficiency at the practice. His charges, sons of a prominent planter, all showed great interest in betting sports, demonstrating an aptitude for pastimes in which they would naturally participate as mature members of the elite. A devout Presbyterian from the North, Fithian was startled to find that even the local parson joined the play. The minister's participation suggested the cultural identification of the Anglican establishment with the planter elite. Gentry and church dominated Virginia society together. The secular seat of their authority resided at the county courthouse, which served as community center and as backdrop for local cockfights. In the later eighteenth century, crowds gathered round the pits to witness the matches. Now secure at their locus of power, "genteel people . . . promiscuously mingled" not only with "vulgar and debased" whites, as in England, but with black slaves as well.[45]

Paradoxically, heightened appreciation for such a bloody diversion as cockfighting implied greater refinement to the colonists because it likened them to Englishmen. Over the course of the eighteenth century, planters in the Old Dominion made conscious attempts to imitate the cultural forms of their English counterparts, including patterns of genteel gaming. The informal horse sprints of the seventeenth century gradually gave way by the mid-eighteenth century to subscription meets at circular race tracks. Members of the gentry began to import English racing stock and to keep horses exclusively for the turf. Moreover, planters' sons more customarily visited London in order to "complete their education in polite society." In that metropolis, the youths of Virginia learned the intricacies of gambling as only savvy sharpers and titled gentlemen could teach them. Such an education heightened in the colony the popularity of household and tavern games like cards and dice, the most fashionable diversions among London nobility. Great planters, who had long preferred outdoor pastimes, gambled increasingly at table games after midcentury.[46]

Colonists in eighteenth-century South Carolina and New York looked similarly to the example of English play. Prior to 1750 Carolinians had also raced horses along open stretches of road. Afterwards, they erected round tracks, gave them English names like York Course and New Market, and established racing seasons. In addition, as in Britain, cockfights often accompanied these race meets, offering that dose of sporting brutality that characterized not frontier conditions but rather civilized society in the Anglo-American world of the eighteenth century.[47] Owing most likely to tolerant attitudes inherited from the first Dutch settlers, New York City had permitted horse racing since the mid-seventeenth century, when the sport earned the governor's approval "'not so much for the divertisement of youth alone,' as for 'bettering the breed of horses.'"[48] By the mid-eighteenth century, New York, like low-country Virginia and South Carolina, had developed a schedule of organized racing.

Horse racing in New York, South Carolina, and Virginia marked the high point of the development of traditional English recreations in the colonies. But as colonists paid more attention to imitating English forms, it must have become clear to them how much American gaming differed from play in the mother country. Though non-Puritan settlers had tried to transplant the traditional games of England to the fresh fields of North America, they ended up with hybrid forms of gambling that departed from British precedents. Adventurous colonists had created new cultural forms appropriate to the western outpost of English civilization.

The single most important barrier to the faithful reproduction of English-style gambling was the absence of a comparable elite. Nobility never made much impact in society on the imperial frontier. The American wilderness swallowed up most vestiges of inherited privilege, and so prevented the successful duplication in the colonies of gaming in England, where aristocrats set the example of extensive betting during the seventeenth and eighteenth centuries.

By all accounts Englishmen gambled more often and more visibly than American colonists. Not even gentry Virginia could match the utter devotion of the mother country to gaming, a pastime that there ran "like a red thread through eighteenth-century life."[49] Englishmen of all classes wagered on all types of play. Observers were particularly struck by the national passion for such blood sports as cockfighting. In fact, this seemingly perverse fascination with cruelty and risk provoked critical reconsideration of British ways.

Foreigners had long disapproved the English lust for such recreations as cockfighting, bull baiting, dog fighting, badger baiting, and cock scaling before William Hogarth became one of the first Englishmen to bring the point home to his countrymen in his print "The Cockpit." Hogarth stressed neither the aggressiveness of the gamecocks nor the cruelty of their handlers, but the sadism of spectators, who typified the national tendency to derive pleasure from betting on a brutal "fight to the death."[50] Additional voices soon joined the call to reform national pastimes. George III was another early opponent of gambling and discouraged it at Court. By the 1790s the urge to improve society by reducing vulgarity, to make the gentility truly genteel, had grown stronger. Perhaps incipient industrialism encouraged a social discipline that revitalized puritan attitudes toward play.

As reformers clamored for change, they yet pointed to two deeply entrenched obstacles. One was the government, which had stoked the flames of the gambling craze by sponsoring regular nationwide lotteries to raise revenue. The other was the intransigent aristocracy. How could reformers suppress the lowly gambling houses that degraded London, and convince sporting Englishmen to refine their pastimes, if noblemen continued to play so excessively in fashionable clubs?[51]

Aristocrats' gaming grew more moderate on the eve of the nineteenth century, but it had prevailed in England for at least two hundred years. Johan Huizinga accounted for the genteel preoccupation with gambling when he explained how the nobility's understanding of virtue, the trait which set aristocrats apart from the rest of society, had changed over the centuries. Medieval noblemen proved their virtue through chivalrous conduct, "by being brave and vindicating their honour." After the Middle Ages the meaning of virtue changed and the nobility adopted different means of demonstrating bravery and garnering esteem. Writing almost as if he had in mind English peers after the sixteenth century, Huizinga suggested that early modern aristocrats might "content themselves with cultivating an outward semblance of high living and spotless honour by means of pomp, magnificence and courtly manners."[52] For English noblemen between 1550 and 1800, gambling provided both a forum for high living and a context for honorable ritual and brave behavior. Encouraged by a rising cul-

ture of capitalism in Britain that increased the fascination with risk and
reward, the aristocracy patronized gaming pastimes as its own and gave
them a legitimacy, an association with virtue, that ensured their endear-
ment to other Englishmen as well.

The lifestlye of the "idle and exhibitionist society" of peers, and its cultural imperative to live conspicuously, contributed to the fondness for
gambling. The "triple vices" of "idleness," "Pride," and "avarice," so
characteristic of courtly manners, encouraged not merely betting but
heavy betting.[53] Throughout the seventeenth and eighteenth centuries,
gambling was a fixture in the leisure of the nobility, as Richard Seymour's
The Court-Gamester (1722), an instructional treatise written for "young
princesses," explained: "Gaming is become so much the Fashion among
the *Beau-Monde*, that he who in Company should appear ignorant of the
Games in Vogue, would be reckoned low-bred, and hardly fit for Conver-
sation."[54] Some modern-minded observers, including Daniel Defoe,
thought intense wagering to be beneath the dignity of noblemen, but aristocrats themselves came to view courtly gambling as a mark of status and
a proving ground for England's elite.[55]

After the 1720s, aristocratic play grew even more notorious when it
became institutionalized in the genteel clubs of London. Establishments
like White's and Almack's arose out of the commercial tradition of the metropolitan coffeehouse. White's started as a coffeehouse open to all classes
during the late seventeenth century. It became exclusive in the early part
of the next century as noble patrons disassociated themselves from the
"infamous sharpers" who had also frequented the place and cheated peers
out of their money. Nonetheless, the heavy bets made inside White's did
not remain private; indeed, gentlemen played not so much to win, but to
achieve wide visibility, perhaps the central purpose of high living. Aristocrats gambled conspicuously and so continued to set the pace for the
entire country. The popularity of gaming throughout England owed much
to the natural leadership of the nobility.[56]

The oligarchy's domination of gambling was but one more instance of
hierarchical ties continuing to prevail throughout the island culture. Try
as they might, English colonists could not duplicate the leadership of the
nobility in the New World, where the imperial frontier militated against
both aristocracy itself and the sort of cohesion imposed by the elite on
British society. The availability of horses in the New World exemplified the
situation. Whereas ownership of horses in England had been a privilege,
the beasts multiplied so quickly in the colonies that they became a common export item.[57] The environment of the New World seemed to work
against most forms of exclusiveness.

By weakening notions of gentility and noble virtue, the American wilderness permitted greater mobility between social strata at the same time
that it encouraged an individualism and a pragmatism that undermined
conventional paths of hierarchical authority. The wilderness also eroded

to some degree the extremes of wealth and status that characterized society in the mother country, and it inhibited the urban and business orientations that were hastening the commercialization of leisure in Britain. As a result, while many colonists strove to follow aristocratic example, the cultural milieu of eighteenth-century America already differed so much from England's that faithful imitation was well nigh impossible.

The distinctive gambling habits of colonists and Englishmen mirrored a broader divergence between the two societies. The colonists adopted many traditional games but often in modified form. They played cards, but without the wide publicity or the enormous wagers that typified high living in London clubs; they raced horses, but not in the opulent and pedigreed manner of the English nobility; they attended cockfights, but never so frequently or enthusiastically as Englishmen. Gambling did become a fashionable pastime in tidewater Virginia and South Carolina, but there was a great difference between a planter staking a hundredweight of tobacco on the outcome of a horse race in the Virginia countryside, and a nobleman wagering thousands of pounds sterling during a single sitting in an exclusive London club.

The message of moderation prevailed among the planters of the Old Dominion. In England some critics of gambling, who feared that excessive play might bankrupt the aristocracy, urged moderation, though seemingly to heedless ears. Virginia gentlemen also worried about preserving the landed basis of authority, but they were surely more concerned with protecting their family estates and their hard-earned personal liberty.[58]

Members of the colonial elite remained ever aware that they had wrested success from the wilderness. They consequently lacked the nobleman's senses of tradition and absolute self-certainty, for what toil had won might also be lost in North America. Along with their estates, planters had acquired an independence. Ownership of land conferred some degree of self-determination, and Virginians guarded that liberty vigilantly. One of the benefits of economic self-sufficiency had traditionally been the right to gamble freely, but now excessive gaming came to be regarded as a threat to that precarious independence.

Landon Carter voiced the opposition of the planter elite to excessive gambling. He viewed betting less favorably than other leading planters, in part because of his "old ill luck" at cards and in part because the practice had supposedly corrupted his intemperate children. Carter noted resentfully that his sons mocked his inept cardplaying, neglected their aged father and their own families by periodically leaving home in order "to push fortune," and ran up high gambling debts that he was expected to pay. He was most seriously concerned, however, that too much betting threatened man's freedom to govern his own life. Fearing that his heirs would gamble away the whole estate as well as the family reputation, the diarist was unhappily sure that his sporting son had become "every man's man but his own and his father's." Carter spoke for the entire gentry when he wrote that "no affrican is so great a Slave" as a man with a "Passion for gaming." He and the rest of the elite strove to protect the autonomy they had achieved as adventurers on the imperial frontier. A gambler's "own liberty is as certainly at stake as his fortune for when he has lost that what can keep him free and independent?"[59]

William Stith, rector of Henrico parish, echoed Carter's sentiments in a sermon delivered to the House of Burgesses in 1752. Gambling was not the best kind of recreation, he preached, but it might suffice as an innocent diversion unless play became too "high." A man of the cloth, Stith naturally felt obliged to enumerate the ungodly habits commonly associated with gambling—swearing, stealing, and drinking, and offending God by blaming Him for losses while not crediting Him for gains. But the rector's audience likely found Stith most persuasive when he warned that excessive gaming evinced a loss of self-control. By staking fate on a toss of the dice or a turn of the cards, bettors jeopardized the independence and self-reliance they had struggled as planters to attain in North America.[60]

Whereas Increase Mather had argued that gaming trifled with God's capacity to determine all things, William Stith and Landon Carter implored gentlemen to preserve the right of self-determination by refraining from extensive gambling. Puritans had seen gambling as a vice in itself, but Virginians regarded gambling as a vice primarily if taken to extremes that threatened social order. A Virginia statute of 1744, which forbade gaming in public places, embodied the attitude that gambling was not an evil per se, but when abused it had the potential to disrupt society. The law tried to limit the pernicious side-effects of the practice by confining it to private homes where participants, it was assumed, would play moderately and not encourage others to follow suit.[61] The same expectation could never have held for English noblemen, who viewed gaming as an essential public display of high living.

Without the money or publicity lent to the activity by the great titled gentlemen of England, gaming in America remained less of a business proposition during the eighteenth century. British culture in the Augustan age was both more aristocratic and more capitalistic than colonial culture. Gambling represented the commercialization of sport, in a way, as people invested in horses or cocks and hoped for capital gains. But English gaming increasingly came to be organized as a business, too.

The emergence of professional gamesters and the rise of commercial establishments that profited from sponsoring games of chance provided two manifestations of the growing enterprise of gambling. Since the early seventeenth century, monied Englishmen had worried about cardsharps, and the problem only seemed to grow larger in the next century.[62] Aristocrats who gambled at White's attested to the problem by converting the public house into a private club, largely in order to eliminate sharpers from their games. Other Englishmen were less fortunate and often found themselves "taken" in what had seemingly begun as innocent games.

There is virtually no evidence to suggest that Americans had the same problem to such an extent. With their preference for private games and smaller stakes, they offered less opportunity to professional gamesters. Eighteenth-century colonists also failed to reproduce the commercial milieu in which so much English gaming took place. Following the nobility, the middle and lower orders of Britain, particularly in London, patronized coffeehouses and taverns in which gaming constituted one of the favorite pastimes. Since public houses were also businesses, they inherently encouraged commercially oriented gambling. Each occupation in the metropolis had its own set of establishments. At the top of the commoners' scale, financiers, merchants, and brokers patronized respectable coffeehouses, while at the bottom the most unsavory sharpers lurked in disreputable taverns. Even had professional gamblers not worked out of these public houses, gaming would still have been somewhat entrepreneurial in the clubs because so many places sponsored commercial games like roulette and faro, and furnished a banker to protect the house's interest.[63] Following the nobility's example, Englishmen developed a stratified network of public gambling shops, providing a milieu for betting that suited the larger society.

Eighteenth-century Americans had no such public and commercial setting in which to gamble. More dispersed throughout the land and with little cash at hand, colonists did not develop an urban hierarchy of public houses in which gaming could flourish. In cities and along roads stood taverns where customers found recreations that included betting, but these establishments were less stratified and less specifically devoted to gaming or any other pastime. Taverns served the colonists more as all-purpose places for all classes.[64] Moreover, though individual patrons might make private wagers on backgammon, cards, or billiards, more commercial games like faro and roulette generally remained unpopular in English North America, and gaming houses as such never really prospered.[65] In the colonies the business of gambling simply lagged behind its development in the more thoroughly mercantile culture of England.

The English aristocracy supplied the money and the example that turned gaming into a popular commercial pastime pervading much of eighteenth-century life. However, the nobility never really made the Atlantic crossing. Members of the new American elites generally had neither the leisure, wealth, nor inclination to gamble like peers of the realm. The imperial frontier offered a chance for new governing groups to rise to power unencumbered by the traditions that encouraged high living and deep play among the nobility in Britain. Mid-eighteenth-century colonists, even in New England and Pennsylvania, showed great interest in borrowing English cultural forms, perhaps to demonstrate the arrival of civilization in the American wilderness. So some imported English bloodstock, built regular race tracks, attended cockfights, and played cards and dice. Yet gambling in the colonies still lacked the commitment, the excess, and the entrepreneurial organization that belonged to the more stratified, genteel, commercial society of Georgian England. Colonists wagered as adventurers, not aristocrats, and American forms of gambling reflected frontier culture more than they mirrored British precedents.

The nobility did not provide the only difference between gambling in the two societies. The extent to which the colonies diverged from the mother country was expressed as well in their approach to the lottery, which evinced the shaping of the frontier. Lotteries in England survived the demise of the Virginia Company and on the eve of the eighteenth century had become an important source of government revenue. The contests remained a Crown monopoly until 1694 when Parliament began exercising the privilege. The government permitted private lotteries from time to time, but for the most part it suppressed unauthorized schemes that competed with state contests. England raised substantial amounts of revenue from lotteries throughout the eighteenth century. The importance of the device was no doubt heightened by the conspicuous failure of other new measures developed to fund government.[66] Lotteries remained a reliable source of revenue while Englishmen considered other methods of raising money. Until reformers protested against them toward the end of the century, the schemes were well-suited to a people intrigued by speculation but unsure how best to turn it to their advantage.

Colonists in North America included the lottery among the cultural freight they imported from England. They sponsored schemes similar in operation to traditional forms, and they often employed lotteries to raise money for the same purposes as Englishmen. Moreover, colonists actually participated in contests based in the mother country. But the continuity between the metropolis and the colonies had its limits. Americans generally scaled their lotteries down in size and used the device to facilitate private as well as public business. Their schemes suited a decentralized society on the western edge of empire.

Relatively removed from the social convention, aristocratic hierarchy, and concentrated government of England, seventeenth-century colonists fashioned a more individualistic culture and a less centralized pattern of government. Over the course of the next century, imperial economic policy perpetuated the colonists' provincial position by subordinating settlers increasingly to the metropolis and contributed to their estrangement from England. Though American society had begun to mature and adopt the cultural forms of English civilization, colonists were never permitted to lose sight of their position on the perimeter of the British world. Both colonial status and frontier conditions generated a demand for such a revenue-raising device as the lottery and ensured that the contests assumed a significance somewhat different from that in England. While the mother country had periodic, large-scale lotteries to fund central government, the colonies employed smaller and more frequent schemes designed to raise money for local and private purposes.

Lotteries were a means to accumulate relatively large sums of money from people who had little cash and to acquire revenue from people who perpetually complained of overtaxation. The perennial shortage of currency in the colonies made it difficult to sell valuable property and to pay taxes. In order to obtain reasonable cash prices for merchandise or real estate, in an age when no single buyer could raise large sums of ready money and when instruments of credit for consumers had not developed very extensively, sellers sold by private lottery, a method that English government generally prohibited. They attained their price by persuading large numbers of small investors to gamble for big prizes of valuable property. Merchants employed this method during the eighteenth century to dispose of their inventory, and developers used it to sell real estate. Lots and houses in New York City, Philadelphia, and the Pennsylvania countryside were sold by lottery schemes at prices which virtually no one individual could afford to pay in cash. Though not a typical kind of business transaction, these private schemes were the first lotteries to gain popularity in the colonies. Because of their enormous potential for fraud, they were also the first to become regulated.[67]

Like England but on a reduced scale, colonial governments also employed lotteries to supplement other forms of taxation. The device was an attractive alternative because it was voluntary, and thus offered relief to the many colonists who felt overtaxed. Moreover, whereas a regular assessment might have drained currency from an already cash-poor society at an inconvenient time, before the harvest and sale of crops, lotteries proved flexible enough to raise money only when it was available in the different sectors of the economy. Local governments, which could not borrow very easily against anticipated revenues, turned to lotteries increasingly during the mid-eighteenth century in order to raise funds for specific projects.[68]

Lotteries to finance public improvements were especially popular in colonial cities. The urban setting provided the best environment for the schemes because of its concentration of people and wealth. Moreover, urbanites, who experienced, too, the shortage of currency, also suffered heavy taxation, particularly during the eighteenth-century wars that involved the western margin of the British empire. Colonial assemblies, in general dominated by rural representatives, tended to tax the cities disproportionately heavily. In recurrent periods of financial crisis, particularly during wartime, urban centers looked to the lottery. Philadelphia's fiscal predicament grew so acute around mid-century that the city actually speculated in lottery tickets itself, but far more commonly city dwellers sponsored lotteries as a method of funding needed improvements. Benjamin Franklin, the quintessential urbanite of the colonial period, organized a successful contest in the 1740s to raise money for strengthening the defenses of Philadelphia during the War of the Austrian Succession.[69]

Franklin's scheme typified the colonists' approach. The rulers of England held regular, nationwide lotteries in order to raise money for the state, but

Americans wove smaller, simpler, more frequent schemes into the fabric
of daily business and local government. Private sponsors conducted the
first lotteries, but complaints that the schemes interfered with commerce,
agitated the lower classes, and encouraged fraud soon moved colonial governments to regulate lotteries. Lawmakers probably hoped as well to
reduce the number of competing contests, since they were turning to the
device increasingly for revenue. By 1776 all but two colonies, Maryland
and North Carolina, required that lotteries have legislative authorization.
This did not stop illegal schemes; in fact, lotteries headquartered near Philadelphia on islands in the Delaware River, in between the enforced boundaries of New Jersey, Pennsylvania, and Delaware, flourished outside of any
apparent legal jurisdiction.[70]

Most colonists did not seem to mind lotteries, whether legal or not, so
long as they did not get out of hand. The raffles were designed either to
facilitate business deals or to raise money from voluntary contributors for
improvements commonly recognized as in the public interest. Some wondered why any good cause needed a lottery to attract funding, and Quakers
opposed the practice on principle, but most people recognized that these
commercial transactions and voluntary taxes generally served everyone. A
lottery held on Pettie's Island, in the Delaware River, in 1772 demonstrated the range of good causes supported by the device. Promoters
pledged to divide the revenue between a Presbyterian church, a German
Lutheran church, the Newark Academy, and "three Schoolmasters in Philadelphia."[71] Besides supporting churches and schools, lotteries were
authorized for the construction of public buildings, roads and bridges,
wharves, defense installations, immigrant halfway houses, and new industries, and for the relief of private debtors and charities. Men as well known
as Franklin, Robert Morris, John Hancock, Samuel Seabury, and George
Washington affiliated themselves with various schemes. In sum, lotteries
were accepted throughout colonial society and continued to be popular
after the Revolution.[72]

Little documentation remains to illustrate exactly why colonists purchased tickets in early American lotteries. The state lotteries of Britain
demonstrated to Adam Smith that "the chance of gain is by every man more
or less over-valued, and the chance of loss is by most men under-valued."[73]
The hope of winning doubtless encouraged colonists to wager as well.
Unlike Englishmen, however, colonists were engaged in building a new
society from the ground up. Lotteries must have lightened the task when
money was short by facilitating commercial transactions, financing public
improvements, and funding charitable causes. The local character of the
schemes, moreover, gave participants a more immediate stake in the venture. Even if a bettor did not win a prize, he likely knew precisely where
his wager went and even approved of the cause to which he had contributed. One felt less of a loss if one's purchase of an unlucky ticket helped
to enhance the immediate surroundings.

Colonists thus participated in lotteries as westering people committed to settling new localities. Lottery schemes indigenous to the colonies were one indication of the self-sufficiency cultivated in the adventure of penetrating a new continent. Therefore, it is not surprising that during the 1760s the lottery became one of the many bones of contention between American and English leaders. The French and Indian War, fought to secure the English frontier in North America, heightened levels of taxation and prompted colonists to resort increasingly to lotteries in order to raise money. When imperial authorities reviewed colonial policies during the early 1760s, preparing to tighten control of the mercantile empire in America, they decided to regulate lotteries in the colonies.

The Board of Trade began the attack by recommending that colonial legislatures outlaw the schemes, and in 1769 it instructed governors in America not to allow lotteries without the Crown's permission. Englishmen feared the effect of the contests on American trade and industry as well as the threat of fraud. They had long been suspicious of the colonial economy and its paper currency; the lotteries must have seemed like another unsound financial institution based on unbacked scrip. Additionally, lotteries held in America competed against schemes authorized by Parliament, including ones to fund English government. In restricting use of lotteries, however, imperial officials seemed out of touch with the importance of the contests in American settlements.[74] The English attitude underscored the differences between the two societies.

When disputes between England and the colonists erupted into war, the Continental Congress, following precedents established by both the English Parliament and the individual colonies, turned to a grand lottery to raise one and a half million dollars for the military struggle against Britain. That the Founding Fathers chose to finance independence through this mode of gambling seems ironic in light of the widespread admonitions against gaming proclaimed by local committees of safety as the rebels tried to galvanize public morality at the outbreak of war.[75] Nonetheless, the United States Lottery got under way in 1777, promoted in words reminiscent of advertisements for the Virginia Company lotteries of 1612–1621: "It is not doubted but every real friend of his country will most cheerfully become an adventurer, and that the sale of tickets will be very rapid, especially as even the unsuccessful adventurer will have the pleasing reflection of having contributed a degree to the great and glorious American cause."[76]

The lottery received considerable support at first, but soon became a source of disappointment to the Continental Congress. Organizers were unduly optimistic that Americans would participate as readily as Englishmen in a nationwide lottery. As members of a more loose-knit society, Americans were accustomed to smaller ventures devised to support purposes more concrete than "the great and glorious American cause." It is no wonder that in the late 1770s ticket sales slowed markedly and sponsors repeatedly delayed drawings. Other contests promoted by states or private

parties to defray military expenses probably detracted from interest in the
national scheme. In addition, prizes offered in the grand United States Lottery declined steadily in value. Winners received promissory notes due in
five years at 4 percent interest per annum, but with drastic inflation the
value of such prizes declined precipitously. The interest rate on notes
awarded to later winners was raised to 6 percent, but that hardly sufficed
to attract new adventurers. Though all the drawings were completed and
publicized, the scheme fizzled and disappeared from sight before all winners received their prizes.[77] The nation's first venture into gambling by lottery raised some cash for the underfinanced war effort, but proved largely
unsuccessful.

The participation of all colonies in lotteries, and the involvement of
every state in the United States Lottery, indicated that to some extent the
polarization between Puritans and cavaliers, between New England and
Virginia, had diminished. Even to descendants of the saints, the evils inherent in lotteries seemed less important than the good causes, such as Harvard College, that they benefited. The relative consensus on lottery contests did not really extend to other kinds of gambling, however. Citizens
in the Northeast invoked the puritan legacy during the post-Revolutionary
period when they set about overturning English legal precedents that sanctioned gambling.[78] Southerners meanwhile maintained that broad toleration of gambling inherited from the planter elite of the early Chesapeake
settlements.

But surely as important as the continuing sway of puritanism in New
England and the heritage of old English customs in the South were the challenges in both regions to century-old traditions. The pioneers of the seventeenth-century imperial frontier had sought social harmony by pursuing
cultural homogeneity. The Pilgrims of Plymouth and the Puritans of Massachusetts Bay did not tolerate such dissenters as Thomas Morton of Ma-re
Mount, the Quakers of Pennsylvania tried to bar traditional forms of recreation, and the Virginia gentry asserted its values unilaterally through
Chesapeake society. The goal of cultural uniformity perhaps seemed
attainable during the seventeenth century, but yielded to diversity afterwards. Economic and territorial expansion, immigration of non-English
peoples, and the divisive force of the Great Awakening all contributed to
increased heterogeneity in the colonies.

Heightened diversity meant that cultural enclaves like New England and
tidewater Virginia, once diametrically opposed in styles of living, grew
more alike because each grew more heterogeneous. In both places the ruling elites encountered challenges to the cultural hegemony they had once
imposed. In the Boston area the threat to traditional notions of recreation
appeared in the form of organized horse racing, which first rose around
1715 and became firmly entrenched after 1765. To the south, particularly
in less settled regions, planters grew alarmed after midcentury as evangelical Baptists, a product of religious upheaval, appeared bent on "destroy-

ing pleasure in the country": "they encourage ardent Pray'r; strong and constant faith, & an active Banishment of *Gaming*, *Dancing*, & Sabbath-Day Diversions," one Virginian worried.[79]

Puritan and planter cultures grew more similar because New England and Virginia societies grew more complex. The course of the development of gambling in the colonies suggests that Americans, in gaining independence from England, did not recapture homogeneity but rather "legitimated" new kinds of conflict over cultural styles within the colonies.[80] Self-determination extended beyond politics and economics to lifestyles, and tended to be subsumed under the heading of religious toleration. Independence mandated that evangelical Baptists, Massachusetts Puritans, Pennsylvania Quakers, or genteel Anglicans coexist with Americans of different religious preferences and, implicitly, different cultural orientations.

Diversification of attitudes toward gambling in individual colonies suggested both a continued ambivalence toward the activity and a broadening heterogeneity throughout American society. The expanding colonial frontier of the eighteenth century served to heighten diversity. Tensions emerged between seaboard residents and backcountry settlers over a number of economic, political, and military issues as well as over cultural orientations. The differences between coastal and interior populations became clearer after the American Revolution as the new republic paid increasing attention to its emerging West.

Observers of the early American frontier pointed to highly visible gambling as one of the characteristic features of the region. In the 1760s Charles Woodmason, an Anglican minister, documented the prevalence of gaming amid footloose peoples in the Carolina backcountry. The itinerant became particularly incensed at the tendency of the unsettled population, allegedly led by New Lights, or dissenting evangelical preachers, to indulge in gambling during and immediately after his religious services. Woodmason ultimately listed "Gaming and Gambling" among the many practices of the backcountry population that in his view prompted vigilantism by Regulators.[81]

Other commentators confirmed Woodmason's observation that gambling flourished in newly settled regions among the many idle people. Fithian, the Presbyterian cleric, noted how quickly a frontier militia in 1775, ostensibly mustered to prepare for war against the British, turned the occasion into a day of drinking and horse racing. "[T]alk of supporting Freedom," Fithian remarked, "by meeting and practising Bacchanalian revels."[82] Similar sentiments were repeated a quarter century later by Timothy Dwight, who noticed the prevalence of "low vices" among the people of western upstate New York, and by an English traveler, who wrote that the inhabitants of western towns were generally devoted to gambling on horse races, cockfights, card games, and billiards, and fighting over the outcome of such contests.[83]

Adventurers were continuing to migrate westward and cultivate new forms of gambling. The unique kind of horse racing that developed in western settlements summed up the novelty of gaming on the early national frontier. By the mid-eighteenth century patrons of the turf in New York City, tidewater Virginia, and low-country South Carolina, following English precedent, had erected circular race tracks, purchased purebred horses, and adopted formal racing seasons. Such developments lent dignity, ceremony, and orderliness to the sport in the older settlements, but they also eliminated all spontaneity and informality.

By way of contrast, frontier versions of racing were "more fun."[84] Backcountry contests descended from seventeenth-century precedents. Without the money and inclination to build formal tracks, the first Virginians had raced common horses in road sprints, but only as an expedient until English forms could be imitated successfully. The rise of civilizing influences along the seaboard ensured that early makeshift matches were replaced by racing seasons comprised of thoroughbreds and circular tracks named after British establishments. "Quarter-racing," however, followed the frontier into the interior and survived as a distinctive sport indigenous to the American West.[85]

Pioneers on the late colonial and early American frontier lacked the means to build tracks and institute racing seasons. They naturally resorted instead to quarter-mile sprints, which soon became more than a frontier expedient. They also cultivated a novel kind of racer, the quarter horse, specifically for their matches. This new breed, which remained distinct from the English thoroughbred stock so integral to formal seaboard racing, was itself a literal product of the frontier. The quarter horse was foaled by cross-breeding English saddle horses, brought by colonists to the British New World, with Indian ponies, which were descended from early Spanish imports and to be found throughout the southern backcountry.[86]

Witnesses of quarter-racing, the forerunner to the modern sport of quarter-horse racing, emphasized how backcountry events differed from the ritualized and sedate racing of tidewater settlements. The organizers of the contests typically laid out courses on fields or straight stretches of road, and almost always next to the local tavern, which served as a kind of community center. The races generally matched two mounts against each other and stimulated a great deal of betting among the owners of the horses as well as the crowd in attendance. John Bernard, an English-born traveling actor, depicted the "motley multitude of negroes, Dutchmen, Yankee pedlers, and backwoodsmen," most of them apparently inebriated, that lined the race path at one such event around 1800. Unlike patrons of the turf in more civilized regions, these spectators and contestants cared little for the rules of racing. Moreover, the sprints were over quickly, in contrast to the drawn out rounds of tidewater thoroughbred contests. The backcountry races were naturally accompanied by boxing bouts, shooting matches, and cockfights, a typically western bill of fare.[87]

Bernard described the tumultuous conclusion of quarter-races, a scene that would have been unthinkable in the tidewater.

> The event was always proclaimed by a tornado of applause from the winner's party, the niggers in particular hallooing, jumping, and clapping their hands in a frenzy of delight, more especially if the horses had happened to jostle and one of the riders been thrown off with a broken leg; whereupon the defeated owner, or some friend for him, always dealt out retribution with his whip, for the purpose, as he termed it, of maintaining order.[88]

Without strict rules or ceremonial procedures, without seasonal calendar or orderly crowds, quarter-racing plainly suited the frontier of the late eighteenth century.

Because it derived from early seventeenth-century origins, and because it typified the adaptation of English forms of gambling to the New World, the spectacle of quarter-horse sprints gives pause to reconsider developments in gaming during the colonial period. Like the lottery, which survived an ill-fated association with Jamestown only to be transformed to suit the needs of eighteenth-century colonists, horse racing migrated westward across the Atlantic and underwent changes in North America. Quarter-mile sprints satisfied early Virginians until the tidewater wilderness had been tamed. Then an increasingly self-confident planter elite began to regenerate the amenities of English culture. But once these low-country sportsmen had erected round tracks, elaborated regular rules, scheduled formal seasons, and imported pedigreed horses, their gambling still lacked the money, the devotion, and the intensity that Englishmen invested in gaming during the eighteenth century.

The importation of thoroughbreds from the mother country, planters discovered, did not make the colonists as gamblers blooded stock. The wilderness had eradicated most vestiges of aristocracy, and no amount of imitation could recapture the ingrained breeding, and the love of gambling, peculiar to the uppermost English class. So the new American society developed novel species of play that were shaped extensively by the adventure lived by westering peoples. Without the example or wealth of the English nobility, gambling in the colonies and early republic never became as deep, as commercial, or as regulated. The emergence of a native-born betting sport such as quarter-horse racing—informal, disorderly, and backwoodsy—confirmed the divergence of American gambling, and American society, from England during the seventeenth and eighteenth centuries, and demonstrated the decisive impact of the frontier on American styles of gaming.

Quarter-racing served as well to mark the advance of the frontier of English-speaking peoples into the interior of North America. The new style prevailed in the westernmost communities of the southern colonies, from the early Virginia tidewater to the Revolutionary backcountry, and continued to move westward as migrants to each new frontier eventually reproduced eastern culture. The passing of the frontier beyond the coastal plain signified the increasing complexity of settlements in New England and the Chesapeake. Once conceived as relatively homogeneous, puritan and planter societies grew more diverse. The cultural uniformity of New England, characterized by a solely puritan approach to gambling and leisure, diminished as time passed. The gentry of Virginia, which tried unsuccessfully to copy the traditional recreational culture of Merrie England, encountered challenges to its cultural hegemony, too. Emergent western societies were seldom predicated on the principle of cultural homogeneity, but rather had diversity as a starting point.

Backcountry betting styles helped to set the region apart from the rest of the young republic. Though Easterners might ridicule the crudity of recreations on the frontier, they treasured the West, too, as a source of national identity and as a reservoir of energy for the new nation. Outbursts of quarter-racing seemed to typify the vitality of the entire section, just as the wide range of spectators at such events mirrored the diversity of its population.

In the early years of nationhood, nobody did more to enhance the reputation of both the region and its gambling than Andrew Jackson, the West's favorite son and most illustrious bettor. Jackson was not the first president to gamble openly, but he wagered with an energy that contemporaries viewed, not generally unfavorably, as representative of the frontier. George Washington and Thomas Jefferson, from settled tidewater Virginia, had been known to bet at cards; they recorded their small winnings and losses in journals as if to caution themselves against excess.[89] Andrew Jackson, on the other hand, played deeply, emotionally, and aggressively. Before he turned thirty he had twice staked virtually all his possessions on gambling events, and in 1805 he killed a man, and nearly died himself, in a duel fought to settle an argument issuing from the terms of a bet on a horse race. Gambling was a crucial ingredient in the General's makeup, a focus for his competitiveness, vanity, sociability, and adventurousness. Two biographers have likened Jackson to a "fighting cock," finding in the man both the strength and weakness of that fierce animal.[90]

Jackson began to gamble as a youth in the piedmont of Revolutionary Carolina, where he participated in cockfighting and horse racing. After the War for Independence, the young man gambled away a small inheritance on horses and dice at Charleston, and as a law student in Salisbury, North Carolina, he gained recognition as "the most roaring, rollicking, gamecocking, horse-racing, card-playing, mischievous fellow that ever lived." After the rising attorney migrated westward to Nashville, he continued to fight cocks for a time, and he once proposed a lottery for a local college, but he became particularly fond of horse racing, a sport that better suited his aspirations and his growing status in western Tennessee. Between 1788 and 1816, Jackson not only raced and bred horses, including some of the very best in the country, but also owned a share of a track and stable near

Nashville, and perhaps another course in the vicinity of Natchez. During this period, and later during his presidency, the topic of racing often permeated Jackson's correspondence.[91] Attention paid to the turf served as a kind of social cement within his circle of family and friends.

Jackson took the pastime of horse racing very seriously. He could not stand to lose a race, for he seemed to stake his pride and status on every event. To Jackson gambling signified living to the fullest the daring and enterprising life of the West. Because each match was a matter of honor to this vain man, it is not entirely surprising that the duel with Charles Dickinson resulted from uncertainty about the terms of a wager on a race that was never run. The showdown cost Jackson a good measure of popularity and good health, but did not cool his ardor for the turf. Rather, his interest in the sport declined only later, after the War of 1812, when his new fame and success launched him into a life that allowed no time for the personal care he liked to give to training and running his horses.[92]

As president, however, when he needed a diversion from the duties of office, Old Hickory maintained two stables of racers, one in the capital and one near Nashville. Against the warnings of political advisers, Jackson ran his horses in the vicinity of Washington, D.C., the only chief executive ever to do so. He also spent considerable time in his correspondence advising an adopted son about the proper care for the stock at the Hermitage and discussing the turf with relatives and friends. The president's advice to a nephew regarding the racing of a filly summed up not merely Jackson's personality and his approach to racing, but in addition the entrepreneurial mood of the entire nation during the Jacksonian era: *"You must risque to win."*[93]

The General made gambling seem as natural an extension of his personality as politics. Betting was altogether suited to the adventurous life of the West's leading light, who approached the practice with the same sense of honor that he brought to all pursuits. For this reason most Americans overlooked his wagering, despite a national reform impulse against gaming. During both the 1824 and 1828 campaigns for the presidency, political opponents made an issue of Jackson's participation in cockfights, horse racing, and other gambling contests, but the charges did little apparent damage to his reputation. Even Jackson's dissolute youth was disregarded by Americans intent on upholding the legend of Old Hickory.[94] People likely accepted gambling as the inevitable consequence of a frontier upbringing and a western code of behavior. They also probably excused Jackson's gaming as the innocent pastime of a gentleman. Gambling seemed so natural for Jackson that he largely escaped the disapproval that gambling received during the antebellum period.

While Jackson was forgiven for gambling because of his reputation as a gentleman, the age of genteel gaming was over and an era of commercial gaming had begun. During the 1820s and 1830s reformers spoke out increasingly against various new kinds of betting. An antigambling crusade sprouted from the same perspective that underlay such other antebellum causes as temperance and antislavery and from the principles of the political economy espoused in this age of the common man. In the four decades prior to the Civil War, gaming and gamblers came under mounting attack. Activists focused their fire particularly on lotteries, a kind of wagering that seemed increasingly offensive to both the moral sensibilities of reformers and the ideals of Jacksonians.

The campaign against lotteries arose in part because, in the early nineteenth century, Americans generally grew more disposed to reform society by removing temptations such as gambling that impeded the pursuit of individual perfectibility. It arose also because the character of lotteries themselves changed after the Revolution. Eighteenth-century lotteries had mostly been small, local affairs conducted with a clear-cut sense of the common good. Participants had purchased tickets in these schemes as a way of contributing to the development of a new country. By the early nineteenth century the scale and organization of lotteries had grown substantially. As an alternative to mandatory taxes and to as yet undeveloped kinds of public borrowing, the schemes continued to provide capital for the same general purposes as before, but they became grander in size and, more important, were turned over almost entirely to private firms of lottery agents who made the wholesaling and retailing of tickets a major line of business. One such agent during the 1820s was teenager P. T. Barnum, who learned some of his showmanship from various schemes and also discovered by selling tickets to foolish buyers that "such bipeds as 'humbugs' certainly existed before I attained my majority."[95]

The money-raising device grew more similar to English lotteries by becoming a larger, more impersonal scheme where the chance to win a prize outweighed all other considerations to adventurers. Moreover, after state legislators turned lotteries over to companies with offices across the country, reformers learned the same lesson that King James I had drawn from Englishmen's experience with the lotteries of the Virginia Company. When delegated to private firms, the privilege of sponsoring lotteries was often prone to abuse.

A committee formed to investigate one Pennsylvania scheme explained how the "corruption" of government-granted privilege could occur. In the second and third decades of the nineteenth century, the state legislature, seeking to promote the building of canals, granted one construction firm the right to raise capital by lottery. The Union Canal company foundered, however, in its early efforts to remain solvent. To keep private investors in the company from placing their money elsewhere, the Commonwealth itself took over the lottery with the intention of raising $27,000 per year to pay as dividends to stockholders in the Union Canal company. The state then contracted with a private firm to conduct the raffles. The lottery agents provided the state with its $27,000 annually, but they also grossed over $800,000 per year themselves on ticket sales of more than $5 million.

Noting the discrepancy between the state's and the company's income, the committee was astounded at such exploitation of privilege and recommended a total prohibition of lotteries in Pennsylvania.[96]

Tales of other "abuse" circulated, too, prompting citizens throughout the nation to join the crusade against lotteries. One recurring argument charged that the schemes subverted the First Amendment to the Constitution by corrupting the free press. By buying plenty of advertising space and by contracting with publishers for the printing of tickets and related literature, lottery agents reportedly undermined the integrity of newspapers and prevented editorial attack.[97]

Not all lottery agents were as corrupt as reformers charged. Some firms managed schemes competently and also pioneered developments in finance and securities trading that ultimately supplanted the lottery as a tool for raising revenue and capital.[98] Such acumen and innovation did not always elevate these entrepreneurs above disfavor, however, because they still were involved in the banking and speculation so characteristic of the "money power" that Jacksonians castigated as a major reason for decline from the virtues of the Jeffersonian republic. To make matters worse, in reformers' eyes, state governments legitimized such practices by authorizing contests and then turning them over to private companies. Consequently, in addition to coming under attack from reformers who equated the schemes with such other "vices" as slavery and intemperance, lotteries fell victim as well to plaints against government-fostered privilege and unearned wealth. The money-raising device could hardly resist such an onslaught. Between 1830 and 1860 every state in the union banned lotteries.[99] Thereafter, in part because of the development of more sophisticated means of raising capital, the lottery did not play an important role, either for western or eastern communities, until the mid-twentieth century.

In its defense of the common man and its similarity to criticisms of the Bank of the United States, the argument against lotteries took on distinctly Jacksonian tones. In 1833 Thomas Man, an ardent opponent of lotteries, asked where the brunt of the schemes' burden fell:

> Who pays the oppressive Tax levied by a few Brokers in Tickets, on the Public? The industrious Mechanic—the hardy Tiller of the Soil. It is the small pittance wrung from the common laborer who lives by the sweat of his brow, and whose family are dependent on him for their daily support. It is bread taken from the mouths of his children.

In contrast to the common citizen as Jacksonians' hero, the lottery indeed seemed a "Horrid Monster—the Hydra with its thousand Heads," making a "monstrous profit" from the pockets of average people. "Crush the *Damned Monster*," Man implored, "or away—your vaunted *Liberty* and *Freedom*."[100]

Such rhetoric derived directly from the sentiments of Old Hickory and his followers. When Jackson wrote to Chief Justice Roger B. Taney in 1836, depicting both the *"paper system"* of the "money power" and its accompanying "gradual consuming corruption, which is spreading . . . stockjobbing, Land jobbing and every species of speculation," as the "greatest threatners" to Americans' pure, simple, "virtuous Government," he might as well have been speaking specifically about lotteries.[101] In such schemes an adventurer would trade in his hard-earned coins for a virtually worthless scrap of paper. Instead of authorizing lotteries and contracting with lottery brokers, the Jacksonians argued, government should work to protect the honestly acquired property of working people from those who sought wealth without labor.

In 1829 John Catron, a justice on the supreme court of Tennessee whom Jackson later appointed to the highest court in the land, decided in one case that government should ensure that dishonest schemes such as lotteries did not deprive people of the fruits of their toil. Catron held government responsible for upholding "industrious habits" and discouraging such aristocratic practices as gaming. He repeated the contemporary sentiment that gambling fostered poverty as well as a host of related problems and created debt which compromised the independence of individuals.[102] That government encouraged gambling and speculation by authorizing lotteries reassured Jacksonian ideologues that, indeed, the purity and simplicity of the virtuous republic truly were endangered by the money power.

There was a certain flexible standard among Jacksonians in condemning all gambling, and lotteries in particular, on the one hand while overlooking the gaming of their General on the other. This inconsistency can be explained in part by the integral place of gambling in Jackson's gentlemanly and western makeup. It can also be understood with the distinction drawn by antebellum Americans between private, recreational betting among gentlemen, and public, business-like gaming conducted by lottery agents and professional gamblers. Jackson played either in private games, in which honorable men supposedly amused themselves in a spirit of moderation, or else at horse racing, a respectable, ceremonious pastime inherited from the Virginia gentry. Neither kind of gambling seemed to threaten society very seriously. Gentlemen like Jackson could clearly afford to play and were apparently immune to the temptations that seduced less worthy men. Moreover, by playing privately they did not encourage others to gamble, too. Finally, these adventurers willingly accepted the risks. They understood that one must take chances to get ahead, a commonplace of antebellum wisdom.

In contrast to such distinguished amateurs stood relative newcomers who viewed gambling as a business. For English aristocrats, gambling was high living; for Andrew Jackson, the epitome of the frontier adventurer, gambling was just plain living; for entrepreneurs, gambling was a living. The lottery agent and professional gambler, types newly visible in early nineteenth-century America, represented the antithesis of the bettors typified by Jackson. They played publicly and commercially, thereby encouraging gambling among all orders of society, including those least able to resist poverty and the other evils associated with gaming. Moreover, they took few chances, relying instead on the inherent percentages of the lottery, or upon fraud and deceit, to win money consistently. Unwilling to "risque to win," these entrepreneurs were not adventurers. They consequently intensified for Jacksonians all that seemed undesirable about gambling.

Antebellum reformers solved the problem of the lottery through legislation, but professional gamblers proved more elusive. Laws designed to check them were difficult to enforce, and the entrepreneurial ethos of the age encouraged all forms of speculation. In addition, the new type of gamester had emerged most successfully where law sometimes had little effect. The transient conditions of life and the frontier intermixture of cultures in the lower Mississippi Valley during the early nineteenth century encouraged the expansion of a kind of gaming that colonists never truly imported from England. This sort of betting, shaped and disseminated by the play of professional gamblers, forcefully redirected the orientation of gambling in the United States.

2

Professional Gamblers

The Old Southwestern Frontier

Late one winter evening during the mid-1820s, William C. Hall, an American writer journeying down the Mississippi River, landed at Natchez and tarried for a short while along the waterfront in order to learn what made Natchez-under-the-Hill "so celebrated throughout the Union." Hall had come to visit the landing that contemporary visitors identified as "a true Gomorrah," "the nucleus of vice upon the Mississippi," and "a repulsive place, the centre of all that is vile, from the upper and lower country." To travelers from England and the eastern states, Natchez-under-the-Hill epitomized the crudity of civilization in newly settled lands in the Mississippi Valley. It harbored the professional gamblers who plagued frontier society in the old Southwest. The reputation discouraged most passers-by from venturing far enough into the district to obtain a closer look, but William C. Hall experienced the riverfront infernos so closely that he was burned, and left a singularly candid account that confirmed other writers' estimation of the place as a "nest of sinners."

The curious traveler strode up a street lined with "grog shops" and "houses of ill-fame." These buildings consisted essentially of abandoned flatboats that had been ordered in rows along the shore and remodeled into remarkably versatile public houses. Out of their doorways and into the street spilled a motley throng that typified the inhabitants of frontier landings on the Mississippi River—"fashionably dressed young men, smoking or lounging, tawdrily arrayed, highly rouged females, sailors, Kentucky boatmen, negroes, negresses, mulattoes, pigs, dogs, and dirty children."

Hall lingered not among this "medley," but instead turned into the first open door he saw and found himself in a brightly lit barroom. There he learned exactly why Natchez-under-the-Hill had become so renowned to antebellum Americans.

The crowd indoors duplicated the mixture of people outside. "Kentucky boatmen" lined the walls of the saloon, watching "two gaily dressed, sylph-like forms" waltz about the barroom. The women danced to the music of two fiddles, a clarinet, a bass drum, and a tambourine played vigorously by a black youth "dressed *à la Turk*." The band responded to Hall's arrival by striking up "an exciting reel" while one of the gaudily attired women invited the newcomer to dance. Hall declined the proposition and retreated farther into the interior of the building through a door that "stood invitingly open." The innocent traveler had just stumbled into a riverfront gambling den. Directly in front of him stood a roulette wheel, "revolving like the flood wheel of a tubmill," and to the side sat six or seven people around a faro table. Hall headed for neither of these suspicious layouts, yet within an instant he was ensnared in a doomed game.

As the writer entered the room he saw the proprietor of the house trying to tell a drunken patron to go home and save his money, but the inebriate, staggering about waving a wad of five hundred dollars in one hand and a pack of cards in the other, insisted that he wanted to play. The proprietor then asked Hall to bet with the drunk at a game fixed in the writer's favor, and to win the drunk's money so that it could be returned safely to him when he was sober. Hall had not decided about the bet when another person, "a plainly dressed man" who seemed to be a local farmer, suddenly appeared to befriend Hall and offered to join in the charitable wager. The farmer then remembered, however, that he had not brought his wallet "in order to avoid the risk of having his pocket picked while under-the-hill." But the bet was such a sure thing that he implored Hall to take it.

By this time the temptation was too much. "I had taken out my pocket book" to make sure that it had not been stolen, Hall recalled, when "my companion and friend, as he seemed to me, half soliciting and half forcing, took from my hand five notes of $100 each, and placed them with the $500 already on the counter, observing with a wink that he would hold the stakes." In that instant the money was as good as gone and the pocket as good as picked. Hall turned to play a game of three-card monte with the drunk and promptly lost his sure thing as the inebriate's sleight of hand manipulated the cards. The drunk, suddenly sober and quite clearly in league with the "farmer" and proprietor, quickly pocketed Hall's money and informed the stunned victim that he had been taken fairly by "My Grandmother's Trick." The writer had surely discovered why Natchez-under-the-Hill had earned its inglorious reputation.[1]

In a manner reproduced up and down the river, Hall had been fleeced in an old confidence game by a relatively new kind of American entrepreneur known as professional gamblers. These sharpers emerged as a distinct group on the southwestern frontier during the first half of the nineteenth century and created novel forms in the culture of American gambling. They developed betting into a business with its own organization and skills, and carried the changed styles of gaming, including many casino games new to the national scene, throughout other parts of the country.

American folklore has commemorated betting in the lower Mississippi Valley with stories of the riverboat gambler, an authentic figure who emerged primarily after the West had begun to move beyond the Mississippi. The riverboat gambler actually imitated and streamlined the practices developed by land-based sharps who operated out of a string of frontier waterfront districts such as Natchez-under-the-Hill, and fattened themselves upon the stream of venturesome travelers flowing up and down the Mississippi. These shore-bound entrepreneurs of the frontier era cultivated novel styles of public and commercial wagering that were borrowed by riverboat gamblers and later gained acceptance throughout the United States.

Whether atop the water or on its banks, gamblers operating along the great river became notorious to the American public as "blacklegs," or outlaws, during the first decades of the nineteenth century. The business of gambling remained suspect, and most states circumscribed the practice by law. Yet, while the public condemned river sharpers, it simultaneously supported the profession in the Southwest by embracing virtually all forms of risk taking and by providing a steady current of players ready to stake their money on a sure thing. Gambling suited the entrepreneurial and individualistic outlook of the young republic and found especial favor in the old South where it became a representative ingredient of the cultural matrix that held slave society together. People along the lower Mississippi Valley frontier demonstrated both national and southern inclinations to gamble at the same time that they resisted the restrictions that other regions placed on betting. The antebellum Southwest consequently became another western source of new styles of American gaming, and the headquarters for the emergence of the professional gambler.

The gaming practices of the old Southwest mirrored the diverse and fluid milieu in which they emerged. A mixture of influences that included Spanish, French, Yankee, Southerner, black, and Mexican ways shaped the youthful society along the lower Mississippi in the years after 1800. Different cultural strains came to be blended together with the waters of the ever-changing stream that dominated activity in the newly settled lands and heightened the transiency of life there. Between St. Louis and the Gulf of Mexico, the great river nurtured a series of towns that focused settlement and facilitated changes in styles of American gambling. Frontier conditions persisted in these inland ports until business flourished in the valley, bringing in its wake such technological advances as steamboats and railroads, and challenging attitudes toward cardsharps.

Once content to live with wide-open, commercial betting, settlers of the old Southwest turned against the professional gambler during the 1830s. Now on the verge of becoming respectable Southerners in a prosperous addition to the Cotton Kingdom, townspeople anxiously identified the sharper and his companions as a vestige of the unruly frontier they sought to put behind them. Communities up and down the river purged professional gamblers, sometimes quite violently as in Vicksburg, Mississippi, where vigilantes lynched five blacklegs in 1835. Such actions, crude as they were, seemed a requisite step toward prosperity and stability, and marked the end of another phase in the development of an American culture of gambling. Newly created styles of betting, however, survived the attack on the sharpers who had first cultivated them. They made their way on to riverboats, later grew popular throughout the country, and continued to influence American gaming well into the twentieth century.

Changes in styles of betting resulted in large part from the shaping of the profession of gamblers, an occupation that Americans first noticed during the nineteenth century. While lottery agents tended to work out of eastern cities, cardsharps typically operated in river towns and on steamboats along the southern frontier, where they came to be recognized as one of the several layers of western society. One traveler's guide to the new territories ranked "gaming adventurers, *black legs*, &c." as the lowest "class of people" in the Mississippi Valley, and advised emigrants to steer clear of the nefarious plots of these confidence men.[2]

While Mississippi Valley gamblers signified the arrival of another profession in the United States, they were little more than a New World manifestation of an old European problem. Englishmen had worried about sharpers since the seventeenth century, when Charles Cotton had pointed out the large number of career "gamesters" fated to "hang as precious jewels in the ear of Tyburn," the English gallows.[3] Professional gamblers naturally accompanied the commercialization of sport and recreation in Tudor-Stuart Britain. Now, as American society also became increasingly commercial in character during the early nineteenth century, professional gamblers appeared in the West to make the most of a new line of business. They adopted the entrepreneurial approach to betting, and from Europe they borrowed the games most suited for making money. Then they tailored Old World practices to suit the American frontier. Riverfront districts in such western towns as Louisville, St. Louis, Memphis, Vicksburg, Natchez, and New Orleans constituted an ideal spawning ground for the new class of professional gamblers and helped to shape the emerging styles of American betting.

Professional gamblers preferred to deal in games that promised the surest profit. These included both banking and percentage games that English colonists had not established in America, such as French favorites faro, roulette, and *vingt-et-un* where the dealer had the odds on his side, as well as card games such as poker and three-card monte in which dealers could easily win by manipulating the deck. By establishing favorable percentages gamblers made sure that they would make money. Then they increased their profits not by increasing volume, as more modern gamblers would, but by increasing the stakes and regularizing cheating. Sharpers also organized into groups like the threesome that fleeced William C. Hall in Natchez-under-the-Hill. While one confederate dealt the cards, others found willing victims and encouraged them to stake more money. Most operators had at least one partner who assisted in the confidence games and shared the income. Professional gambling was generally not an individualistic enterprise.[4]

By commercializing betting games, sharpers remade American gambling for good. They paved the way for the widespread introduction of such casino games as twenty-one, roulette, and the frontier favorite, faro, that were well suited to a businesslike approach to betting, and they quickened the pace of cultural change by constantly reshaping games of chance in order to accommodate both their own needs and the shifting preferences of the American public. Professional gamblers helped to popularize poker, for instance, during the antebellum period. They carried it from its port of entry, New Orleans, up the river frontier and eventually to eastern and western centers of population where it became a favored pastime after 1850, and they modified the rules to conform to national tastes. The addition of wild cards and bluffing helped to Americanize this Old World game. Sharpers added the draw to stud poker, too, partly because the extra round of discarding and dealing enhanced opportunities for cheating, and partly because the prospect of new cards added excitement and stimulated betting.[5] In such a manner Westerners adopted and modified games for American consumption.

Perhaps even more significantly, professional gamblers on the river frontier remade American gaming by helping to eliminate the influence of social rank that betting in the early republic had inherited from the English aristocracy. The sharper often disguised himself as a gentleman, knowing that some men of status would refuse to play with lesser opponents, but he hardly cared whose money he won. Participants in betting games were no longer regarded so much by their social status, but rather by their position at the table. Bettors were divided into players and gamblers; one viewed gaming as recreation while the other saw it as business.

The new type, the professional bettor, diverged sharply from the genteel ideal that southern colonists had tried to cultivate. Robert Bailey, a Virginian rakehell who sat on both sides of the gaming table during his long career, differentiated between the two kinds of participants in 1822. He defined "a sportsman" as a "high minded liberal gentleman, attached to amusements regardless of loss or gain; his motto is honor, his shield his judgment." A gambler or professional sharper, on the other hand, pursued only "the business of general gaming, destitute of all honor and integrity."

The one sought his pleasure discreetly and moderately, while the other made profits publicly and dishonestly.[6]

The rise of sharpers along the rivers of the old Southwest added a new dimension to gambling culture in America and helped to define a distinctive sporting style for the rest of the country. Professional gamblers belonged to that broad spectrum of tricksters and confidence men, indigenous to the cotton frontier of the old South, that came to be immortalized by a popular body of regional literature. These *chevaliers d'industrie* pioneered the gamesmanship that set American sport further apart from English and European traditions.[7] They helped to create a fashion of play that their countrymen accepted roundly, yet they were also targets of scorn and condemnation. Sharpers thrived in a society that embraced the hazards and adventure of thorough-going free enterprise at the same time that it feared the consequences of speculation and commerce when they were pushed to extremes.

The nation's ambivalence toward gamblers paralleled the mixture of attitudes that Marvin Meyers has termed "the Jacksonian paradox." Many Americans followed the logic of market capitalism to its conclusion, engaging in business adventures of all kinds, but they simultaneously retained their "ideal of a chaste republican order, resisting the seductions of risk and novelty, greed and extravagance, rapid motion and complex dealings."[8] Jacksonians remained unprepared for the cultural consequences of the business practices that they so heartily adopted. Similarly, they condemned the professional gambler at the same time that they flocked to his table to thrill at the risks and rewards offered by his games. The period's enterprising mentality sanctioned chance taking, but fears that the future would differ too sharply from the virtuous republic of Jefferson ensured that such bold products of the new era as professional gamblers received widespread condemnation.

In a society attuned to risk taking, gamblers were vulnerable because they minimized risks to themselves in games designed to turn around pure chance. Reformers, however, generally attacked the profession from another perspective. Antebellum Americans tended to place the sharper at the bottom of the class of "idlers"—"lackeys, servants, lazy sons of the rich, mere men of fashion, 'lottery people,' and a few 'gentlemen' who occupy themselves with breeding horses"—that compared so unfavorably with the "industrious producers" who comprised the common man in contemporary belief.[9] Because he created nothing of value and got by on trickery rather than on honest labor, the gambler stood outside respectable society in settled regions. Moralists likened his trade to thievery. Betting amounted to little more than an "attempt by one person to deprive another of his property or possessions, against his consent, and *without the return of an equivalent*," one critic explained, and it clearly led to even graver crimes.[10]

The nation's willingness to perceive sharpers as out-and-out criminals meant that gamblers were frequently identified as blacklegs, especially in southwestern territories where they apparently congregated and operated freely. Foreign visitors to the Mississippi Valley learned from their American hosts that although these outlaws were labeled "gamblers, as such was their ostensible profession, they were ready for any crime which might offer an advantage to them."[11] There seemed to be simply no legitimate place for the sharper in American civilization. In a country filled with people of chance, however, there also seemed to be no effective barrier to separate the gambler from respectable society.

While most citizens probably agreed that gamblers were distasteful, the profession nonetheless took shape and flourished in the early nineteenth century. The prosperity of a sizable class of sharpers suggests that to many people the arguments against gaming remained largely unpersuasive. Americans were caught up in the risks and rewards of free enterprise and westward expansion during the antebellum period, and gaming often seemed a natural extension of daily economic life. Just as they speculated in business, they wagered extensively and willingly, both against each other and against gamblers who often disguised their true identities. European travelers, especially those who toured the Mississippi Valley, went home convinced that betting amounted to a national pastime in America. These observers doubtless exaggerated the trait, perhaps in order to document a common European stereotype of American vulgarity on the frontier, but their perceptions clearly contained a kernel of truth.[12] Gambling and gamblers thrived, despite rhetorical disapproval, in an atmosphere congenial to wide-open, commercial betting.

Foreigners explained Americans' fondness for gaming in terms of the overall cultural climate. Alexis de Tocqueville contended that the dynamics of capitalism and democracy in the new republic generated a restlessness and an infatuation with risk that heightened the urge to wager. The life of an average American, the French aristocrat marveled, "passed like a game of chance," and every endeavor came to be structured around risk taking. The national trait appeared most clearly in the country's commerce, which Tocqueville likened to a "vast lottery," and in the westering process; each adventure was undertaken "not only for the sake of the profit it holds out to them, but for the love of the constant excitement occasioned by that pursuit."[13]

A style of risk taking had blossomed as a cultural attribute that marked Americans as a distinctive people. Their attachment to risk and change intensified their urge to gamble. Gaming seemed to be an amusement that suited Jacksonians' self-image perfectly. It reiterated the nation's egalitarian premise at the same time that it generated the vital differences, the wins and losses, that distinguished between equals.

On the one hand, betting games created for participants the "conditions of pure equality denied them in real life."[14] The mixture of chance and competition, in a sphere set apart from the working world, appealed to this generation of egalitarians, for all white male adults who gambled stood as equals before the goddess of fortune. On the other hand, although all shared the opportunity to gain, gambling differentiated between winners and losers, and so provided the distinctions that individuals hoped would set themselves apart from each other. Almost every American prided himself on his country's democratic condition, but he simultaneously strove to prove that he was better than others by making the most of his opportunities to stand apart from the undifferentiated mass. Gambling facilitated this quest ideally. A man displayed his equality by sitting down to play in the first place, but hoped that the game's outcome would make him more equal than other citizens. Gambling reiterated both the egalitarianism and the enterprising individualism of the antebellum period.

While nationwide attitudes reinforced the urge to wager, within the United States the residents of different regions approached gambling in different ways. Timothy Dwight, a staunch New Englander, resented European accounts that portrayed vulgar betting as a national pastime in the new republic, and insisted that his own chaste region be distinguished from southern and western societies. Within several years foreign travelers' perceptions had sharpened enough to recognize the distinctions between North, South, and West. Frederick Marryat found that bettors "carried on very quietly" in northeastern cities during the 1830s, while in Dixie and along the Mississippi River they played "as open as the noon day."[15] The English observer thus described the regional differences that helped to explain the emergence of the Southwest as source of American gambling culture.

The Southerner's fondness for gambling received some attention from those seeking to understand the distinctiveness of the Slave States. The South and its frontier contained not only the sharpers who flourished along the rivers of the region, but also the national "fountain-head" of gaming, New Orleans, and the majority of American race tracks. The section's tolerance for gaming has mostly been explained as a consequence of European cultural orientations that took deep root in southern, rather than northern, soil. Gambling as practiced in New Orleans resulted in part from the weight of Spanish and French tradition. Moreover, Southerners inherited colonial Virginians' preference for English fashions of horse racing and card playing.[16]

British gambling traditions no doubt appealed to a slave-owning gentry that liked to identify itself with English gentlemen.[17] Elite Southerners consequently continued to try to imitate the customs of their supposedly genteel English forefathers, and, like colonial Virginians and Carolinians before them, they never quite succeeded. There were some similarities, of course. As in England, gaming continued to help distinguish between classes. Many a Southern gentleman bred and ran thoroughbreds less for the sport than for the honor and distinction that his participation brought.[18] As in colonial Virginia and Jackson's Tennessee, horse racing remained a proven means of establishing and maintaining bonds between men of kindred status and spirit.

Yet, horse racing and other forms of gambling generally lacked the excess and form that had connoted high living to British noblemen, and continued to disappoint those seeking to imitate English example. When Southerners compared their racing to that which took place across the Atlantic, they found that their mounts ran the wrong direction—counterclockwise—on the wrong surface—dirt—around the wrong type of track—a flat oval.[19] The American wilderness had altered Old World styles of racing altogether.

Like the colonists, Southerners tried with little success to borrow English customs. As a result, their cultural practices inevitably reflected the nature of their own slave society more than their imitation of Europeans. Gambling was encouraged by the same distinctly regional conditions that fostered dueling. The planter elite cultivated a pessimistic world view that stressed restraint of such passions as competitiveness and aggression, instincts which, if left unchecked, threatened to undermine a precarious social order. To defuse disruptive tensions, Southerners tended to personalize and ceremonialize potentially explosive disagreements. The symbol and ceremony of the duel helped to minimize social dangers by reducing conflict to purely personal terms and formalizing it as a drawn-out ritual.[20] Gambling likely served a similar function in planter society by ritualizing competition and confining aggression in a personal context that still managed to uphold codes of honor and manliness. Like dueling, card playing and horse racing assumed considerable cultural importance in the old South as valuable outlets for troublesome passions. Gambling thus became an integral strand in the fabric of southern civilization.

When Southerners migrated to the frontier, their attitudes toward betting became even more tolerant. In the North and the South, gaming had been encouraged by national and regional orientations, but it had remained comparatively moderate in tone and stagnant in form. Few new styles appeared and few professional gamblers thrived in eastern settings. Society in the frontier Southwest, on the other hand, not only distilled the antebellum orientations that encouraged all Americans to take chances in order to get ahead, but also placed fewer restraints on the substance and style of betting games. In the lower Mississippi Valley gambling became a legitimate, highly organized enterprise. In that region professional sharps and their gaming practices mirrored frontier ways of life, came to be identifyed closely with unsettled frontier conditions, and changed as the frontier itself evolved into a more stable society. Gambling along the western rivers assumed both the openness that Northerners tried to repress and the passion that Southerners sought to subdue. As a result, gaming practices new to the American scene, such as casino games and draw poker, took root there and eventually branched out to the rest of the nation. Between

1800 and 1848 the old Southwest served as the principal point of origin for new kinds of American betting.

The southern frontier consisted of two geographic components. Between the settled coasts and river valleys stood numerous backcountries in the forests and hills of the interior that comprised an "inner frontier."[21] These patches, dispersed and heterogeneous, are difficult to conceptualize as one geographic or social entity. Similarly, because the areas were settled at different times and at different paces, they defy description as a single chronological frontier. When pioneers entered these diverse locales, they did not often stay for long, so circumstances of life there, including gambling games, sometimes retained a degree of western unsettledness.[22] Patches of the southern interior are best viewed as backwoods districts, not as a well-defined frontier.

The lower Mississippi Valley between 1800 and 1840, on the other hand, constituted an American frontier in the more classic sense. This river frontier featured not only the more definite, linear shape that is traditionally pictured as the westering edge of civilization, but also a more clear-cut timetable of development. Stretching roughly from the port of Natchez to the towns of St. Louis on the Mississippi River and Louisville on the Ohio, the frontier of the lower Mississippi Valley was opened fully to American penetration by 1815. And while the backcountry districts of the southern interior quickly turned into rural patches, the river frontier was tamed more gradually by trade and transportation. By 1840 the forces of commerce, technology, and urbanism had closed this mercantile frontier by planting the dominant economy and civilization of the South in towns along the river banks. The culture of the lower portion of the great mid-continental valley was finally more southern than western, and the change found expression in the transformation of gambling.[23]

The foundations for an American gambling frontier had been laid during the eighteenth century by French and Spanish colonists in the Southwest who imported European gaming practices to that corner of North America. Although their colonizing efforts ultimately proved unsuccessful, the two waves of European settlers left a lasting legacy of Continental betting that diverged notably from the English-based gambling of the eastern seaboard. New Orleans served as both the center of Spanish and French attempts at colonization, and a port of entry for European gaming practices in the New World. Once Americans broke through the barriers that isolated them from the lower Mississippi, novel forms of public and commercial gambling began to flow from the Crescent City up the river frontier and, eventually, throughout the young republic.

American attempts to penetrate the Franco-Spanish sphere of colonization during the late eighteenth century began fittingly with the speculations of the Yazoo land companies. Defying the national governments of both Spain and the United States, the legislature of Georgia "granted" enormous tracts of Spanish and Indian land to private American companies

in 1789 and 1795, for the purpose of opening for settlement the uncharted
territories adjacent to the eastern bank of the Mississippi River. These real-
estate bubbles burst quickly, but they demonstrated Americans' interest in
the Southwest and foreshadowed the role that gambling would play in
shaping that frontier.[24]

The United States made more successful inroads into the great valley during the late eighteenth and early nineteenth centuries. A royal order from
the king of Spain tried to entice alienated Americans into Spanish colonizing schemes in 1788, but the youthful republic had greater designs on the
western territories. In 1795 it concluded Pinckney's Treaty with Spain, an
agreement that opened New Orleans to American water-borne commerce,
and made the Mississippi into a major western commercial artery.[25] Finally,
in 1803 the United States complemented its holdings along the eastern
shore of the great river by buying the enormous western territory from
France. The Louisiana Purchase did not stimulate an immediate influx of
settlers to the lower valley, for lands remained insecure in that remote territory. However, it did complete Americans' acquisition of the Mississippi
River and laid the groundwork for future settlement. Moreover, it
cemented the stream's role as a crucial avenue of trade, and transferred
New Orleans to United States possession. The gamblers' frontier had begun
to take shape.

Prior to 1815, a singular class of pioneers populated the river frontier
and established gambling as an essential aspect of life in the new territory.
From the agricultural and forest hinterlands of the Ohio and Mississippi
valleys, adventuresome boatmen floated downstream in an assortment of
river craft. These deck hands and pilots, who numbered between two and
three thousand by 1815, manned the rafts, barges, keelboats, and flatboats
that protected the role of the Mississippi and Ohio rivers as arteries of commerce in the early nineteenth-century West. They guided their craft to
Natchez and New Orleans, where cargoes of farm and lumber products
were sold or transferred to ocean-going vessels. The boatmen then began
the arduous upstream journey. With extensive labor some keelboats were
poled and pulled upriver. Other boatmen dismantled their craft in order
to sell them as lumber in New Orleans, and then returned northward by
land. The introduction of regular steamboat traffic on the western rivers
made the return trip much easier by 1820, though the new vessels did not
soon displace the cheaper flatboats and keelboats as downstream carriers
of cargo. Large numbers of boatmen continued to work, and gamble, on
the Mississippi until the Civil War.[26]

American folklore was quick to inflate the boatmen into figures larger
than life. Legends depicting these "Kentuckians" as "gigantic" or "rough
and hardy" men soon obscured the actual nature of life along the river.[27]
Underlying the topsoil of legend lay the reality of homeless and womenless
men, the bedrock of tall tales about such other heroic drifters as mountain
men, cowboys, and hobos. In 1826 Timothy Flint colorfully depicted the

hard migratory life, punctuated every so often by bouts of abandon, that boatmen led. From all points on the trans-Appalachian frontier and with all kinds of cargo, he noted, these sailors floated downriver through the western wilderness. Their long, friendless journey was interrupted on occasion when the boats converged in "fleets" at such landings as Natchez or New Madrid, Missouri. For one evening the transient men socialized and caroused, but by dawn each boat had resumed its solitary southward trip, not to encounter another crowd until the next big landing. And so the boatmen traveled downstream, enduring long "indolent" stretches interspersed with bursts of dangerous work and playful excitement.[28]

The alternating pace of life that Flint described not only left boatmen plenty of spare time for gaming but also encouraged them to seek the thrills of chance. They consequently became prodigious bettors who wagered both among themselves, while on the river, and against the professional gamblers who increasingly awaited their arrival at frontier landings. Toward the middle of the century, artists George Caleb Bingham and Jacob A. Dallas portrayed the boatmen's card playing while aboard their craft, and captured the small scale of these private games. Deck hands never gambled too extensively while floating downriver, because the voyage was often rough and boatmen liked to save their money for sprees at the ports of Natchez and New Orleans or, after 1820, for betting while heading upstream aboard steamers.[29]

If boatmen restrained themselves aboard their barges and craft, they gambled with abandon while on shore. In the small towns that dotted the banks of the lower Mississippi and its tributaries, and in the terminal port of New Orleans, waterfront districts evolved that catered specifically to the boatmen making their way north and south. Each landing offered drink, food, and gaming to the homeless river travelers. Pilots customarily gave their deck hands a holiday in these inland ports in order to reward them for the strenuous work on the river. As the only significant station between New Orleans and St. Louis or Louisville prior to 1820, the town of Natchez gained early and lasting notoriety as a boatmen's paradise. Those journeying downstream viewed it as the end of the most difficult stretches of water and celebrated every time they stopped there. For men returning upriver by land, the town served as the final river settlement before moving on to the long and lonely Natchez Trace.[30] The hearty gambling in Natchez-under-the-Hill and other landings nourished a growing body of sharps, and gamblers armed with novel modes of betting flocked to the towns to take advantage of the steady flow of players. New forms of public and commercial betting, imported from France and Spain through New Orleans and modified for American tastes, thus began their penetration of the North American continent. By the mid-1820s, gambling had become a well-established feature of life under-the-hill.

For the first twenty years of the nineteenth century, Natchez stood by itself as an important river port between St. Louis and New Orleans. American flatboatmen who floated down the Ohio and Mississippi saw few other signs of settlement. Between the rude farms of western Pennsylvania and Ohio, and the levee-sheltered plantations below Natchez, river travelers passed dense forests interrupted but rarely by rundown outposts of Spanish and French colonies. In the second decade of the century, steamboats began to ply the western rivers, creating a host of insignificant service points. By that time, also, a few favored overnight landings for flatboats and keelboats were beginning to emerge as logical sites for towns along the lower Mississippi. Not until after 1815, however, did Americans begin to occupy in numbers the land that bordered southwestern streams.

The initial white inhabitants of the region came as part of the Great Migration that inundated western territories after the War of 1812. The conclusion of that conflict in 1815 opened the southern frontier to uninhibited American settlement by securing the area from Spanish and English claims, and by initiating a series of military and diplomatic advances that forced Indians to cede their lands to the American government.[31] Flatboatmen floating southward would first have noticed the white man's livestock grazing along the river banks in the years around 1815, for herdsmen comprised the first wave of pioneers moving to the newly opened lands of the South. Close upon the heels of drovers came land-hungry farmers eager to divide the vast public domain into an extension of the Cotton Kingdom.

Keeping to westbound paths, settlers moved from the tired soils of Virginia, eastern Kentucky and Tennessee, the Carolinas, and Georgia, on to the fertile lands of western Tennessee and Kentucky, central Alabama, and west-central Mississippi. They settled not up against the river, where their holdings would have been flooded periodically by the stream, but rather at a slight distance inland, preserving the line of forest that bordered the rivers. The massive migration continued into the early 1830s as Indians ceded more and more land. As late as 1832 much of the northern and western portions of the state of Mississippi, including that part bounded by the river, remained reserved for Choctaw and Chickasaw Indians. The presence of these tribes prolonged the pioneer phase of society and restricted the growth of the nearby river towns, Memphis and Vicksburg, by occupying potential hinterlands. With the removal of the few remaining native Americans during the mid-1830s, one last influx of newcomers capped the Great Migration to the cotton frontier along the lower Mississippi, and marked a turning point in the development of this gamblers' West.[32]

The perpetual motion and speculation of westering migrants likened the old Southwest to other American frontiers. Prevalent chance and change not only encouraged the rise of gambling as the characteristic pastime of the area but also added to the uncertainties of life. The instability of the new country became especially apparent in Arkansas on the western side of the river, a territory that retained its frontier character for an unusually long time. Peopled by numerous displaced Indians, and burdened with swampy terrain and inadequate roads, Arkansas remained unsettled long after lands just east of the river had been subdued by the culture of cotton and slaves. Emigrants hesitated to push beyond the Mississippi into the interior of the territory. Consequently, it remained a no man's land "admired" by "*bankrupts, homicides, horse-stealers,* and *gamblers.*" The territory perpetuated frontier conditions throughout the lower river valley by serving as a refuge for the blacklegs chased out of other communities.[33] While Arkansas was exceptional in the extent of its unruly population and slow development, the territory nonetheless demonstrated the uncertainty of life in newly occupied lands along the western rivers.

The people of the river frontier diverged markedly from the cotton planters migrating to new lands in the Southwest. The first comprised a commercial and fast society of towns right next to the rivers where pioneer conditions endured, while the second formed an agricultural society, inland from riverbanks, that was disciplined by the presence of black slaves. The two groups of settlers depended heavily upon each other, for farmers mostly shipped their produce through river towns and often purchased goods from townspeople; yet they each cultivated their own styles of living. Town residents thrived in a speculative and transient western setting that welcomed new forms of public, commercial betting, while planters quickly reproduced the rigid order and restraints of the slave South.

The transformation of river towns from crude flatboat landings to full-fledged cotton markets proceeded slowly and fitfully, but large plantations founded in the surrounding hinterlands passed through the frontier stage fleetingly. One year growers would bring in slaves to clear the land; the next year the same laborers sowed and reaped cotton.[34] In a brief span of two years the plantation became fully established and the social controls necessary to the slave economy were firmly in place. This short process took place forcefully in the lands surrounding Natchez, which before 1800 had been divided up thoroughly into large plantations. The huge proportion of black slaves in the countryside compelled white planters to eliminate as quickly as possible any disruptive influences. When John James Audubon depicted the vicinity in 1822, the peaceful and tame landscape he painted mirrored the well-ordered rural society of the Natchez District.[35] The western wilderness had given way rapidly to southern respectability. At the same time that Audubon portrayed the orderly life of the Natchez countryside, however, William C. Hall experienced the disorder of waterfront infernos and attested their uncontrollable frontier population. The diversity of town inhabitants, once the consequence of Spanish, French, British, and Indian interests in the area, persisted in the guise of free blacks and river travelers whose social and geographic mobility added to the fluidity of society along the river.[36]

Residents of such fledgling communities as Natchez, Vicksburg, and Memphis, isolated from the plantation South by forest and swampland, behaved exactly like "a race of men placed on the extreme limits of order and civilization," according to Timothy Flint. They were ill-mannered and given over to crude habits such as carrying knives and firearms.[37] Unlike Southerners, who tried to channel passion into rituals, these Westerners seemed to live for lust and paid little attention to established authority or eastern convention. Unlike planters, who toiled to maintain a rigid sense of hierarchy, these migrants adhered to a frontier code of informality and rough egalitarianism for white males. Travelers were surprised to find army officers, cotton planters, and other successful men playing cards with common clerks and roguish gamblers, "laughing together, swearing together, and the names of Bill, Dick, and Harry, passing familiarly between them!"[38] Eastern proprieties seemed to dissolve in the riverfront setting.

The urge to gamble was heightened by the speculation of westering people who hoped to turn migration into quick profit. "Sudden vicissitudes" and perpetual excitement, Michel Chevalier surmised in 1835, characterized business and society among American pioneers.[39] Unsettled territory seemed to intensify the traits of individualism and chance taking that encouraged gambling throughout the nation, while at the same time the West lacked the inhibitions that had limited Northerners' and Southerners' participation in betting. So along the lower Mississippi river frontier, games of chance not only constituted one of the "prevailing vices" but also took their place alongside real-estate schemes, commodities markets, and currency manipulation as accepted forms of frontier enterprise.[40]

The commercial orientation of southwestern society further strengthened the inclination to gamble. The Mississippi headed a network of southern streams that served as avenues of trade for farmers and merchants. Those who settled in towns along the rivers often devoted their lives to the risks and rewards of inland commerce and land development, and the entire valley seemed alive with travelers who had a great deal of currency at their disposal. Boats plying the waterways carried plenty of cash-laden businessmen, preoccupied with money, who also proved a strong temptation to sharpers.[41] Many of these passengers were southern planters taking a vacation as they escorted their crops to market. With profits either in hand or on the near horizon, these men relished the trip to and from New Orleans. Like other river travelers, they made ideal marks for the confidence men who infested waterfront towns.

Although the traveler's money made him ripe to be picked by gamblers, he was generally done in as well by his own willingness to wager, a trait that likened him to residents of the western region. Seduced by the bright prospects for their business deals as well as by the transience of the river frontier, these excursionists, including "many eastern and northern men of good character at home," seemed to leave behind all restraint when journeying down the Mississippi.[42] The British actor Joseph L. Cowell recalled that "a trip down the river" often meant an uncontrolled yearly opportunity for the young merchants and their clerks *to go it with a perfect looseness*, mixed up indiscriminately with "a sort of vagabonds" of all nations, who then made New-Orleans their *"jumping-off place."* All moral and social restraint was placed in the shade—*there Jack was as good as his master*—and never was Republicanism more practically republicanized.

Although river travelers often lost hundreds of dollars to sharpers in these sprees, the Englishman preferred to sympathize with the gambler, who had all too often been misrepresented. Victims might complain about being taken by the blackleg, Cowell noted, but they nonetheless played against him regularly, and would have cheated the gambler out of "every dollar [he] had, *if they knew how."*[43]

The unrestrained behavior of river travelers typified the restlessness and riskiness of the lower Mississippi Valley during the first third of the nineteenth century. To the essential gamble of migration westward were added the fluidity of life along the river, and the hazards and excitements of a commercial frontier. Consequently, settlement in the old Southwest remained a chancy proposition. Moreover, it came to be focused not in rural districts but in waterfront communities where western ways of living resisted the penetration of conventional southern culture. These towns, often little more than real-estate ventures themselves, presented gambling as a natural ingredient of life and permitted the constant operation and refinement of public games of chance. They fostered the growth of betting in the region and served as a springboard for the distribution of new kinds of American gambling to the rest of the country.

The character of raw inland ports like Memphis, Vicksburg, and Natchez derived in large part from the archetypal riverfront town of New Orleans. Unlike many of the communities upstream, New Orleans was no longer a full-fledged frontier town, but it shared with other river settlements certain elements that linked the towns in an unholy alliance. The Crescent City had its own waterfront district, the "Swamp," located inside the Old Quarter of the metropolis, that differed in size from landing districts upriver, but catered just as successfully to the thousands of boatmen and steamer passengers arriving each year. In addition, although Americans "pioneered" New Orleans less by migration than by diplomacy, the city did comprise a unique ethnic frontier for Spanish, French, English, African, Creole, Mexican, and American cultures. People from a variety of backgrounds learned the customs of different groups and came to tolerate heterogeneous attitudes and behavior regarding betting. The diversity of the local population thus contributed to an atmosphere which encouraged such activities as gambling, helping to make New Orleans the Babylon of the South and the center of gaming in the United States.[44]

French and Spanish settlers of the eighteenth century had cultivated gambling extensively in New Orleans and the surrounding lowlands. Many

of these colonists viewed Louisiana as a temporary residence, an outlook
that heightened the impermanent character of the place and reinforced the
willingness to take chances. In addition, the pestilential environment of
the lower Mississippi made New Orleans but a seasonal home for some,
and encouraged a sort of secular fatalism that elicited further the gambling
instinct. Crowds of visitors naturally regarded the Crescent City as a resort.
Its streets always seemed to be filled with male travelers—merchants, boatmen, soldiers, sailors, and planters—who, "not looking upon New Orleans
as their homes, [were] all more devoted to mere pleasure, and less scru-
pulous as to the shape in which it [was] enjoyed, than in their native cities."[45] Early nineteenth-century observers of the port seldom failed to mention the quadroon balls, the promiscuous dancing, the violations of the
Sabbath, and the dens of drinking and gambling for which the city became
so notorious to the English-speaking world.[46]

If observers were shocked at the apparent sinfulness of the town, they
nonetheless understood quite well that gambling flourished more successfully in New Orleans than elsewhere in the United States, and sought to
explain why. The first colonists from France and Spain had introduced
wide-open betting to the vicinity, but the metropolis became the American
center for gambling only with the explosive growth initiated through the
takeover of the town by the United States in 1803. Yankee newcomers
could hardly resist the unfamiliar temptations that Louisiana offered. By
1810 New Orleans reportedly had as many gaming halls as the four largest
American cities combined, and by 1815 the city had begun to license and
tax gambling dens, forwarding the revenues to charity.[47]

Louisiana legislators sanctioned public and commercial gambling in
New Orleans by permitting it at the outset of statehood in 1812. While
reformers succeeded in outlawing the activity on a few occasions, gambling in the Crescent City flourished during the nineteenth century
whether legal or not. The Panic of 1837 drove some gaming houses out of
business by reducing the supply of currency, but by the mid-1840s the
steady flow of soldiers through the town to the Mexican War had revitalized the industry. At the end of the decade, between four and five hundred
gaming dens were operating. Furthermore, in the 1850s the metropolis
became known as the "horse-racing capital of the nation," with no less
than five tracks open every winter season. The unprecedented extent of
betting on thoroughbreds confirmed visitors' claim that New Orleans stood
alone as the principal focus of American gambling.[48]

The city's reputation as a "modern Sodom" derived not only from the
extent of its gambling but also from the new styles of play that made their
American debut there. New Orleans served as the nation's port of entry for
such European games as poker, craps, and faro, and for the Mexican game
of three-card monte. In that metropolis and up the Mississippi River Valley,
each of these diversions appealed to American tastes.[49] During the latter

half of the nineteenth century these new forms of betting emerged as the most popular gambling games in the United States.

Faro, craps, monte, and poker became popular in large part because a certain class of entrepreneurs promoted them, and because they corresponded to the increasingly commercial and public character of American betting and recreation. The newly arrived styles of play were tailored to the professional sharper who pursued gambling as a profitable line of work, because they could be operated either as banking games in which the dealer's income resulted from odds or percentages fixed in his favor, or as ostensibly private games in which the gambler's slippery skills assured a steady profit through deceit. Sharpers consequently made the novel games their livelihood and spread them quickly to the great valley above New Orleans and, later, to other parts of the country. Westerners accepted these imports quickly because they appreciated their entrepreneurial character and found them suited to frontier tastes.

The new games became mainstays in the growing number of public gambling houses in New Orleans. The city acquired a great many commercial establishments that foreshadowed the clubs and casinos of the Far West. In 1827 John Davis opened one Crescent City house that was perhaps the first full-blown American gaming casino. The club provided public halls for betting at the more commercial games, including faro, roulette, and *vingt-et-un*, as well as secluded rooms where more illustrious citizens played such private games as brag, *écarte*, and Boston. All gambling took place in a rich and ornate setting, yet the club was open to virtually any white male bettor who wanted to play.[50] Davis had arrived at a popular American formula that combined aristocratic appearance with democratic participation in casino play.

John Davis's elaborate club in some regards illuminated the future of American gambling, but it remained an exception in the old Southwest. Most waterfront gaming houses on the river frontier were modeled after the smaller, cruder dens located near the levee in the New Orleans Swamp. Gaming remained just as open and commercial in riverside clubs, but it relied on a different range of customers. The *"infernos"* of the district, according to clergyman Joseph Holt Ingraham, attracted not men of status who played in private rooms, but rather "the *canaille* of the city, sailors, Kentucky boatmen, crews of steamboats, and poor Gallic gentlemen, in threadbare long-skirted coats and huge whiskers."[51] Largely ignored by lawmakers and lawmen, games in the Swamp were generally rough and crooked, but most participants took such conditions in stride because they knew of no other kind of gambling in the lower Mississippi Valley.[52]

North of New Orleans, waterfront communities with their own landing districts fell within the commercial orbit of the Crescent City and borrowed many of its ways, including its styles of gambling. Yet such settlements as Natchez, Vicksburg, and Memphis had histories of their own as products of the westward migration of the early nineteenth century. These towns arose to enhance water travel and regional commerce in the old Southwest. The river naturally stood out as the strongest influence on the development of these frontier towns. It shaped not only the chronology of their evolution but also the geography. The most enduring settlements on the lower Mississippi were located on high bluffs that overlooked the river. These elevated sites remained relatively impervious to the constant erosion and shifting of the river banks below. To accommodate water-borne traffic, each community built a landing at the foot of the bluff. Comparable in some regards to the New Orleans Swamp, these riverfront districts contained the attractions that appealed to boatmen, gamblers, and other river travelers. Respectable citizens generally dwelt atop the bluff, away from the water and the underworlds fittingly located beneath the "hill-cities."[53]

The streams that determined the shape of the towns in the old Southwest also governed their pace of settlement. At first the great river served to intensify frontier conditions, particularly in waterfront districts, by heightening the transience of life, delivering heterogeneous populations of migrants and travelers, and providing an avenue of escape as well as an accessible border for shifty elements in pioneer society. The fluidity of river settlements made the Southwest an ideal environment for professional gamblers, who dominated those parts of town that lay closest to water. Operating openly under-the-hill between St. Louis and New Orleans, and along the lower Ohio River, sharpers exploited the perpetual motion that seemed to characterize town life.[54] They also took advantage of the speculativeness of westering people, the holiday mood of many travelers, and the enterprising spirit of businessmen. Gamblers found that the rivers facilitated their trade by enhancing the risks and rewards of frontier life.

If the streams helped to postpone settlement of the old Southwest, however, they also ultimately brought the forces that tamed frontier conditions and curbed the practices of professional gamblers. The rivers of the region functioned both as routes of migration and as paths of commerce. They brought more and more settlers from the East who were eager to civilize western towns by supplanting frontier culture with refined ways of living. The growing numbers of businessmen who depended upon water travel encouraged the elimination of disruptive and unreliable elements from inland ports in order to enhance the commercial climate. Entrepôts like Natchez, Memphis, and Vicksburg, which competed against one another for river trade and transport, resolved increasingly to confront the lawlessness in under-the-hill districts. The technological advancement of steamboats and railroads reinforced the efforts of the "better class" by expediting commerce and by tying western towns more closely to settled regions. In short, the great inland waterways brought civilization to the frontier.[55]

Because of their prominence under-the-hill, gamblers were among the first targets of townspeople bent on refining southwestern communities. Sharpers and their compatriots in river landings increasingly seemed too incongruous a vestige of the frontier to coexist safely with the ever-growing numbers of merchants. For one thing, the presence of blacklegs in waterfront districts clearly interfered with commercial growth. Gamblers occupied the same landings that respectable businessmen needed, thereby inhibiting the free flow of trade. In Memphis, where decent citizens were afraid to approach the wharves to do business, merchants worried that cardsharps and faro dealers repelled prospective customers. Furthermore, as one Natchez newspaper bluntly asserted, the presence of gamblers simply tended to drive down property values, a serious threat to western towns obsessed with real-estate prices.[56]

Sharpers challenged more than local business prospects, however, for they also seemed to threaten the safety of society itself. As southern culture replaced western ways in the lower Mississippi Valley, professional gamblers offended the traditional sense of a stable social order. Even more than Northerners, Southerners felt very keenly the need to establish and preserve social distinctions. Their peculiar institution tended to sharpen social gradations and heighten concern throughout the region. Planters generally viewed their society as a well-ordered but fragile structure that needed plenty of protection. They consequently strove to build and maintain a rigid social hierarchy that would lend stability to southern life. The pursuit of hierarchy naturally clashed with a considerable amount of social mobility, especially in newly settled parts of the region, but it nonetheless helped to satisfy Southerners' yearning for order and security. Once people knew where they stood in the hierarchy, it was thought, they would understand and observe the proprieties of human relationships, and society would function smoothly.[57]

Here gamblers caused a special problem, for they tended to ignore social distinctions completely. To them, as to prostitutes, it seemed unprofessional to differentiate between paying customers. They consequently played indiscriminately with all potential victims, from the most upright planter to the meanest flatboatman or, even worse, the black slave. Too often for the taste of upstanding townspeople, sharpers did not stay in their place under-the-hill, but instead walked about river towns promiscuously, completely beyond the control of civil authorities.[58] They violated notions of social hierarchy and flouted the respectable class of Southerners that continued to grow in river towns.

In frontier settings, where gamblers were virtually legitimate businessmen, they might have rubbed elbows with anybody and broken laws with impunity. But as the culture of the settled South began to take hold along western rivers in the 1830s, and as commercial prospects in the cotton trade grew brighter by the day, townspeople throughout the lower valley objected increasingly to the presence of presumptuous sharpers. Unable to control low life through lawful means, the "better class" turned to violent lynching to bend the gamblers to its will. Beginning in the mid-1830s, at a host of places between Cincinnati on the north and Natchez on the south, citizens formed vigilance committees that ran professional gamblers out of town. By cleansing communities in this time-honored western fashion, townspeople announced both the closing of the river frontier and the coming of respectable southern civilization.[59]

The purge of the gamblers was perhaps the most clear-cut symptom of social change in the old Southwest, but it was not the only one. As the frontier region absorbed southern culture, it also gained greater respect for the South's peculiar institution. Once relatively indifferent to the imperatives of black slavery, river towns paid increasing deference to the labor system upon which their cotton trade depended.[60] Similarly, western communities had long disregarded Southerners' apprehensions of unbridled violence, but they now worked to confine aggression and fighting and to ceremonialize personal conflict.[61] Vigilantism constituted one stage in the modification of southwestern violence, and in fact exemplified the transition from frontier river landing to southern cotton entrepôt.

All these developments came into sharp focus in July 1835, at Vicksburg, Mississippi, where settlers struck the first and most resounding blow for respectability by lynching five gamblers and declaring martial law. The episode, which had far-reaching repercussions throughout the great valley, dramatized the process of transition from western flatboat town to southern inland port and provided a case study of gambling and society along the western rivers.

Located high on a bluff overlooking the junction of the Yazoo and Mississippi rivers, Vicksburg clearly belonged to the far western frontier of the 1820s and 1830s. Like Memphis, the chief rival to the north, it had been founded in 1819 as a steamboat landing and farmers' market, and its hinterland remained incompletely developed for fifteen years. By the mid-1830s the town, "a raw-looking, straggling place," consisted of approximately 2,500 people.[62] The population was quick-tempered and excitable, and apparently cared little for stability. Men walked the streets armed with pistols and knives, and decent women avoided walking through town altogether. In addition, citizens placed no trust in the law. Faced with venal authorities, jurors feared to convict criminals. "The law has no power here," a local clergyman lamented; "the civil officers are afraid to do their duty, and they have good reason to be so, for they are as often the offenders themselfs."[63]

If residents of Vicksburg seemed less than interested in establishing community order, it was perhaps because they devoted more time and money to the tremendous economic boom driving the young town. Visitors passing by the village found inhabitants "run mad with speculation. They do business in a kind of phrenzy," one Alabaman reported. "Money is scarce, but credit is plenty."[64] The excitement revolved in large part around sales of the "rich cotton lands" in the area, just recently surrendered by Indians, which had attracted "adventurous spirits of every description." The "mania" was intensified throughout the decade as builders started and completed a railroad line from Clinton, Mississippi, to Vicksburg that promised to facilitate the shipment of cotton to the river town and make Vicksburg the state's leading inland port.[65] Such bright prospects made the village a popular destination for speculative migrants, and attracted plenty of hopeful plungers who made prime targets for professional gamblers.

Scenting the opportunities in a town rife with speculation, sharpers "flocked there from all parts of the Union" and by 1835 had made Vicksburg "the liveliest gambling place in the whole Southwest," one reformed cardsharp recalled. The gamblers had found a community whose very spirit welcomed betting of all sorts. Moreover, in contrast to Natchez where the steep bluff acted as a barrier between under-the-hill gamblers and respectable townspeople, the more gradual bluff at Vicksburg permitted easier travel between one part of town and another, and did not confine sharpers to the waterfront district. Gamblers in Vicksburg boldly set up shop all over town, "both on the hill and under the hill, in log cabins, board houses, canvas tents and flat boats."[66]

The blacklegs' presence both above and below the bluff indicated how little the western town had adhered to southern notions of social hierarchy. Local residents hardly seemed to distinguish between underworld and respectability, for they accepted the gaming dens as legitimate businesses. In fact, "some of the most prominent people" in Vicksburg patronized the gambling shops regularly. G. W. Featherstonhaugh, an English geologist traveling down the Mississippi by steamboat, learned of the character of the town in early 1835 when a group of local "gentlemen, some of whom were planters of great respectability," boarded his vessel at Vicksburg and spent the entire voyage to New Orleans wagering, drinking, and carousing with an unsavory collection of blacklegs.[67] These leading residents seemed to exemplify the local preoccupation with gambling.

The speculation that obsessed frontier Vicksburg heightened the townspeople's urge to gamble and increased their tolerance for sharpers. Yet most investors' expectations for the town simultaneously envisioned a rapid growth that would ultimately transform the rude outpost into a prosperous and stable settlement. Local residents who looked ahead impatiently to the town's bright future as cotton railhead and commercial center must have realized that, once it had been fully integrated into the southern economy, Vicksburg would have to become more refined. These citizens wanted the town to conform to eastern standards of civility, which in this case derived from the planter elite of the Slave States. They wanted to reform the community, and made gamblers the primary focus of their attention.

By 1835 rumor had long indicted and convicted local blacklegs as guilty of all crimes in the vicinity and responsible for all limitations on economic growth, but none of the suspects had ever been brought to satisfactory justice. Then in early summer a series of events stirred respectable citizens to

concerted action against the gamblers, touching off a storm of vigilantism
that blew throughout the southern frontier.

On the third of July townspeople heard a terrifying story that implicated
gamblers as conspirators behind a slave insurrection in central Mississippi.[68] The tale derived from the popular legend of John Murrell and the
Clan of the Mystic Confederacy, an alleged band of outlaws and sharpers
whose design to incite slave rebellion and to plunder the stricken Southwest had been "exposed" the year before. There was no truth to the
charges of conspiracy, and Murrell, the blacklegs' leader, had been impris-
oned since 1834, but fearful Southerners continued to believe in the plot
and expected its outbreak at nearly every turn. The region became particularly sensitive to the threat of insurrection during the summer of 1835 as
northern abolitionists initiated a stunning direct-mail campaign in the
Slave States that heightened whites' apprehensiveness and provoked violent protests throughout the region. Southerners tended to see the blackleg, the slave conspirator, and the abolitionist as one and the same threat,
and in some cases struck out furiously against it.[69]

The fright reached a peak in the newly settled counties of Mississippi,
just to the east of Vicksburg, where blacks overwhelmingly outnumbered
whites. Acting first on rumors that predicted a July fourth uprising by the
Clan of the Mystic Confederacy, and then on dubious confessions beaten
out of both slaves and whites, the local elite acted to prevent a suspected
uprising by forming armed vigilance committees that terrorized supposed
conspirators into submission. The furious violence took the lives of fifteen
slaves and six whites in Madison County alone, and then began to turn
against those who opposed the unlawful proceedings. Meanwhile, the vigilantes spread their message of fear throughout the state.[70]

When the citizens of Vicksburg heard of the reported uprising in central
Mississippi, they prepared to defend their town by readying the militia and
staying alert. Insurrection never reached the river port, of course, and residents proceeded with their Fourth of July festivities the following day.
The townspeople's preparations, however, were not wasted. Accounts of a
nearby slave conspiracy and whites' retaliation provided an opportune
moment for the inhabitants to set matters straight in Vicksburg. Now prepared and organized to defend their community, they devoted their attention to the gamblers whom they increasingly viewed as the source of all
the town's troubles. The days of the blacklegs' reign in Vicksburg and other
river communities were now numbered.

At an Independence Day picnic hosted by the militia, the Vicksburg Volunteers, the troubles began when a drunken gambler named Francis
Cabler, and perhaps some comrades, disrupted a series of toasts. When a
militia officer "attempted to enforce order and silence at the table," the
sharper, "who had impudently thrust himself into the company, insulted
the officer, and struck one of the citizens." Several eager Volunteers
grabbed the offender, ready to punish him, but their commander made sure

that Cabler was released and sent away, and the picnic continued. At the end of the day the militiamen paraded through town, where they once again encountered the troublesome gambler at the public square. Seeking revenge for his earlier embarrassment, Cabler had armed himself with "a loaded pistol, a large knife and a dagger," and set out to assault the Volunteers responsible for his indignity. The militiamen disarmed the blackleg and punished him summarily.[71]

The Volunteers' rationale for taking the law into their own hands illustrated the origins of vigilante violence in frontier Vicksburg, for it expressed the growing frustrations that respectable citizens felt in the face of the uncontrollable class of blacklegs. To permit Cabler to go free, a sympathetic resident explained,

> would have been to devote several of the most respectable members of the [militia] company to his vengeance, and to proceed against him at law would have been mere mockery, inasmuch, as, not having had the opportunity of consummating his design, no adequate punishment could have been inflicted on him. Consequently it was determined to take him in the woods and *Lynch* him—which is a mode of punishment provided for such as become obnoxious in a manner which the law cannot reach.

In the antebellum South, lynching, primarily a frontier phenomenon, meant either hanging or tarring-and-feathering. The militiamen tarred and feathered Cabler for his insolence, and, after a whipping, ordered him to leave town.[72]

Fearful that blacklegs might protest the lynching, and anxious to complete the reform they had at long last undertaken, the citizens of Vicksburg met that very night in the courthouse to settle once and for all the problem of the professional gamblers. There they passed three resolutions. One ordered all sharpers to leave town within twenty-four hours, another warned that local courts would hereafter prosecute the owners of all houses that permitted faro dealing, and the last mandated the posting of one hundred copies of the citizens' resolutions around town the next morning.

The people's ordinances agitated the population of gamblers residing in the town, for most of them left Vicksburg the next day. On the following morning, July 6, a vigilance committee made up of "better citizens" and led by the Volunteers convened to enforce the popular will. It marched through town to known gaming dens, pulling faro tables, roulette wheels, and other betting apparatus out into the streets to be burned, until it reached a barricaded house where five of the "wretches" defied the townspeople's wishes.[73]

The vigilantes demanded the gamblers' surrender, but their entreaty met with still more defiance. When the mob of citizens began to batter down the door of the house, the occupants responded with gunshots, instantly killing one of the vigilantes and sealing the fate of the blacklegs inside.

Members of the committee, "their indignation overcoming all other feelings," returned the fire, rushed into the sharpers' den, and took the holdouts prisoner. They then marched the captives quickly past the courthouse, as if to give the ceremony the briefest of legal sanctions, and directly to the scaffold. There the crowd hanged the five "desperadoes" without hesitation. The townspeople let the bodies dangle until the next morning, long enough to warn off other blacklegs, and then buried them in a ditch. Professional gamblers got the message, apparently, for they reportedly never bothered Vicksburg again.[74]

Not content to stop at lynching, the vigilantes pressed on to root the gambler out of their community. After hanging the five desperadoes they returned to the streets to destroy the sharpers' equipment, and then established an antigambling society. Members of the new organization spread the message up and down the river, and joined the Volunteers in nightly armed patrols of Vicksburg. The extra policing of the town expressed the force of the martial law imposed by vigilantes and the militia in order to secure the gains they had made. L. S. Houghton, a newly arrived resident who later served as a local judge, depicted the extreme measures taken during the week following the execution of the five sharpers:

> at this time while I am writing they are whipping, tarring and feathering for stealing. They have driven the gambler from this town and all law is according to the will of the victors. All gamblers that can be found are hung, insurrectors hung, other offence, whipping. If a man says aught against the [militia] Company's proceedings he is either whipped or hung.[75]

The townspeople reacted to gamblers with virtually as much ferocity as planters in central Mississippi had reacted to threats of slave insurrection. Indeed, Vicksburg drew inspiration from the vigilantism in Madison County. But the population of the river town responded more as Westerners closing the frontier than as defenders of slave society. When gamblers acted up on July fourth and sixth, they were merely behaving as they had many times before. This time, however, they touched on the fear of the "better citizens" who, now more prepared to resort to extralegal violence, decided to settle the old aggravation of gamblers once and for all.

The gamblers, the *Vicksburg Register* explained, had with impunity interfered with business, endangered the streets, committed numerous crimes, "poisoned the springs of morality, and interrupted the relations of society." Moreover, they had perpetuated these misdeeds shamelessly while scorning the respectability to which many of the residents aspired. Cabler's daring antics, in front of a population finally disposed to vigilante justice, proved to be the final straw. Local citizens at long last felt compelled to defend their "insulted laws," "offended virtue," and "slaughtered innocence," if only to regain a modicum of the self-respect that gamblers had won from them. "We had borne with their enormities," the *Register* stated, "until to have suffered them any longer would not only have proved us to be destitute of every manly sentiment, but would also have implicated us in the guilt of accessories to their crimes." The towns-people regretted the violence, but society, they felt, "can sometimes be purified only by a storm."[76]

Although they increasingly shared Southerners' concern for social hier-archy and rigid discipline, Vicksburg residents began to strive for the respectability of more settled society in a manner that mirrored the usual unsettledness of frontier people. They struck out violently, at gamblers rather than slave conspirators, as if to repent all at once for the sins that they committed when their attention had been fixed not on building social order but rather on migration and speculation. The town would never have had to cleanse itself "by storm" if citizens had been vigilant enough to restrain the gamblers lawfully in the first place. Eastern and foreign cor-respondents, who viewed the mob violence as uncivilized, seemed to understand that the "outrageous" vigilantism, like the bold gamblers themselves, typified both the inadequacy of "law-courts" and the generally crude tenor of life on the western edge of American civilization.[77]

While sharpers had epitomized pioneer conditions at a peak, vigilantism signaled the beginning of the end of the river frontier. The winds of change that had first blustered in Vicksburg soon stirred throughout the lower val-ley of the Mississippi. In the Kentucky towns of Lexington, Covington, and Danville, in New Orleans and Mobile, St. Louis and Cincinnati, and throughout Arkansas, westering people intent on conforming to eastern standards increasingly viewed gamblers as a dividing line between frontier disorder and southern respectability. The citizens of Natchez, prodded by a delegation from the Vicksburg antigambling society, began to cleanse their own under-the-hill beginning in 1835. They were assisted in 1840 when a hurricane that leveled the waterfront district literally purified lower Natchez "by storm." In Memphis, the drama began familiarly in July 1835, when respectable citizens chased sharpers across the river into Arkansas. After the two groups later reached a modus vivendi that permit-ted peaceful coexistence, Memphians turned their attention to lawless boatmen who represented more of an obstacle to prosperity and stability. The townspeople finally stood up to the boatmen in 1842 when a crowd of citizens scuffled with and killed a pilot who refused to pay wharfage fees. Like the lynching of the gamblers in Vicksburg, the death of the defiant boatman marked a turning point in the transition from western river town to southern port city.[78]

Up and down the Mississippi, violent popular justice heralded the clos-ing of the frontier in the old Southwest. While vigilantism still belonged distinctly to western societies, it often constituted the first step in a some-times rapid process of transition that ultimately asserted eastern culture over western ways. To residents of river towns, the professional gambler appeared more and more as a barrier to growth and refinement. They objected neither to betting itself, which had a certain place in the civilization of the Slave States, nor to the popular new games of chance that gamblers introduced into the country. Rather, they felt as if their budding sense of decorum was being undermined because the sharper observed none of the proprieties expected by planter society and stood for backwardness in communities increasingly devoted to progress. The blackleg consequently became the focal point for townspeople's fears and frustrations during the mid-1830s as they looked forward to a more stable and more prosperous future. His elimination, or at least his subjugation to the "better class" of people, became an important phase in the changeover from a western to a southern outlook.

In river communities the new attitude toward gamblers was accompanied by shifting views of both blacks and violence. After 1840 residents increasingly turned their attention from the frontier problem of disreputable blacklegs toward the uniquely southern problem of betting among slaves. Because slaves were not supposed to own any property to wager, and because gaming tended to attract both blacks and whites into promiscuous games of chance in defiance of southern ideals of rigid social stratification, settlers now devoted much of their antigambling efforts to enforcing laws against wagering by slaves.[79] They simultaneously adopted more typically southern styles of violence. Dueling replaced vigilantism as the preferred "unpeaceful mode of settling disputes" in Vicksburg. During 1835, in consonance with the frontier character of the town, a lynch mob punished gamblers' transgressions. Ten years later, in a series of deadly duels between rival newspaper editors, citizens supported the recourse to the more individualistic and ceremonial code of violence advocated by the planter elite.[80] Like the changing attitude toward gamblers, the different form of violence indicated the passing of the frontier.

While sharpers' new styles of play survived and gained popularity throughout the nation, the closing of the river frontier meant the demise of one ideal setting for gamblers. Professional sharps had flourished in the fast and fluid society of the lower Mississippi Valley before 1835, for southern notions of hierarchy and stability grew but slowly in crude waterfront towns. The development of new forms of betting had been encouraged in an atmosphere of speculation and movement where sharpers came to be accepted as legitimate businessmen. Without a devoted body of permanent residents, an effective judicial system, or a commitment to eastern respectability, Southwesterners permitted boatmen and blacklegs to have the run of their towns. The gambler consequently became an integral feature of western life. His destiny seemed so intertwined with that of frontier settlements, in fact, that when townspeople finally determined to make their communities more respectable, they turned first against the sharper as if he personified the unsettled frontier.

In the decade after 1835 the conditions that had encouraged gaming in southwestern towns changed. While the gambler was not driven out of the valley for good, save perhaps in Vicksburg, he became less prominent and less threatening in communities that lined the banks of the great rivers. Sharpers persisted by finding another ideal milieu for betting, the western steamboat, which both supplanted under-the-hill districts as a center for gaming and continued to generate additions to the culture of American betting. This vessel produced a new type of entrepreneur, the riverboat gambler, who quickly overshadowed the land-based sharper of frontier times. Yet the two types were very closely related, for the riverboat gambler essentially borrowed the games and the methods that his predecessor had cultivated in the region, and continued to disseminate the new forms of gambling originating in this part of the nation.

Public and commercial gaming in the United States always thrived in climates of transiency, for in just such settings did family and hometown inhibitions disappear. In later years, gambling halls in Gold Rush San Francisco and modern-day Las Vegas depended heavily for their patronage upon travelers, either Argonauts or tourists, who bet more readily because they were in transit. Similarly, Mississippi riverboats, like the waterfront districts, contained that essential element of travel in their makeup that stimulated gambling. The Mississippi and its tributaries in a sense constituted a perpetual frontier, even as their shores settled down into respectability. Technological advances such as the steamboat appeared to tame society along the river, but the riverboat was also an unsettled world unto itself, not exactly within the legal jurisdiction of any state or city, and certainly not always bounded by the morals of stable and fixed communities. The transient conditions that had encouraged gambling in frontier society consequently continued to prevail aboard the steamers, perpetuating gambling along the river throughout the nineteenth century.[81]

Steam-powered vessels first appeared in the western territories in 1811, and gamblers, no doubt, appeared on board soon afterwards. Yet for more than twenty years, most sharps tended to operate out of landing districts rather than on boats. As late as 1835, when national reporters discussed the problem of gamblers in the great valley, they located blacklegs not aboard riverboats but "at all the principle points on the western rivers."[82] Soon, the reforms of the mid-thirties directed more sharpers away from landings and on to steamboats. Riverboat gamblers began to receive wider recognition and enjoyed their halcyon years between 1840 and 1860. The class thus flourished after the frontier had begun to disappear in the Southwest. Nonetheless, an analysis of the reality behind the mythical riverboat gambler helps to illustrate the nature of gaming in the unsettled Southwest, for betting aboard steamboats in many ways resembled the gambling in towns along the river frontier.

Riverboat gambling took after under-the-hill gambling in large part because the two social settings resembled each other. Passenger populations generally mirrored the heterogeneous, fluid, and unpolished society of the river frontier. Travelers' descriptions of their company aboard the vessels generally agreed with portrayals of western townspeople. Even in cabin passage, the steamboat equivalent of first-class accommodations, the diverse crowds proved to be ambitious, impolite, informal, mobile, and energetic. As the touring Frenchman Michel Chevalier commented, river passengers' lack of refinement merely mirrored the crude society from which they came.[83] And among the many traits that they shared with westering people, river travelers loved to gamble. Sharpers regularly boarded the steamboats to take advantage of this particular inclination.

As riverboat design progressed, travelers encountered increasingly an ideal physical setting for gaming that complemented the atmosphere of tolerance and transience on board the "floating palaces." The gradual emergence of an elegant main cabin or "saloon" produced a pleasantly luxurious environment for first-class passengers that, like gambling itself, provided welcome relief from the dreary scenery of the river banks.[84] Most fares, of course, booked deck passage where accommodations remained crude at best, and not all vessels included a richly appointed main cabin. But after 1820, as passenger comfort grew steadily in importance among competing steamboat lines, growing numbers of craft featured an upper deck which became more elegant and more popular. By the 1840s the perimeter of the second story had been given over to staterooms, and the interior had been divided into a women's parlor astern, a bar in front, and a dining hall and men's lounge amidships. The bar, dining hall, and lounge comprised the saloon, the "showpiece and chief embellishment of the western steamboat."[85] Richly furnished like a fancy New Orleans club, the appearance of the main cabin enhanced the gaming that naturally gravitated to the plush setting.

Just as the sophisticated and civilizing technology of the steamboat contrasted with the common and unpolished character of the passengers, so the elegance and refinement of the saloon seemed incongruous with the roughness and crudity of gambling in the antebellum Southwest.[86] Folklore suggests that betting in saloons on the river was quite extravagant and polished, but although it took place in a much more elegant setting, riverboat gambling reflected more nearly the essentially western society that had fostered widespread gaming in the lower Mississippi Valley in the first place.[87] Similarly, the gamblers themselves often divided their time between riverboats and river towns. Through them and their games the frontier of the old Southwest persisted on board steamboats.

The observations of Aleksandr Borisovich Lakier, a Russian who toured the United States during 1857 when the era of the steamboat and the riverboat gambler had peaked on the Mississippi, captured the coarse nature of betting aboard "floating palaces." On a southbound journey from Ste. Genevieve, Missouri, Lakier criticized his fellow passengers' crude and single-minded devotion to gaming. The activity never seemed to stop, he wrote. "On the upper deck or in the private salons, the tables had hardly been cleared after breakfast or dinner when card games were set up." Bettors often played through the nights as well. And much to the Russian's confusion and chagrin, many people participated energetically in the games, playing with seemingly reckless abandon. "Money obviously had little value. The tables were piled with gold."

Just as in the flatboat landings along the river, the feverish betting appeared to be a main attraction aboard the vessel, a diversion that appealed to the heterogeneous and bored travelers. "Except for the ladies," Lakier noted, "everyone took part, some with their gestures, some with their eyes, and some by placing bets on one side or the other." Black servants even approached the table "in a free moment" to watch their masters play, "grinning at every stroke of luck and bitterly shaking their heads at a loss." Although the play occurred in the relatively exclusive main cabin, which was quickly crowded with passengers, Lakier commented that the card-players were "not at all a select group." As the boat steamed southward, picking up more travelers along the way, the throngs around the tables grew even more dense. Some sharps found conditions too congested and sought a more congenial setting for their profession. "Entrepreneurs with limited means and dirty cards went down to the second deck where the immigrants were, and there tried to take away from the poor whatever extra they might happen to have." To Lakier it seemed that the vice took hold in the boat like a cancer, spreading through the body of passengers.

Clearly troubled by the goings-on, the Russian took refuge in the galley, but even there he was unable to escape a quarrel that broke out among the bettors. Many a game along the river, either on land or water, ended with just such a disagreement. This time, the argument "arose as a result of an insult that a passenger who had lost his money hurled at the player who had beaten him and whom he called a cheat." With all the ardor and vengeance that seemed to characterize Westerners in European eyes, the antagonists drew pistols, and, "had it not been for the interference of others and the fright of the ladies, the matter would have ended in bloodshed." In this case and in numerous others, the behavior of players on board steamboats differed not at all from that of players in riverfront towns.

The unsophisticated nature of a society just beyond its frontier days was exemplified as well in the bettors' treatment of the elegant saloon in which they gambled. Lakier depicted the "awful" scene the morning after one all-night bout. "The whole floor was covered with torn, bent, and folded cards and tobacco ashes; the place was dirty and stuffy." In the midst of such disarray several players "had fallen asleep in the very spot where since evening they had been playing euchre or poker." Though the steamboat had elevated gambling to a milieu more refined than a flatboat town, the bettors themselves retained many of the rough-and-tumble qualities incongruous with southern respectability.

Riverboat gamblers helped to transmit western ways on to the steamer. As in communities like Vicksburg, the professionals who plied the river took on competitors from all levels of society and promoted commercial games of chance. The Russian traveler did not quite know what to make of the gamblers. He needed the captain to tell him "that there are people who do nothing but play cards. They board the steamboat only for short distances." To Lakier the idea of a professional gambler was foreign, perhaps something imaginable only in an entrepreneurial culture like that of the United States. The Russian spent so much time trying to avoid the games that he never figured out who the sharpers were. In fact, he may have bunked with one, though he seemed not to comprehend the fact. "I had to share a cabin," he recalled, "with someone I never even saw; by day he slept, all evening and night he played cards, and his coming to bed was a signal that it was time for me to get up."[88]

Lakier had likely shared a stateroom with one of the sharpers whom Americans were quick to immortalize in folklore. The Russian, of course, did not hold the professional cardplayer to be worthy of idolization, but Americans have generally felt differently. When analyzing the Mississippi riverboat gambler one must compete against a substantial legend that has distorted the type beyond reasonable belief. It was aboard the riverboats that the term "gambler" began to become divorced from its frontier association with the phrase "blackleg." In the 1820s steamboatmen, perhaps taken in by the gambler's deceptions, started to regard the sharper as a token of good luck aboard their craft. Also, as a result of American storytellers' glorification of the trickster, the gambler soon became a romantic figure in fiction, and the public regarded him, along with the flatboatman and mountain man, as a hero. By the late nineteenth century the popular stereotype had blossomed fully to depict gamblers as chivalrous individuals. "They were usually consummate actors," one author concluded, "handsomely dressed and immaculately groomed, with a tradition of gentlemanly behavior, and their own strict code of honor." Few people doubted that gamblers cheated, but it was widely held that they won money primarily from "suckers" who did not deserve to have it or could easily afford to lose it. Victims were frequently portrayed as members of groups out of social favor—Jews, foreigners, slave-holders, immigrants, or the spoiled sons of wealthy families.[89]

This folklore stereotype has actually distorted the reality of the riverboat gambler. First, it obscures the functional aspects of the sharper's style, like his purposeful dress. People noted that gamblers tended to wear a lot of jewelry, and made the embellishment out to be representative of the gentleman's fashionable flair. The sharper's watch chains and diamond breastpins, however, constituted ready sources of cash, liquid assets in a world where currency was not always easy to come by. Observers also noted the almost obsequious politeness that characterized the sharper's gentlemanly behavior, and even critics mockingly called him "genteel."[90] But gamblers acted politely and chivalrously not because they were fundamentally good-hearted and respectable, but rather because they hoped to enhance their business prospects. Understanding sharpers to be kind and genteel was akin to stereotyping slaves as "Sambos"; in both cases the observer reported as reality the masks that his subjects had donned.

Furthermore, although gamblers were identified as the polite, well-dressed, bejeweled men aboard riverboats, that particular type comprised a minority of the entire floating population of sharpers. Gamblers tended to travel in teams of from two to six men, and not as the talented individuals suggested by figures of legend. In fact, levels of co-operation, as indicated by gamblers traveling in groups, were so extensive that they suggest a strong sense of common self-awareness as an occupational class. The group consciousness took several forms. One was the reluctance of gamblers to compete with one another aboard the same vessel; sharpers tended to respect each other's territory.[91] Another was the extensive use of teamwork within each group of gamblers. While one member of the team might dress and behave like a stylish gentleman, his partners would dress and act differently, and pretend not to know their confederates. Gamblers posed in such roles as naive hayseed, Irish immigrant, itinerant preacher, Yankee merchant, and dull-witted cowboy. In such disguises they would encourage other passengers to play, raise the stakes of a game, and sometimes win money in order to keep "suckers" from becoming too suspicious of the bejeweled gentleman, who often served as dealer.

The deception fooled many people. In 1829 Joseph Cowell observed a high-stakes card game aboard the steamboat *Helen McGregor* in which, unknown to the observer, two partners fleeced their opponents. The game had been under way for a time when it was interrupted by the boat running aground. Like the other passengers, all the card-players left the table to see the problem, except for one "gentleman in green spectacles, a guard-chain long and thick enough to moor a dog, and a brilliant diamond breastpin." This sharper remained in his seat shuffling and cutting the cards until the other players returned and the game resumed. He then dealt out three extremely strong hands to the other players, and a weak one to himself. After a furious round of wagering, the huge pot of over $2,000 was won by a young participant who seemed not to know the extent of his good luck. Cowell noticed the irritation of the bejeweled dealer and concluded that he had mistakenly dealt out his own winning hand to the "green" youth.[92] Gamblers seldom made such mistakes, however. It is more likely that the obvious sharper and the young winner were partners. The youth had pretended inexperience in order to encourage the other players to bet more and to allay suspicions about a fixed game. Because the supposedly unhappy dealer and the big winner acted as if they did not know each other, the dealer, too, remained above suspicion, despite attire that gave his identity away.

Like Cowell, other observers of riverboat gamblers have misinterpreted their actions and produced a lore about the type that divorced sharpers from both the practical and the historical contexts in which they operated. The riverboat gambler has been viewed solely as a creature of the steamboats, not as a product of the river frontier. In fact, the river sharp was amphibious and could never distance himself too much from the shore-bound society of the old Southwest, where he and his games had arisen in the United States. The steamboat setting admittedly encouraged some minor modifications. Riverboat sharpers generally avoided games that required a lot of cumbersome equipment, like a roulette wheel, because it was inconvenient for boarding and leaving the craft. They stuck primarily to playing cards, a field in which they adapted games to fit their techniques. They also learned to time their play more precisely on steamboats. Sharpers tried to finish games near a stop on the river so they could leave the vessel promptly if they needed to avoid reprisals by angry victims.[93] Such prudence had not been necessary in riverfront districts where the gamblers had operated more or less on their own turf.

On the whole, however, gambling aboard steamboats differed little from the betting that developed in river towns during the frontier era. Steamboat passengers such as Aleksandr Borisovich Lakier described play that seemed almost as rough and disreputable as that in any flatboat landing. The sharps who had fleeced William C. Hall in Natchez-under-the-Hill during the 1820s employed many of the same ruses that gamblers used aboard riverboats in the following decades. As towns like Vicksburg strove to become more settled and respectable in the 1830s and 1840s, professional gamblers, whose activities were increasingly circumscribed on land, found greater opportunities afloat. Gentlemen who might have ignored or shunned the sharper on hometown streets would still sit down to play with him aboard steamboats where the pressures of family and community were not always felt. The river continued to function as a commercial artery upon which traveled cash-laden merchants, planters, emigrants, tourists, and farmers, bored with the scenery and interested in speculative diversions.[94] The conditions that had originally nurtured gaming among flatboatmen and migrants in river towns continued to exist on steamboats and among many kinds of river travelers. As a consequence, the gambling that had grown up in a frontier region continued to thrive throughout the antebellum years, even though the frontier had closed.

In the late 1850s and the 1860s, the emergence of railroads in the Mississippi Valley and the outbreak of the Civil War began to erase many such vestiges of a bygone frontier as river gambling. Steamboats passed through a critical period during the 1850s, a decade at once the "golden age" of the vessels as well as the initial years of decline. Railroads started to supplant steamboats as the favored vehicle of transport in the great valleys of the mid-continent. Trains moved more rapidly, regularly, and reliably than riverboats and enjoyed better financial backing and organization. They also prompted the construction of bridges spanning the waterways, and thus obviated some of the need for boat traffic. In the early 1860s the Civil War interrupted virtually all river travel, and gambling along the river declined abruptly. It picked up again after the war, and held on through the late nineteenth century, but it never regained the prevalence, the vitality, nor the renown it had once known.[95]

The professional gambler managed to hang on in the lower Mississippi Valley even after the close of the frontier and the demise of river travel, but his heyday had clearly passed in that region. The sharper had thrived most prosperously in the transient, hazard-filled setting of the old Southwest where people took risk and change for granted. He had capitalized on the mobility and the speculativeness of footloose Westerners. As conditions in towns on the river frontier began to settle down, he took his act increasingly to steamboats where society remained loose-knit and fluid. There the professional gambler continued to refine and to broadcast the new styles of betting that had originated in the old Southwest. First from frontier towns and then from riverboats, he disseminated new forms of gaming to the rest of the country.

The kinds of betting that Americans learned from the professional gambler reflected the nature of society on the southwestern frontier during the early decades of the nineteenth century. They mirrored the cultural mixture of New Orleans, the commercial orientation of river towns, and the speculative instincts of westering people. But if the frontier had remade styles of gambling, one should remember that gambling helped to shape the frontier, too. The two became so closely identified, in fact, that townspeople who hoped to subdue the frontier turned first against that class of blacklegs that seemed to perpetuate hazard and instability along the river. By putting the sharper in his proper place, settlers began to construct an orderly hierarchy that would soon make their culture more southern than western.

Southwesterners purged the gambler from their society, but they could not eliminate the kinds of gambling that he had cultivated. The games of faro and poker and three-card monte appealed to all Americans' appreciation for speed and risk and enterprise. In addition, they marked a departure from traditional forms of wagering that had paid so much homage to rank and status, and they set a new standard of commercial and public betting that would ultimately develop into casino gaming.

The nation took to the new styles of play eagerly, embracing the frontier shaping that had energized American gambling. River sharps distributed the new forms of play in two different directions. They first introduced their kind of gambling to urban syndicates in the East and Midwest, where gaming became the initial enterprise to be exploited by modern organized crime.[96] Then they took the new styles of betting to Gold Rush California. Forty-niners encountered the professional gambler all along the overland route—on steamboats and in camps along the Missouri River, at way stations along the trip, and at the end of the trail in the cities and towns of the Pacific Coast.[97] The new modes of betting accompanied the migration to the newest gamblers' frontier, where they continued to evolve. From San

Francisco and from a host of mining camps and commercial centers, the farthest West emerged. Because this West was both a final and an enduring frontier, its influence on the nation's gambling was deep and lasting, stretching from mid-nineteenth-century California to mid-twentieth-century Las Vegas.

Notice.

AT a meeting of the citizens of Vicksburg on Saturday the 4th day of July, it was

Resolved, That a notice be given to all *professional* GAMBLERS, that the citizens of Vicksburg are resolved to exclude them from this place and its vicinity, and that *twenty-four hours* notice be given them to leave the place.

Resolved, That all persons permitting Faro dealing in their houses, be also notified, that they will be prosecuted therefor.

Resolved, That one hundred copies of the foregoing resolutions be printed and stuck up at the corners of the streets, and the publication be deemed notice.

Vicksburg, July 5, 1835.

This broadside evinced a change of attitude toward sharps in the old Southwest. Professional gamblers in Vicksburg, Mississippi, learned that citizens intent upon erasing vestiges of the frontier would back their resolutions with popular vigilante force. *Courtesy of the Mississippi Department of Archives and History, Jackson, Miss.*

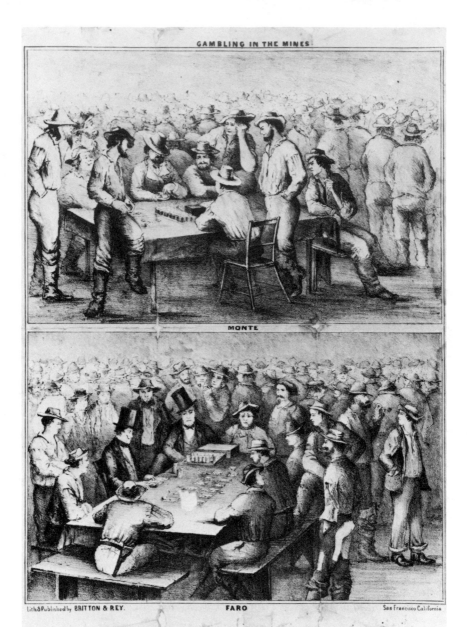

These lithographs from the 1850s illustrate the diverse crowds attracted to games of chance in Gold Rush California, where even in mining camps gambling became a high-volume industry. *Courtesy of the Bancroft Library.*

Located at the very center of early San Francisco, the El Dorado gambling saloon was a spectacle appreciated by bettors and non-bettors alike. The varieties of comforts and customers are shown in this illustration from *The Annals of San Francisco* (1855) by Frank Soulé, John H. Gihon, and James Nesbit. *Courtesy of the Bancroft Library.*

In the wrong place at the wrong time, dealer Charles Cora died in 1856 at the hands of vigilantes who had been persuaded that San Francisco had to eliminate gamblers, and other examples of frontier disorder, if it hoped to become a respectable city. *Courtesy of the Bancroft Library.*

The throngs that gathered in San Francisco streets to buy and sell shares in Comstock mining companies during the 1860s and 1870s resembled in many ways the crowds that had patronized California gaming halls during the early years of the Gold Rush. In the foreground are faces that caricature prominent street traders of the day. *Courtesy of the Bancroft Library.*

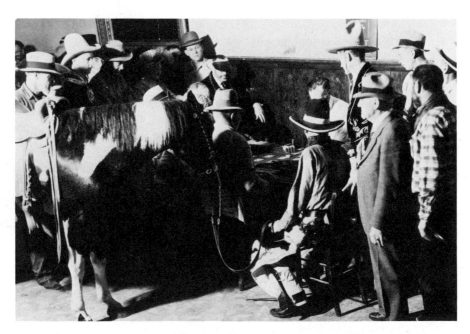

Last frontiersmen dismounted during Helldorado festivities, probably during the late 1930s, long enough to observe a faro game in a typically unsophisticated early setting. *Courtesy of the Logan Collection, University of Nevada, Las Vegas.*

A sharp contrast to the barren desert background, Fremont Street in downtown Las Vegas served as the principal focus of gambling activity during the early 1940s. Its casinos stood within walking distance of the Union Pacific depot located at the bottom of the picture.   *Courtesy of the Las Vegas News Bureau, Convention Center, Las Vegas.*

Tourists visiting the gaming halls of Glitter Gulch during the 1940s often stayed at motor courts, located on the main routes into town, where luxury was hardly the watchword that it became at Strip hotels.   *Courtesy of the Manis Collection, University of Nevada, Las Vegas Library.*

The Last Frontier, here captured around 1945, was the second hotel completed on the Strip. Its old Western theme likened it to downtown establishments, but its location, size, and amenities (note chapel at right) represented departures from the old railroad town. *Courtesy of the Manis Collection, University of Nevada, Las Vegas Library.*

"The Early West in Modern Splendor" greeted guests at the Last Frontier in the mid-1940s. Ranch-style design permeated the hotel complex. *Courtesy of the Manis Collection, University of Nevada, Las Vegas Library.*

The Hotel Last Frontier received a facelift during the mid-1950s that brought it into line with the futuristic vision embodied by postwar Strip hotels. *Courtesy of the Las Vegas News Bureau, Convention Center, Las Vegas.*

The Flamingo, Bugsy Siegel's contribution to the Strip, brought a new emphasis on modern luxury to Las Vegas when it opened in 1947. The Caribbean-like hotel was the first establishment that did not pay homage to the last frontier. *Courtesy of the Manis Collection, University of Nevada, Las Vegas Library.*

This publicity gimmick, a floating craps game at the Sands hotel, demonstrated how convenient and plush the setting for gambling became on the Strip during the 1950s. *Courtesy of the Las Vegas News Bureau, Convention Center, Las Vegas.*

This shot, probably from the early 1960s, of the futuristic convention center (foreground), Landmark hotel (center), and Stardust, Riviera, and Thunderbird hotels (from left to right on the Strip), illustrates how parking lots and sprawling development characterized land use in roadtown Las Vegas. *Courtesy of the Darrel Bradford Collection, University of Nevada, Las Vegas Library.*

Intent players gathered around the roulette layout at the Fremont Hotel and Casino, which opened in 1956 as downtown's answer to the Strip. *Courtesy of the Las Vegas News Bureau Collection, University of Nevada, Las Vegas Library.*

The cloud from an atomic test blast serves as backdrop to the skyline of Glitter Gulch, bringing into focus "the past and the future of that gigantic and fabulous paradox which was America itself." *Courtesy of the Las Vegas News Bureau, Convention Center, Las Vegas.*

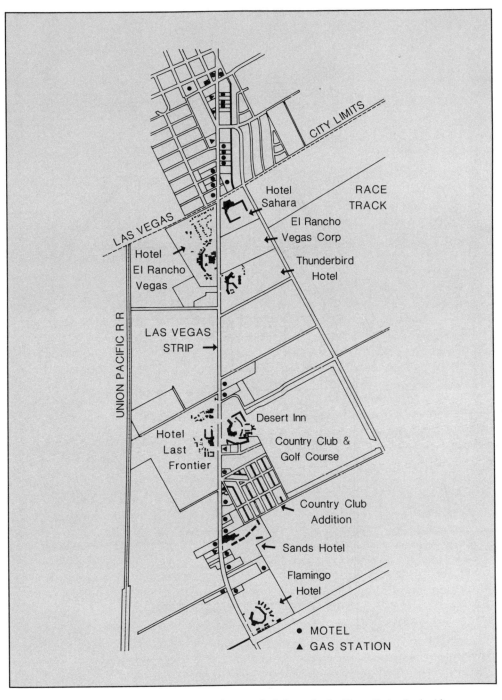

By the early 1950s, seven resort hotels sprawled along the Las Vegas Strip, flanked by a variety of roadside businesses.

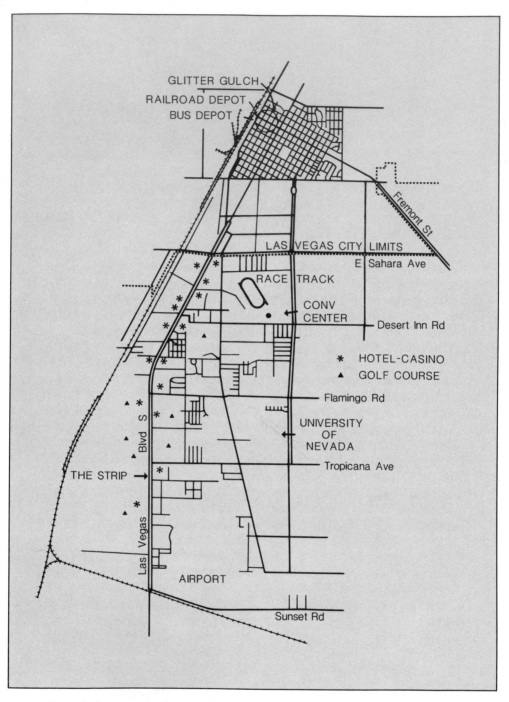

Las Vegas had two saturated gaming districts by the mid-1960s, downtown's Glitter Gulch and the Strip to the south of the city limits.

* * * * * * * * * * * * * * * * *

3

A Fast People

California and the Far Western Frontier

* * * * * * * * * * * * * * * * *

When one well-traveled European set out to write about typical sites in Gold Rush California, "A Night in a Gambling House" came immediately to mind. Gambling seemed such an integral part of life on the American mining frontier that Friedrich Wilhelm Christian Gerstäcker had no choice but to include it in his *Scenes of Life in California* (1856). This enterprising man of letters had visited San Francisco and the gold fields from late 1849 to late 1850 in order to gather information for German emigrants and to dig up material for new literary ventures. Like most participants in the Gold Rush, he was attracted to the gaming halls of California, and spent enough time in them to learn that the betting he witnessed typified the unprecedented society on the Pacific Coast at midcentury. Gambling in a San Francisco temple of fortune "was an abnormal condition," he wrote, "as was that of the entire country."

While Gerstäcker spent some time at gaming houses in San Francisco and the mining camps, he was no friend of gambling on the California frontier. He deplored its prevalence in far western society, but expected that it was so deeply rooted there that respectable citizens would have to resort to lynchings, as Southwesterners had, in order to eliminate the gambler from their communities. In no uncertain terms the German condemned gaming as the peculiar institution of the Pacific Coast. "Those gambling houses," he wrote, "are now to California what slave-holding is to the United States." They sheltered "rogues" who "intended neither to work, nor to trade, nor to buy, nor to sell," men resolved "to enrich themselves by *fair* or *foul*." Gaming halls represented all the troubles that plagued a frontier society, and they loomed so large that an objective reporter had to include them in his depiction of California.

For the edification of his readers, Gerstäcker described the interior of the plushest gambling house in early San Francisco. The El Dorado at the city center was designed in a manner that "seduced" a newcomer so that "in a measure he loses his senses." Whether one was a raw American pioneer or a seasoned European traveler, the glaring and lively establishment presented an overwhelming spectacle. The huge room stood out at night as one of the few signs of life and pleasure in a city otherwise given over to darkness and discomfort. Bright chandelier lights reflected off the shiny white ceilings, and "paintings calculated to arouse the instincts" lined the walls. A charming young woman offered refreshments to patrons who clustered round just to gaze at this rare instance of femininity in California, while across the way a bartender, intermittently summoned by dealers to pour free drinks around their tables, served wines and liquors to players. And penetrating through the smoky din, a "full band orchestra" played, on and on. The El Dorado provided all the comforts that men away from home might desire.

Many features recommended the "gambling saloon" to people in early American California, but its allure resulted primarily from its games of chance. Argonauts had come to the Far West not for bright lights, warm comforts, or charming femininity, but for the opportunity to make money rapidly. They appreciated the attractive women, the fine liquors, and the cozy surroundings, but they were most fascinated by the piles of gold dust atop each gaming table. The prospect of quickly winning that gold lay very near the heart of their own rationale for coming to the distant coast.

Gambling had a powerful appeal to fortune-seekers on the mining frontier, and houses like the El Dorado thrived as a result. Diverse throngs of bettors gathered around layouts where only the speediest commercial games took place. They played at monte and twenty-one, dice and roulette, faro and three-card monte, all fast-paced diversions appropriate for a fast-paced society. When a bettor made a small gain, Gerstäcker reported, the dealer would point out his "run of luck" and urge the player to "make the most of it, force it." There seemed to be no time to hesitate or to play at one's leisure, just as there was no thought of making one's fortune slowly. Amid the frenzy fights often broke out, thieves picked pockets, and losers complained to winners, but disagreements over the course of fate only evoked the fascination that attracted players into gaming houses. They loved the winning and the losing, the money that changed hands so quickly, and the varieties of action that surrounded the tables.

Friedrich Gerstäcker cut a curious figure inside these early California gambling halls. He disliked the gaming and seemed to shake his head at the greed and the lust that the strange environment elicited. Yet the German spent enough time at the temples of fortune to sketch a roughly accurate picture of them. Unlike most buildings in Gold Rush towns and cities, the gambling saloons were well-lit, well-heated places where a lonely traveler could while away an evening in comfort and among crowds. In addition, as a keen student of human character, Gerstäcker found the gaming halls an ideal laboratory for his research.

During one evening at the El Dorado he learned of a betting episode that illustrated attitudes toward gambling in early American California. For seven nights running during the height of the Gold Rush, "a man in a dark coat, in pantaloons of deeper color," appeared at the same table at eight o'clock to play a single hand of monte. As was the custom, he placed his wager by putting a small bag of money on the card of his choice. On the first evening the bettor won and shook twenty-eight silver dollars out of his bag, a sum that the dealer matched. On the following five occasions the man lost each time, emptied the inevitable twenty-eight dollars out of his bag, pocketed the limp pouch, and walked out. On the seventh try, the player finally won again. Smiling, the dealer was preparing to count out the standard sum when, much to his astonishment, the bettor shook the twenty-eight coins onto the table and then proceeded to extract from the purse $800 in bank notes and a letter of credit for $3,000. The man in the dark coat had staked nearly four thousand dollars, and he demanded his winnings.

The dealer, his grin turning to a frown, balked at the thought of paying out so much money and protested that he had been cheated. He did not have to reward the winner with more than twenty-eight dollars, he explained, because he had been misled about the size of the bet. To this argument the player responded by pointing out that the dealer, had he won, would surely have kept the entire wager. A crowd of spectators, clustering around the table to enjoy just the kind of excitement they had come for, agreed with the winner and told the dealer that it was his own fault that he had not inspected the pouch of money in the first place.

Now losing his composure, the dealer took another tack. Why should he have to pay, he asked, when the player had surely staked the bank notes and money order in his bag on previous nights, but had not relinquished the money after losing? This charge counted for nothing with the winner, however, because it could not be proven. The onlookers, now pressing in more closely, once again agreed with the player and insisted that the loser cover his debt. They watched on as the dealer, after conferring with a colleague and examining the player's paper money, finally paid off the winner in bags of gold dust. As the stoic bettor left with his fortune, the crowd cheered. For them, Gerstäcker explained, "such a trick was not a fraud, it was nothing but cleverness; moreover, the dealer has his advantages also; he must be alive to what is taking place."[1]

Gerstäcker's tale illuminated the changes that reshaped the culture of gambling on the Pacific Coast. In the old Southwest a professional card-sharp would never have let himself lose in such a fashion. Professional gamblers in the Gold Rush, however, relied less on tricks and more on percentages and high turnover, which made them vulnerable to an occasional stroke of luck. Moreover, while blacklegs in the towns of the lower Mississippi Valley had mostly operated on their own turf, dealers on the far western frontier were susceptible to the pressure of crowds. Their games took place in a setting more wide-open and public than ever before; they now worked in an environment unprecedented for American gambling. Finally, the differences between gambler and player were no longer so great. Gamblers still made money, perhaps even by deceit, but in the early Gold Rush they were regarded as legitimate businessmen, and they often wagered against players who were as clever as they were. Everybody seemed to be fast and sharp in California. Everyone needed to "be alive to what is taking place."

In this far West and in others, gambling expressed the character of a new society. The restless region was full of migrants seeking an angle in their quest for fortune. "It must be remembered that there was never a place of such temptation as California," Charles Loring Brace explained in 1869. "The prizes for 'sharp-practice' are enormous, and public opinion is not strict."[2] Brace's conclusion summarized the dynamics of the monte episode that Gerstäcker recounted. "Sharp-practice" certainly included seeking an edge in gambling games, but the young society offered many similar opportunities—digging gold ore, disputing land titles, manipulating mining stocks, speculating in real estate, cornering commodity markets— where profits might be made quickly and easily. In no other place did the fluctuations of fortune seem so intensely followed, Friedrich Gerstäcker decided. "California will always . . . be a land in which to make money— or lose it."[3]

The German's prediction proved accurate, because for more than one hundred years after the discovery of gold the residents of the state retained both their speculative orientation and their reputation as "a fast people."[4] Beginning with the Argonauts and continuing into the post-Second World War era, American California remained a destination for westbound migrants seeking new lives, new chances to get ahead, new opportunities for wealth. The Golden State was peopled by adventurers intent on taking risks in order to make rapid gains.

The influx of population came in two major currents. One headed toward San Francisco and the Mother Lode during the first twenty-five years of American occupation, and a second, longer and deeper stream ran toward Southern California, beginning in the late 1880s and continuing through the mid-twentieth century. The two flows created distinctive societies whose differences signaled a dramatic change in the relationship between East and West. While San Francisco anchored a frontier that continued to look eastward for cultural standards, Los Angeles became the capital of an innovative frontier that created new cultural forms and exported them to the rest of the country. The differences were epitomized in each city's system of transportation. San Franciscans struggled to become the terminus of a transcontinental railroad that bound their city tightly to the East, but Southern Californians pioneered adaptations to the automobile that soon became standard throughout the country.

Yet, despite the different outlooks on culture and the different periods of settlement, the two parts of the state were equally prominent in remaking American betting. San Francisco and Los Angeles both served as primary points of origin for new styles of gambling in the United States. Like other westering migrants, those who came to California during the nineteenth and twentieth centuries were "a gambling people" who fostered novel ways of betting and disseminated the modified forms to the rest of the country.[5]

The shape of what Hubert Howe Bancroft termed "California gambling" first became clear in early San Francisco and the other "fast cities and towns" of the Gold Rush. In gaming halls, more wide-open and more commercial than ever before, people played all day and all night at games that had been organized and refined into a high-volume industry, a business where the dealer relied more and more for profits on percentages and odds rather than cheating and deceit. And once players understood that a gambler with the percentages on his side could not really be beaten, they looked at betting a little differently. With the odds against them, it came to matter less whether players won or lost, so long as they got a chance to participate. Again, gaming practices mirrored the frontier society in which they emerged. Bettors resembled those veteran miners who kept rushing off to the latest unverified strike in the Far West, not because it seemed a sure thing but because it meant excitement. To restless miners and to thrill-seeking bettors, "the fun would be worth a fortune almost."[6]

California at first lived wholeheartedly with the new fashions of gaming, but as Gold Rush society settled down it grew less tolerant of the prevailing pastime. Guided by eastern standards of respectability, the state struggled to reduce its notorious wagering. Citizens turned first against the professional gambler, using lynching and legislation, and soon extended reforms by outlawing all public, commercial gaming. Their opposition interfered with the free play of bettors, but it did not subdue the deeply ingrained gambling instinct of the population. Californians continued to wager in violation of the law and sought out other, more legitimate arenas for taking chances.

San Franciscans gambled respectably by investing recklessly in commodities and city lots and mining stocks, but their excitements eventually played out along with the gold and silver ore. Southern Californians, on the other hand, speculated on a never-ending series of booms in fruit, climate, oil, movies, autos, aerospace, and, above all else, real estate. The risk-taking atmosphere of Los Angeles sustained through the twentieth century the heritage of gambling as a way of life that Argonauts had first cultivated on the mid-nineteenth-century frontier. That mentality was in large part responsible for the rise of Las Vegas after 1940, when casinos similar to Gold Rush gambling saloons grew increasingly popular among Southern Californians. The success of California gambling in southern Nevada signified that since 1848 the Golden State and the Far West have been the primary source of American gambling culture, for together they have comprised a final and enduring frontier.

The emergence of California as a fountain of betting styles illustrated the state's special relationship to the rest of the nation. California represented the culmination of the westering process and epitomized frontier social development. Familiar patterns of western economic adventure and cultural striving appeared once again in the Golden State, but developed more quickly, more lastingly, and more thoroughly than on other American frontiers.[7] The discovery of gold instantly attracted to the Far West hordes of sojourners whose restless and acquisitive spirit came to typify the entire society. Their arrival in such large numbers intitiated an intense bout of development that never let up as successive waves of migrants continued to flock to the state to mine its array of resources. Whether the newcomers headed to San Francisco, to Southern California in later years, or to some other boom on the Pacific slope, they took after the Argonauts who had first set the rapid pace for far western society.

Observers have generally agreed that the Golden State's distinctive western character stemmed in large part from its beginnings as the focus of the Gold Rush. Later generations of Californians were deeply influenced by the ways of their mining forefathers, pursuing fortune impatiently as if trying "to outrun old Time himself."[8] One Easterner figured that urgent risk taking would forever be the nature of Californians' economic endeavors: "Plodding, patient industry will never stand in as high esteem on the Pacific coast, as with us. People have a passion for achieving great results at once, and are too often indifferent to the means."[9] The inclination to take "great chances" for "great results," and the disregard for the propriety of the path to success, made California an ideal setting for the rise of new forms of gaming. The population was not only more willing to gamble, but would also gladly try out any novel kind of betting that might appear.

Californians' attachment to gambling pursuits set them apart in degree but not in kind from other Americans, for they mainly followed to an extreme the material orientations that affected all of society. When Englishman James Bryce reached the Pacific Coast on his epic journey through the United States, he found there in most concentrated form all the qualities that differentiated the New World from the Old. He viewed the Far West as "the most American part of America, the part where those features which distinguish America from Europe come out in strongest relief." And in large part because of its Gold Rush experience, the Golden State excelled the entire region: "What America is to Europe, what western America is to eastern, that California is to the other Western states."[10]

The development of California epitomized other far western societies because the state served as the metropolis for frontier expansion on the Pacific slope. To new mineral strikes throughout the region, California dispatched restless people who became, in effect, agents of frontier culture wherever populations gathered to dig their fortune from the earth. First in Nevada and British Columbia, and then in Colorado, Oregon, Idaho, Montana, South Dakota, and Arizona, inexperienced migrants looked to "old Californians" for leadership. New mining camps borrowed proven Californian styles of digging, of self-government, of vigilantism, and of gambling. Moreover, the Golden State became the source of technology and capital for the extractive industry, and San Francisco acted as the principal entrepôt for far western mining frontiers.[11] Consequently, California, with its special role as the "most American" of American states, had a profound influence on the shape of society on the Pacific slope. Other western states borrowed its impatient and speculative spirit, and its interest in all matters of gambling.

The traits of acquisitiveness and risk taking that had long been pronounced among westering people prevailed in early American California and continued to permeate society in the Far West long after the Golden State was settled. Yet, as James Bryce suggested, these were not exclusively western characteristics, but typified much of American culture. California put the singular nature of nineteenth-century citizens of the United States into bold perspective. It was to Gold Rush California that Josiah Royce looked in his effort to study "the American character," for on the Pacific Coast the distinguishing features of the national type could be seen clearly amidst migrants arriving from all sections of the country.[12] The average person that those features defined capsulized the American as enterprising man. Life on the Pacific Coast elicited in clear form the "speculating, enterprising, and go-ahead" mentality that so many foreigners regarded as a common denominator in nineteenth-century society.[13]

California was the product of an extended generation of entrepreneurs that stretched from the adventurous businessmen of the Jacksonian period to the captains of industry ascendant during the Gilded Age. On the Pacific slope this era ranged from the first mountain men who set foot in coastal territories to the domineering railroad and land monopolists in the second half of the century. California society developed in an economic age that cherished above all else the chance to get something for nothing, the very same prospect that lay at the heart of the urge to gamble. The gold seeking of the 1840s and 1850s not only helped to define California society for years to come but also summarized the nation's style of risk taking.

Argonauts came seeking prosperity and, as in matters of gambling, they remained open to innovations in the matter of making money. Never a people to do things on a limited scale or in a dated fashion, Californians took to modern economic ways, including industrial and scientific advances, more quickly than most other Americans. Between 1848 and 1970, they pioneered new forms of gambling; between 1870 and 1970 the state led the rest of the nation in adopting new technologies and organizations for large-scale production.[14] Having endured hardship and migration in the hope of bettering their lots, Californians eagerly embraced any novelty that promised to make them more prosperous more quickly.

Californians' devotion to fast material gain skewed the version of American society that they regenerated on the Pacific Coast. The restless and youthful population of the state aspired not merely to become richer than Easterners, but also to build a more perfect example of United States civilization. Californians hoped to distill only the best of eastern culture, and intended to keep out of their state the disruptions and constraints that afflicted the East. In their devotion to acquisitive pursuits, however, they lost the opportunity to improve on nationwide standards of culture, and ended up imitating eastern styles for the most part. By the late nineteenth century the *Overland Monthly* proudly boasted that "Pacific civilization" had become the "most completely realized embodiment of the purely commercial civilization on the face of the earth," and therefore represented "in almost every respect an intensification of the American spirit." But the region had not yet begun to generate cultural refinements. Its residents remained "recipients of letters and science and art" rather than "producers."[15] California excelled America not in taste and learning but in pursuing money.

Throughout the last half of the nineteenth century, Californians primarily applied their innovation to aspects of business and gambling. The state only gained recognition as a cultural pacesetter during the twentieth century when, led by Los Angeles, it pioneered the nation's adaptation to automobiles and motion pictures, and became a point of origin for new ways of living. Many of Southern California's styles became apparent in the gaming resort of Las Vegas, an outgrowth of Los Angeles, where the experience of betting epitomized the contributions of Southern California to American civilization. California had been generating new styles of gambling, however, since 1848. Twentieth-century Las Vegas casinos were, in effect, just another manifestation of California gambling, a practice which since the mid-nineteenth century had exemplified the Golden State's contribution to the national character.

The contours of California gambling, like those of California society, took shape during the Gold Rush when newcomers overran the Mexican outpost and turned it into an American state. Styles of gambling helped to distinguish Americans in California by setting them apart from other inhabitants. Argonauts who portrayed Mexicans as exhibitionist, backward, and indolent tried to find justification for their charges in Latinos' betting contests. In sharp contrast to the crisp and speedy games that most Americans preferred, Mexicans often engaged in colorful and drawn-out rituals. After witnessing Californios betting on fights between bulls and grizzly bears, Americans outlawed such sports as bull-baiting, thus encouraging Spanish-speaking bettors to share increasingly in gaming tailored to Anglo-American preferences.[16] Virtually no interaction, however, occurred between whites and Chinese around early California gaming tables. Seeking relief from the drudgery that characterized debt bondage in the American West, the Chinese imported their distinctive games of chance and regarded them, along with opium and prostitutes, as familiar freedoms in an unfamiliar world. One Asian pastime, *"pák kòp piú"* or the game of the white pigeon ticket, eventually formed the basis for the twentieth-century casino game of keno, but Americans during the Gold Rush regarded the forms of gambling available in Chinatown as too foreign for their tastes, and generally kept their distance.[17] Neither Mexican nor Chinese precedents contributed very much to the rapid emergence of an American style of gambling on the Pacific slope.

The history of betting in California, Bancroft noted, leads one back to "the barbaric splendor of 1849."[18] Indeed, it did not take long for Argonauts to make gaming not only *"the* amusement" of their society but also the typical approach to "every department of business"—agriculture, commerce, real estate. But it was gold mining that, throughout the early period of American control in California, made gambling "the life and the soul of the place."[19]

Gold mining stimulated gambling because it encouraged people's trust in luck and speculation. Once migrants arrived on the Mother Lode, they realized that they had undertaken something less than a sure thing. Dame Shirley referred to the quest for gold as "Nature's great lottery scheme," and many concurred.[20] A few quickly became pessimistic about prospects for success in California, and warned those back East to save themselves the trouble: "You at home had better buy lottery tickets with your money," Charles Nash advised in a letter in 1850, "than come here expecting to be one of the lucky ones."[21] But many remained optimistic and stayed in the Far West longer than they had planned. If the mines did not pay off, one was bound to find better odds at other business ventures, or even at the gaming tables. To his family and friends, William H. Dougal praised the opportunities of California in 1849: "there never was and probably never will be such a chance as there is here for acquiring a fortune."[22] Dougal's attitude typified the outlook of a century of migrants to the Pacific Coast. While hazards discouraged some new arrivals, many more were caught up in the risks and rewards of the chase for wealth.

Gold mining conditioned early Californians to take a chance on almost any economic prospect. At the dawn of the Gold Rush it seemed that "the rashest speculators were the most fortunate," so people threw caution to the wind in their haste to accumulate money. The state's population, noted Albert D. Richardson, "go fast, have the best, and despise the expense."[23] In a society intent upon turning quick fortunes, people spent money freely because they expected to strike it rich again the next day, or even the next hour. Californians held such high expectations that some disdained working to secure the future. Few had time to plant crops and wait for a harvest; few planned to build up a livelihood over the years. Everyone hurried to accomplish a lifetime of business in a year, and a year's worth of business in "a few hours only."[24] Argonauts' outlook on tomorrow made them gamblers by second nature.

Gambling, Hubert Howe Bancroft explained, was simply "a more direct expression of the spirit of speedy accumulation" that guided "mining, merchandising, real estate operations" during the early years of American occupation. Even migration to the gold fields, the "staking of time, energy, and health against the hidden treasures of the Sierra," was a wager.[25] In such an environment, where people understood that fortune was determined by luck, where commerce "fluctuates with every hour, and profit and loss are not matters of calculation, but chance," it was difficult to resist the temptations of gambling saloons.[26] Risk taking as a way of life shaped both individual personality and social character. "Speculation becomes a passion," James Bryce discovered, "and patient industry is distasteful; there is bred a recklessness and turbulence in the inner life of the man which does not fail to express itself in acts."[27] Moreover, the gambling psychology militated against the formation of a society that might inhibit risk taking. Gold-seekers hurried about pursuing fortune and gave little consideration to the future of their community, because for many home remained in the East. The Pacific Coast at first lacked the social cement provided by the presence of women and children. The youthful, virtually all-male society cared more for chance than for any principles that might limit the prevalence of gambling.[28]

With society so loosely knit, and with fortune making and chance taking so highly regarded, gambling flourished. The pastime took hold in old Mexican communities like Monterey, in new mountain towns like Mariposa, and in growing cities like Sacramento. Professional sharps not only followed prospectors to each new settlement on the Mother Lode, but also gathered in central urban districts where Argonauts consistently sought them out. At the time of its admission to the Union in 1850, California licensed gambling and assessed quarterly fees for every table. The state government, followed in turn by towns like San Jose which needed to finance municipal debt, thus recognized the public's general approval of gaming. Among the "many vices peculiar to California," wrote Alfred Doten in 1856, gambling stood "first and foremost."[29]

By permitting and taxing gaming, California recognized professional gamblers as legitimate businessmen. *Chevaliers d'industrie* flocked to the state from other parts of the United States, from gaming houses in France and Latin America, and from the betting dens of China. Although gamblers often administered to the needs of their fellow countrymen first, there was much intermixture around gaming tables as bettors tried out the new games introduced to the West from afar. No matter what their country of origin, dealers in Gold Rush California found a surfeit of customers around gaming tables, and players found plenty of dealers. The great influx of gamblers made the class a prominent one in the state, and no place had more resident sharps than San Francisco. John W. Audubon, writing from "this pandemonium of a city" in late 1849, found gamblers so prevalent that he compared the Gold Rush metropolis unfavorably to the old Southwest:

> The place full of gamblers, hundreds of them, and men of the lowest types, more blasphemous, and with less regard for God and his commands than all I have ever seen on the Mississipp, [in] New Orleans or Texas, which gave us the same class to some extent, it is true; but instead of a few dozen, or a hundred, gaming at a time, here, there are thousands, and one house alone pays one hundred and fifty thousand dollars per annum for the rent of the 'Monte' tables.[30]

It seemed that all available space had been rented out to gamblers, that the entire population of the city had devoted itself to that form of play.

In San Francisco Audubon had discovered the center of early California gambling, the site where westering Americans practiced gaming on a scale grander than in the old Southwest and promoted new styles of betting vigorously. Since the beginning of the Gold Rush, the city had served as the funnel through which poured thousands upon thousands of migrants intent upon taking risks in order to make easy money. Populated by citizens eager to turn a quick fortune, San Francisco was renamed "San Fastopolis" by a clergyman who lamented the sinfulness and "sharp-practice" of frontier urbanites. The city easily lived up to its reputation, for it contained both hundreds of establishments devoted to the various forms of gambling, and thousands of residents who, one reformed gambler recalled, would "bet on anything, from a dogfight in the street, to a presidential election."[31]

Perhaps because it seemed so inevitable in early California, San Franciscans embraced gambling without hesitation during the community's rapid growth. Instead of outlawing the practice, they initially looked to it as a source of income for a municipality that thrived on speculation and risk. Why struggle in vain to eliminate betting, asked alcalde and first mayor John W. Geary in 1849, when the city can license, regulate, and tax gaming? So until 1855 San Francisco permitted licensed gambling and took a percentage of the money wagered. Even when citizens became less tolerant of betting, they continued to permit it because they appreciated the revenues that it generated.[32]

By betting in the two-, three-, and four-story brick buildings clustered at the city center, players attested the legitimacy of gambling in San Francisco. Gaming clubs functioned as one of the few forums for society in the raw metropolis. In addition, the establishments served as respectable businesses that attracted money to the town and provided revenues for municipal government. Although some Easterners and foreigners condemned the halls, early Californians generally welcomed them as additions that contributed constructively to their city.

In regarding gaming as a legitimate enterprise in the years around mid-century, San Franciscans gave implicit approval to the professional gambler, whose respectability was bound up with that of his games. Argonauts perhaps understood that, like themselves, the gambler had come to California to make money quickly and easily, although the profession was not an automatic ladder toward upward mobility. More importantly, although the gambler still liked to have an edge in his line of work, he operated games that were more "square" than those on the river. He became known less as a sharper than a dealer, he made his money less by cheating than by maintaining sizable percentages in his favor, and he maximized income not by increasing the stakes but by increasing the volume. All of these changes indicated that gaming had turned into a more refined industry.[33]

There was some confusion on this point, in part because various forms of cheating and deception still occurred, and in part because to many from the East or from Europe, public and commercial gambling remained immoral. Even as Alfred Doten spoke of gamblers as "dealers" and discussed the percentages they employed, he continued to call them "professional blacklegs."[34] Europeans suspected corruption, too, perhaps because they mistrusted the democratic style of play or the unfamiliarly high percentages that San Francisco dealers used to their advantage. When Frenchman Albert Benard de Russailh likened far western gaming to "organized robbery," he may simply have been taken aback by a system of odds that gave operators such an unbeatable edge.[35] But those who knew best agreed that gamblers were relatively honest. Both the residents of early California, who frequented gambling dens and regarded dealers as respectable citizens, and reformed and retired gamblers, looking back on golden years, concluded that most games were comparatively clean and straightforward.[36]

The gamblers marketed their product in a fashion that may have brought disrepute upon themselves. They no longer worked so hard to create the illusion that their games offered a sure thing, but observers remained suspicious. Dealers' stoic behavior probably suggested that they expected to win one way or another, and their tables piled high with gold and silver seemed to demonstrate to critical spectators that they never lost. But the impassive demeanor was a professional stance and a confidence in the inevitable profit to come from favorable odds, while the precious metal and coins atop the layouts mainly served as advertising that attracted customers effectively.[37] While gamblers often drew comparison to their predecessors in the lower Mississippi Valley, they had evolved beyond that stage of commercial and public betting. Sharpers in the old Southwest had fleeced river travelers while operating in groups on their own turf, and for a long time they proved beyond the reach of the law. Dealers on the Pacific slope faced different conditions. They tended to rent table space from proprietors instead of operating out of their own haunts; rather than fleecing players one at a time for large sums, individuals took on crowds of bettors every day and night and depended upon repeat business; they faced the more likely prospect of mob justice if they cheated too flagrantly; and, as Friedrich Gerstäcker explained, they played against opponents who were often as intent upon "sharp-practice" as they were. These conditions encouraged dealers to rely increasingly upon the more predictable and more secure profits provided by odds fixed inflexibly in their favor.

Once gamblers realized the benefits of the more industrial form of gaming, at least in sites that could attract high volume, they made it the accepted style of play. The business of betting now depended more on players of more moderate means. The size of most wagers became smaller—Bancroft suggested between fifty cents and five dollars—but the number of bettors expanded tremendously. By becoming more honest and by attracting a wider range of customers, gambling became a more legitimate enterprise. Dealers, with their handsome dress and professional appearance, heightened the image of respectability.[38]

Of all the places in early California, gambling became most respectable in the grand houses that bordered the old Mexican plaza at the center of San Francisco. While gambling took place in the drinking saloons of small towns and mining camps, cities fostered more specialized establishments where gaming reigned supreme and the bar was incidental. As the largest and most prosperous town of the Gold Rush, San Francisco developed the specialized gaming hall to its logical conclusion and devoted an entire block to the new betting palaces. The city had its lesser clubs as well, comparable to small-town saloons, "scattered through the less frequented streets."[39] Once residents determined that grand gambling halls did not belong in the city center, the more modest houses would become predominant in the town's gaming, surviving through the latter half of the nineteenth century. But the spectacular establishments that lined Portsmouth Square, flourishing from 1849 to 1855, marked the apex of early California betting and set a new pace for American gambling.

The great gambling saloons assumed an unprecedented significance in San Francisco that was embodied both in their central location and in their finances. When migrants spoke of their days in Gold Rush San Francisco they noted that the establishments near the plaza overshadowed other buildings and that "much of the life of the throbbing town centered in that locality." The plaza constituted the "great centre of attraction," and its halls served as the favored public houses, offering to Argonauts the most appropriate pastime for their society.[40] For the privilege of operating out of those crowded places, gamblers paid fantastic rents that drove the prices of surrounding real estate skyward. As early as 1849, landlords for the Parker House hotel, "'the place' in San Francisco," collected between $1,800 and $2,400 monthly from dealers operating out of small rooms on the second floor, taking in a total of $60,000 per year from the trade. Next door, gamblers leased the El Dorado, at first a canvas tent measuring fifteen by twenty-five feet, for $40,000 annually. Rents were due in advance, in gold dust.[41] That gamblers willingly paid such overhead attested to the lucrative nature of their work.

While all San Francisco boomed during the early years of the Gold Rush, "gambling-houses" proved to "prosper best in the growing town," wrote Friedrich Gerstäcker. Gambling halls began as cloth shelters or crude structures, but they quickly became the most solid and distinguished buildings in young San Francisco. They were not only among the first to be rebuilt after fires, but also among the first to be reconstructed in stone. When one of early San Francisco's notorious fires broke out one night, it burned down a gaming hall first and then spread to engulf other buildings until it finally died out the following morning. The first structure to disappear was also the first to be replaced. By afternoon carpenters had already begun rebuilding the gambling saloon, stopping every so often to throw water on the hot ashes around them. They erected a lightweight frame, stretched canvas over it, and opened the establishment for business the next day. In a few more months, brick buildings had supplanted the cruder structures as landlords strove to make their shelters fireproof.[42] Gambling hardly ever stopped, not even to accommodate catastrophe.

By 1851 the "handsome brick houses" that housed games of chance seemed "already fairly old" in relation to the rest of the city.[43] The population of the growing metropolis confirmed the prominent stature of the establishments by regarding them as evidence of cultural achievement on the far western frontier. Anxious to demonstrate to the East that they, too, enjoyed the refinements of civilization, San Franciscans adopted the gaming houses as an indication of taste and success. In May 1850, the *Daily Alta California* welcomed the "new Empire" gambling saloon: "We do not know of any public room in any portion of the United States of so great an extent or possessing such elegant decorations and embellishments. Our New Orleans and New York friends would scarcely believe that they could be so far excelled in California."[44] But the West, of course, always preceded the East in the culture of public and commercial gambling.

The central gambling houses of early San Francisco marked an important turning point in styles of American betting. They made gambling more public and commercial by turning it into a high-volume industry, and they elevated the practice above the disrepute engendered in under-the-hill dens in the old Southwest. The gilded establishments surrounding the plaza foreshadowed Las Vegas casinos by combining luxurious furnishings with a clientele composed of all classes. And with the more wide-open styles of gaming and the brand-new setting, the nature of gambling itself changed. Players still hoped to win, but, true to the commercial character of gambling and society in California, they looked upon betting more as a commodity for sale by respectable retailers, as an experience worth purchasing with losing wagers. Thrills that came from taking risks had become almost as important as winning; the excitement of the speedy games and the unusual surroundings combined to make even losses seem worthwhile.

The size and decor of the gambling saloon enhanced the enjoyment of the play. Many observers found it difficult to resist the temptations offered by the elaborate halls. "They look more like palaces than gambling dens," reported French journalist Etienne Derbec, and they glittered with all that was bright and cheerful. After each consuming fire the gaming houses always "rose from their ashes more beautiful and more magnificent" than before.[45] The chandeliers and glassware seemed more radiant, the food and drink more plentiful, the women and music more charming, and the paintings of nudes more suggestive. Running all day, all night, all week long, the palaces provided every inducement that might attract bettors into the room. Piles of gold atop the gaming tables no doubt constituted the primary appeal, but they were supplemented by "every device that art could suggest to swell the custom" of the establishment: "once the rubicon of temptation is passed, . . . the dazzled vision vanquishes all virtuous resolves, tinges the acquisitive senses, and those who came to scoff remain to *play*."[46]

The effectiveness of the unusual setting was heightened by comparison to the rude surroundings. San Franciscans wagered in style even while they resided in crude hotels and canvas hovels. Instead of spending the evening in the boredom and misery of a cold, wet tent, or a crowded boarding house, Derbec explained, one went to a gaming hall. "You meet your acquaintances there, and you shake hands; you chat about the weather or business; you speak of your homeland, always dear to the heart of emigrants. There are newspapers to read, musicians serenading you, women to accompany you or invite you to play."[47] Such temptations were irresistible to Argonauts and, once inside, they found themselves drawn to the gambling tables, too.

The gaming palaces increased their popularity by welcoming citizens from all backgrounds. Just as they epitomized the commercial and risk-taking orientations of frontier society in the Far West, so the gambling houses mirrored its open and egalitarian nature, and in this regard finalized the divorce of American gaming from notions of status. Migrants to California, especially foreigners accustomed to European betting establishments where rank meant something, never ceased to wonder at the diversity of crowds patronizing the clubs around the plaza. "Absolute equality reigned," one Frenchman surmised; "Bankers and porters rubbed shoulders at the same tables." Gamblers dealt to "Mexicans, Miners, Niggers, and Irish bricklayers," one Englishman recalled. Even a few women joined the play, though more frequently they served as dealers or employees in the elegant halls.[48] A few private rooms were given over to more select customers, but such exclusiveness proved the exception in the general free-for-all that Gold Rush gambling saloons provided.[49]

The wide-open policies of gamblers in early San Francisco reduced gaming to what life was all about in California. Some people dressed as gentlemen and others as laborers, J. D. Borthwick recalled, but "appearance, at least as far as dress was concerned, went for nothing at all. A man was judged by the amount of money in his purse,"[50] by his willingness to risk it, and by his reaction to the outcome of his wagers, for such were the crucial ingredients of Gold Rush character. Moreover, Argonauts preferred to play at games that exposed this character the quickest. Californians had no time for pastimes that required "some little thought and reflection," just as they showed little taste for patient industry. Players preferred faro, monte, roulette, twenty-one, and other banking and percentage games that appealed to the fast-paced acquisitiveness of the society.[51]

For Americans in early California, the betting experience provided by San Francisco palaces was generally new and different, and they often reacted to it in a fashion that displayed their unfamiliarity with both gambling itself and the novel shapes that California gaming assumed. Unlike the stoic dealer and the expressionless Mexican or Chinese, Americans tended to get excited in the heat of the moment, and often "ill concealed their disappointment over losses."[52] Albert Benard de Russailh, writing in 1851, drew an unflattering portrait of Americans after observing those who lost at gambling and then engaged in fights. "The Americans are enterprising, inventive, and clever; they scarcely admit that the word 'impossible' exists; but they have many bad faults, and they are not always pleasant to live with." Moreover, the lack of refinement that gambling exposed prevailed throughout the population because, as the Frenchman added, "Nearly everyone is maddened by the gambling fever."[53]

As many a European observed, it was not always easy for Americans to embrace the risks that they undertook. Gambling had less and less to do with social rank on the far western frontier, so one's stakes seemed more important to players in early California. "It is the money men gamble for here," explained Hubert Howe Bancroft late in the century, "and they have no hesitation in saying so." But bettors saw money increasingly as a measure of their participation rather than as just the goal of their play. Because gamblers behaved more predictably, relying on odds tilted infallibly in their favor, players increasingly understood that one could hardly get rich at betting. So while they continued to gamble for money, they did so in larger and larger part for the thrills that it provided. "It is a fine thing to get a peck or a bushel of gold just by betting for it," Bancroft realized, but "the tremulous rapture of mingled hope and fear is almost compensation enough even if one loses." Additionally, speedy games, and moderate stakes that prolonged participation, maximized excitement by intensifying the experience. "Next to the pleasure of winning is the pleasure of losing," the historian wrote; "only stagnation is unendurable."[54]

The gambling that thrived around the plaza of San Francisco between 1849 and 1856 typified an adventuresome people devoted to chances for rapid accumulation of money. It captured the essence of the Gold Rush frontier of the mid-nineteenth century, and it suited the style of Argonauts flocking to the Pacific Coast. Set in a milieu as fluid and as gilded as society itself, gaming constituted a second chance for those who had not been lucky in other ventures.[55] It seemed to prolong the opportunities that the California frontier offered, and at the same time it distilled those characteristics that made the Far West the summation of American civilization.

While San Franciscans' devotion to their gaming palaces was strong, it was short-lived and unable to survive citizens' attempts to reestablish eastern morality. The midtown gambling house lasted only as long as the peculiar condition of the society that nurtured it. The fleeting career of the El Dorado illustrated the quick rise and fall of the new institutions. In the late summer of 1849, the El Dorado consisted of a blue canvas tent. By November it had grown into "a commodious two-story edifice," only to be burned to the ground the following month. A series of brick structures soon followed as the El Dorado, once owned by former riverboat gambler James McCabe, ran "full blast from 1850 till 1856." By the latter year the four-story building had begun to fall into disrepair, its upstairs windows shattered and its downstairs neglected. The San Francisco City Hall, now located next door, gave sign that civic leaders and land developers had started to reassign the block to purposes more suited to the central district of a respectable metropolis.[56] The brief heyday of the midtown gaming hall had come to a close.

The prominent place of gambling in Gold Rush culture was undermined during the 1850s as the frontier settled down. Although the process was not always peaceful, Californians gradually redefined gaming as beyond the borders of respectability as they set about taming their society. In San Francisco the changeover began as early as 1851 when such competing forms of amusement as theaters, gymnasiums, reading rooms, and private clubs began to siphon off some of the customers who had frequented gambling saloons. The new alternatives suggested the growing complexity and domesticity of the golden metropolis as well as citizens' struggle for respectability. Americans increasingly attributed the surviving corps of gamblers to foreign influences, and gradually proceeded to curtail and then to outlaw altogether public and commercial gambling. On April 17, 1855, the state legislature made illegal most common forms of wide-open gaming. The event, in the words of Dale Morgan, "from one point of view marks the end of California's frontier era, Frederick J. Turner to the contrary notwithstanding."[57]

The new laws, weak and difficult to enforce, likely had little effect on gambling in California, but they did illustrate a new spirit afoot in the state. They resulted from an outlook that perceived gaming establishments not as evidence of cultural refinement but as unwanted remnants of the frontier. As in the old Southwest, the target of reformers was not so much gaming itself as the professional gamblers who made their living from the pastime. Chance taking remained an integral aspect of life in the state, but those who made betting a career were cast out from respectable circles of society because they seemed increasingly incongruous in communities intent on conforming to eastern standards. This process was dramatized vividly in San Francisco during the course of events leading to the rise of vigilantism in 1856.

The Second Vigilance Committee of 1856 took shape largely for the political purpose of replacing an allegedly corrupt Democratic regime with an independent businessmen's government in San Francisco, but its reform rhetoric focused relentlessly on gamblers and portrayed public gaming as an obstacle to the stability of society. James King of William, editor of the city's *Daily Evening Bulletin*, led the antigambling hysteria of 1855 and 1856 in a newspaper campaign against municipal corruption. A banker who had been bankrupted by the statewide depression of the mid-1850s, King took avidly to journalism where, using sensation and controversy to the fullest, he built a leading newspaper by touting the need to establish social and fiscal respectability in San Francisco. Much of his success resulted from spiteful attacks on prominent city figures, and "his particular *bête noire*," his "pet villain," was the gambler.[58]

James King launched his campaign against gamblers in late November 1855, upon reporting the killing of General William H. Richardson, a federal marshal, by the dealer Charles Cora. Cora reputedly had come to San Francisco from the old Southwest, where he was said to have grown up in Natchez-under-the-Hill and become a "lucky" faro dealer. An Italian gambler and paramour of one of the town's leading madams, Charles Cora stood for all the things that the *Bulletin* opposed, and in King's eyes his arraignment for murder provided the city with an opportunity to put all undesirable citizens on notice that their day had passed in San Francisco. Convinced from the outset that Cora was guilty of murder, the editor stated that the gambler "*must and will be hung.*" He also proceeded to warn all of Cora's associates, including the Democratic sheriff who reportedly used to run a gambling hall, that any efforts to liberate the prisoner would be met with intransigent popular force:

> we warn the sheriff and the gambler friends of this man Cora, that any attempt at rescuing him either by a packed jury or by influence of gold, will raise such a feeling in this community as will end with more fearful consequences than attended the expulsion of such parties from Vicksburg. And now we want to know why the laws of this State against gambling are not enforced?

If the gambler somehow escaped from confinement or conviction, King feared, San Francisco would be rent by the forces of good and evil competing for control of the city—"War between the prostitutes and gamblers on the one side, and the virtuous and respectable on the other!"[59]

Confident from the outset that the gambler was unmistakably guilty and that the courts would agree, King became incensed in early 1856 when

Cora's trial ended in a hung jury. The gambler was held over for retrial, but to King it seemed that he had escaped. Less passionate observers believed that Cora's counsel, hired by the gambler's lover, had convinced enough of the jury that the accused had actually shot Richardson in self-defense. The *Bulletin* viewed things differently, however. Alleging that justice had been corrupted by "the money of the gambler and the prostitute," King believed that right would ultimately prevail over wrong, either through the courts or through popular tribunal. "Gamblers, we warn you! remember Vicksburg! You may yet be set adrift with this impious woman, Belle Cora, to drift where the ebb tide may carry you through the entrance to our harbor! Beware!"[60]

Complications soon made matters worse for gamblers by tainting them even more thoroughly as suspected allies of the corrupt political machine in California. During the early months of 1856, United States Senator John B. Weller recommended that President Franklin Pierce select James Y. McDuffie as the new federal marshal, replacing the man Cora had shot. The *Bulletin* attacked the Democrats' candidate by publishing reports that McDuffie had worked in 1850 and 1851 as a dealer in a Marysville gambling saloon where he had met Charles and Belle Cora. With this information King immediately jumped to the conclusion that Cora had shot Richardson so that his friend McDuffie, another sharper, could fill the vacancy. It seemed that the gamblers were colluding with the Democrats to take control of the state. In a letter to the *Bulletin*, McDuffie denied most of King's allegations. He admitted that he had worked as a dealer when gaming had been acceptable, legal, and licensed in California, but noted that he had long ago given up the occupation, denied connections to Charles Cora, and recalled his liking for General Richardson. Other letters to the editor offered similar arguments on McDuffie's behalf. Some people were willing to forgive his past because they understood that different standards had prevailed during the first years of the Gold Rush.[61]

King was appalled that his readers had actually submitted letters in support of McDuffie, and took it as a sign of California's failing condition. "In what other State of the Union would such a thing be done?" he asked. The editor saw no reason to encourage the rest of the country to think that "gambling is a *legitimate* business in California" any longer. "It is about time gamblers were taught that success cannot gild their vices so effectually as to hide their deformity from public view. Gambling is a dishonest calling and of the most pernicious level. No amount of gold can wipe out the stain."[62] King made it clear that norms had changed since 1850, and insisted that the state leave behind its frontier era once and for all by adopting eastern attitudes toward practices like gambling.

California's need to reform itself seemed especially keen in early 1856 because of the region's recent depression. A victim himself of the hard times, King came to regard gamblers as one of the roadblocks preventing California from taking its rightful place as the richest and most virtuous state in the country. The editor argued that the tremendous influx of new migrants to the West had slowed terribly. For a society dependent upon increasing population for economic growth, this was a serious blow, and King searched for the causes. He found one answer in the moral tenor of the population. Californians shunned patient industry and established vocations, he wrote, and plunged "into every kind of speculation and enterprize which presented the alluring prospect of increasing a quick or brilliant fortune."[63] Such an approach to business inhibited slow and steady economic growth and compounded the unstable character of the population.

Even more discouraging to potential immigrants, King reasoned, was the state's permissive attitude toward gamblers. "What honest man," he wondered, "comfortably situated in the East, will leave a land of law and order and morality for a country where gamblers are recommended to office, supported by the U. S. Senator, and endorsed by the largest political party in the state?" According to the *Bulletin*, Californians had corrupted themselves by tolerating gamblers as acceptable citizens. Now the sharpers seemed on the verge of controlling government, and that in itself would drive potential residents away. In order to continue to attract newcomers, the state had to reform its ways. Some practically minded men argued that completion of a transcontinental railroad would encourage growth, but James King of William disagreed. So long as gamblers are accepted as legitimate businessmen and permitted to hold political office, he advised Californians in April 1856, "you may thread the plains with a network of railways and you cannot expect any advancements in the prosperity of the state. Families will continue to leave our shores for a society and a code of morals more congenial to their tastes and better suited for rearing children in virtue and sobriety."[64]

By the time the editor's abrasive and fiery columns provoked his murder the next month, King had convinced many San Franciscans that the city's political establishment was, in the words of one private citizen, "under the controle of the Vilest of creation, desperadoes of every caste, the gambler, the thief, the Murderer and Assissin."[65] The editor's death made him a martyr to the antigambling cause and provided opponents of the Democratic regime with sufficient excuse to take the law into their own hands. As the ranks of the vigilantes swelled, they perpetuated the slain editor's battle against gamblers. Whereas the vigilance committee of 1851 had only thought about barring gamblers from membership, the committee of 1856 made a large point of it.[66] Moreover, King's crusade against gaming ensured that, when the vigilantes lynched the editor's killer, they also hanged Charles Cora, who had been awaiting his new trial in jail. The lynch mob thus fulfilled James King's prophecy of another Vicksburg episode. The *Bulletin* had finally gotten its man.

The vigilantism of 1856 reenacted a familiar western ritual of purification, played out within the context of local politics in San Francisco. Its unfolding highlighted the changing attitudes of Californians toward the public business of gaming. By taking on the gambler, residents of the state challenged not the risk taking and speculation that characterized Pacific civilization, but the unrestricted commercial betting that had flourished most in the early years. They seemed to be turning away from their own frontier past in order to regain the standards they had supposedly left behind in the East. In 1850 the palaces of fortune at the heart of San Francisco, teeming night and day with professional gamblers and Argonauts, had been celebrated as indications of cultural refinement and achievement in the Far West. A mere six years later, gamblers and wide-open gaming halls were viewed as obstacles to continued economic growth and social responsibility. The dramatic shift fell into step with the other measures undertaken to recreate Atlantic Coast civilization on the Pacific slope.

Californians' struggle to become more typical American citizens took shape in changing statutes against betting. After the first weak antigambling bill of 1855, the state legislature steadily strengthened laws against public and commercial gaming. In 1860 it banned most banking games by making it a misdemeanor to operate them. This measure was directed not at gaming itself so much, nor at ordinary players, but at professional gamblers. In a state that cherished risk taking, it remained more or less acceptable to play at games of chance, but not to run them for fixed percentages of profit. An 1863 bill reiterated the legal distinction between players and gamblers by giving losers at banking games the right to sue dealers in order to recover losses. Nine years later the state legislature approved a more stringent version of its previous ban, but omitted a few select games. Finally, in 1885, it became illegal in California not only to operate the prohibited games but also to play in them, and in 1891 punishments for gamblers and players were made equal.[67] The state had finally taken the last step to drive lawful gaming from inside its borders.

Legislation provided an official record of the Golden State's changing views on casino-type gambling. Laws did not necessarily affect residents' behavior, however. For much of the time between 1855 and 1885, the statutes did not outlaw every kind of game, proved difficult to enforce, and provided mainly light penalties. Government found it hard to deter citizens from wagering at their favorite diversion, for the gaming instinct was deeply ingrained in the population. William H. Brewer, an eastern professor who led a scientific survey of the state during the early 1860s, sniffed at the people's willingness to wager on anything. "You cannot differ with a Californian in the slightest matter," he complained, "without his backing his opinion with a bet."[68] Such an inclination turned much antigambling legislation into a "farce, a moral morsel that tastes well abroad" but stimulates no appetite at home.[69] Californians had tried to uphold the cause of James King by striving to regain eastern standards, but their continued interest in gambling, through the late nineteenth century and into the twentieth, demonstrated how Gold Rush sentiments persisted in the Far West.

The campaign to banish gaming from the Golden State did not succeed, but it did help to modify the shape of betting. The conspicuous and egalitarian style that prevailed at Portsmouth Square in early San Francisco, foreshadowing casino gambling in Las Vegas, quickly lost favor. Changing forms of gambling in the western metropolis reflected social fossilization. The Gold Rush had been a leveling influence at midcentury, and gaming then had been as open as the rest of the society, but Californians, and particularly San Franciscans wrestling with the complexity and divisions of an urban center, began to regenerate stratification rapidly.[70]

After the early 1850s, gaming establishments were increasingly geared to accommodate not everyman but rather specific groups of bettors. Local elites, which had always been able to afford to play in less public places, grew larger and began to gamble more exclusively among themselves. Like the upper classes of any city, they naturally preferred to play against each other in surroundings that catered to their monied tastes, rather than facing the prospect of losing to citizens of lesser stature. Meanwhile, the lower strata of society increasingly played games that seemed less than reputable in saloons distant from the city center.[71] These dives, which tended to flourish along the waterfront and on the Barbary Coast, were devoted less specifically to gambling than earlier midtown gaming halls. Yet, through them, and through the luxurious clubs that appealed to local elites, San Franciscans continued to gamble abundantly.

Gaming in the golden city had essentially adjusted to eastern notions of respectability. Urbanites continued to wager, for gambling remained an important ingredient in the makeup of Californians, but different forms of betting permitted San Franciscans to wager in a fashion more appropriate to a cosmopolitan center. A hierarchy of clubs and dens accommodated the social divisions that grew more steadily prominent in the city. Consequently, the amount of betting appeared to decrease. People now gambled in less public and less heterogeneous groups located at a greater distance from the city center. Betting was not as visible as before.

Moreover, Californians embraced different games that conformed more to the modified settings. Faro, monte, and roulette still thrived at special occasions like state fairs, "as openly played as in the palmy days of '49 and '50," Bret Harte reported in 1866.[72] But those speedy games had already begun to give way to an ever more popular California pastime. Poker flourished during the last half of the nineteenth century on the West Coast, partly because it remained legal so long as games were not operated by professional dealers. Some proprietors tried to cut themselves in for a percentage of the stakes, but the game was mostly played as a private diversion, and that suited both the upper- and the lower-class bettors who played at the more exclusive sites. Poker became king among sporting men in California, "the land where the game has been most favorably received and industriously cultivated as a science," according to Bancroft.[73] The betting contest was slower and less commercial than faro, monte, and roulette, but it was an American favorite appropriate for a more settled population.

Californians' conversion to poker signaled that their frontier society had begun to recede. Out of the grasping and daring days of the Gold Rush had come the indigenous western gambling that mirrored the speculation and "sharp-practice" of the population. Once Californians determined to leave the frontier behind them, they set about replacing their original forms of gaming with styles more suited to a people intent on garnering eastern approval. The kind of play that had flourished from 1849 to 1856, a practice marked by professional dealers, public settings, and fast-paced games, gradually disappeared in California, but it did not die out altogether.

Professional gamblers joined the "old Californians" leading the way to other mineral strikes in the Far West, where new strains of Argonaut society sprouted. By 1859 Colorado had become "an almighty fast country, owing to the number of fast men that have emigrated there," according to one newcomer. In 1863 William Brewer described the public gaming in one Nevada camp in terms that echoed earlier depictions of San Francisco, and would have applied to any number of mining towns in the nineteenth-century Far West: "Here men come to make money—make it *quick*—not by slow, honest industry, but by quick strokes—no matter *how*, so long as the law doesn't call it robbery."[74] The gaming halls were wide open, the crowds diverse, the dealers professional, and the games fast-paced, just as they had been in early American California until the frontier stage of society had passed.

Californians had reduced the prominence of their gaming by turning to less public, less promiscuous, and less professional forms of betting. Reformers made the dubious claim that people simply played less frequently. If in fact Americans were not gaming as much as before on the West Coast, it may have been because they speculated more in commercial and financial ventures. Californians rejected professional dealers, but they accepted gambling as a way of conducting their business affairs. They "passed laws that drove it under cover," Bancroft explained in 1888, "but its spirit still stalks abroad, and enters into almost every avocation." Workingmen tended to speculate with, rather than save, their earnings, the historian commented, and merchants inevitably had an adventurous sideline apart from their regular business.[75]

A gambling spirit was probably inevitable among a population with its mind on tomorrow. Like the Argonauts before them, residents of the Golden State lived for the future rather than the present or the past. The trait stood out most boldly in San Francisco. "Plainly a city of expectations" during the late 1860s, the metropolis seized upon every prospect for growth as a wager on tomorrow.[76] San Franciscans regarded their town as a bettor's windfall to be parlayed into even greater winnings. They seemed to have gotten something, an "instant city," where little more than nothing had existed before, and that made them distinctly intent on other chancy pursuits. Citizens continued to speculate in real estate, attempted to corner commodity markets, staked their money on the transcontinental railroad, and bought into such schemes as the Great Diamond Swindle of 1872.[77] But on no sure thing did they speculate so avidly as mining stocks.

By 1860 individuals' opportunities in gold and silver mining had all but disappeared as the economic activity became modernized and industrial, much as gaming had become more businesslike and predictable in Portsmouth Square establishments.[78] In other circumstances, Californians might have resorted more and more to the gaming tables in order to recapture the risky opportunities and the rapid fluctuations that more highly organized kinds of mining had eliminated. The industrialization of far western mining, however, was conducted in such a way that individuals from every social rank could still partake in the adventure by gambling on shares of mining companies.

Observers had commented on Westerners' propensity to invest quickly and recklessly since the beginning of the Gold Rush. After witnessing Americans' behavior in San Francisco in 1849, Patrice Dillon, the French consul, concluded that the "Yankee is a stockjobber by nature; no one understands the 'puff' better than he." James King of William, during his campaign to reform the morals of his adopted city, had also complained about the "vice" of "stock gambling," a practice that he ranked far below more patient and virtuous methods of making money.[79] Yet King and Dillon had seen nothing compared to the "mania" that broke loose after the discovery of the Comstock Lode in western Nevada. As large companies organized and capitalized to exploit the new find, Californians dug deep into their pockets and began an intense bout of speculation in mining firms that lasted from the early 1860s through the late 1870s. People invested in mining stocks with the same fervor and speed, the same outlook and commitment, that they had brought to faro tables, roulette wheels, card games. Like gambling before it, "stock-jobbing" became "*the* business of San Francisco."[80]

The "speculator's paradise" of the Far West was centered at the stock exchanges on California and Montgomery streets in downtown San Francisco, just a few blocks away from where the El Dorado gambling saloon had prospered at the old Mexican plaza.[81] Throngs gathered daily on the city streets in front of the trading offices, eagerly awaiting news of developments in the Washoe district. William Laird MacGregor, a Scot touring the Far West in 1876, paused in his travels to bring the fantastic scene home to his readers.

> Stand on a slight elevation for a few minutes, and look down on the mass of humanity who take part in this vast gamble for wealth. See how the crowd sways to and from with every fresh canard; how with one impulse they all

seem to move in the same direction to read the latest telegram or price list. I have been in the saloons of Hamburg, Baden, Wiesbaden, and Monaco, when those gambling establishments were at their zenith, but in none of them have I witnessed the same excitement.[82]

Californians did not monopolize the excitement, but rather exported it to the Nevada hinterland. Virginia City and other Comstock communities each had their own stock brokers who posted San Francisco prices just as soon as they could be telegraphed over the Sierra Nevada. The townspeople of Washoe clogged streets and sidewalks, too, by crowding around bulletin boards to learn the latest information. Like San Franciscans, they thrilled at the roller-coaster ride that mining stocks provided. William Wright, who covered the Comstock as newspaperman Dan De Quille for the *Territorial Enterprise,* was fascinated by the addictive nature of the speculative excitement. Those who had lost out on previous occasions always seemed to invest anew, swearing that this time they would sell their shares more quickly. But plungers inevitably held on too long, Wright noted, forever trying to recoup earlier losses by pushing their luck to achieve a top price. The reporter was just as surprised by the way that speculators in Washoe relied so resolutely on information relayed from California stock exchanges. "Men were not dealing in the big bonanza as it existed in Nevada," the journalist recalled, "but as it appeared on California Street, San Francisco."[83] Those living atop the Comstock Lode thus made investment much more of a game of chance. They cared less about actual conditions in the mine shafts directly beneath them than they did about the opinions of dealers in San Francisco.

Californians and Nevadans invested as gamblers in Washoe strikes, and imitated the style of play that bettors had adopted in early San Francisco gaming palaces. Mining stocks seemed to recreate the widespread opportunities that had characterized the Gold Rush and invited people from all classes to participate. "Every man you met was a president" of a mining company, remembered Bret Harte, "every other one a trustee, and all stockholders. Your washerwoman had ten feet in the 'Highflier,' your office-boy held certificates for 50 shares of 'Aladdin.' Everybody talked stock."[84]

By buying shares on margin, even those who lacked plenty of cash engaged in the frenzy, often to their misfortune. The speculative fever that encompassed San Francisco and Virginia City ensured that these Westerners, too, kept the future foremost in their minds. They spent money freely and lived life intensely, always nurturing the expectation that tomorrow would bring fortunes. Good luck would hardly have halted their speculations, however. Unlike Europeans who might try to purchase status or security with newfound wealth, Americans in the Gilded Age, and especially in the Golden West, aspired mainly to amass more, to stay involved in the game of accumulation as long as they could, even if their paper profits came tumbling down around them.[85]

After frantic investment had subsided one last time during the late
1870s, observers agreed that mining stocks had served as another mode of
"sharp-practice" by which confidence men fleeced innocent players. One
big loser protested that silver mines were much bigger swindles than poker
games run by riverboat gamblers, and another critic charged that the
"Kings of the Comstock" had taken unfair advantage of the "enthusiastic
and speculative, free, liberal, and even extravagant" character of the population of the Pacific slope.[86] Whatever the accusations, few failed to see
that the craze had stemmed from the same pursuit of quick fortune that
had encouraged Argonauts to try their luck. Doubtless more than one person found it ironic that Westerners passed laws "to suppress gambling with
cards where the chances are fair and the games honestly dealt," and at the
same time tolerated and even patronized untrustworthy stock exchanges,
or "mammoth gaming establishments," where upright citizens were "regularly victimized by rich and reputable sharpers."[87] Reforms had had
apparently little effect on the gambling proclivities of Californians.

Comstock mining had proven once more that, while the Far West still
lacked the learning and the taste to put it on a par with the more refined
East, the region remained a fertile source of new forms in the culture of
risk taking. Pacific civilization had developed the mines of Washoe
through innovative technology as well as through sophisticated finance
that permitted average people to gamble in the adventure. The extraction
of Nevada silver became a highly advanced industry that in some regards
predated the forward-looking changes in the United States during the late
nineteenth century. By pushing the logic of nineteenth-century enterprise
to an extreme in activities given to high risk and reward, California and
Nevada had plainly reached the Gilded Age long before other American
states.

Far western society similarly led the rest of the country in modernizing
styles of gaming during the last half of the nineteenth century. Inspired by
gold-seekers come to dig a quick fortune, newly arrived settlers embraced
novel kinds of betting that suited the distinctive way of life. They proved
most inventive in early San Francisco where high-volume gambling flourished near the city center in buildings quite similar to the modern casino.
As with mining, agriculture, and tourism in later years, Californians were
the first Americans to organize gaming into a modern industry.

This stage in the development of betting endured only as long as the
population regarded gaming as a legitimate enterprise operated by ordinary businessmen. Once people turned against professional gamblers and,
more gradually, against public and commercial betting, the original innovations gave way in California to tamer styles of gaming that seemed more
appropriate for a settled society. Residents of the Golden State hardly gambled any less, however. They maintained their reputation as a fast people
by continuing to speculate in commodities, land, and stock. Regarded as
more legitimate endeavors, these gambles demonstrated that betting still

prevailed on the Pacific Coast and served notice that the Far West would continue to act as the fountain of American gambling culture.

Despite the efforts of opponents of gaming, California society retained its predilection for betting. Gambling as a style of life gained reinforcement from the rapid growth of metropolitan Los Angeles during the late nineteenth and the twentieth centuries. Southern California came to resemble Gold Rush San Francisco in some respects when it spawned a series of speculative booms after 1880 that defined the fluid and acquisitive character of society south of the Tehachapis. At the same time that San Franciscans' preoccupation with California gold and Nevada silver diminished, a new burst of economic excitements stirred society in Southern California. Consequently, Los Angeles and its copious suburbs became the single most fertile source of new American forms of betting.

Southern California reveled in its own Gilded Age during the fifty years from 1880 to 1930, when prosperity stemmed from unprecedented growth. In the 1880s, the population of Los Angeles quadrupled, in the next decade it doubled, and then it tripled, doubled, and doubled again to overtake San Francisco in size. Demographic expansion laid the groundwork for economic booms. Prior to the 1880s businessmen had proceeded cautiously in Southern California because new demand for their services and products depended upon an unsteady stream of newcomers. Following the start of the boom, however, entrepreneurs had to anticipate the needs of an increasing population.[88] They willingly made advance commitments and took speculative risks because the profits resulting from growth seemed to be a sure thing. Angelenos gambled as capitalists on their bright future, and hedged their bets with prodigious public works, like a man-made harbor and a stunning aqueduct, that assured continued growth.

The characteristic venture of this speculative era was real estate, a field where people of even modest means could profit quickly as land values climbed. Every newcomer to the region needed a place to live, so the lands surrounding the former Mexican pueblo were subdivided again and again to accommodate an ever-increasing market. Those who saw city lots as a sure thing were occasionally disappointed when busts followed booms, but an optimistic attitude toward land prevailed because the general trend of prices was clearly upward. Other economic activities added to the venturesome mentality. The petroleum industry that boomed from the 1890s into the 1920s became a "charnel house of speculation" reminiscent of the Comstock; citizens wagered not on the oil wells underfoot but on corporate stocks marketed by questionable dealers. During the 1920s the automobile's influence on Southern California proved similar. The money that circulated around the auto trade fueled additional bursts of economic activity.[89] It did not take much to become an entrepreneur in Los Angeles, and, with the city's fantastic rate of growth and civic commitment to expansion, there seemed to be luck enough for every plunger. Blessed with such favorable odds, Angelenos accepted risks eagerly. Gambling became the outlook of an entire metropolis as residents sought to get something for nothing in their rush to succeed.

Because the boom in Southern California provided so many opportunities for people looking to get ahead, the region attracted hundreds of thousands of migrants eager to test their fortune. The numbers of these newcomers naturally served to prolong the economic explosion in Los Angeles. Even more importantly, the high expectations of recent arrivals reinforced the speculative outlook of the region. Migrants were taking a chance in coming to Southern California, and they proved willing to make additional bets to see that their life's gamble paid off. The city emerged as a center of gambling culture because, as destination for wave upon wave of westering people, from the late nineteenth through the mid-twentieth centuries, its society remained a frontier governed by the attitudes and movement of westward migration.

Even if the frontier as place had disappeared, the frontier as process endured in society on the Pacific slope, particularly around Los Angeles. Migrants brought to the region the individualistic quest for opportunity that they had taken to other Wests. In Southern California they found their pursuits enhanced by technological advances such as movies and automobiles, which not only enriched the good life that this frontier promised but also generated new styles of living. Many Angelenos hoped to reestablish eastern cultural standards in their adopted home, but they had also come to the West Coast in reaction against the East and its crowded cities, foreign immigrants, and harsher climate. By adopting new technologies and new patterns of urban living, they set themselves apart from Atlantic Coast civilization.

By the early twentieth century, it had become clear that Southern California would be different, yet it was also evident that the Pacific Coast had not relinquished its role as a most representative fragment of United States culture. Southern California distilled American culture in part because its society was made up of people from all corners of the nation. Boom-town conditions perpetuated the nineteenth-century trait of acquisitiveness that had characterized Gold Rush and Gilded Age, while advances in technology brought all that was modern to bear on life in Los Angeles. In 1928 one observer labeled Los Angeles the "Great American Mirror" because "no other community in America represents so fully what, to European eyes, seeing us in perspective, is so inexplicable because so incongruous." Against "its mushroom growth, its sprawling hugeness, its madcap speed, its splurge of lights and noise and color and money," Los Angeles balanced its "cultural charm, mature discrimination, intellectual activities." The mixture plainly "sprung from American soil, and could come from no other. If we are a nation of extremes, Los Angeles is an extreme among us."[90] More simply, Louis Adamic, an Austrian immigrant writing in 1927, called Los Angeles "the most American city in America any way one looks at it."[91]

Southern California put many national traits into bold relief, often by carrying them to extremes. Like gold-seekers, Angelenos reproduced a version of American civilization that was skewed toward the material and the acquisitive, for the Far West remained a fresh territory for economic adventures of all kinds. Scheming and speculating in their own special "diggings," Southern Californians retained for the Golden State its heritage as a residence for fast and sharp people.

Gambling in Southern California developed in stages roughly analogous to earlier phases in San Francisco. Gaming at first flourished conspicuously in downtown Los Angeles on a street known as Calle de los Negros, or "Nigger Alley," during the third quarter of the nineteenth century. Although the gambling saloons had somewhat more of an Hispanic accent because of the larger proportion of Mexicans in the population, they offered betting as openly and commercially as it had been provided by the grand gaming halls in early San Francisco. Dealers, importing American games into the changing pueblo, were mostly regarded as legitimate businessmen, Harris Newmark recalled. They were "generous, honest in methods, courageous in operations and respected by everybody."[92] Only with the beginnings of large-scale growth in Southern California did residents turn against the public business of betting. As promoters advertised the town as a healthful and clean-living community, and as Midwesterners poured into the Los Angeles basin, wide-open gaming became less acceptable. The city approved an ordinance closing all gambling houses in 1889. Angelenos' increasing vigilance drove betting under cover into illegal clubs and into permissive little suburbs like Vernon, "the tiny sin city of the 1910s," where the practice survived well into the twentieth century.[93]

Citizens outlawed public and commercial gaming because it contradicted their vision of the progressive and virtuous city that Los Angeles would become. But they simultaneously embraced a pattern of metropolitan development that hinged upon Californians' gambling outlook on the future. Angelenos speculated feverishly in economic bursts that became the essence of growth in Southern California. The first real-estate boom peaked in 1887 after railroads slashed fares to the Coast and stepped up their promotion of Los Angeles. Dubious dealings created short-lived paper fortunes for many local investors, but the boom broke in 1888 and took many participants with it. Upon retiring from speculation after his losses in the late 1880s, T. S. Van Dyke waxed philosophical about winning and losing in Southern California booms. "Life is but a game anyhow," he concluded, "and he beats it best who plays for the smallest stakes."[94] Unless they were playing at gaming tables, however, relatively few Angelenos confined themselves to modest wagers. They picked up the pieces after every bust and prepared to invest anew in the next day's sure thing.

Following previous generations of Westerners, Southern Californians viewed risk taking as a crucial ingredient of their way of life. Their attachment to chance and speculation stimulated betting games of all kinds and encouraged acceptance of new styles of play. Gambling furnished Southern Californians with a thrill even more genuine than the movies, because it reiterated the spirit of the entire metropolis and reduced the speculation that pervaded Los Angeles to an intense and speedy interval. The city inherited from San Francisco the legacy of California gambling.

In the twentieth century, California gambling thrived best not in the Golden State but in Nevada. Californians had been exporting their fast ways to other states since the 1850s when miners left the Mother Lode for additional opportunities on the Pacific slope. In the desert climate of the Silver State, the California style of betting finally blossomed to the fullest during the mid-twentieth century and gained nationwide recognition. One hundred years before, this fashion of gambling had been a short-lived aberration in downtown San Francisco; now it emerged as a cultural fixture that gave succinct expression to many aspects of modern American civilization.

Prior to the importation of California gambling, Nevadans played on a small scale. While the practice was legal from 1869 to 1910, betting tended to be a second line of business in barrooms, dance hall, and bordellos. Rather than running wide-open, games of chance were generally relegated by law to back rooms and second floors. Most establishments provided only a few tables for bettors, and players primarily staked only modest sums. Table limits seldom topped two dollars, and most wagers ranged from twenty-five cents to one dollar. The only features that set Nevada's gaming apart from most other states' were its legal status and the high rate of participation by residents of the state.[95]

Gaming in Nevada never really took shape during the nineteenth century on a scale to match Gold Rush gambling in downtown San Francisco. As virtual colonists of California, Nevadans shared mining as an economic base and speculation as a way of life with residents of the Golden State. Yet, save for temporarily at Virginia City, they never built urban centers where gambling could develop as a specialized enterprise. Even on the Comstock, people regarded San Francisco as the favored location of most gambling endeavors and spent their free time in that metropolis. Investors in mining stocks looked not to their own towns in Washoe where the ore was mined, but to exchanges on Montgomery and California streets where the betting line was established. In later years, prior to 1930, Nevadans looked not to Reno but to San Francisco for the best and widest range of sinful pleasures, including illicit gaming.[96] In this fashion the Golden State remained pre-eminent in the Far West.

The tables turned when twentieth-century Californians began to direct their attention to Nevada after the Silver State legalized wide-open casino gambling in 1931. Residents of the coastal state now had to travel beyond their own borders to partake fully of the kinds of gaming originally cultivated in California. Angelenos led the way to Nevada casinos. Their predominance ensured that Las Vegas would quickly surpass Reno as Californians' favorite gaming resort, in the same fashion that Los Angeles had surpassed San Francisco as the leading city in the Golden State.

Las Vegas generated new fashions of betting just as Argonaut San Francisco had during the mid-nineteenth century. The desert city marked the culmination of Californians' shaping of American gambling culture and demonstrated that Pacific Coast civilization, still being shaped by westbound migrants, remained an innovative frontier. By the mid-twentieth century, gambling was just one of many new cultural forms that California and the Far West transmitted to the rest of the country. Paradoxically, though, this hallmark of a bold new West was first dressed up as a remnant of the old West of the nineteenth century. No longer interested in imitating eastern styles, Far Westerners looked initially to their own immediate frontier past for clues about the proper packaging of casino gambling.

4

Last Frontiersmen

Downtown Las Vegas

* * * * * * * * * * * * * * * * * *

Few Americans ever made so much of the relationship between gambling and the westward migration as the people of Las Vegas, Nevada, in the middle third of the twentieth century. In toiling to convert the old railroad townsite into a thriving tourist resort, Las Vegans packaged the regional past and marketed it as a commodity essential to the promotion of their town to visitors. And because the invocation of the last frontier implied defiance of the constraints of modern life, gambling naturally became a part of the Las Vegas package after its legalization in 1931. The activity of gaming at first played a secondary role in the formula for town growth, more or less equivalent to such local attractions as Hoover Dam, dude ranches, and court houses offering convenient divorce. As gambling assumed an increasingly prominent place during the late 1930s and early 1940s, however, it heightened the community's identification with images of the old West. In a downtown district designed to duplicate the past, all casino betting reaffirmed the city motto—"Las Vegas, Still a Frontier Town."[1]

The town's career as relic of yesteryear was limited. Even while Las Vegans posed as last frontiersmen during the early 1940s, the resort began to change in directions that foreshadowed the future rather than recalling the past. New patterns of growth, which exposed the shortcomings of the last frontier theme, resulted primarily from the influx of Southern Californians beginning around 1940. These newcomers imparted to Las Vegas an uninhibited approach to betting that made southern Nevada an important outlet for novel styles of life originating in the Los Angeles basin. By heightening the presence of gambling, Californians liberated the town from the confines of railroad and old West and reclaimed it from the shadows of Hoover Dam. By 1945 casino gambling had replaced the last frontier as the trademark of Las Vegas.

When Californians superimposed new styles on the railroad town and last frontier village, they catapulted Las Vegas into nationwide prominence. The growth of the gambling resort ultimately relegated the old West theme to a subservient position, but the city center retained its close attachment to the past throughout the postwar period. As the focus for betting during World War II, the downtown district had ushered in another era of American gambling. There, full-blown casinos emerged anew, not as exceptions to the rule or temporary expedients, but as a dominant context for gambling in the twentieth-century United States. Decorated in a fashion that reiterated old Western themes, the downtown casino was a new form in the national culture of gambling that commemorated the affinity between gaming and frontiers. It provided a uniquely single-minded environment that enriched the betting experience and, at the same time, it illustrated the continuing influence of Californians on American forms of gambling.

In one way or another Las Vegas has long been on the road to Southern California. During the nineteenth century the springs and streams of shallow Las Vegas Valley made it an ideal desert way station. The site served as an oasis on the Old Spanish Trail between Santa Fe and Los Angeles, in the 1830s and 1840s, earning praise as "The Diamond of the Desert" for its "capital water." Around midcentury Mormons incorporated the camp into their projected corridor connecting Salt Lake City with the California coast. The Latter-day Saints even built a mission there in 1855, consisting of a "little mud fort" and a farm where local Indians received instruction in religion and agriculture, but they abandoned the site less than two years later. "It is easy to foresee," two French travelers commented during the mid-1850s, that the isolated desert settlement "will never become considerable."[2]

Over the next fifty years, as in so many other spots in Nevada, small-scale mining, ranching, and farming characterized economic life in the vicinity, yielding hardly enough income to support a town. In 1905, however, the oasis regained importance as way station on the route to Southern California when it became a division point along the San Pedro, Los Angeles, and Salt Lake Railroad.[3] For the following three decades the railway dominated the development of Las Vegas in virtually every regard. The community became the entrepôt for the mines of southern Nevada, the nearest train station to Hoover Dam, and a company town.

The railroad brought people and prosperity to Las Vegas. The population grew from 945 in 1910 to 5,165 in 1930. Most of the residents depended directly or indirectly for their livelihoods on the business of the railroad, which established shops and offices in or near its yards in Las Vegas. The railway also formed the Las Vegas Land and Water Company to manage the town, which it did quite paternalistically until the San Pedro, Los Angeles, and Salt Lake line sold out to the Union Pacific Railroad in 1921. As over-seers of a much larger rail network, the new owners were more indifferent to the small division point. Conflict between labor and management soon broke out, and in 1922 the Union Pacific moved its railroad shops north-east to the town of Caliente. The local economy slumped considerably, and efforts to diversify town business by building tourist facilities met little success.[4] Las Vegas remained tied to the fickle fortunes of the railroad.

The dominance of the railway was underscored by the physical form the community assumed. Rather, than construct roads along north-south and east-west axes, as virtually all later planners did, the Las Vegas Land and Water Company laid out downtown streets in a grid that followed the train line. Numbered streets ran from southwest to northeast, parallel to the rail-road, and cross streets ran perpendicular to the tracks. The grid formed a compact desert townsite of roughly forty blocks. Other additions, mostly following north-south and east-west axes, later appeared adjacent to the initial grid laid out by the railroad, but they were primarily residential sub-divisions subordinate to the central townsite. The train station, within walking distance of each of the forty original blocks, was both the eco-nomic and geographic center of life in Las Vegas, the focal point of a cen-tripetal community.

Local architecture enhanced the sense of cohesion. The railroad com-pany designed and built many of the early homes in the town using a stan-dard "cottage" pattern. Heavy reliance in construction on concrete blocks, an inexpensive and indigenous building material, added to the relatively uniform appearance of Las Vegas. Furthermore, the inward organization of the community was reinforced by its isolation. Only rough dirt roads con-nected the town to nearby mining camps in the mid-1920s, and neither roadway, telephone, nor railroad placed Las Vegas in direct communica-tion with Reno, the preeminent city in the state. The only highway con-structed through Las Vegas prior to 1930 paralleled the railroad line. Con-sequently, the Union Pacific tracks that constituted the town's major artery were also the primary link to the outside world, a link that favored South-ern California rather than northern and western Nevada. Early twentieth-century Las Vegas was in virtually every sense a railroad town.[5]

Up to 1930 Las Vegas had but slowly acquired the amenities of a small but permanent division point. The presence of the Union Pacific line, how-ever, soon unleashed the forces of expansion by making the community an ideal center of transshipment for the Boulder Canyon Project. With the building of Hoover Dam in the early 1930s the pace of growth quickened.[6] The influx of men and money, slowly gaining during the 1920s in antici-pation of the project, gave Las Vegans their first taste of a boom. Residents readily staked the future of the community on the construction and tourist appeal of the dam and newly created Lake Mead. Although the state legislature legalized gambling in 1931, they viewed that activity as only a secondary factor in the growth of their city. It remained for construction workers on the dam and Californian visitors in the vicinity to demonstrate the economic primacy of gaming. While Hoover Dam promised to revitalize the railroad town without changing it fundamentally, visitors and builders of the dam fueled the industry of gambling that was to remake Las Vegas altogether.

Preparations for the dam had been under way for years, but actual construction began in the summer of 1930 upon passage of the Boulder Canyon Project Act and requisite appropriations in Congress. The builders completed the dam in 1935 and the power plant in 1936. During construction the project employed an average of thirty-five hundred workers on a mean monthly payroll of $500,000. This was a bonanza to Las Vegas, which at thirty miles northwest of the dam was the nearest established town. Las Vegans also welcomed the new state highway and spur line that connected their town to Boulder City, the construction townsite near Hoover Dam. Off-duty workers streamed steadily into Las Vegas along the roadway to enjoy the hard liquor and gambling that were not available in federally managed Boulder City. Sudden prosperity so boosted the local economy that residents generally looked past the numerous transients and unemployed who naturally accompanied work projects during the Depression. Moreover, private growth in town was matched by federally funded civic improvements as New Deal monies poured into Las Vegas in amounts disproportionate to the small population. While most of the nation shivered through the hard times of the early 1930s, Las Vegans basked in the relative warmth of federal largesse and economic expansion.[7]

The flush of growth buoyed town residents. In addition to reaping long-awaited gains in business and population, they enjoyed sharing the nation's limelight with the dam. More than 200,000 visitors combined tours of Hoover Dam with side trips to the town in 1933. In Las Vegas travelers found a place that seemed at once relaxed and wild. One newcomer sized up the town.

Las Vegas impressed me as being different from any other American town. It had a touch of Mexico's Tijuana, where people loitered in the streets and the tempo was slow. There was a lack of formality in the air and absolute disregard for social distinction. The people were friendly and money was loose and plentiful. The bars and gambling halls were packed to capacity, and the Boulder Dam workers were pouring their earnings into the town. Loafers and moochers roamed the streets and women of questionable reputation rubbed elbows with society. Tourists were having a gay time and newly married people were celebrating, mingling with divorcées, the latter displaying an attitude of reckless abandon.[8]

The easy-going nature of the town invited comparison to frontier society, an allusion relished by local boosters intent on touting the community as a living remnant of the old West. Townspeople had already begun to promote downtown Las Vegas with a theme that would endure through the middle decades of the century. In the early 1930s, however, promotion did not appear to be a crucial ingredient in the formula for local prosperity. The construction project on the Colorado River provided a steady supply of customers for town businesses, and when completed the dam would continue to attract travelers.

Promotion became much more important in the last half of the decade. The completion of the dam drained away the captive audience of construction workers who had deposited their paychecks into the local economy. As the number of regular customers diminished, businesses began to move away, and residents began to worry about the future. The closing of The Meadows, the most elaborate gaming club in the area, seemed especially significant. Located on the highway to Boulder City, The Meadows had catered to dam workers. When they were laid off as the project was completed, the club could no longer afford to stay open.[9] Its closing signaled more than the demise of one gambling hall; it portended as well the reappearance of the railroad town. The Boulder Canyon project brought cars, trucks, and highways into the area, and clubs like The Meadows depended on motor traffic between Hoover Dam and Las Vegas for their business. As that traffic began to decrease in the mid-1930s with the completion of the work, it looked as if the town might once again become dependent on the domineering railroad.

With the decrease in the number of travelers between Boulder City and Las Vegas, town boosters had to find a new supply of customers. Las Vegans still saw their future bound up with Hoover Dam and Lake Mead, but now instead of relying on the regular patronage of construction workers, they hoped that travelers to the dam would stop in Las Vegas along the way.

The town had never really advertised itself to tourists before. It had not needed to appeal to the young, male construction workers who had eagerly sought out the town on their own. In addition, like many Westerners in the early twentieth century, Las Vegans had previously looked to travelers not for their tourist dollars but rather as potential residents and investors in the town. In the 1920s they hoped to attract farmers to the limited agricultural hinterland, and in the early 1930s they pointed out the potential of cheap electricity from Hoover Dam for the possible industrialization of southern Nevada. Even as they turned to tourism they held out hope for the development of manufacturing: "Las Vegas CAN become a combination of Pittsburgh and Niagara Falls," one columnist wrote.[10]

Appeals to industry and to new residents met with minimal response. With the completion of Hoover Dam and the possibility of local slump, Las Vegans earnestly undertook the unfamiliar task of tourist promotion. They initially had but partial success, for they were hampered by a lack of vision and self-confidence. Residents of the late 1930s tended to perceive their town as little more than a sideshow to the greater spectacle on the Colorado River. Las Vegans figured that while the dam would draw the tourist into the vicinity, they would have to make the town appealing enough for a side trip. At first they did not see gambling as a foremost attraction, even though construction workers and dam visitors had demonstrated its strong allure in the early 1930s. They looked instead to other ideas.

Las Vegans viewed the divorce and marriage business as one tourist staple. Nevada strove to be the most lenient of American states in its divorce statutes, requiring only six weeks' residency to qualify for final legal separation in the 1930s. Reno had attracted most of the unusual trade ever since movie star Mary Pickford sued Owen Moore for divorce in that vicinity in 1920. In part because it was closer than Reno to Los Angeles, and with that to Hollywood, Las Vegas garnered some of the business for itself during the 1930s. The town gained national recognition in 1939 when local boosters publicized widely the action filed in Las Vegas between Ria and Clark Gable. One local newspaper honored the momentous event with a special page devoted to the prospects of the divorce trade in southern Nevada, reporting that a 42-day stay netted between $350 and $400 for the town. During her six-week visit, which culminated in a five-minute court hearing, Mrs. Gable helped the town's cause by announcing that she preferred Las Vegas to Reno as a temporary residence.[11] The endorsement not only marked the escalation of divorce into a major local industry, but also signified the beginnings of local promotion using Hollywood personalities.

Movie stars further publicized Las Vegas by wedding there, as the community played both sides of the matrimony trade. The town's efforts in the wedding business culminated in 1940 upon the opening of a marriage-license bureau in the new Union Pacific depot on the eve of America's entry into the Second World War.[12] The location for the new agency was fitting, for both the railroad and the trade in matrimony offered only limited opportunities for growth. Neither the railroad nor the industries of marriage and divorce promised to establish the town as an urban resort.

Townspeople's limited vision for the future also found expression in the shortsighted theme of the old West, which dominated virtually all publicity campaigns between 1935 and 1945. Las Vegans sought to enhance the appeal of the town to travelers by playing up its frontier character. Other struggling communities in the American West used a similar approach during the early twentieth century, writes Earl Pomeroy, but Las Vegas proved one of "the most patently commercial Western charades that snare the tourist."[13] It no doubt started innocently enough, for townspeople had naturally identified with the local frontier heritage ever since downtown streets had been named for western explorers in 1905. In the 1930s, however, the packaging of the old West became much more pronounced as boosters emphasized not the modern comforts and opportunities that attract new residents and industrial investors but rather the gimmicks and ballyhoo that appeal to tourists.

Townspeople appeared to spare no effort to demonstrate that Las Vegas was, as the slogan promised, "Still a Frontier Town." Parties of mounted horsemen greeted arriving trains carrying special passengers, and innkeepers hired live prospectors with mules to adorn hotel entrances. Residents strove to recreate the casual atmosphere of the old West by wearing western-style clothing, and civic groups first sponsored Helldorado, the annual western festival, in 1935, and added a yearly professional rodeo to the event in 1936. Such ploys offered to travelers a piece of the bygone frontier. Both tourists and promoters relished the contrast between the duplication of the frontier past in Las Vegas and the futuristic technological advances at Hoover Dam. The same chamber of commerce sign that heralded the old West town also described Las Vegas as "Gateway to World's Greatest Engineering Project," and visitors, including J. B. Priestley, contrasted those "roughing it still" in Las Vegas and Reno with "the man of the future" responsible for awesome Boulder Dam.[14] Although the dam overshadowed the town, Las Vegans' frontier theme complemented the structure on the Colorado River and thereby served to make the town attractive to tourists in the Southwest.

Even more than tourists, however, Las Vegans themselves saw the frontier image as the foremost characteristic of the town. Travelers were already identifying Las Vegas with "all night gambling,"[15] much as they equated Reno with "divorcing." But local residents preferred to describe Las Vegas as an old West town above all else, and then to list the features that evoked the last frontier—convenient marriage and divorce, low taxes, friendly residents, licensed prostitution, permissive laws, abundant self-promotion, plentiful alcohol, cowboy attire, western rodeos, 24-hour entertainment, and legal gambling. To Las Vegans the promotional motif of the old West took precedence over a secondary feature like gambling. They were reluctant to become known as denizens of a community with an economy based on betting, preferring instead the function of a tourist stop. In this quest Las Vegas enjoyed some success. In 1938 roughly three-quarters of all those visiting the dam traveled through Las Vegas to get there; in 1939, when 630,900 travelers visited Hoover Dam and Lake Mead, 539,000 people also stopped in Las Vegas. The outbreak of war in Europe that year promised to divert even more Americans to the town as travel abroad came to be proscribed.[16]

Yet even if prospects appeared brighter in 1939, Las Vegans remembered still more booming times during the building of Hoover Dam. Although the town had enhanced its tourist appeal through promotion since the completion of dam construction, it had not recaptured the rapid growth of the early 1930s, and rapid growth, after all, was the quintessential purpose of any frontier community. Las Vegas remained a western sideshow to Hoover Dam and Lake Mead, lacking the vision that would later enable it to overshadow the dam.

The promotional motif of the last frontier probably imposed a limit on growth. It not only obscured the potential of the business of gambling, but also shortened the range of boosters' imaginations. The old West could be regarded as quaint, but the theme also reiterated the relatively unsophisticated and uncomfortable life of the frontier. Las Vegans lacked the requisite facilities, like a resort hotel, to keep tourists in southern Nevada.[17] Traveling Americans shied away from the prospect of "roughing it" in a village setting. Finding little of lasting interest besides "wide-open" gambling, most visitors did not stay very long or spend very much. Many no doubt agreed with Secretary of the Interior Harold Ickes when he described the community as an "ugly, rotten little town."[18] Such reactions helped to illuminate the limitations on development in 1939. Townspeople had contrived a frontier town that suited the promotional needs of the gambling business, but they viewed gaming as secondary to the actually less promising notion of the old West.

It seemed doubtful that the resort could ever develop to meet the expectations of its boosters so long as the townspeople viewed gambling as less than the leading attraction. The attitude found expression in 1937 when one local editor predicted that Helldorado would ultimately surpass other far western festivals, such as the Pendleton Round-up, because Las Vegas offered extra attractions, like brothels and casinos, that intensified the "last frontier" atmosphere. "Gambling," he wrote, "goes with those wide open days of the west."[19] Such an approach, which rated gaming a subsidiary feature, ensured that Las Vegans built a tourist stop, in which gambling served as one of many contributing features, rather than a resort, in which gambling prevailed, and the frontier theme contributed as a secondary influence. Consequently, true to its beginnings as a railroad town, Las Vegas remained a division point on the road to more significant destinations.

The shortcomings of Las Vegas as a tourist center stemmed in part from a relatively provincial mentality. Southern Nevadans were not prepared to exploit fully the opportunities bequeathed to the town by the state of Nevada. While Las Vegas had acquired connections to the outside world, and especially to Los Angeles, that would ultimately shape it into a cosmopolitan resort, it remained a cultural backwater, not only in the Far West but even in Nevada. As railroad station on the Union Pacific line, Las Vegas had come to identify more with Los Angeles than Reno, and as "gateway" to Boulder Dam, Las Vegas belonged more to the Southwest than to the Great Basin. These orientations distanced Las Vegans slightly from the state's heritage of exploiting "vices," prevented them from recognizing fully the potential in the statewide legalization of gambling in 1931, and blinded them to the forthright attitudes of Reno to the north.

Of all the states of the Union, only barren Nevada had a social history that made it the logical choice to legalize casino betting in the 1930s. For most of its existence Nevada had permitted gambling, in one context or another. Even during those periods when law forbade the activity, from 1864 to 1869 and from 1910 to 1931, games of chance played for profit continued to flourish. They seemed as much a part of the Great Basin state as the desolate landscape and the sparse population. Chroniclers have often pointed out that gambling resembled the chancy pursuit of precious metals, which had defined the state's economy from its earliest days. In addition to the psychological similarities between gaming and mining, the cyclical patterns of mining encouraged Nevadans to accept lawful gambling.

Well into the twentieth century, the state depended heavily upon the extractive industry not only for its social character but also for its economic development. As a result, Nevada did not advance far beyond the modes of production typical of the miners' frontier of the late nineteenth century. Residents sought new economic opportunities only when mining booms diminished, first in the 1880s and 1890s, and later in the 1920s and 1930s. Responses to the first depression included the divorce trade and lawful prizefighting, as well as state and federal reclamation programs. Responses to the second depression included additional reclamation, as in the Boulder Canyon project; greater dependence on federal largesse; even more permissive attitudes toward marriage, divorce, and gambling; and the beginnings of the tourist industry.

After the United States Congress created Nevada Territory in 1861, the first territorial legislature, responding to an appeal by Governor James Nye, outlawed gambling. The prohibition continued through the first five years of statehood, but was repealed in 1869. Gambling had flourished in the state despite the prohibition, remaining as popular on the Comstock Lode as it was elsewhere in the Far West. By legalizing the practice, the state legislature recognized the prevalence of gambling in Nevada at the same time that it began to regulate and tax betting games. As a source of private income and public revenue, gambling no doubt gained importance during the late nineteenth century when the mining economy of Nevada collapsed. As an adjunct to betting, and as another source of money, the state legalized prizefighting in 1897, shortly after California and a host of other states outlawed it. With boxing, betting, and the first few illustrious divorces, Nevada earned a reputation for permissiveness in the first decade of the twentieth century. The return of prosperity in mining after 1905, however, enabled the state to afford to follow the nation's progressive impulse. Seeking greater respectability in the eyes of other states, Nevada outlawed gambling in 1910 and extended its required length of residency for divorces in 1913. The longer residency minimum lasted only two years, but the prohibition on casino gambling lasted some twenty years.[20]

In open violation of the law, Nevadans continued to gamble after 1910. Then, upon the decline of mining in the 1920s and 1930s, residents of the state set out to find new sources of income. Unlike Las Vegas, most of Nevada suffered along with the other forty-seven states during the Great Depression and searched for any new source of money. Gambling was one of the most obvious options, and in 1931 the legislature reversed its stand on the activity. Six other western states also legalized betting in the decade, establishing pari-mutuel wagering on horse races. Nevadans went even further, however. Over the strident objections of the state's leftover progressives, the legislature legalized wide-open casino gaming, returning to the permissive policy of the late nineteenth century. Although a few other American states legalized one or two casino games during the first three quarters of the twentieth century, none except Nevada permitted full-scale, public casino gambling. Moreover, in the later 1930s the Silver State authorized betting on other states' horse racing, and for a time even considered a state lottery.

Gambling was seen as part of a larger effort to attract people and capital. Advertising itself as "One Sound State" in the midst of nationwide economic collapse, Nevada disregarded some of the welfare burdens that other state governments had assumed and strove to maintain a balanced budget and to prohibit taxes on income, corporations, inheritance, gifts, and "intangibles." Permitting games of chance would complement economic policies designed to attract businessmen and other residents to the state. Nevadans made these conditions out to be part of the same "free & easy, individualistic spirit" that licensed gambling and prostitution and permitted convenient divorce.[21]

When Nevada embraced easy divorce, open gambling, and low taxes, it was merely "exploiting the federal commodity," as Daniel Boorstin explains. Throughout American history different states, particularly those small in population or size, have profited from each state's sovereign right to set its own guidelines for licensing corporations and regulating morals. Nevada had merely followed the examples of New Jersey and Delaware in making itself more attractive to businesses by promising low taxes and lenient regulations. Similarly, Nevada had several predecessors as divorce center of the nation. Recognizing that the most tolerant laws in moral matters would attract the patronage of residents from other places, states like Indiana, Illinois, and the Dakotas in the nineteenth century had conceived their statutes regulating divorce with the specific intention of attracting the dissatisfied spouses of less permissive states. Pecuniary gain to the tolerant states resulted from the costs of the required length of in-state residency and from legal and court fees. Whereas other states had looked upon divorce as a sideline during the nineteenth century, however, "divorce actually became a major force in the economy" of Nevada.[22] Especially in the 1920s, after the deflation of the statewide mining boom, Nevada pushed its competitive advantage to new lengths, lowering residency requirements from six months to three months in 1927 and to six weeks in 1931. Whenever other states threatened to legislate even shorter residency requirements, Nevadans proposed to reduce their minimum, too, and discussed liberalizing definitions of legal grounds for divorce. Nevada became widely known as the country's haven for unhappy wives and husbands, granting around one thousand divorces annually in the early twenties, 2,500 in 1928, and 5,260 in 1931 after passage of the six-weeks' law.[23]

Once the state of Nevada had created these opportunities, it was up to local communities to realize them, and none pursued them more earnestly in the first four decades of the twentieth century than Reno, Nevada's largest city and America's divorce capital. Reno differed substantially from Las Vegas in that history and location encouraged it to exploit permissiveness more quickly. Reno lay closer to the mining heritage of the Comstock Lode and as the state's leading city had a greater sense of Nevada tradition. It lived in the shadows of neither Boulder Dam nor Los Angeles; if it identified with any other city, it was San Francisco, with its "sinful" Barbary Coast.

Unabashed Reno had few qualms about the "divorce trade," particularly during the hard times of the 1920s and 1930s. The local economy was clearly bolstered by the traffic in marital separations. Between 1936 and 1938, visitors to Reno filed 8,156 divorce suits, compared with 2,010 for Las Vegas. Because each of the plaintiffs had to reside in the state, usually in Reno motels or on dude ranches, and had to pay for the services of local attorneys, a $3 million yearly trade resulted. Reno residents of the 1930s accepted this business with a sense of detachment and self-satisfaction. Neither proud nor ashamed of the peculiar economic staple, they took divorce, and the nation's condemnations, in stride. Unlike Las Vegas, which, Renoites thought, debased itself with gimmicks in an effort to become "what the week-end visitors from Los Angeles and Hollywood would want Las Vegas to be," Reno calmly accepted the legacy bequeathed by Nevada tradition and exploited it with few second thoughts.[24]

Las Vegas ultimately surpassed Reno, primarily by catering to the preferences of Southern Californians, but at the conclusion of the 1930s, residents hesitated to shape their town into a recreational suburb for Los Angeles and Hollywood. The public equated Reno with divorce, and Renoites accepted that connotation happily, but when Las Vegas came to be identified with gambling, residents seemed reluctant to accept such a reputation. Las Vegans tried to mold their town into what they expected tourists would want. On occasion they admitted that gambling and prostitution were major attractions, but those activities assumed secondary status in their picture of what Las Vegas should be—a tourist stop that utilized the motif of the last frontier and offered recreational opportunities consistent with the "spirit of the old west." Tourists could see the sights, partake of convenient marriage and divorce, and enjoy the "freedom of the great outdoors," as well as visit the gambling halls and bawdy houses. Each activity was seen as another dose of the frontier for visitors.[25]

Las Vegans understandably felt no compulsion to base the promotion of their community solely upon the enterprise of gambling. In addition to a reluctance that doubtless derived from Americans' traditional ambivalence toward the activity, they had no familiar examples of gambling resorts for tourists, other than such exclusive spas as Saratoga, New York, and Hot Springs, Arkansas. Moreover, Las Vegas through the mid-1930s remained isolated and provincial, little more than railroad division point and gateway to Hoover Dam. Residents naturally hitched their fortunes to the tourist potential of the dam, the very project that had so forcefully revitalized the town during the 1930s.

As a result of this cautious perspective, gambling developed in but a limited fashion as an economic force during the decade. Both during and after construction of the dam, city commissioners restricted the number of licenses the town could issue to casinos, just as they curtailed the number of permits to liquor stores and taverns. Those interested in operating gambling clubs easily evaded the law by setting up shop outside city limits, but the restriction nonetheless typified a lack of confidence in the business of gaming. The publisher of the Las Vegas *Review-Journal*, A. E. Cahlan, epitomized townspeople's reluctance to embrace casino betting wholeheartedly. Six gaming clubs and sixteen saloons in the town, he concluded in 1939, were perhaps the maximum if Las Vegas intended to remain "a somewhat 'nice' play center" instead of becoming a "gaudy" and "rowdy little community like Tijuana." Two years later the newspaperman reiterated his unwillingness to promote gambling when he suggested that the city restrict the commercial activity to only two downtown blocks and the few "bona fide hotels" in the community.[26] Las Vegans did not envision gambling as their town's major industry.

The form that casino gaming assumed in southern Nevada pointed to its low status on the eve of the Second World War. Legal, public betting remained a limited enterprise. Early operations were known as "clubs" rather than casinos, suggesting an atmosphere of intimacy and exclusiveness. These clubs, more akin to corner groceries than to the supermarkets of gambling that appeared afterwards, functioned with none of the sensation that later casinos created. Bettors generally risked only little sums, and observers mostly agreed that the business was small, even harmless. Instead of the shady and corrupt gambling dens that they had anticipated, visitors found insubstantial and seemingly innocent clubs. Local residents prided themselves not on the economic success of gaming but rather on its upright character.[27]

It is not difficult to explain why gambling proceeded on such a small scale in southern Nevada. Local operators had virtually no experience in big-time betting. They possessed neither the resources nor the skills to build gambling into an extensive enterprise; only an infusion of money and knowledge could do that. Similarly, local businessmen lacked the inclination to develop gambling in order to attract tourists. This shortcoming found expression in Las Vegans' modesty in the shadows of Hoover Dam and their overconfidence in a short-sighted promotional motif. Without a widely successful publicity campaign, and with no more than a slight familiarity with the Southern Californians who would ultimately comprise the bulk of travelers to Las Vegas, local gaming clubs in the late 1930s depended mostly on visitors who did not value the town as their primary purpose for touring the Southwest, a perilous clientele at best.

Tourists generally regarded the dam as the major attraction in the area. Young, federally employed dam builders had at least been steady and paying customers, unlike the excursionists to the Colorado River who might pass through the dusty town without spending money or stopping there. Unable to attract for itself a dependable patronage from dam visitors, Las Vegas needed another captive supply of customers, men who like the construction workers had nowhere else to spend their money. With the onset of the Second World War, the town acquired these patrons. Around the same time, southern Nevada began to appeal more successfully to Southern Californians, the tourists who shaped the city so profoundly during the 1940s and 1950s. Not coincidentally, experienced operators and promoters arrived in Las Vegas, recognized the potential windfall there, and began to remake local gambling into a large-scale enterprise.

Prior to the spectacular rise of legal gambling in Nevada, most casino betting in the United States was illegal, and gambling operators, the nation's only source of expertise in that particular business, were naturally outlaws. Entrepreneurs in organized crime, who had dominated the profession since the days of riverboat gamblers, gained experience in promotion, mass merchandising, and finance during the bootlegging era, and naturally gravitated to illicit gaming after the repeal of Prohibition.[28] Because of their experience in large gambling halls, and because of their participation in the complex enterprise of organized crime, these underworld operators provided the ideal catalyst for big-time betting when they transferred their skills and resources to southern Nevada.

The first to appear in the area were the Cornero brothers, two ex-bootleggers from Los Angeles who ran The Meadows club until it closed down after the completion of Hoover Dam. More significant for the growth of gambling in Las Vegas was the relocation of casino operators purged from Southern California by municipal reforms of 1938–1939. A host of well-known gaming dens had flourished on Spring Street in Los Angeles during the 1920s and 1930s. Guy McAfee, the "overlord" of these operations and a former vice squad captain on the police force, first sensed the imminent crusade for purification in 1938 and began to relocate his interests to Las Vegas. He brought both experience and capital to the southern Nevada town, taking over one downtown club and one operation located on the highway to Los Angeles. As reformers closed in on Los Angeles clubs in

1939, other operators moved away from the metropolis. Some, like Tony Cornero, launched gambling ships anchored off the Southern California coast. When state and federal officials closed down such floating casinos as well in the years between 1939 and 1942, another swarm of professional gamblers descended on Las Vegas. In addition to Cornero and the legendary Benjamin "Bugsy" Siegel, this second influx included Chuck Addison, Bill Curland, Farmer Page, and Tudor Scherer, the foursome that opened the downtown Pioneer Club in 1942, one of the city's best managed casinos.[29] Bold men like these, experienced in large-scale gaming operations as well as in the general business of "vice," helped to transform local gambling into a more sophisticated, more successful enterprise.

The significance of the coming of Angeleno casino operators to Las Vegas was twofold. They made up the first clearly defined group of emigrants from the world of organized crime to set up "legitimate" business in southern Nevada. Men like McAfee foreshadowed the arrival of both seasoned personnel and tainted funds from underworld activities. Figures from the realm of organized crime, who ranged from petty shills and dealers to full-fledged gangsters, ultimately spawned a host of problems for Las Vegas and Nevada. As the *Review-Journal* covered the municipal reforms in Los Angeles during the late thirties, its editors proudly assured readers that state legalization and local regulation would forestall any such corruption in Las Vegas. Initially confident that the last frontier town could remain impervious to organized crime and municipal corruption, the paper grew apprehensive by 1942. Editors now warned that an influx of known racketeers jeopardized the development of Las Vegas into a "'nice' play center" or an "industrial capital of a great inland empire."[30]

Yet illicit gamblers also contributed constructively to the rise of commercial gaming in modern Las Vegas. They provided funds in an age when most investors would not or could not finance casinos in southern Nevada, and they brought the experience and skills necessary to remake gambling into a big business. This infusion was essential to the growth of the city, because it was not about to succeed as a "'nice' play center" or an "industrial capital." The legal nature of betting in the Silver State enabled gamblers to practice their livelihood respectably, bringing them above ground from the underworld, so they in turn helped to ensure the success of the urban gambling resort which gave legitimacy to their way of life.

The most important contribution of professional operators from Los Angeles, however, was the strengthening of the bond between Southern California and Las Vegas. Gamblers like McAfee, Cornero, and Siegel had all worked in the Los Angeles area and encouraged many of their former customers to visit southern Nevada. Moreover, relocated casino entrepreneurs knew how to cater to Southern Californians. When Guy McAfee timed the opening of his 91 Club, on the Los Angeles highway, to coincide with Ria Gable's divorce from Clark Gable, he demonstrated the knack for publicity that was essential to the rapid growth of the gaming industry in

Las Vegas. McAfee and his California colleagues not only compelled local competitors to expand their clubs and work to build up business, but also forged the final link between Las Vegas and Hollywood. The movie crowd had regularly patronized the gambling dens along Spring Street before the municipal reforms of 1938 and 1939. Now it made its way increasingly to southern Nevada, and attracted other Californians to the desert town in its wake. Taking a cue from the newly arrived entrepreneurs, the Las Vegas Chamber of Commerce readily incorporated Hollywood personalities into a promotional campaign by urging tourists to rub elbows with "writers, movie stars, directors, and other vacationists" around the gaming tables, a ploy certain to appeal to a population enamored of its celluloid heroes.[31] The migration of experienced casino operators from Los Angeles at long last made Las Vegas a full-fledged satellite of Southern California.

A mere trickle during the 1930s, the swelling current of Angelenos streaming through Las Vegas after 1939 washed away old limitations and drastically reshaped both gaming practices and the resort town. A certain fondness for southern Nevada and a pronounced inclination to gamble openly channeled Californians' thorough-going impact on the desert community. Angelenos had demonstrated an attachment to the area by visiting Hoover Dam constantly during the 1930s.[32] Southern Nevada lay close enough to the Coast to be an ideal automobile excursion, its climate seemed familiarly pleasant, especially with the growing use of air conditioning, and it offered recreational opportunities that appealed to Californians but, after municipal reforms in Los Angeles, were less readily available in the Golden State. Moreover, once they began traveling to Las Vegas regularly, Southern Californians found the town congenial. Chapin Hall, columnist for the *Los Angeles Times*, authored two glowing articles that typified Angelenos' response to southern Nevada. The journalist found that Las Vegans kept their community decent and tasteful, and promoted the resort with "showmanship," tact, and "initiative," traits that likened them to the populace of Southern California. In fact, Las Vegas appeared to sprout from the very soil that nurtured Los Angeles. "This town is really the infant prodigy of our immediate hinterland," Hall concluded. "If you go once it's all off. It will become a habit."[33] And so it did.

Las Vegans were timid about the business of gambling, but Southern Californians had no such restraints. Angelenos visited Las Vegas not to experience the last frontier but to gamble. The trappings of the wild West may have attracted visitors to southern Nevada a first time, but such gimmicks gradually lost their appeal. Southern Californians returned repeatedly to Las Vegas because they enjoyed the thrill of gaming. They consequently made gambling the predominant feature of the desert resort. They accepted the old West motif, but they subordinated it to the activity of betting. The town changed to suit the preferences of Southern Californians, and so began its rise to become gambling capital of the United States.

The new Las Vegas appeared most dramatically in a series of resort hotels built along the Los Angeles highway after 1945, where Southern California culture had full rein from the outset of development. Even in downtown Las Vegas, however, Californian styles of gambling penetrated the railway townsite and reoriented the outlook of the last frontier town. Full-fledged casinos steadily supplanted the gaming clubs of the 1930s, automobiles constantly undermined the primacy of the railway, and Hollywood techniques increasingly governed promotional efforts. A B-grade movie called "Las Vegas Nights," which supplied favorable publicity in 1941, aptly symbolized the much more powerful role that Southern California had begun to play in the desert resort.[34] The arrival of ever-increasing numbers of Angelenos in Las Vegas at the close of the 1930s marked the start of the transformation from tourist stop to urban resort.

Wartime social patterns reinforced the reorientation that Southern Californians initiated in Las Vegas. Mobilization for war directed to Nevada thousands of men uprooted from home and family. These migrants included servicemen preparing to face tremendous risks as well as war workers toiling in oppressive conditions. Conventional moral standards wilted in such a climate as everybody tried to grasp pleasure in the time available. Like Angelenos, soldiers and war workers cared more about Las Vegas as a recreation center than as a showcase for Western Americana. They perhaps enjoyed the last frontier on a first visit, but they returned to play at the gaming tables.

The onset of war served to accclerate change and growth. During the Second World War the military made ample use of the vacant federal lands throughout the state of Nevada. Even before the Japanese attack on Pearl Harbor, preparations were under way to build a military base and a defense plant in the vicinity of Las Vegas. In mid-1941 the Army Air Corps established a training facility north of the town at an old airport. Later converted to Nellis Air Force Base, the gunnery school initially cost more than $2 million to construct. The number of soldiers stationed there grew from 2,000 in July, 1941, to an average between 8,000 and 11,000 from 1943 to 1945, with a monthly payroll of around $1 million. Soldiers on maneuvers in the nearby Mojave Desert and black military policemen stationed at Hoover Dam joined the Air Corps trainees in considering Las Vegas an off-duty refuge from military camps. Other servicemen stopped at the train depot on traveling orders to and from the West Coast. These many soldiers were generally young, male, and on their own. Military service often exposed men to gambling and encouraged them to play at casinos. Soldiers tended to spend just as freely as the federal government did in the area and increased local business substantially.[35] The soldiers of the early 1940s constituted a steady supply of customers for Las Vegas casinos.

They were joined at the gaming tables by employees from Basic Magnesium, Incorporated, an industrial townsite located ten miles south of Las Vegas. Planned in late 1941 and completed in stages from mid-1942 to mid-1943 by an army of more than 10,000 men on a weekly payroll of approximately $1 million, the factory took advantage of Nevadan minerals and Boulder Canyon hydroelectric power to process magnesium, a lightweight metal essential to the Allied war effort. After its completion the huge facility employed thousands of workers on a weekly payroll that remained around $1 million. Because of grossly inadequate housing, unbearable working conditions, and heavy demands for labor throughout the region, the turnover rate of employees at Basic Magnesium soared. More than 20,000 workers toiled at between 3,600 and 6,500 jobs in the plant from 1942 until it closed in 1944. Many of them became acquainted with Las Vegas and contributed some of their wages to the booming town.[36]

Wartime conditions inaugurated unprecedented prosperity and growth in Las Vegas. A town of 8,400 in 1940, the population exploded to 20,000 in mid-1942 and grew even higher in 1943 and 1944. Postwar relocation siphoned off some of the increase, but by the end of 1945 the number of residents had more than doubled since the beginning of the decade. Shortages of housing, a perennial problem for Las Vegas between 1930 and 1960, were particularly acute during the war as newcomers lived in canvas tents, cars and trailers, tarpaper shacks, hastily built barracks, and old mine shafts. Motels rented out rooms in two or three shifts per day to accommodate recently arrived workers and visitors to Las Vegas. The flood of newcomers represented a financial bonanza to the young city, which quickly seized the opportunities at hand. Local construction grew precipitously until bridled by shortages of building materials, and optimism prevailed as boosters at long last tasted the fulfillment of their efforts on behalf of the town.[37]

Local businessmen had good cause for confidence in the early 1940s because Las Vegas had suddenly become a popular recreation center. Soldiers and plant workers, of course, proved to be a broad and deep supply of steady customers. The value of these generally young men resided not only in the wartime business they stimulated but also in the postwar return trips they would make to southern Nevada. Civilians kept coming to Las Vegas, too, despite the rationing of gasoline. In fact, the town surpassed the popularity of Boulder Dam for tourists. While tight military security on the Colorado River discouraged travelers from stopping there, Las Vegas appealed to visitors increasingly and became the primary tourist attraction in southern Nevada.

The optimism and easy-going style of the last frontier community seemed like welcome relief from the routine and anxiety of wartime society. Southern Californians, perhaps trying to escape coastal blackouts, continued to travel to Las Vegas, frequently by train, and left their unmistakable imprint on the impressionable resort town. Largely as a result of military relocations, the marriage business reaped a harvest of desperate servicemen, especially in 1941 and 1942, who took advantage of the quick and easy weddings that Las Vegas provided, just as dissatisfied spouses

flocked to the area in record numbers to seek divorces during the immediate postwar years. The town ideally suited the needs of servicemen.
Among its most prized attractions was Block 16, the neighborhood to
which licensed prostitution was confined in Las Vegas. Block 16 did a land
office business through 1941 and part of 1942, but pressures from military
and civilian officials and from real-estate developers finally closed down
the brothels and dispersed their occupants to more discreet locations.[38]
Prostitution naturally continued to thrive at other nearby sites, but it lost
its wide-open character and its status as the town's penultimate attraction.
By reducing the visibility and availability of prostitutes, ironically, federal
authorities heightened the primacy of gaming. Gambling became the
undisputed trademark of the town in the early 1940s.

Residents and visitors increasingly identified Las Vegas primarily with
gambling and set out to exploit the opportunities that gaming presented.
Growth in the fledgling city now depended on expansion in the betting
industry. A series of new casinos opened so that the area had a total of
thirty-four clubs in 1945. Businesses ran day and night until late 1942
when proprietors, at the request of military officials, jointly decided to
close down between 2:00 and 10:00 A.M. as a contribution to the war effort.
Many of the new investments and wagers in Las Vegas appeared to come
from black market sources that could find no better place to spend or
"launder" ill-gotten funds. Such pursuits reinforced the bonds between
Las Vegas gambling and experienced casino operators. But "legitimate"
prospects abounded, too, as one writer noted: "There isn't a citizen in Las
Vegas who hasn't his hands in several deals, all of which stem from the
boom. Business mushroomed overnight, and it's a smart hombre who can
remember the enterprises he's backing. Everybody owns half of something,
nobody owns all of anything."[39]

The sudden prosperity of Wilbur Clark demonstrated the available
opportunities. From 1941 to 1945, Clark parlayed his initial stake of
$2,200 into ownership of a casino and small hotel, four bars, and two card
rooms, and part ownership of two other gambling halls and a "string of
horses." Even women joined the boom. The shortage of male operatives
allowed female dealers to take their place alongside Rosie the Riveter in
the wartime economy. Indeed, the entire complexion of the town changed
in the midst of rapid growth.[40] Gambling had become the predominant
industry in Las Vegas by 1945, and its remarkable success gave great
encouragement to local residents. Less concerned with posturing as a tourist sidestop, Las Vegas gained confidence and a better sense of its future.
Optimism surged and plans for the postwar era proliferated. Las Vegas
appeared to be realizing its boosters' dreams.

The rise of gambling as the sine qua non of Las Vegas necessarily weakened the prevailing theme of the old West, for the frontier ethos had to
assume a supporting role beneath the primary attraction of wide-open gambling. Yet, although the promotion of the betting industry ultimately

required more variety and flexibility than the narrow western theme could
provide, in that flurry of growth during World War II, developers perceived virtually no other style to which they could turn for guidance. Consequently, even as the preeminence of the last frontier image diminished
in relation to the significance of gambling, the old West enjoyed its most
pronounced revival in Las Vegas from 1940 to 1945. Many new casinos and
hotels—like the Western Casino, the Pioneer and Frontier clubs, and the
Last Frontier, El Cortez, and El Rancho Vegas hotels—were named and
styled with the wild West in mind, and observers repeatedly echoed boosters' claims that Las Vegas was "still a frontier town." In 1944 this western
revival reached its zenith when civic leaders proposed that all new downtown architecture conform to frontier styles.[41]

In addition to the contrived sense of history derived from period architecture, an even more fundamental attachment to the past persisted in the
burgeoning city. Almost all the new wartime business was centered downtown in the original forty-block townsite adjacent to the Union Pacific
depot. The gaming clubs of Las Vegas, decked out in the fashion of the old
West and elevated to paramount status in the resort town, were mostly
located within walking distance of the train station and stockyards. The
centripetal railroad town had merged fully with the last frontier. The con-
vergence of the two designs was ill-fated because it occurred at the same
time that gambling became the overriding factor in local development.
The imperatives of the gaming industry rapidly came to control the shaping forces in Las Vegas. Just as in architecture and promotion, the city's
function as America's twentieth-century gambling capital required an
urban form that was more diverse than the nineteenth-century shapes of
the railroad and old West could provide. Yet even though railroad town
and last frontier had begun to give way to the complexly formed urban
resort of the postwar era, they combined in the early 1940s, at the first
blossom of urbanization, to lend to Las Vegas a cohesion in geography and
architecture that it would never regain.

Railroad town and last frontier endured in Las Vegas in the guise of
downtown casinos, centers of betting that survived the demise of the old
tourist stop. The downtown casino, another new form in the culture of
gambling indigenous to the American West, captured the past of the frontier as well as the future as portended by Southern California. It represented the grafting of new ways on to traditional practices of gaming in
southern Nevada, and it gave the central district a distinct identity.

Like the clubs of the 1930s, these new establishments lay close to the
train depot and featured western styles of architecture and decor. In location and design, they perpetuated attachments to yesterday. In addition,
most downtown casinos were not connected to hotels. Overnight tourists
generally stayed either at separate downtown motels or in the many motor
courts that lined highways leading into the center of town. The heyday of

the resort hotel, another cultural form that coupled casinos with hotels on the same grounds, had not yet arrived.

At the same time that downtown casinos preserved Las Vegas traditions, however, they also illuminated the direction of change. The new establishments were no longer called clubs nor regarded as small or petty, for they had expanded substantially in order to accommodate the increased trade. Moreover, they were now given over almost entirely to the business of gambling. The clubs of the 1930s had evolved from late nineteenth-century saloons where betting had to compete against liquor for the customer's attention. Now gambling became the uppermost attraction in downtown establishments, much as it had prevailed in the early gaming halls around the plaza in Gold Rush San Francisco, while the bar and the old West decor merely contributed to a setting conducive to gambling. The change from club to casino demonstrated the growing influence of the tourist from Los Angeles. The Californian visited Las Vegas with gambling in mind, and downtown casinos as supermarkets of betting best suited his purpose.

The downtown casino enjoyed its prime during the boom years of the early 1940s when it underwrote local growth and contributed to the unity of the city center. Fremont Street came to be the center of nightlife. Gambling clubs, as well as many other types of downtown businesses and even private residences, had located there through the 1930s, and by the end of the decade the block had acquired its first bright neon lights. Beginning around 1940, with the sudden growth of the gaming industry, casinos and closely related businesses, like hotels, bars, and restaurants, multiplied along Fremont Street and quickly supplanted other businesses and remaining residences. Railroad passengers to Las Vegas, whose numbers grew as a result of wartime gasoline rationing and the movement of soldiers, disembarked within view of the casinos and walked but a short distance to reach them. A spate of new downtown clubs and hotels opened during the war within just a few blocks of the train depot on or adjacent to Fremont Street. Novelist Erle Stanley Gardner, taking a cue from the local architecture, recognized in 1941 the "frontier" shaping of the railroad town:

> Las Vegas keeps to the traditions of western towns by having one main street that shoots the works. A few cash-and-carry grocers and businesses . . . hang on to the side streets. Two main districts branch out at each end of this main street: One of them a two-mile long collection of tourist camps containing some of the best air-conditioned auto cabins in the country. At the other end, like the arm of a big Z, is the stretch of houses where women sit around— waiting. The length of the main street is sprinkled with gambling casinos, eating places, hotels, drugstores, and saloons. Virtually every form of gambling runs wide open.[42]

Even before Fremont Street had been stripped of its unnecessary shops, Gardner acknowledged its central role in the budding gambling resort of

Las Vegas. The "main stem" or "Great White Way," as the avenue was nick-
named, overflowed with patrons in those prosperous years. Customers
streamed off the trains stopping next door, rushed in from nearby military
bases, flocked up Boulder Highway from the magnesium plant, and poured
in from the auto courts that lined the road to Los Angeles. Yet the very
success of the downtown gaming district also revealed most clearly its limits as a resort center in the mid-twentieth century. Despite wartime shortages of gasoline, so many tourists drove cars to the downtown center that
in mid-1942, before curfew was imposed on local businesses, one journalist complained, "You can't find a parking place on Fremont Street at five-
thirty in the morning." Wartime Las Vegas witnessed the beginnings of a
parking shortage that lasted into the 1950s.[43]

The overcrowding that afflicted the downtown during the 1940s indicated that if Las Vegas continued to grow, another city district altogether
would be needed to accommodate postwar resort development. Parking
problems and other symptoms of congestion illuminated the shortcomings
of the railroad town in an automobile age at the same time that the primacy
of gaming began to undermine the motif of the last frontier. The enormous
number of cars, which indicated the popularity of Las Vegas, had also
begun to reshape the city profoundly. Already, row upon row of auto
courts and hotels stretched out toward Los Angeles and Boulder City,
halted only temporarily by restrictions on civilian building during the
war.[44] Once those constraints had been removed, a new gambling district
called the Strip would blossom along the highway to Los Angeles, less
devoted to local traditions and more attuned to California culture, and the
cohesive community of Las Vegas would be fragmented irreparably.

The growth of the new "roadtown" district would ultimately split Las
Vegas in two by introducing architectural and geographic diversity, but at
first it did not challenge the prevailing stereotypes of the old West.[45] The
first two resort hotels erected along the Strip in the early 1940s, El Rancho
Vegas and the Last Frontier, were named with the untamed West in mind,
and both were fashioned in styles similar to downtown clubs. El Rancho
Vegas featured several one-story buildings of wood and stone composition
that sprawled over a wide lot alongside the highway. A local attorney compared the ranchlike complex to "a Spanish village in a desert setting." The
operation included a casino, dining room, bar, main hotel structure, pool,
and guest cottages, all surrounded by green lawns. Brick chimneys topped
all the buildings and range-style wooden fences enclosed the grounds.
Interiors were adorned with open beams, wood paneling, mounted tro-
phies, fringed leather drapes, and paintings of the historic American West.
A windmill tower stood atop the hotel office, and the slogan "Howdy, pod-
ner, come as you are" greeted tourists.[46] With stylings such as these, El
Rancho Vegas suggested that the last-frontier motif so popular in downtown Las Vegas might reach new heights in the undeveloped expanses
along the highway to Southern California.

Western styles of architecture, however, never really developed extensively on the Strip. They did appear there on occasion, thereby preserving
the tenuous connection between the two districts. Up until the opening of
the Riviera hotel in 1955, most establishments followed the low-slung,
ranch-style pattern of construction begun by El Rancho Vegas and the Last
Frontier. But as befitted resort hotels, rather than just plain casinos, the
newer buildings generally shed the wood and stone exteriors, the brick
chimneys, and the cattlemen's fences. Most of the decorative motifs inside
and out drew inspiration not from the American West but from African
deserts, Mediterranean resorts, or tropical settings. Hotel bars in particular
paid homage to the bygone West in their ornamentation, no doubt inspired
by Americans' mythology about the hard-drinking cowboys, miners, and
lumberjacks in the westward migration. Murals in cocktail lounges at the
Thunderbird and Sands hotels depicted cowboy scenes on the American
prairie, and the Navajo dining room at the Thunderbird featured Indian
styles of decor and open wooden beams. The Last Frontier, however,
exceeded all other Strip hotels in using western styles. It even created a
hollow replica of a real frontier town complete with a museum of artifacts
from the historic West.[47]

Such were exceptions, for the most part, among the numerous motifs
that characterized the Strip. Last frontier styles may have suited Las Vegas
when the town was little more than a tourist stop in the shadows of Hoover
Dam, but post-war innkeepers along the Los Angeles highway realized that
different, more exotic decorative themes would better promote their distinctive blend of casino gambling and cosmopolitan luxury to the Southern
Californians who made up the bulk of tourists.

Meanwhile, the past lived on in downtown Las Vegas where advocates of
the last frontier idea seemed virtually oblivious to its rejection on the Strip.
Throughout the postwar period the motif of the old West lent to the central
district a unity that reinforced the lingering impact of the railroad's shaping. In the effort to recreate the old West totally, even those businesses
displaced by downtown gambling halls adopted "last frontier" designs,
but casinos were the most unrelenting in their use of stylized architecture
and interior decoration. The Horseshoe and Las Vegas clubs reached new
heights in their blunt juxtapositions of western images with the lure of
money; the former framed a glass display of one hundred $10,000 bills
with a huge golden horseshoe, and the latter featured slot machines cast
in the figures of one-armed bandits. At the Lucky Strike club a picture of
two prospectors panning for gold adorned the casino entrance.[48]

The Golden Nugget casino was the most avid in commemorating the
frontier. One writer termed its style "Early Western Saloon." The plushly
carpeted club featured innumerable nude figures—on the walls, in the
bar, and atop slot machines. Indian heads decorated the one-armed bandits, and signs posted throughout the building imitated productions of the
1890s. As usual, the casino lounge went to the greatest lengths. In addition

to old-time barroom woodwork and furniture, the saloon featured a ceiling that must have been inspired by San Francisco's nineteenth-century Barbary Coast; it was "held up by two carved [unclothed] maidens who are ever mindful of their responsibility even though they have been set upon by two carved satyrs." Tony Lucy, owner of the Golden Nugget, naturally dressed to conform to the style of his casino. He sported a bright green "stockman's suit," a cravat embroidered with the figure of a naked woman woven in gold thread, and cowboy boots with plates of solid gold on heels and toes. Dealers, croupiers, waitresses, and other employees all wore western-style uniforms in the clubs along Fremont Street, and Country and Western music filled the lounges, eateries, and gaming rooms.[49] By exploiting every possible opportunity to expound the last frontier, casinos created an overwhelming effect.

Downtown Las Vegas maintained its last frontier identity throughout the postwar era. Those who observed the district between 1945 and 1960 acknowledged the pervasive atmosphere of the old West, which spread beyond casinos to characterize the general appearance, special events, local journalism, and persistent promotion of the urban area. National journalists reiterated perceptions of the old West as they flocked to the sensational new resort in search of stories. "This is where the wild west went when it couldn't go farther westward," one reporter decided.[50]

Local boosters never lost sight of the promotional pitch that identified downtown Las Vegas with frontier freedoms and western informality. The town continued to promote Helldorado just as before, and in 1946 the Chamber of Commerce added a new gimmick—it decided to name more fittingly the three-block stretch of Fremont Street where casinos had become so densely packed together. When the chamber elected to call the neighborhood "Glitter Gulch," it incorporated not only the last frontier theme but also the influence of Hollywood. Local boosters later had second thoughts about the new nickname, and ultimately reverted to the blander "Casino Center" to delineate the downtown glut of gambling halls.[51] The label "Glitter Gulch" stuck nonetheless. As gaudy and compact as the downtown district itself, it well described central Las Vegas after 1940.

New and expanding casinos, named and decorated with the frontier heritage in mind, continued to eliminate virtually all other forms of downtown life on Fremont Street during the late 1940s and the 1950s. By 1955 only one drug store, complete with slot machines; one telegraph office, where losers wired home for money; and one bank, for cashing travelers' checks; remained on those busy blocks of Glitter Gulch. The district consequently presented a singlemindedness of design and function matched nowhere else in the metropolitan area. No luxurious resort hotel along the Strip would be able to rival the intense devotion of downtown to gambling.

In a sense the roadtown district had rendered obsolete the earlier downtown, with its mixture of residences, businesses, and casinos. In sprawling resort complexes on the Strip tourists could find all the facilities they wanted without leaving a single air-conditioned building. It thus acquired a certain edge over the downtown area as a tourist attraction. In response, however, Glitter Gulch abandoned its all-purpose nature and specialized in one central feature for tourists. While Strip hotels tried to achieve the appearance of luxury by featuring swimming pools, gourmet dining, night-club shows, and sport facilities, Casino Center offered gambling in its purest, least diluted form: "In Glitter Gulch, the approach to the tourist is straightforward. The Golden Nugget, a large gambling house in the heart of the Gulch, is the richest vein in the big rock candy mountain of Las Vegas. It offers no entertainment, just a multitude of ways to gamble, from wheels of fortune and penny slots to big-time poker games in the back rooms."[52] Without many frills or comforts, downtown Las Vegas retained a distinctive identity in the urban resort.

Differences between downtown and roadtown have been explained by the notion that Glitter Gulch was "more proletarian" in its appeal and clientele. While more luxurious hotels on the Strip came to be identified with "high rollers," the downtown motif of the old West, it was said, catered to the "working class."[53] This idea received widespread acceptance, but it essentially misrepresented the nature of downtown and road-town customers as well as the significance of the last frontier theme. Whether rich or poor, players patronized the "less plush casinos" of the central district "to economize." The clientele in both districts was essentially middle class. Downtown players "are essentially no different from the tourists on the Strip; they are simply less obviously affluent and considerably more single-minded. For Glitter Gulch is where the real action is, the thing in itself, with no pretensions to glamour or luxury, or even holiday-making. The people are there purely to gamble." Moreover, Las Vegans, who were less likely to need all the services that resort hotels offered, tended to patronize downtown establishments when they gambled. The Fremont Hotel, which opened there in 1956, made a concerted effort to attract local customers.[54]

The solitary purpose of gambling in Glitter Gulch appealed to all economic classes, and so did the frontier idea. Like casino gambling itself, the heritage of the American West was not more attractive to one social stratum than to any other. It functioned downtown not so much as a promotion that discriminated between different classes of customers, but rather as a buttress to the singleminded purpose of the district.

The theme of the last frontier served to intensify the gambling experience. It has been hypothesized that any device that helps to remove the bettor from his normal environment actually enhances the experience of betting and allows players to become more deeply involved in the game. The greater the player's sense of distance from the setting that makes up his daily reality, the more he is "released" from "conventional responsibilities and controls." Furthermore, any sort of visual or auditory "noise" that creates an "unusual sensation" also heightens the thrill and the pleasant tensions of gambling.[55]

Both downtown and roadtown casinos effectively enriched the experience of gaming by creating unusual environments in which to bet, but the clubs of Glitter Gulch developed the more consistent theme and created the more singleminded atmosphere. In addition, the motif of the old West perhaps evoked more response from casino patrons. They were not only familiar with that particular historical setting, but also readily equated the old West with permissiveness and risk, and willingly abandoned "conventional responsibilities and controls" in such an atmosphere.[56] The contrived environment was unusual enough to detach gamblers from daily inhibitions and restraints, but it also conjured up attitudes that encouraged participation by reminding Americans of the frontier heritage. That gambling could be pursued in a setting that recalled the pride and glory of the westward movement must have lent a sort of legitimacy to an activity toward which most Americans were ambivalent. In this manner the motif of the last frontier, while clearly subsidiary to the dominant role of gambling, nonetheless remained significant in the appeal of downtown Las Vegas to tourists.

While Glitter Gulch continued to recall the heritage of the frontier, hotels and casinos on the Strip were designed using different motifs. Underlying the resulting diversity of images, though, was gambling, the activity that more than anything else held together an increasingly amorphous city. On the Strip gaming took place in a distinctly resort setting. The hotel complexes along the Los Angeles highway offered tourists every possible convenience, thereby making the shops and services of downtown Las Vegas unnecessary to those travelers who stayed on the Strip.

If the old railroad townsite lost some of its significance as an urban center, it nonetheless retained a specialized appeal. There commercial gambling emerged in its least adulterated form. Unencumbered with wedding chapels or guest cottages, gift shops or parking lots, gourmet restaurants or show rooms, downtown casinos presented but one major service to customers. Bettors from all classes continued to flock to Glitter Gulch for the straightforward dose of gambling, the last frontier environment which heightened the intense sensation, and the convenience of a glut of casinos located literally next door to one another. After 1940, gambling came to dominate all aspects of downtown life, and the last frontier theme enhanced the experience of the the downtown casino by setting the proper tone.

Americans, and Las Vegans in particular, in this manner perceived the ties between gambling and the westward migration. Period architecture, western styles of music and dress and decoration, and events like Helldorado served to condition tourists for gambling, just as frontier conditions earlier had encouraged people to take risks. The last frontier image first merged with and then replaced the railroad as a unifying force among the casinos of downtown Las Vegas, helping to sustain the vitality of the old railway townsite through the mid-twentieth century.

Gambling and the American frontier merged on Fremont Street as they never had before, but Glitter Gulch was only the beginning of the evolution of the western city of Las Vegas as gambling capital of the United States. In the years after 1945 when the resort metropolis grew at an unprecedented pace, the underlying dynamism of expansion derived not from the downtown district but rather from the flourishing Strip on the southern outskirts of town where the influence of Southern Californians was most pronounced.

Californians had proven instrumental in redirecting the development of downtown Las Vegas. They had prompted the rapid shift from tourist stop to Casino Center and helped to subordinate the old West motif to the more powerful theme of gambling. In central Las Vegas the changes produced a new form in the American culture of gambling, the downtown casino, which embodied both the last frontier recreated by Nevadans and the new cultural frontier originating in Los Angeles. Within the framework of railroad town and last frontier, the downtown casino so magnified the importance of gambling that it became the "main pattern of life" in Glitter Gulch.[57]

While downtown Las Vegas was singlemindedly devoted to gambling, roadtown Las Vegas dispensed gambling as one ingredient in a whole new style of living. Gaming dominated development on the Strip during the postwar period, but in resort hotels the practice stood out less boldly because it took place in a setting even more sensational than Glitter Gulch. The casino remained the heart of the resort hotel, for the lessons learned by downtown clubs about the business of betting had not been lost upon roadtown establishments. The Strip constituted a unique urban environment that created yet another American form of gambling. This new configuration, the hotel-casino on the Los Angeles highway, drew its inspiration from not the old West but the ultimate West. Gambling on the Strip distilled the pacesetting culture of Southern California and transmitted it to the entire country.

5

New Frontiersmen

The Las Vegas Strip

On the evening of April 4, 1955, the owners of the Last Frontier Hotel turned their backs on the bygone era of old West nostalgia and opened their doors to the age of the future. As they closed up the casino of the original hotel, they directed patrons around the corner and up the Strip to the entrance of a recently completed addition called the New Frontier. Like the updated name, the new annex could hardly have expressed better the mood of Americans in midcentury Las Vegas. Instead of the old West style that had prevailed at the Last Frontier, opening-night crowds now encountered modern luxuries couched in the most futuristic designs in the resort city. A switch in hotel slogans, from "The Old West in Modern Splendor" to "Out of this World," summarized the changed outlook and announced the space-age decor.

Inside the New Frontier, the ranch-style design of the original edifice, complete with bar stools shaped like saddles, walls studded with trophy heads, and dealers clothed in cowboy outfits, had given way to ornamentation that combined plush luxury with the wonders of tomorrow. Originally laid out in the design of an old West fort, the hotel suddenly epitomized the civilization of the new West. A cocktail lounge called the Cloud Nine, walled with three-dimensional murals showing celestial bodies, superseded the Gay Nineties Bar of the Last Frontier, which had been decorated like an old Western saloon. The Planet dining hall supplanted the Ramona Room, a restaurant with walls of intricate Zuni stonework, and the new Venus dinner-theater contained a revolving stage set atop a hydraulic orchestra lift.

The old lobby, complete with double fireplace and western gift shop, had combined stone blocks, wood paneling, and split logs in its decor. The new entrance featured shiny floors of Italian marble, lengthy sofas of pink and white leather, and a picture of "six little men from outer space making a bee line" for the gambling tables. The deep-pile, lilac-colored carpets covering the new casino floors matched walls painted in rich violet and magenta. The ceilings, once made of rough-hewn wood, were now red and pink, and from them, instead of low wooden beams and wagonwheels, hung flying saucers, spinning planets, and chandeliers shaped like creatures from another galaxy. Finally, although the hotel had originally relied heavily on its Western Americana museum and Last Frontier Village to interest tourists, in 1955 it employed such entertainers as Ted Lewis, Gypsy Rose Lee, Sammy Davis, Jr., and Liberace to attract visitors. The transformation confirmed one reporter's suspicion that Las Vegas had become "unquestionably the new frontier of America."[1]

The conversion from Last Frontier to New Frontier, from small, woodsy, auto court to large, garish, resort hotel, exemplified the dramatic changes that Las Vegas underwent after World War II. By the mid-1950s the population of the city proper had reached 50,000, while close to 100,000 people resided in the metropolitan area of Clark County. Eight million tourists spent $160 million in Las Vegas during 1956, demonstrating its nationwide popularity and providing the economic underpinnings so essential to its runaway growth.[2] The dynamism of rapid expansion sprang not from Glitter Gulch, where decorators still enshrined the old West, but from the Strip, which stretched toward the future because it led to Los Angeles.

The centerpieces of the emerging gaming district were the novel resort hotels, like the New Frontier, which comprised yet another American form of gambling to appear first in the West and then gain acceptance in the East. For Las Vegans, the resort hotel served as a unit by which to measure the city's fantastic growth. For other Americans, it served as a travel destination, as the scene of the vacation experience in southern Nevada, and as a glimpse of tomorrow.

Like previous additions to the American culture of gambling, the Strip hotel reflected the particular western society in which it developed. Its predecessor in Las Vegas, the downtown casino, had blended certain aspects of modern far western culture with remnants from the old West to produce a resort establishment devoted single-mindedly to gambling. The Strip hotel continued to offer gambling above all else to visitors, but because it consolidated so many components of Southern California culture, it also conveyed to its patrons a distinctive and new mode of living. In the roadtown district south of the city limits, futuristic styles took root at the outset of postwar development and dominated the shape of the emerging resort district.

As a source of new ways of life, Southern California reached its peak during the postwar period. The region had already pioneered the new cultural forms suggested by automobiles, moving pictures, and suburban housing. Now it led the nation in adapting to the social conditions of postindustrialism as well. Californians explored the shifting relationship between work and play, the changing role of the individual in mass society, and the novel dimensions of postwar affluence. Leisure activities placed the new way of life into sharp focus for the nation because many of Californians' cultural innovations during the twentieth century converged to generate distinctive forms of recreation. The hotel-casinos of the Las Vegas Strip comprised one prominent playground where a most modern culture came to be distilled and dispensed for the entire country.

The Los Angeles blend of automobility, affluence, risk taking, and individualism that tourists encountered in the roadtown gambling district was promoted and marketed as an industrial commodity. Casino gambling grew into an enormous business that mass-produced vacation experiences for average people in much the same fashion that Hollywood movie-makers created pictures for widespread consumption. Industrial methods of production increasingly shaped the Strip hotel as a cultural form and defined the boundaries of the future as embodied in the urban resort; they also enabled large numbers of tourists to act as new frontiersmen in Las Vegas.

The futuristic Strip captured the imaginations of Americans. The resort city presented to visitors, in packages of three days and two nights, the attitudes and leisure of tomorrow. To a nation preoccupied with affluence and technology, roadtown Las Vegas appeared as a city designed for comfort and convenience. To a generation less burdened with doubts about gaming, Las Vegas offered a permissive atmosphere in which people freely took chances without seeming to suffer injury. To a people increasingly comfortable with the processes and commodities of large-scale consumer and service industries, Las Vegas proffered mass-produced, mass-merchandised vacations at prices great numbers of Americans could afford. The culture of the coming decades appeared to be on preview today for tourists in southern Nevada.

The postwar rise of the desert resort was in a sense a tale of two futuristic cities, for the development of the Las Vegas Strip amounted to little more than another subdivision of metropolitan Los Angeles. Increasingly during the middle decades of the century, observers recognized the close bond between the two urban areas. The legendary sleuth Lew Archer deduced the connection as he observed midday traffic in Las Vegas: "It came from every state in the Union, but most of the license plates belonged to Southern California. This carney town was actually Los Angeles's most farflung suburb."[3] In the middle of Hollywood in 1960 appeared an advertisement that attested Southern Californians' fondness for the desert playground. On the Sunset Strip, atop a sign for the Sahara Hotel in Las Vegas, stood a thirty-foot figure, "an immense twirling plaster statue of an almost naked lady in a green bikini, holding a sombrero in her upraised hand" and beckoning people to visit the resort.[4] Many answered her invitation, gratifying the southern Nevadans who had striven to attract Angelenos to the gambling center since the 1930s. In fact, throughout the postwar years, Southern Californians amounted to between three-fifths and three-fourths of all visitors to Las Vegas.[5] The resort catered successfully to the preferences of Angelenos and consolidated their novel values and styles of living.

Southern Nevada served as a backyard to which Angelenos retired for recreation. There they found the kinds of leisure that resembled in form and substance the amusements that Los Angeles itself had cultivated extensively. In the production of movies and television shows, and in the utilization of such theme amusement parks as Disneyland which had spun off from the entertainment industry, Southern Californians developed particularly commercial types of leisure that revolved in part around fantasy, that is, around the participant's willing suspension of disbelief. Recreation in Las Vegas not only borrowed the very personalities, economies, and architecture of leisure from Los Angeles; in gambling it also relied on the same element of fantasy among players.[6] In both places the suspension of disbelief in play activities made all things seem possible.

Movie making and Las Vegas gambling were closely linked as industries devoted to mass-producing leisure that incorporated fantasy. Strip hotels ceaselessly identified themselves with film stars in their promotion. The prevalence of famous entertainers in southern Nevada contributed to tourists' willingness to suspend disbelief by making vacations less an aspect of everyday life and more an excerpt from the movies. Moreover, a risk-taking outlook bound Hollywood to Las Vegas visitors even more tightly, for movie making exemplified the speculation that pervaded life in Southern California. Denizens of Hollywood seemed to be bettors by second nature; they thrived in an atmosphere of tension and anxiety, expected easy money, and regarded each picture "as an enormous gamble."[7] Actors, directors, and writers accepted casino gaming as just another opportunity for taking chances in a life that they viewed as predominantly one of hazard and luck. Movie-makers' presence in southern Nevada reiterated the similarities between casino gambling and the fantastic amusements of Hollywood.

Disneyland, an offshoot of the movie industry that opened for business in the same year as the New Frontier, also resembled Strip hotels as a provider of amusements. Disneyland served American families as Las Vegas served American adults.[8] Both constituted fantasy worlds set apart from daily life, and both marketed on a wide scale recreation experiences designed to appeal to transitory customers. Both Las Vegas and Disneyland conveyed to visitors from across the country a streamlined and exaggerated version of Southern California culture.

The automobile forged still another link between Los Angeles and Las Vegas, for the two cities were but three hundred miles distant along a con-

venient highway. The car lay near the heart of the way of living that Angelenos held out to the rest of the nation. Southern Californians had elevated
the automobile to the basis for a new pattern of urban life. The sprawl, the
mobility, and the rootlessness that characterized Los Angeles society were
all attributable in large part to cars. The influence of autos steadily became
more visible throughout the land, although nowhere more spectacularly
than on the Strip in Las Vegas. Once utterly dependent on the railroad, the
urban resort became just as reliant on automobiles during the mid-twentieth century.

The importance of the automobile became immediately apparent in Las
Vegas. By the 1920s and 1930s tourists from the Far West had already
accepted automobile travel as a prominent form of vacationing. After curtailed use of autos during World War II, people throughout the United
States took avidly to car touring. By 1953 fully 83 percent of all vacationers, in the East as well as the West, traveled by automobiles and supported
a blossoming highway tourist industry. More than 85 percent of the visitors
to Nevada traveled by car, and almost half of all cars headed for Las Vegas
came from Southern California.[9]

As the auto brought tourists to Las Vegas in record numbers after 1945,
it also contributed to the atmosphere for gaming. Automobiles helped to
recreate the feeling of transiency and adventure that had urged previous
generations of westering people to gamble. Americans in the postwar
period, like Angelenos before them, became increasingly aware of the rootlessness that car travel induced.[10] While the auto sped tourists away from
hometowns, it also loosened the conventional psychological restraints that
would otherwise inhibit activities like casino gambling, and kindled an
appreciation for movement and speed. Like the city of Las Vegas, and much
like gambling itself, automobiles seemed to put all desirable things within
reach. Both driving and betting heightened senses of action and fantasy,
and enlarged people's perception of what seemed possible. Both activities
were rapid and transitory experiences to be consumed for their own sakes
and then forgotten with little regard for ultimate consequences or costs.
In this manner cars reinforced the willing suspension of disbelief upon
which depended commercial leisure in Los Angeles and casino gambling
in southern Nevada.

Automobiles shaped the resort city physically as well as psychologically.
The landscape and architecture of the Strip conformed to the needs of the
car. The resort hotels along the Los Angeles highway made Las Vegas the
"ultimate achievement of the motor-court civilization" and underscored
its appeal to American travelers who were increasingly dedicated to auto
tourism. Southern Californians no doubt felt especially comfortable in the
gambling district, for few appeared to mind the five- or six-hour drive to
southern Nevada.[11] As residents of the Golden State, they belonged to a
restless society that had long thrived on speculation. Moreover, Southern
Californians found Las Vegas just far enough removed from the environs of

Los Angeles to relieve them of hometown inhibitions, yet so similar in its orientation to autos that it seemed convenient and familiar. After all, the Sunset Strip, the Miracle Mile on Wilshire Boulevard, and other Los Angeles roadtowns were at bottom the ancestors of the Las Vegas Strip. In roadtown Las Vegas, Southern Californians could see, in an intensified form, the same type of cityscape they knew in Los Angeles.[12] The physical and cultural resemblance between the two cities helped to explain Southern Californians' fondness for the desert gambling resort.

At the same time that they led the way to Las Vegas, Angelenos led the rest of the country in creating the culture of the future. Other Americans retained more ambivalence about the promises of modernity, but Southern Californians embraced the future without hesitation. They incorporated moving pictures, theme amusement parks, automobiles, and other cultural advances into a new way of life for average citizens, and then transmitted the new styles to the rest of the country by way of such spectacle suburbs as Hollywood, Disneyland, and Las Vegas, where many Americans first encountered Southern California culture.

Angelenos' wholehearted acceptance of tomorrow stemmed from the same social conditions that encouraged them to gamble. They resided in a state that continued to serve as destination for westering Americans through the mid-twentieth century. Like migrants to previous frontiers, new arrivals brought high expectations to a golden land of promise. Having already staked their futures on California, they were inclined to accept the additional risks that modernity presented. Residents of the state adopted new technologies and styles that promised to heighten the prosperity and enhance the good life that had drawn them westward to the Pacific Coast in the first place. The future held out to mid-twentieth-century Californians the same positive prospect of chance and change that gold had offered to Argonauts one hundred years earlier, and that betting had offered throughout the history of the state.

Since the early years of American settlement Californians had acted as pioneers of the nation's economic culture. The state had generally been among the first to industrialize mining, agriculture, and tourism, and led the nation in using and producing modern technologies. After 1940, huge increases in defense-related spending and a continuing influx of migrants and new technologies made California the nation's first postindustrial society.[13] Residents adjusted eagerly to the conditions that accompanied the aftermath of industrialization, illustrating for other Americans the direction of tomorrow.

Los Angeles played the same role within the state that California played for the nation. The metropolis became the preeminent city in the Far West, the fastest changing part of the Golden State, and the most fertile source of new cultural styles during the twentieth century. There westering migrants arrived in the largest numbers with the loftiest expectations; there new methods of production and ways of living gained the earliest acceptance; there postindustrial society blossomed first. Southern California had been the most forward-looking part of the state since the rapid expansion of the late nineteenth century taught Angelenos to expect and plan for growth, and to view technological progress as essential for mastering an improbable natural setting.[14] Southern Californians lived for tomorrow. Their future tended to be organized in a series of speculative booms that engaged Angelenos in projecting their lives beyond the present. Southern Californians gambled continuously on the future, and so explored the only frontier left to the American West. They simultaneously developed novel cultural forms, such as casino betting in Las Vegas, that suited the new day.

Los Angeles relished its role as cultural pacesetter for the nation, but it also paid a price. The future never quite turned out as anticipated; some expectations remained unfulfilled, and gambles did not always pay off. The troubles resulting from automobiles in the metropolitan area demonstrated the pitfalls of such a headlong leap into modernity and suggested that the future, like other frontiers, had its limits. Yet Southern Californians' enthusiasm for tomorrow never seemed to diminish through the mid-1960s.[15] As cultural leaders for the rest of the nation, and as residents of an increasingly rich and influential urban center, Southern Californians shared with other Americans the lessons of their encounter with the future. Attitudes toward affluence, automobiles, technology, work, and leisure emanated from Southern California to the rest of the nation, making Los Angeles the heart of the cultural frontier reshaping American society from West to East during the mid-twentieth century.[16]

Las Vegas assumed a prominent place on this cultural frontier because, especially on the Strip after 1945, certain of the changes originating in Southern California appeared there in accelerated form. The urban resort was slower to acquire the high-tech enterprise and diversified economy that Los Angeles seized so rapidly, but in southern Nevada, where commercial play provided the economic base, the cultural changes involving leisure appeared quickly and came into sharp focus. They made the city "the new frontier of the entire West in its way of life."[17]

Observers often overlooked the modern economy of Los Angeles and concentrated on its unique recreations as an essential measure of the metropolis. Edmund Wilson, for one, called it a "great anti-cultural amusement-producing center," implying that residents devoted more time to shallow amusements than to serious pursuits.[18] Such a perception was hardly accurate, however, because Angelenos participated in an advanced and vital economy. In Las Vegas, on the other hand, visitors devoted themselves to play every day of the week. If "amusement" seemed to be one of the major contributions of Los Angeles to American civilization, it could be discerned most clearly in Las Vegas. The desert city accelerated and concentrated Southern California trends that were remaking leisure by heightening the senses of freedom, luxury, and mobility, the commercialization

of play, the significance of recreation, the feelings of fantasy and rootlessness, and the availability of the fruits of affluence. The urban resort
provided a streamlined version of Southern California leisure. Just as
metropolitan Los Angeles emerged as a cultural frontier for the nation, Las
Vegas became the leisure frontier for Angelenos and, implicitly, for all
Americans.

As a center of changes in the nature of recreation, the gambling capital
had a disproportionately large role in transmitting new styles to the rest of
the country. Americans could test novel forms of leisure more easily than
they could experiment with other aspects of futuristic culture. Easterners
may have been too tied to the central city to embrace suburban living, too
attached to subways or elevated trains to accept automobility, or too
reliant on traditional modes of production to participate in postindustrial
economic activities. Outside of working life, however, they could be
exposed to new cultural trends more readily. At home they could see the
movies and television shows that Hollywood produced, and on vacations
they could try out Californian styles of play. Trips to Disneyland, and later
to Disney World, became a common experience for young Americans, and
gambling vacations in southern Nevada permitted adults as well to taste for
themselves the futuristic ways of life taking shape in Southern California.

The desert resort offered a combination of pleasures that could be experienced in such an easy and single-minded fashion nowhere else in the
United States. Las Vegas operators toiled to provide a wide variety of pastimes for visitors. Each Strip hotel featured a number of bars or cocktail
lounges, different restaurants and coffee shops, and at least one dinner-
theater. Golf courses, swimming pools, tennis courts, riding stables, and
still more athletic facilities were laid out on hotel grounds for guests.
Resort hotels competed among themselves to attract the finest, most popular entertainers, often paying astronomical salaries even while charging
minimal admission. Moreover, they all obtained not just one major show
for the dinner-theater, but also a variety of lesser acts for other lounges and
auditoriums in the different resort complexes along the Los Angeles highway. Nonetheless, the distinguishing feature of Las Vegas, the activity that
set the town apart from other American resorts in substance rather than
degree only, the financial centerpiece of the city, was casino gambling.
Although other attractions gained popularity among tourists, betting prevailed as the major drawing card in southern Nevada. Gambling played a
central role in the vision of tomorrow that Las Vegas projected.

Casino gaming was probably neither more nor less appealing to postwar
Americans than it had been to other peoples in other times, for gambling
has held a timeless interest around the world. From both the experience
of casino betting and the setting of Las Vegas Strip hotels, however, Americans derived a significance that reflected the orientations of their society
in the 1940s and 1950s.

Most contemporaries tended to see Las Vegas and casino gambling not as integral strands of the general social fabric, but as loose threads on the fringe of everyday behavior. Many tourists explained trips to southern Nevada as efforts to "get away from it all," and scholars agreed that gambling vacations functioned as a form of escape from daily existence. Roger Caillois, a student of the role of play in civilization, categorized Las Vegas in 1958 as one of the world's several

> specialized metropolises [that] attract in the main a transient clientele who have come to spend several days in the stimulating luxuries of pleasure and ease and then return to a more laborious and austere way of life. . . . The time passed [in Las Vegas] is merely a set of parentheses in their ordinary lives. The basic pattern of culture has not been appreciably affected.[19]

The resort city seemed to belong outside the mainstream of American civilization because gambling vacations appeared unrelated to the realities of daily life.

While Las Vegas vacations were hardly typical moments in the lives of postwar Americans, they nonetheless expressed broad social trends; the basic pattern of culture *was* appreciably affected. Tourists in southern Nevada perhaps left behind their hometown existences and indulged in fantasy, but they neither escaped reality nor denied the rigors of work and the tensions of Cold War society. Rather, they tested a vision of the years to come. As an offshoot of Los Angeles and as the nation's gambling capital, Las Vegas figured prominently in the cultural reshaping of the United States. More than a "set of parentheses" in people's lives, the city, and the Las Vegas Strip in particular, portended what the future held in store for Americans of the postwar period. The tremendous attention paid to the desert resort, the huge number of visitors, and the enormous sums of money spent there all certified that, in its own completely secular way, Las Vegas stood "as a city upon a hill" for Cold War Americans, demonstrating the direction and meaning of cultural change. Tom Wolfe, ace reporter of contemporary styles, concluded in 1965 that the gambling capital represented "the super-hyper-version of a whole new way of life."[20]

Las Vegas proved particularly instructive about the implications of a veritable revolution in recreation in the United States. After decades of a gradual shift in the balance between work and play, Americans became increasingly preoccupied with the consumption of leisure after World War II. The unforeseen affluence, the relaxation of wartime restraints on travel and purchasing, and essential technological advances all compelled Americans first to recognize leisure clearly as a division of their lives' time, and then to devote more attention to spending that time in a satisfying manner. The experiences of depression and war doubtless helped to lay the groundwork for these changes. The forced idleness of the unemployed and underemployed during the 1930s and of servicemen during the Second World War taught people how to find and structure amusement, and the "moral lapse" that presumably follows upon the heels of war prepared the nation to accept more diverse modes of recreation.

In the years around midcentury Americans were persuaded that the amount of leisure was growing and would continue to grow in the future. Whether they truly had more free time remains unclear, and the extent of their off-hours never matched predictions of an increasingly work-free society.[21] Nonetheless, that Americans thought they had more time for play, and that social scientists devoted more attention to recreation, certainly evinced the growing significance of leisure in the United States. The importance of time devoted to leisure increasingly gained ground on the importance of the working week. Such a transformation signified the emergence of a postindustrializing society.

The blossoming of postindustrialism in the years after World War II marked the culmination of many changes under way since at least the late nineteenth century. With the economy geared less for industrial growth and more for personal consumption, many people regarded their jobs differently. Greater numbers of Americans looked to the workplace less for the personal challenge or the potential for personal fulfillment, and more for the security it offered in the way of rising per capita income, heightened corporate, bureaucratic, and union organization, and greater emphasis on social welfare programs. As many jobs seemed less satisfying and grew less distinctive, Americans sought fulfillment and a sense of self less from the work world, and more from their consumption activities, including the consumption of leisure time.[22] The shift contributed to the perception that the working week was shrinking. People did not need to visit Las Vegas or any other resort in order to escape work; indeed, in bits and pieces work appeared to be escaping them.

The postwar economy generated another important change in the relationship between work and leisure. Since the onset of the industrial revolution in the Anglo-American world the two spheres of work and play, which had overlapped extensively in preindustrial societies, became increasingly separated from one another. In industrializing countries people reordered their lives so that hours devoted to leisure were differentiated sharply from periods of work. Such compartmentalization of daily life endured well into the twentieth century, until the imperatives of a postindustrializing economy began to dissolve conventional divisions of time. More laborers interrupted the working day with breaks, more businessmen took extended lunches, and more people attended conventions, often in resort cities like Las Vegas, where job-related activities came to be intermixed with play. David Riesman observed that, "reminiscent in some ways of the pre-industrial age," the strands of work and leisure became "increasingly indistinct" and more intertwined as the boundaries between the worlds of "application" and diversion began to disappear.[23] The meaning of leisure was consequently redefined. As Americans incorporated forms of leisure into their working hours, they also began to work harder at play. It quickly became clear that leisure would no longer be so leisurely any more.

Americans had long been taught to fulfill themselves as producers in an ever-expanding economy. Now as the economy reached an affluent plateau and became less oriented to industrial growth, they increasingly gave meaning to their lives by consuming services, goods, and leisure time, an activity that stood diametrically opposed to the traditional ethos of work and delayed gratification in the United States. The novel importance of play, coupled with Americans' general unfamiliarity with the serious consumption of leisure, made it difficult for people to accept this particular cultural shift and helped to explain why adjustment to the new conditions was somewhat troubled. Americans turned increasingly to leisure activities for fulfillment, but play did not yet provide "the moral equivalent of work" for their lives, Riesman noted. As a result, Americans tended to work at play: "Many of the physical hardships of the older frontiers of production and land use have survived in altered, psychological form on the newer one of consumption." People found themselves unprepared to make leisure a source of purpose for their daily existence and remained uncertain about new styles of play. Leisure consequently induced at times a sense of "aimlessness."[24]

The tensions that change produced came into clear focus in Southern California, where the rearrangement of work and play naturally proceeded quickly. Newcomers who arrived in Los Angeles during the 1920s and 1930s, expecting to fill empty days with satisfying leisure activities, found time hanging heavy on their hands. Nathanael West suggested then that Angelenos had not "the mental equipment for leisure, the money nor the physical equipment for pleasure."[25] Technology and affluence helped Southern Californians to organize and spend leisure time more easily after the Second World War, earning for the metropolis a reputation as a society devoted too seriously to amusements. In the early 1960s, however, an English observer found that Angelenos continued to seem "neurotic" about recreation and relaxation.[26] They still had not adjusted fully to the new balance between work and play.

Once again Southern California was but the bellwether for the rest of the civilization. People across the country followed Angelenos in devoting to leisure the same nervous energies they had previously reserved for the working day. With leisure no longer as relaxed as before, students of play anticipated widespread psychological turmoil. Roger Caillois suggested that the intermixture of play and work produced a "perversion" of the normal and healthy functions of leisure. "What used to be a pleasure becomes an obsession," he wrote. "What was an escape becomes an obligation, and what was a pastime is now a passion, compulsion, and source of anxiety."[27]

Caillois overstated the problem because he believed that the spheres of work and play must remain largely separated, a concern that disregarded the inclinations of preindustrial and postindustrial societies to mix one with the other. Nonetheless, he attested the pervasive uneasiness that accompanied change in the relationship between play and work, and helped to explain the sense of compulsion that Americans brought to recreation in the mid-twentieth century. Denying the deep-rooted patterns of their culture, Americans became less anxious about work and more anxious about leisure. Certain that they must play, but unfamiliar with so much play and unsure about its benefits, Americans tended to exhaust themselves at leisure while seeking in it some of the personal fulfillment they had previously derived from their jobs. The result was the most unleisurely play imaginable, a sort of frantic leisure epitomized by casino gambling in Las Vegas.

All of the terms that Caillois used to describe the "perversion" of play—obsession, obligation, passion, compulsion, and anxiety—have also been applied to gambling, and gambling more than anything else determined the pace and intensity of life for tourists in Las Vegas. In fact, the frenzied leisure produced by casino gaming characterized entire vacations in the resort city. Often going without sleep, tourists made dizzying rounds from one resort hotel to another, from casino to restaurant to golf course to swimming pool to dinner show and back to casino. Polled in 1958 as to why they visited Las Vegas, tourists responded that they came mainly for the gambling, the night life, and the entertainment. Only 3 percent claimed they traveled to the urban resort for rest or relaxation.[28] Trips to Las Vegas were taken not for replenishing but for spending oneself. Contrary to the traditional notion of a vacation from the strain of work, vacations in southern Nevada offered all the exhaustion and self-depletion that a person could desire.[29]

In intensity and pace, gambling holidays in Las Vegas became the prototype for vacations in the postindustrializing United States. Growing participation in organized athletics and outdoor life, as well as heightened attendance at amusement parks, illustrated how Americans worked harder at recreation, but in Nevada gambling sprees the changes in the nature of play reached new extremes. Seemingly unconcerned that casinos had arranged vacation activities so as to require the minimum of effort, tourists consumed leisure as earnestly as they could, particularly in the gambling halls where players slaved away at games as if there were no tomorrow and no yesterday. With no clocks provided by the management, gamblers lost all track of time in casinos. Moreover, encouraged by an atmosphere of fantasy and by casinos' policy of converting currency to plastic chips, vacationers also lost track of the customary value of money. It was as if players' psychological moorings to the industrial culture of America, their senses of time and money, had unraveled. John Pastier, an architectural historian, suggested that, without keeping conventional track of time or money, gamblers in Las Vegas could "experience the present moments as intensely as the inhabitants of a preindustrial society."[30]

Perhaps the diminished senses of time and money that enabled tourists in Las Vegas to experience play so intensely did not resemble preindustrial conditions so much as they characterized the nature of leisure in postindustrial society, especially as it emerged in Southern California and southern Nevada. Gambling vacations encompassed the most far-reaching changes in the relationship between work and play. As the cutting edge of the revolution in recreation, Las Vegas offered tourists not a place to get away from it all but rather a sleepless and timeless atmosphere of excitement, tension, and pressure. There visitors consumed leisure time in a most unleisurely manner, spending themselves and their money heatedly at a variety of diversions and places. All activities revolved around casino betting, which epitomized frantic play in the resort city.

Casino betting appealed to postwar society not only because it suited the new balance between work and leisure but also because it helped people develop a stronger sense of self. Finding individuality threatened by the rising economic culture of mass production, average Americans turned more and more to consumption of goods, services, and leisure time as a mode of personal expression. Observers noticed the trend relatively early in Los Angeles, where residents commonly defined individuality in terms of such possessions as cars and homes.[31] As pioneers of the new age, Southern Californians seized very quickly the opportunity to pursue individuality less through economic endeavors and more through cultural channels. Consumption of material goods constituted one source of identity and individuality, but Angelenos also achieved personal fulfillment as accomplished consumers of leisure. They and other Americans invested play with a greater importance, as indicated by the serious, worklike attitude they brought to it. They also sought out those activities, like casino gambling, that promised to demonstrate most clearly where they stood as individuals in the mass society of the mid-twentieth-century.

Contemporary social scientists who analyzed gambling generally agreed that the games were well suited to the process of defining personal identity. In an era when individuality and economic risk seemed to dwindle in importance next to the stress on collective security, betting made up an arena of endeavor where individuality continued to flourish, where chance could still be enjoyed at an intensely personal level. Erving Goffman explained that gambling provided people with an opportunity to "achieve character," to develop personal reputation. In a society where risk had been "all but arranged out of everyday life," people could still prove themselves through play in public casinos. Character established at gaming tables was regarded as an accurate measure of one's mettle because it was attained in the face of hazards undertaken "without obligation." Character came to be enhanced not so much by winning or losing, but by maintaining "full self control when the chips are down."[32] Reputation depended first upon whether a person gambled at all, whether he would expose himself to unnecessary risks, and second upon how, not how successfully, he played the game. Character came to be gambled, then, along with money. Casino betting enabled people as consumers of leisure time to define for themselves a stronger sense of reputation.

The atmosphere inside casinos located along the Los Angeles highway facilitated the pursuit of individuality and character that betting entailed. Strip casinos offered patrons a blend of sociability and autonomy that proved ideal for wagering character. Unlike downtown gambling halls, which relied more on solitary games like the slot machines, keno, and bingo, roadtown resorts emphasized more social games such as craps, roulette, and twenty-one, where players gathered around tables.[33] These games provided an audience in front of which individual bettors had to establish reputation. The presence of other players increased the psychological stakes by making the wager of character a public event.

Yet few players actually paid much attention to each other. From all walks of life and from all corners of the globe, people crowded into downtown and Strip casinos largely unaware of one another. The anonymous throngs induced a sense of self-reliance. Bettors almost inevitably played Las Vegas as individuals, and that helped them perceive more directly the character they were establishing. The anonymity and permissiveness of casinos, and the solitude inherent in gambling, lent to players a feeling of autonomy that once again served to heighten individuality in an age of the "lonely crowd."[34]

The quest to develop personal reputation through gaming seemed to be particularly masculine, an orientation also forcefully enhanced by the atmosphere of Las Vegas casinos. Given the traditional domination of all aspects of gambling by men, one could only expect the resort city to cater especially to masculine tastes. At first Las Vegas hardly knew what to do with women. Virtually all casinos preferred to employ only male dealers, and female tourists were generally relegated to the less esteemed, less challenging games like keno, bingo, and slot machines. In fact, one gambler commented that the "slots" were essential for attracting auto tourists because they occupied wives who would not otherwise have driven to Las Vegas with their husbands. Though casinos kept banks and banks of one-armed bandits, and though some hotels even distributed instructional pamphlets to teach women about gambling, the notion prevailed that only men constituted the truly serious players.[35] The tenor of the resort consequently remained heavily masculine. After all, like gambling itself, individualism in the United States had traditionally connoted masculine traits.

The individualistic nature of casino gaming kindled a sense of enterprise among players. Much like the legendary captains of industry of the nineteenth century, gamblers thrived on risk taking. They behaved aggressively and competitively, though often behind a calm facade that suggested strong character. Moreover, they displayed a sense of initiative that enabled them to feel more like creative participants in games at which they were often little other than paying spectators. Such behavior defied the prevailing ethos of collective security which stressed accumulation, rationality, cooperation, routine, and minimal risk, and heightened the feeling, which was especially strong among Southern Californians, that there was still a place for the self-reliant individual in a mass society.[36]

In gambling, Las Vegas tourists could challenge the stifling conformity and affluence of the Cold War era and resist the sense of aimlessness that accompanied postwar change. Although the risks undertaken were generally small and safe, gamblers derived disproportionately strong senses of personal satisfaction and identity from betting, senses that helped them to understand and to accept where they stood as individuals in the fluctuating culture of the United States. The experience appealed especially to Californians and other Westerners, whose restless and atomistic society was predicated on private confrontations with chance and change.

That people developed a sense of individuality while gambling in Las Vegas proved paradoxical. Americans rushed en masse to southern Nevada and acquired a greater sense of self amidst huge crowds at supermarkets of gambling. Although betting was experienced at an intensely personal level, it was undertaken by large numbers thronging together at gaming tables. Casinos manufactured and marketed their product as if by assembly line processes with virtually no regard for the individuality of consumers.

Gambling casinos resembled such other novel forms of commercial leisure originating in Southern California as theme amusement parks, television programs, and moving pictures. Each entertainment industry mass-produced a form of recreation meant to be consumed individualistically. These amusements paralleled the sensation of automobility as pioneered in Los Angeles.[37] Drivers relished the privacy, self-direction, and identity that their cars provided, sustaining an illusion of autonomy despite the extensive social cooperation necessary for successful auto travel, the enormous traffic jams that swallowed up any sense of personal freedom, and the yearly harvest of standardized car models. Like driving, amusement industries such as casino gambling mass-produced the sensation of individuality and permitted crowds of participants to establish character en masse.

Moreover, although bettors hoped to develop senses of themselves that would set them apart from the crowd, gaming tended to reduce everything and everybody to a single common denominator—money. The sound, the feel, and the appearance of money pervaded each gaming table and each casino and hotel interior, from downtown clubs that displayed tens of thousands of dollars in cash in their lobbies, to roadtown hotels decked out in the most luxurious furnishings. Because the common denominator of money seemed to underlay all aspects of the desert resort, William Saroyan concluded that Las Vegas had developed a single-mindedness about it. "Some place in the richest nation in the world," he mused, "there has to be a city with no other excuse for being than money."[38] But money was the means as well as the end in Las Vegas, the medium as well as the message. It lent significance to games that would otherwise have been empty, even though from the outset players understood the probable outcome of the action.[39] In other words, satisfaction, excitement, and even reputation came from gambling with money, and with character, not necessarily from winning or losing. Beyond the actual games, money served as a medium of communicaton, of advertisement, of architecture in Las Vegas; it prevailed everywhere in one form or another.

The primacy of money in Las Vegas proved to be as paradoxical as the mass achieving of individuality in gaming. On the one hand money translated into luxury beyond the means of the average citizen. From the deep-pile carpets to the space-age chandeliers, wealth permeated resort hotels on the Strip.[40] Publicists dramatized the lives of the rich and famous, and at every turn patrons might be reminded that casino gambling had traditionally been the exclusive province of upper classes around the world.

On the other hand, however, gambling vacations in Las Vegas were generally tailored to the great American middle class, because there lay the profits for the resort industry of the mid-twentieth century. Prices in the desert city remained mostly moderate and the atmosphere remained largely informal. Contemporary observers stressed the egalitarian and unexclusive nature of Nevada gambling. Comparing Las Vegas to European gaming resorts, English playwright Noel Coward found crowds in Las Vegas composed of "the most ordinary people."[41] The urban resort catered to the middle strata of society, and in this way more than any other demonstrated that it was an achievement of mid-twentieth-century American civilization. As a resort for the masses, it broke with the long tradition of gambling spas for the rich, and the contrasts appeared everywhere. Whereas aristocratic Monte Carlo in 1879 had celebrated the completion of an opera house and theater and the debut of the exclusive *salle privée* with a poetry reading by Sarah Bernhardt, "Bugsy" Siegel's Flamingo Hotel opened in the late 1940s with the comedy team of Abbott and Costello.[42]

Employing a facade of luxury and wealth, hotels and casinos on the Strip appealed as successfully to the middle classes as the downtown clubs adhering to the more common motif of the old West. Entrepreneurs in Las Vegas quickly realized that in the gambling business the most money would be made from high volume, so they mass-produced and mass-marketed gambling vacations for the wide American public. The astounding prosperity of the resort city was predicated not on a few wealthy "high-rollers," nor on serious gamblers who might work the casinos skillfully, but on millions of small-scale bettors whose average length of stay spanned three days and two nights. These tourists lost just enough money to provide sizable profits for the casino industry, but never enough to deter them from return visits to Las Vegas. Such consumers were the raw material for the gambling industry which grew up in southern Nevada, an industry that mass-merchandised the transitory leisure experience of gambling in an unprecedented environment.[43]

The desires and the methods of the entertainment industry, shaped in large part by Southern California styles, profoundly influenced the experience of tourists in the resort city and determined the image that Las Vegas projected to the nation. The tremendous success of the gaming business depended on several factors. First, entrepreneurs enjoyed favorable odds from the beginning because of their proximity to Los Angeles, the peculiar nature of the business, and the friendly environment in Nevada. They displayed a shrewd capacity for advertisement and promotion that kept the resort prominently before the American public. Gambling entrepreneurs on the Strip also understood well the imperatives of commercial leisure for the masses, marketing the play world of tomorrow with a sure grasp on business realities of the present. Finally, they shared a well-defined sense of mutual interest, partly out of defensiveness about their suspect line of work, that enabled business rivals to cooperate extensively. As a result, all industrialists at bottom marketed the same basic product clothed in varying styles and colors, much like autos rolling off Detroit assembly lines. Players hardly noticed the similarities, however, as they experienced Las Vegas on their own terms. The result was a tremendously lucrative leisure industry.

The prosperity of the desert resort after World War II was remarkable. In 1945 Las Vegans feared that the conditions that created rapid wartime growth would disappear, but the decline never fully materialized. Developers planned newer and bigger hotels, primarily along the Los Angeles highway, and numbers of visitors grew steadily. By 1952 local casinos hosted seven million tourists annually and handled gross receipts of $43 million; ten years later seventeen million tourists left $200 million on the playing tables of Las Vegas. Including what one lost gaming, the average auto tourist spent more than $100 per visit to the resort in 1958. That kind of money helped to employ more than thirteen thousand workers in the industry by 1962. Moreover, twelve huge resort hotels stood on the Strip that year where only two had been before 1946. Journalists who hurried to cover the sensational boom town reported that hotels and casinos were packed and often had to expand their capacities immediately after opening.[44] Las Vegas had no dearth of patrons in the two decades after the Second World War.

The financial success of the casinos resulted in part from special circumstances surrounding the business of legalized gambling. Nevada had a national monopoly on full-fledged casino gambling, and Las Vegans saw to it that Reno no longer rivaled their city as the nation's gambling capital. Once casinos were well established, they usually had little difficulty in turning profits so long as they maintained high volume, because gaming odds remained inflexibly in the house's favor. Moreover, casino doors never closed; gambling tables generated profits day and night. And unlike other American vacation spots, particularly those in southern states where business ebbed during summer, visitors streamed to Las Vegas year round.

More travelers, including family groups, actually came in the summer, undaunted by the desert heat because virtually every resort building was fully air-conditioned. Fewer people came during the winter, but they generally spent more money per person.[45] With odds so overwhelmingly in their favor, and with gaming tables busy every hour of the year, casinos mass-produced the thrills of gambling that so many vacationers sought.

The industry benefited from the tolerance of state officials, who were generally reluctant to interfere with the business unless operators appeared to be injuring either themselves or the image of Nevada gambling. The state's inclination to protect the "pariah industry" resulted in part from its dependence on tax revenues generated by casinos, particularly in Las Vegas, and in part from the crucial role of gaming in Nevada's economy. Permissiveness was most widely publicized in the matter of licensing casino operators who had either criminal records or alleged connections to organized crime. Largely overlooking the charges of moralists and federal authorities, Nevada generally accepted figures whose pasts were shady but not too shadowy. Some of these men reciprocated with good will gestures for the city and state, happy to have the respectability that Nevada provided for their livelihoods. Like government officials, they hoped to ensure that legalized gambling kept an upright reputation in the resort city.[46]

Local publicists initially worried that if Las Vegas came to be associated with unsavory types its reputation would suffer, but the gaming industry actually seemed immune to such negative influences during its postwar heyday. Any news coming from the city served primarily as favorable publicity for southern Nevada. Hearing that representatives from organized crime appeared in casinos, visitors came with the hope of rubbing shoulders with gangsters around the gaming tables. Furthermore, having learned from Hollywood, Las Vegans demonstrated a remarkable and shameless knack for making the most out of any news item, thereby elevating to new heights the midcentury art of advertisement. They milked an endless succession of publicity stunts for every last drop of attention, and reached unprecedented levels of extemporaneous self-promotion during the early 1950s when they capitalized on the publicity value of the nearby testing of nuclear weapons.

In 1950 the Atomic Energy Commission selected a large tract of the gunnery range of Nellis Air Force Base as its continental testing center, and during the next twenty-five years detonated more than four hundred "devices" where Las Vegans could feel, hear, and sometimes see the blasts. Until mid-1962 many of the tests took place above ground and attracted the attention of the nation to southern Nevada. Local residents at first worried that the danger associated with the bombs would deter potential visitors, but exactly the opposite happened. Reporters, military and civilian officials, and curious citizens inundated the town during tests, giving Las Vegas perhaps the least expensive national publicity it ever received.[47] The dangers associated with the explosions apparently only added to the number of risks that tourists relished in the gambling center.

To most Cold War Americans, the nuclear detonations were causes for celebration. Visitors to southern Nevada gathered all night in local casinos and lounges, awaiting the dawn explosions that lit up the skies and shook the town. With that bewildering huckster's genius so peculiar to residents of the resort city, local celebrities and merchants commemorated the blasts in a manner sure to draw the national limelight. When the first explosions shattered display windows, one shopkeeper placed the glass fragments in a barrel outside his store and advertised "'ATOM BOMB SOUVENIRS— FREE!' Within an hour, the barrel was empty." Similarly, a local hairdresser created an "'atomic' coiffure," ostensibly shaped like a mushroom cloud, a hotel filled its pool with two thousand mushrooms, and a local beauty queen was titled Miss Atomic Blast. One locally famous stripper tried to upstage them all. She timed her wedding ceremony to coincide with a nuclear test in 1955, and then served her guests a cake shaped like "an atomic-blast-mushroom."[48]

If Las Vegans proved themselves experts at instinctive and spontaneous advertising, they also demonstrated considerable persistence in a more planned publicity campaign, for promotion could not be left up to chance. Anticipating a precipitous business slump after World War II and ever conscious of the rivalry with Reno, entrepreneurs agreed during wartime to sponsor a more professional promotion of the city. A competent, businesslike chamber of commerce replaced the amateurish and inefficient staff of the early 1940s and quickly raised the nation's largest per capita promotional fund. So began a sophisticated publicity campaign that targeted the most desirable types of customers, appealed to the entire nation with special emphasis on Southern California, and created a plethora of trademarks and slogans that characterized the city for potential visitors. Every possible angle was exploited as Las Vegas was first identified with the old West and then with "fun in the sun." Next came portrayals of the city as a superior family resort at bargain prices, and then an emphasis on Hollywood personalities and bathing beauties. This effort lasted into the early 1950s and enhanced the reputation of the desert town across the country.[49] It prepared tourists to accept gambling as a vacation activity and Las Vegas as a resort city.

The publicity offensive had been the product of cooperation within the gambling industry, but when the willingness to collaborate diminished, the promotional campaign lost its support. Downtown clubs and Strip hotels each wanted more favorable promotion, at the expense of the other, and individual casinos hoped to compete more successfully by advertising on their own.[50] This turn of events during the early 1950s exemplified a trend of alternation between competition and cooperation among Las Vegas entrepreneurs that was not unusual in American business but became especially pronounced in the gambling industry. Commonly defensive about their involvement in a suspect business and aware of the relative absence of outside competition in the United States, Las Vegas casino owners generally tried to work with one another to advance what they agreed were the best interests of the industry. The tendency to pull together became especially visible when the industry was threatened by economic or political crisis. A general pattern of mutual assistance was punctuated by heightened competitive tensions as new casinos opened and tried to overcome late starts by offering more for the tourist's dollar. This balance between competition and cooperation helped to shape the vacations that tourists consumed in Las Vegas.

In the decade after World War II, growing competition within the industry, exacerbated by nationwide recessions, contributed to two significant crises in Las Vegas, both of which were solved in part by intra-industrial cooperation to check potentially ruinous rivalry. During the national economic slump of 1947–1948, after a brief burst of expansion downtown, Las Vegas casinos became embroiled in a fierce price war. Each gaming hall claimed to offer better percentages to players by lowering the house advantage in table games and increasing the payoff ratio on slot machines. Recognizing the dangers in this struggle, casino owners, first on the budding Strip where expenses were higher and then more hesitantly in the downtown district, agreed to standardize odds for every game at a fixed level. These new percentages were more favorable to bettors than odds before the price war, thereby underlining the ever-increasing commitment to high volume and turnover.[51] However, the player's range of choices in selecting a casino was reduced. This indirect form of price fixing proved to be one of the crucial steps taken to ensure the uniformity of the gaming that Las Vegas mass-produced for the nation.

The settlement of the price war, combined with economic recovery, ushered in a flush period of cooperation between the casinos. The extent of the consolidation among owners was dramatized by the lone exception to the new rates among the major establishments. Located, of course, in Glitter Gulch, Benny Binion's Horseshoe Club not only offered more liberal odds to bettors but also accepted higher wagers. Furthermore, the maverick Binion paid his employees substantially more than was dictated by the pay scale used by other casinos. He consequently earned the resentment of his competitors, for he remained the lone exception to uniform policies regarding wages, odds, and size of bets.[52]

Cooperation between casinos took other forms as well. Virtually all establishments subscribed to the city-wide publicity campaign prior to 1953 and most accepted one another's betting chips as valid currency. Strip hotels went to the greatest lengths to achieve concerted action. First they organized into the Resort Hotels Association to settle "matters of mutual financial interest." Then they incorporated into two independent townships in order to resist annexation and taxation by the city of Las Vegas. In 1951 the aptly named township of Paradise had seven Strip hotel executives on its board of commissioners.[53] This political expression of mutual interest confirmed the rise of a second cohesive district in the urban resort and marked a high tide of cooperation along the Strip.

Casino owners coexisted agreeably in the late 1940s and early 1950s because the number of competitors grew quite slowly in proportion to the rapid increase of business. By 1955, however, the ratio had reversed. Revenues grew by 25 percent in that year, by almost any standard a sizable increase in volume, but the number of resort hotels nearly doubled. In the first half of 1955, five new hotels opened for business, the New Frontier started up adjacent to the Last Frontier, and several developers planned still more new hotels for the area. The additions to Las Vegas, mostly located along the Strip, generally fared poorly, for the less rapidly growing number of tourists could not keep them filled. By early 1956 most of the new resort hotels had either folded, sold out, or reduced operations. As debts piled higher and rates of occupancy declined, operators began to lay off employees and considered other means of reducing costs. The problems became especially acute when several prominent publications, including *Time, Life,* and the *Wall Street Journal,* ran articles about the recession in Las Vegas, and banks and other lending institutions, already wary about loans to the gambling industry, lost confidence in borrowers in southern Nevada.[54]

The economic crisis sent shock waves through established owners on the Strip. They had survived with relative ease the inroads made into the business by newcomers, but now they faced problems much graver than declining profits, for the future of the resort city appeared to be in jeopardy. Stable owners met the crisis by adopting another form of cooperation that reinforced the uniformity of Las Vegas gambling. They began to pump money into some of the failing establishments. The Flamingo Hotel saved the Riviera, the Desert Inn took over the Royal Nevada, and the Sands bailed out the Dunes. These actions rescued the new Strip hotels for at least a short while and, coupled with substantially higher earnings in 1956, pulled the resort out of its slump. Las Vegas regained its characteristic confidence, expectations for rapid growth returned, and developers continued to plan new hotels along the increasingly saturated Strip.[55]

In the crisis of 1955 the leading owners of Las Vegas demonstrated their sense of mutual interest, and homogenized the conditions of casino gambling, not only by saving certain hotels but also by not choosing to save another establishment. The new Moulin Rouge Hotel, like other shaky newcomers, was poorly managed and insufficiently capitalized from the beginning, but three additional marks against it ensured its failure. First, it broke precedent by having no racial restrictions. Blacks and whites both could play and stay there, unlike all other resort hotels which practiced racial segregation. The tolerance of the Moulin Rouge contributed to the second count against it—popularity. As a favorite after-hours place for black entertainers who performed elsewhere for all-white audiences, the

Moulin Rouge attracted substantial crowds.[56] Furthermore, the interracial establishment, unlike other hotels and casinos, was located in neither downtown nor roadtown, where it might share its customers with nearby competitors, but rather lay west of Glitter Gulch on the border of the black neighborhoods of Las Vegas. Combined with its desegregated clientele and its noted popularity, the location of the Moulin Rouge likely made it a competitor that established owners would prefer not to save. Though its popularity indicated that it might have eventually become a successful business, the new hotel died a sure death, first reducing its scale of business and then closing up altogether, another victim of local recession.[57]

The economic slump of the mid-fifties accelerated another process which reduced competition and diversity in the tourist industry. Since the late 1940s observers had described a gradual shift in business practices from operation by "old-time gamblers" to more impersonal methods that maximized profits through stricter cost-accounting. Casinos run by experienced operators had competed with one another by offering free drinks, inexpensive rooms, low-cost entertainment, and bargain meals in order to attract high volume. They willingly sacrificed profits in secondary enterprises because they expected to compensate with generous revenues from gaming. This policy has been influential throughout the modern period in Las Vegas, but it began to lose some favor during the late 1940s after house percentages were reduced by the price war. Newer methods really took hold during the financial crisis of 1955–1956, when the cost of rooms, meals, drinks, and entertainment increased as entrepreneurs became ever more reluctant to finance such "loss-leaders" out of gaming revenues. Once more, Strip hotels made the shift in virtual unison, refusing to compete with each other over prices.[58]

All the trends within the gaming industry during the 1950s—standardizing prices, wages, and odds, devising sophisticated publicity campaigns, regulating growth and competition in favor of a well-defined collective security, taking over smaller or less competitive businesses, and developing tighter cost-efficiency measures—represented the growing domination of casino gambling by economic mass culture. The Nevada gaming industry, which had only recently been a relatively small-scale business run in part by marginal operators, was being restructured along corporate lines. One reporter referred to the process as "industrial integration." It seemed natural that only the largest companies could best marshal resources and master economies of scale in the mass consumer industry that casino gambling had become. The new hotels of 1955 and after discovered just how much of an advantage the larger, more established firms enjoyed as they struggled, often in vain, to break into the business. Many newcomers, such as the independent Hacienda Hotel, went to great lengths to attract customers, but nonetheless found success elusive.[59] Gambling on the Strip was now dominated by big business.

Cooperation between major operators on the Strip gave them cultural hegemony in Las Vegas. Following the dictates of mutual interest, they adopted noncompetitive policies that assured a certain uniformity of selected features of the resort city. Big business in Las Vegas displayed a conservative attitude, not only toward political change but also toward innovation and risk, that once again likened gaming to another cautious mass-entertainment industry, movie making.[60] In the manner of studio moguls in Hollywood, the big industrialists of Las Vegas cleaved excessively to proven and predictable formulas for success. They standardized the commodity of the gambling vacation, especially in its monetary aspects, so that tourists found that the details of gambling hardly varied from one resort hotel to the next, or from the Strip to downtown. Although gambling stood as a kind of last bastion of individualism in a society increasingly reshaped by a consumer culture of the masses, the actual conditions of betting at the various casinos became rigidly identical.

As in matters of economics and politics, owners on the Strip stood in unison on the more practical aspects of hotel design. Recognizing that in some respects of architecture and landscape form must follow function in order to maximize volume, certain exterior and interior features of resort hotels were the same up and down the Strip. One was the devotion to the automobile. All the major hotels had spacious parking lots. The centrality of the car in the district was underscored as in between the different hotels arose a host of roadside businesses, including drive-ins, motels, and service stations that, in part because of the absence of useful sidewalks or buses, could best be reached by car. Moreover, above the highway the major establishments erected huge flashy signs, unprecedented in style and size throughout the world. These beacons gave the Strip a distinctive and unified skyline; more importantly, because the signs spoke more directly to those speeding by in cars than to stationary or pedestrian observers, they reiterated the Strip's commitment to auto tourists.[61]

The major hotels followed profit-maximizing formulas on the inside as well. One dictated that each inn strive to achieve autonomy from other businesses, so that under one roof guests could find virtually every desirable commodity and service. An architectural historian coined the term "island palaces" to depict the string of self-sufficient resort hotels along the Strip.[62] Even more prominent was the central location of the casino within each complex, a placement that guaranteed as much play as possible. Observers commented that visitors could hardly move from one part of the hotel to another without passing by the gaming tables. In the 1956 mystery *Diamonds Are Forever*, protagonist James Bond attributed the architecture of casino placement to "the Gilded Mousetrap School, its main purpose being to channel the customer-mouse into the central gambling trap whether he wanted the cheese or not."[63] The uniformity of gambling vacations in the desert resort, the "industrial integration" evident in odds, prices, and mergers, extended as well to exterior and interior design of Strip hotels.

The dictates of mass-production ensured that one Las Vegas vacation resembled all the others in certain important regards, yet the tourist hardly seemed to notice. Despite the high volume and the economies of scale, he still enhanced his sense of individuality and found fulfillment while visiting Las Vegas. Entrepreneurs may have imitated each other in marketing gambling, but the standard recipes they followed nonetheless concocted enjoyable vacations for which people hungrily returned again and again. Moreover, though gambling vacations could be duplicated, Las Vegas could not. There was simply no place like it.

The presence of legal casino betting made the resort unique. No matter how businessmen packaged and promoted it, casino gambling in Las Vegas retained its powerful appeal to mid-twentieth-century Americans. Regardless of the crowds around him doing the same thing, a player could still experience gaming at an intensely personal level, could continue to suspend disbelief, could yet indulge the illusion of infinite possibilities that arose from betting. Gambling seldom seemed as if it were mass-produced, and Las Vegas certainly never seemed that way either.

The desert resort was singular not so much because it provided casino gambling but rather because casino gambling as practiced on the Strip epitomized a new way of life for tourists. Downtown clubs and casinos did not serve to set Las Vegas apart fully from Reno or to establish it as a capital on the cultural frontier remaking American life from West to East. Resort hotels along the Strip, on the other hand, placed gambling at the center of a style of living that belonged to tomorrow, and encouraged visitors to regard Las Vegas as a city where all things seemed possible.

Much of the distinctiveness of the place resulted from the ostensibly enormous range of choices that the Strip offered. Gaming industrialists generally did not rival one another in more practical matters, but in areas in which they did compete, encompassing the more superficial aspects of the vacation experience, resort hotels went to extremes to differentiate themselves. Competition for customers became a matter not of prices or odds, but of extra attractions. Hotel-casinos strove to create the most sensational spectacles, offer the broadest range of facilities, and present the most popular entertainment. Their efforts resulted in a resort of such seeming diversity and choice that at first glance it seemed to provide everything for tourists. Yet even in the narrow range of competition over outward appearances, success was so frequently reduced to predictable formulas that what had been spectacular in 1946 almost seemed routine by 1960.

The trend developed in a number of areas. Operating on a level at which smaller establishments could hardly compete, the big Strip hotels each added a variety of restaurants that ranged from the most exclusive gourmet dining rooms to inexpensive, all-night, "chuckwagon" buffets. Wilbur Clark's Desert Inn, among the more successful hotels, could no doubt attribute some of its popularity to the many adjuncts to gambling that it offered. In 1950 the Desert Inn made a direct appeal to family business by boasting its playhouse where children played under the supervision of a child psychologist, and in 1952 it hosted the first annual Tournament of Champions for professional golfers. Each such addition, of course, provoked other resort hotels to respond in kind: "When Wilbur Clark opened the Desert Inn in 1950 with a fancy pool, the Last Frontier across the highway promptly filled in its old pool and built a heated one of AAU dimensions with a subsurface observation room at the deep end and a deck-side bar. Whereupon the Desert Inn tore up its brand new pool and dug a bigger one. Then the Sands created a thing of free flow design large enough to float a cruiser." A few years later the Hotel Tropicana made its bid in the rivalry by equipping its shell-like, semicircular pool with canned music that could be heard underwater.[64] Pool wars had supplanted price wars among Las Vegas competitors.

Entertainment provided an even more spectacular arena of competition. Most of the shows took place in rooms so close to the casino that audiences had to pass through it, and ran on tight schedules so that customers were not kept from gaming by long encores or other delays. Major resort hotels had competed to offer the most appealing acts since the beginning of the postwar era, but the significance of entertainment expanded during the 1950s when promoters realized its popularity with touring wives who seemed generally less inclined toward gambling vacations than their husbands. Strip establishments normally relied on musicians, actors, and comedians of national fame, presented with a professional competence, but they also passed through stages of featuring more extraordinary acts. One such phase at the end of the 1950s introduced a series of imported French extravaganzas that revolved around what Americans considered nude showgirls. Some people expressed concern over whether such entertainment belonged in a "family" resort like Las Vegas, but the revues proved exceedingly popular with tourists and enjoyed lengthy runs in several Strip hotels.[65] That so many establishments joined the trend, however, reiterated the industry's preference for proven formulas and its tendency to mass-produce the same vacation commodity.

Coupled with the range of restaurants, the swimming pools, the athletic facilities, and other Strip features, the wide array of entertainment contributed to a vision of unfettered choice in Las Vegas which overlooked the uniformity in more practical concerns. The range of selection in so many matters reinforced the sense created by casino gambling that anything and everything was possible, that no limits existed to restrain tourists in southern Nevada. Like the motif of the old West in Casino Center downtown, the sense of total possibility on the Strip helped to lift conventional inhibitions and hometown restraints, and encouraged visitors to gamble more freely. Similarly, the pervasive opulence among the resort hotels imparted a sense of extreme affluence to tourists, which in turn weakened conventional valuations of money even further. "The illusion is created that we are all rich," one journalist discovered, "that money means nothing. It is changed into chips, which are buttons, sort of; losing them on the gaming tables can seem trivial."[66] At the core of the fantastic world of choice and luxury remained games of chance. Players who were no doubt aware of the odds against them inhaled deeply the surrounding atmosphere of total possibility and plunged into casino gambling.

On the Strip the major resort hotels served as the axes around which the world of fantasy and spectacle revolved. Unlike the Glitter Gulch casinos, which tried to outdo each other in exploiting a single design motif, island palaces differentiated themselves in numerous ways. Downtown clubs had but casino and saloon interiors, and a solitary format, with which to work, but each Strip hotel had the space and the means to make itself clearly unique. These establishments had such a variety of factors to combine— architecture, restaurants, lodging rooms, grounds, theaters, athletic facilities—and so many cultural forms to incorporate—Hollywood stars, French revues, desert and tropical motifs, and historical periods—that the range of alternatives seemed endless.[67] The resulting Strip hotels were so spectacular and distinctive that they immediately became the symbols that identified Las Vegas to Americans nationwide.

The Strip hotel constituted another western contribution to Americans' culture of public and commercial gaming. Although it blossomed on Nevada soil, the resort inn had its roots in Gold Rush San Francisco, where plush, high-volume gambling halls had first sprouted, and in greater Los Angeles, where the seeds of a new civilization had been planted. Its design typified "the convulsions in building style," so characteristic of California, "that follow when traditional cultural and social restraints have been overthrown and replaced by the preferences of a mobile, affluent, consumer-oriented society."[68] The Strip hotel not only marked the culmination of Pacific Coast styles of betting as they made their way eastward, but also expressed boldly the direction of cultural change. Its significance as harbinger of a new way of life heightened the preeminence of the Strip in southern Nevada.

The prominence of the roadtown resort hotel only confirmed what Europeans had long before discovered about travel in the United States. "In Europe," wrote one French tourist in 1887, "the hotel is but a means to an end. In America it is the end. . . . Hotels are for [Americans] what cathedrals, monuments, and the beauties of nature are for us."[69] And on the Las Vegas Strip, the function of the hotel as ultimate destination was intensified threefold—first by the presence of gambling casinos within the hotel complexes, next by the autonomy of each self-sufficient inn, and finally by the paucity of comparable attractions in the southern Nevada desert. Of course, tourists stayed at accommodations besides those on the Strip and played at other casinos in the resort, but visitors nonetheless regarded Strip hotels as the most important sights to see and the choicest places at which to gamble. They became units of measurement for the entire town, dominating the attention paid to the resort by media, visitors, and publicists.

The sensation and uniformity created by hotel-casinos along the Los Angeles highway resulted in a second cohesive district in the resort city, as separate and identifiable as Casino Center. The Strip challenged the shaping of the railroad in Las Vegas. Whereas the original townsite had been laid out in a standard grid that centered on the train station, the new gambling district emerged in a linear pattern that straddled the Los Angeles highway, just outside the southern city limit of Las Vegas. In sharp contrast to the segregated belts of commercial and residential buildings downtown, radiating out from the railway depot, the new linear district contained primarily commercial buildings that were just as likely to be located at any one point along the Strip as any other. Moreover, roadtown hotels supplanted previous lodgings that had supported downtown casinos. By the early 1940s, numerous auto courts had grown up along the roads to Hoover Dam and Los Angeles, within the city limits.[70] These motels hardly challenged the cohesion of the central gambling district, however, because they offered none of the betting games found downtown. Rather, motor courts merely housed tourists along the major access routes to central Las Vegas, funneling them toward the casinos in the middle of town. On the Strip, however, hotels had their own casinos, as well as their own wedding chapels, restaurants, bars, shops, and recreational facilities. Their spacious parking lots, which attracted auto traffic away from downtown congestion, reiterated their self-sufficiency, their dedication to the automobile tourist, their independence from both downtown and railroad, and their orientation toward Southern California.

Initial development along the Strip began at the inception of the 1940s, just before the war curtailed construction and auto travel. Local promoters had long tried to persuade someone to build a new resort hotel in Las Vegas, a larger, grander, plusher complex along the lines of famous hotels at such resorts as Miami Beach and Palm Springs. They finally convinced a retired Los Angeles hotel operator, Tom Hull, to build a small version in 1940, and El Rancho Vegas opened along the Los Angeles highway in the spring of 1941. A Texas hotel magnate, R. B. Griffith, agreed that Las Vegas had great potential for tourism and opened the larger Hotel Last Frontier on the Strip in 1942. The additions differed substantially from other Las Vegas inns in that they were dominated from the outset by gambling. They offered all services to the tourist—rooms, meals, drinks, weddings, and shows—but from the beginning they viewed him primarily as a bettor. Establishments like El Rancho Vegas and the Last Frontier were in fact complete little cities in themselves, miniature replicas of the western town recreated in central Las Vegas. These new resort hotels seemed to be virtually no threat at all to downtown facilities in the early going. Nobody foresaw their multiplication into the enormously successful Strip of the postwar period. El Rancho Vegas only slowly became a profitable business, changing ownership after the first few seasons, and upon the debut of the Last Frontier, habitually timid local residents feared that Las Vegas tourism could support no more than one resort hotel.[71]

Skepticism about the new hotels disregarded the town's potential for growth as its bonds to Los Angeles solidified. The downtown area proved successful during the war and continued to thrive afterwards, but it actually contained little room for further expansion. The inundation of the district from 1940 to 1945 had demonstrated its limits as a resort center, for overcrowding threatened to choke off some of the tourist business. Since the downtown had been laid out as a railroad townsite, it had a diminishing appeal to the ever-increasing numbers of auto tourists in the mid-twentieth century. Strip hotels, on the other hand, were more convenient for car travelers and nearer to the Southern Californians who comprised the bulk of customers for Las Vegas. They were also closer to the future site of the Las Vegas airport. The Strip hotels, like the automotive and aeronautic vehicles to which they beckoned, were self-contained. They represented liberation from the congestion of the old railroad town. While the downtown district remained tied to the past of the railroad and the last frontier, the roomier Strip came to be designed along more modern lines after World War II.

El Rancho Vegas and the Last Frontier first suggested the location of the Strip, but the Flamingo Hotel, completed in 1946–1947, constituted the first full-blown resort complex with a modernistic bearing that distinguished it completely from the rest of Las Vegas and set a new precedent. Around the end of the Second World War many talked about erecting large hotels in southern Nevada, but only Benjamin "Bugsy" Siegel proved willing and able to marshal the necessary resources in a time of scarcity and delay in the construction business. Siegel had risen to prominence in the East Coast world of organized crime during the 1920s and early 1930s. Dispatched from New York and Miami to Los Angeles in the mid-thirties, where he tightened underworld connections, ran offshore gambling ships, and took over West Coast bookmaking, Siegel stumbled upon the potential of the gambling resort in the early 1940s and persuaded his eastern partners to finance a new resort hotel there. Recognizing the opportunity to make legal and respectable a lucrative underworld specialty, he set out to construct the Flamingo with Caribbean motifs in mind. Operating outside the monetary and legal restraints that confined others, Siegel completed the hotel in 1947 and invited guests to "Come As You Are to America's Monte Carlo." But he did not live long afterwards to enjoy it. Perhaps in part because of delays and cost overruns that arose during construction, or because of early losses suffered by the Flamingo casino, gunmen executed Benjamin Siegel in a Beverly Hills mansion in June 1947.[72]

Siegel's vision as realized in the Flamingo survived the gangster's death as a guiding perspective for Strip establishments. Drawing upon Miami hotels as examples, but also demonstrating his acculturation to Los Angeles, Siegel erected a spacious, low-slung, glass-doored luxury hotel, appointed inside with the most modern and comfortable furnishings and surrounded outside by lush lawns and tropical gardens installed, with characteristic Las Vegas timing, the night before the casino opened. The exterior appearance of the building spoke loudest of all, for the hotel stood out from the strange and arid landscape in a manner that no ranch-style inn could begin to match. Tom Wolfe captured the scene successfully.

> Everybody drove out Route 91 just to gape. Such shapes! Boomerang Modern supports, Pallette Curvilinear bars, Hot Shoppe Cantilever roofs and a scalloped swimming pool. Such colors! All the new electrochemical pastels of the Florida littoral: tangerine, broiling magenta, livid pink, incarnadine, fuschia demure, Congo ruby, methyl green, viridine, aquamarine, phenosafarine, incandescent orange, scarlet-fever purple, cyanic blue, tessellated bronze, hospital-fruit-basket orange. And such signs! Two cylinders rose at either end of the Flamingo—eight stories high and covered from top to bottom with neon rings in the shape of bubbles that fizzed all eight stories up into the desert sky all night long like an illuminated whisky-soda tumbler filled to the brim with pink champagne.[73]

Observers noted the pronounced influence of Hollywood. Newspaper reporters described the hotel as a movie "set that M-G-M wanted to build but couldn't because of budget limitations" and listed the film stars, including Jimmy Durante, Lucille Ball, William Holden, Veronica Lake, George Jessel, Ava Gardner, and Peter Lawford, who attended the grand opening.[74]

Combining Californian with Floridian motifs, the Flamingo presented a new image that announced the desert city's arrival as a leading American resort. Virtually all the hotels that succeeded Siegel's creation incorporated the dual themes of exotic location and luxurious surroundings, even though the specific styles varied. No longer would any major inn be confused with auto courts, as the Last Frontier and El Rancho Vegas had been. No longer could Las Vegas be regarded as a tourist stop.[75] The resort city had advanced in one bound, so to speak, from the backwater of the old West to the cutting edge of a cultural frontier.

By 1953 four more hotel-casinos, the Thunderbird, Desert Inn, Sahara, and Sands, had been added to the burgeoning Strip. Among the newcomers, the Desert Inn stood out for several reasons. The "Bermuda-pink" hotel received the widest national attention of any Strip establishment, for it opened just as Americans began to give more consideration to Las Vegas. The Desert Inn soon earned a reputation for elegance that helped to dispel further the old image of the last frontier.[76] It also brought into the limelight its host, Wilbur Clark, a local favorite who benefited both the hotel and the entire city with his ceaseless promotion. In addition, the Desert Inn initiated a design formula that capitalized on the arid climate. Followed closely by the Sahara, Sands, and in 1955 the Dunes, the Desert Inn made the first attempt to recast the desert of southern Nevada in a more favorable light. Its initiative gave way later in the decade, however, to the theme of the tropics, when hotels like the Riviera, Martinique, Tropicana, and Tradewinds followed the lead of the Flamingo in drawing inspiration from Mediterranean and Caribbean gambling spas. In comparison to the plush and hectic resort hotels popping up all around, the dry landscape of Las Vegas Valley must have diminished in appeal.

In the late 1950s the new Tropicana and Stardust hotels continued the tradition of luxury for the masses on the Strip. The Tropicana and Stardust spared no frill or expense, on the assumption that new hotels needed to pull out all stops in order to compete against older establishments. Opening in 1957 with 300 rooms, and adding 150 more by 1959, the Tropicana aspired to be the most sophisticated establishment in Las Vegas. Its spacious quarters were decorated in a variety of Asian and European styles, and it claimed to serve the finest foods and wines available in Las Vegas. Whereas the Tropicana appealed to the craving for luxury, the Stardust appealed through sheer quantity. The world's largest resort hotel when finished, the Stardust sprawled over forty acres; it was so big, in fact, that new guests were chauffered to their rooms in electric golf carts. Adopting the New Frontier's outer-space formula, the Stardust named different clusters of accommodations after planets and constellations. The hotel's huge sign, "a gleaming earth turning in a welter of flashing planets, comets and flaring meteors," spanned more than one block of road front, and its casino dwarfed all others on the Strip. In addition, exemplifying industrial integration within the gaming business, the Desert Inn corporation owned the Stardust.[77] Together, the Tropicana and Stardust epitomized the trends begun with construction of Bugsy Siegel's Flamingo in the mid-1940s.

The Riviera Hotel added a new dimension to Strip architecture when it opened in 1955, for it became the first resort building to exceed three stories along the Los Angeles highway. Prior to its completion most hotels had featured low, rambling designs that covered wide acreages, with only their towering signs standing vertical. By early 1955, however, when prices for frontage along the Strip reached $1,500 per foot, roadtown was ready for the skyscraper formula of the nine-story Riviera. The new island palace advertised itself as "A Resort City in a Tower of Luxury," and borrowed both style and management from similar hotels in Miami. By 1963 the remodeled Sahara had also extended skyward to the height of twenty-four stories, and just off the Strip stood the "29-story, mushroom-shaped 341-foot-high Landmark Hotel, the tallest building between Denver and the West Coast."[78] The days of the sprawling resort complex, modeled after El Rancho Vegas or the Last Frontier, had passed.

The new heights scaled by the Riviera and Landmark, and the extremes of luxury and size reached by the Tropicana and Stardust, marked the conclusion of a long spurt of expansion. Between the completion of the Stardust in 1958 and the opening of Caesars Palace and the Aladdin in 1966, the pace of growth slackened. Those who sought to erect new hotels or expand old ones found funding in short supply as a result of a narrow investment base, and Nevadans who depended upon the casino industry encountered increasing outside suspicion of the business.[79] New Strip development would have to await the prosperous era after the mid-1960s, when most growth would take place atop foundations that had been laid between 1940 and 1960.

The character of the roadtown gambling district had nonetheless become plain by the late 1950s when the uniformity of hotel styles was evident. The Strip hotel, a new cultural form which represented the changes of the future, had itself become rather inflexible. The elaborate Stardust and Tropicana added nothing qualitative to previous decorative themes. Rather, they offered more and more of the same luxury, architecture, motifs, and size. By so doing they demonstrated the success of Strip styles in the postwar period, but they also suggested that by 1960 successful design on the Strip had been reduced to a few standard equations in which the coefficients only got larger while the variables remained fixed. The millions of visitors who continued to gape at the spectacles confirmed one reporter's quip that "nothing succeeds like excess," but critics could also detect a "bland norm" among resort hotels.[80]

In the twenty-five years after the completion of El Rancho Vegas, the Riviera was the last major project in which quantitative change resulted in qualitative change, for the extra floors generated a new, upright style that broke with the sprawling, low-roofed patterns of other structures on the Strip. Built on cheap land along the Los Angeles highway during the 1940s, the Last Frontier and El Rancho Vegas had pioneered modes of land usage with their widely scattered buildings which made inefficient use of the real estate. By the time El Rancho Vegas burned to the ground in 1960, "the compact structure of the high-rise" put the now expensive property to better use.[81]

The rise of the Riviera in 1955 pointed out the limits of sprawl in roadtown, just as ten years before downtown had also felt the sharp pains of congestion. Stretching southward from the Sahara just outside the city limits of Las Vegas to the Hacienda and Tropicana adjacent to the airport, the Strip became increasingly saturated during the 1950s, and the growing density gave it an affinity to the downtown district. In fact, the nine-story Riviera at first seemed more suited to the centripetal Casino Center than to linear roadtown.

While in its flush of success the Strip came to resemble downtown in some respects, the downtown district made more conscious efforts to imitate the Strip during the last half of the 1950s. Relatively stagnant from 1947 through 1955 and overshadowed by developments along the highway to Los Angeles, the Casino Center emerged from its doldrums in 1956 upon the debut of the fifteen-story Fremont Hotel and Casino. The Fremont, which was the first downtown resort complex, and the Mint Casino, which opened the following year, both deviated somewhat from the original old West theme of Glitter Gulch by featuring shows and paying greater attention to comfort. Furthermore, recognizing the problems that traffic congestion imposed, downtown owners renewed efforts to provide more parking spaces for customers.[82] In these ways the businesses of Glitter Gulch began to pay homage to the modernistic cultural orientations emanating from Southern California and shaping the Strip so extensively. Such undertakings did not substantially dilute the last frontier flavor of Casino Center, but they did indicate that the designs and the tone of the Strip had become preeminent in Las Vegas.

The development of the roadtown district not only reshaped the city but also heightened its visibility and stature. With the rise of the Strip after World War II, Las Vegas became America's ultimate resort. No longer could it be confused with the tourist stop that had struggled through the 1930s in the shadows of Hoover Dam. Now, in its single-minded devotion to mass tourism and its unprecedented array of new forms of leisure, including casino gambling in particular, the city had no rival in the world.

If by comparison Las Vegas was unique, however, one would be mistaken to portray it as atypical of major social currents. The enormous popularity of the gaming capital indicated that it catered successfully to the preferences of postwar Americans. People responded positively to the direction of the cultural changes that the Las Vegas Strip represented. Tourists flocked there to partake not only of casino gambling but also of a new way of life appropriate for postindustrial society. As a spectacular outpost on the cultural frontier sweeping from West to East, the Strip permitted tourists to embrace tomorrow.

While the Strip allowed Americans to experience the future, Glitter Gulch continued to recreate the past. Las Vegas stood both behind and ahead of its times; it represented old frontier as well as new, yesterday's West as well as tomorrow's. Novelist Frank Waters found a metaphor for the significance of Las Vegas in the scene of a Helldorado parade during the 1950s. One segment of the town was typified in the procession by sheriffs mounted on Palominos, a band of Paiute Indians, a line of covered wagons, and the "Twenty Mule Team Borax Wagon that had hauled borax out of Death Valley . . . driven by the last aging mule skinner." On the other hand, a model of Hoover Dam, "resort hotel floats swarming with chorus girls," a brigade of bathing beauties as well as a "squadron of new jets overhead," and, in the distance, a mushroom cloud signaling another atomic blast, represented a second segment of the desert resort. In Waters's novel, a news photographer "caught it all in a single frame—the past and the future of that gigantic and fabulous paradox which was America itself."[83]

With the term "paradox" Waters illuminated the significance of the gambling capital as a signpost of social and cultural change, and described the vacations that visitors took there. Tourists worked at play and played at work in Las Vegas, where leisure no longer seemed leisurely. Bettors derived a sense of individuality even while they consumed mass-produced vacations, and lived out illusions and fantasies in an environment predicated on inflexible casino percentages and rigid design formulas. Rival hotel owners erected luxury accommodations for visitors of relatively modest means, and strove to top one another in some aspects of the industry while refusing to compete in others. Everywhere the tourist turned, he encountered the inconsistencies that accompanied rapid cultural change.

In Las Vegas social trends appeared in accelerated or intensified form. The city served as a satellite of Los Angeles, the nation's most futuristic metropolis. Visitors experienced vacations in southern Nevada as a purified version of the postindustrial society that Southern Californians were pioneering, for the Strip portended affluence, leisure, and amusement, fulfilling a popular vision of tomorrow during the postwar period. Yet at the same time Las Vegas expressed a popular vision of yesterday by recalling the heritage and virtues of bygone years. Visitors rediscovered the past in southern Nevada, not only in the trappings of Glitter Gulch, but also in the sense of individualism and enterprise that gambling elicited and in the general atmosphere of permissiveness and liberation that had traditionally connoted the frontier.

Of all parts of the country, this particular juxtaposition of past and future was most likely and most appropriate in the midcentury Far West. In that region one never felt too removed from the frontier of yesteryear or too distant from changes that were shaping the future. The proximity of yesterday and tomorrow was symbolized in Las Vegas by the side-by-side placement of the Last Frontier and New Frontier. The original hotel and casino, with its old West decor and attractions, embodied the ideal of a freer, simpler life, of a kind of society that Americans had always associated with the past and which was now especially linked to the particularly short and retrievable heritage of the final frontier of the Far West. Like many other residents of the region, Nevadans kept the ideal ever apparent to visitors by continuously reviving the past in such places as Glitter Gulch and such practices as casino gambling. These features suggested that the West, and Nevada in particular, constituted the last bastion of liberty and individualism in the United States.[84] There the frontier loomed so nearby that the less desirable aspects of modernity, such as the mass economic culture and threats to individuality that accompanied postindustrialism, had ostensibly made but few inroads.

Yet even as the region remained closely tied to the past, it also grasped the future. In part because Westerners had so few deeply rooted traditions, in part because they prided themselves so much on liberty and individualism, and in part because they experienced such rapid growth in the years after 1940, convention exerted less influence and people accepted changes more readily on the Pacific slope during the mid-twentieth century. As the fastest changing city in the Far West, Los Angeles became the source of an eastbound cultural wave that provided Americans with futuristic technologies and lifestyles. The tomorrow of Southern California appeared especially clearly and conveniently on the Las Vegas Strip where a new form in the culture of gambling, the resort hotel, epitomized Angelenos' devotion to autos and amusements, affluence and speculation. The New Frontier Hotel, with its space-age theme, luxurious furnishings, and casino betting, characterized the new ways of life that Southern California and the Far West represented to the nation. Like its adjacent predecessor, the New Frontier also embodied an ideal society to Americans, a civilization of ease and pleasure, of individualism and possibility, that seemed to lay in store for the confident generation of the postwar period.

Like all visions of the future, Las Vegas was too fragile to endure for long without setbacks or limitations. That even tomorrow had its boundaries was indicated first by the crisis of 1955, which demonstrated that rapid growth was not automatic, and then during the later 1950s by the predictability of architecture and the cautiousness of the gaming industry. In those years the future as embodied in the resort city was reduced to formulas that resulted mainly in quantitative change, not the qualitative change necessary to set tomorrow apart from today. Americans could no longer imagine the years to come as anything other than more and more of the affluence, leisure, and technological progress that seemed to typify society during the 1950s.[85] It is perhaps the hallmark of a postindustrializing society, of a people oriented toward consumption rather than production, that the future is envisioned as a richer version of the present rather than a different story altogether.

Events of the 1960s and 1970s challenged the promise of a better life that Americans had equated with tomorrow, and reminded them that every frontier, even the future, entails hardship. Geopolitical, social, and environmental crises jeopardized the climbing standard of living that Cold War society had presumed constant. In the Far West the cultural frontier was blunted by such changes, its cutting edge intact but somewhat duller. The problems appeared most plainly at the source of the new way of life. Southern California continued to thrive, but ecological plight and social dilemmas produced doubts where only confidence had prevailed before. A British writer suggested that Los Angeles had "lost the exuberant certainty that made it seem . . . the City of the Future, the City That Knew How. None of us Know now."[86] Las Vegas survived as well, but without the aura of invincibility that characterized it during the late forties and the fifties. The gaming industry and the resort city continued to grow impressively, but along with Los Angeles they were past their prime as harbingers of tomorrow. They had lost much of the promise that they once held out to the postwar people of America.

Both the pitfalls and the paradoxes of the future that Southern California and southern Nevada expressed resulted in large part from the rapidity of social and cultural change. In Las Vegas the future materialized before the past could give way. Since the legalization of casino gambling in 1931, the transformation of the area had virtually never stopped gaining speed. The city hardly had time to come to grips with its frontier heritage, which reached its fullest embodiment in Glitter Gulch during the early 1940s, before another age and another vision blossomed suddenly into a quite different resort district along the Strip. Save for times of unusual financial crisis as in 1955–1956, postwar Las Vegans had little interest in coordinated planning or imaginative city building. Like Angelenos, they grasped the future as eagerly as they embraced gambling, without weighing carefully the costs or planning fully for the consequences. Lacking much sense of tradition and any general agreement on direction, the spectacular resort grew recklessly after 1940. It incorporated into its rapid expansion diverse and often inconsistent elements that made it a showcase for the shifting and heterogeneous culture of the United States and the Far West, as well as an index to the limits of tomorrow.

Most Americans came to know Las Vegas as a gambling resort and hardly noticed the problems that it foretold for the future, but the city also served as home for more than one hundred thousand people by 1960. Although most southern Nevadans applauded rapid growth and contributed to rapid change, they also gradually recognized the toll that growth and change exacted from their community, and tried to shelter themselves from the resulting problems. At the same time that it reached out for the promise of the future and came face to face with limitations, Las Vegas grew like a frontier boom town from the past and so replicated many of the old problems of westering societies. The fast pace of change, the devotion to risk taking, and the prevalence of cultural paradox did not always sit well with local citizens, even though they, too, were people of chance. Las Vegans, more than other Westerners and other Americans, lived intimately with public, commercial gambling and its trappings. They had to shape a hometown out of a resort city at the same time that they reconciled the future with the past.

6

Las Vegans

The Hometown Frontier

After holding hearings in Las Vegas during November 1950, the members of Estes Kefauver's Senate committee on organized crime came away full of disapproval for the desert city. The senators' reproach began with the influence of racketeers in legalized gaming, the ostensible object of their investigation, but it extended well beyond to indict virtually all aspects of life in southern Nevada. The committee pronounced the milieu of casino betting "not healthful" for the local population. A "short tour" of either Las Vegas or Reno, it decided, demonstrated conclusively that "gambling is the major preoccupation of the residents in both places." Kefauver even resented the western informality of the resort; one hotel owner had the presumption to address "everyone—even the dignified Senator Tobey of New Hampshire—as 'fellow.'"[1] After only a brief stay in the town, the senators found all of Las Vegas incapable of meeting their standards. They condemned not just casinos, but an entire style of living that seemed to revolve around gambling.

The senators' disapproval of the gaming resort reflected their attachment to stuffy eastern standards. Las Vegas broke with the past too sharply for the tastes of traditionalists. It had no familiar shape, no conventional economy, and no existence apart from casino gaming. It prospered by catering to Americans' taste for "vices," so Easterners naturally wondered about the fate of those who lived there. In Las Vegas, it was well known, visitors did that which they were forbidden to do at home and then they departed the city, leaving behind their money and their abandon. Residents of southern

171

Nevada could leave neither the gambling nor the resort behind so easily, however. They were Las Vegans, and other people's "sinful" playground was their home.

The presence of legal casino gambling made Las Vegas an unusual hometown. As residents of the nation's gaming capital, southern Nevadans not only dispensed the new ways of living to other Americans in the form of gambling vacations, but also lived with new cultural forms intimately. They dwelled not only on the frontier of gambling but also on the frontier of society, for gambling accelerated in southern Nevada the development of postindustrial trends. Even Angelenos described the place as "extreme" and "bizarre."[2]

Like the members of the Kefauver committee, many Las Vegans blamed the peculiar condition of their community on gambling, but they were not the first American Westerners to encounter the dilemmas presented by gaming to society. From colonial Virginia to modern California, frontiersmen had tolerated wide-open gambling for only so long before supplanting it with more respectable activities. In Nevada, however, casino gaming was an economic staple. Las Vegans could afford neither to outlaw nor to minimize gambling. More than other Westerners, they had to accommodate the practice within their society and resolve the dilemmas that it presented.

This they accomplished by building a hometown that at once promoted gambling while insulating inhabitants from the side-effects of the practice. They devised a residential culture that distanced them from gaming casinos, but in so doing found that they had also distanced themselves from each other. Las Vegans found it difficult to maintain a strong sense of community in southern Nevada. The surrounding desert made permanent settlement seem improbable, and the fast pace of growth, typical of other far western cities during the mid-twentieth century, made society relatively atomistic. Most of the problems faced by residents, however, stemmed directly or indirectly from the social impact of casino gaming, which not only threatened to corrupt hometown morality and attracted widespread condemnation, but also accelerated cultural change. The atmosphere of gambling drove Las Vegas society to extremes.

In evoking both the old West and the new, casino betting in Las Vegas exemplified the continuities between the nineteenth-century frontier and the futuristic West of the twentieth century. The geographic frontier had presumably passed, but modern overland migration to southern Nevada kept the attitudes and behavior of the westward movement alive. The gaming industry generated such growth and opportunity that the resort soon resembled the frontier boom towns of an earlier period. In prospering beyond residents' wildest expectations, however, the expanding city came to be characterized by an underlying restlessness. Southern Nevadans experienced the same transiency, the same lack of permanent commitment, the same fortune seeking, and the same tensions and shortages that typified previous settlements of westering Americans.

Gambling inhibited the development of a traditional community in more than the moral sense that had preoccupied Kefauver's committee. As centerpiece for the resort city, it attracted through Las Vegas an endless flow of travelers who presented problems for home-seekers. Residents found it difficult to make the city their own at the same time that they shaped it into what the tourist desired. Gaming also helped to fragment the city both spatially and socially. As the resort industry took over the city center and encouraged the dispersal of inhabitants to outlying areas, the desert metropolis lost its core. Moreover, the gaming industry fostered an elite of businessmen whose interests often seemed opposed to the welfare of the larger community. In short, living in Las Vegas was a gamble where success came at a high price.

Residents of Las Vegas ultimately responded to the abnormal conditions as new frontiersmen rather than last frontiersmen. They built a forward-looking city that resembled Los Angeles in its shape, outlook, and prosperity, and they adopted postindustrial ways of living that defied conventional standards. To outside observers, and even to many residents, southern Nevada, like Southern California, always seemed a troubled version of the future, a vital metropolis that somehow lacked a center and a direction. In many respects, however, Las Vegas was merely experiencing changes that the rest of the country would eventually face as well. In serving as the basis for the success as well as the malaise that characterized life in southern Nevada, casino betting placed in bold relief the mid-twentieth-century evolution of American culture.

Rapid growth, predicated on the gaming industry, dominated social development in the city. Between 1940 and 1965 Las Vegas ballooned like a lucky Comstock camp where the lode consisted of legalized gambling rather than mineral ore. The population virtually tripled between 1940 and 1950, from 8,422 to 24,624, and expanded another 2½ times to 64,405 by 1960. Then, when it seemed as if the boom had to level off, the population nearly doubled again during the next five years. Such explosive growth could hardly be contained within the borders of the old railroad townsite, and in 1960 Clark County gained recognition as a Standard Metropolitan Statistical Area. The county then contained more than 127,000 residents, 90 percent of them clustered in greater Las Vegas.[3]

The burgeoning population, during and after World War II, consisted primarily of newcomers. The metropolis served as a magnet for those who equated a better life with a real chance for personal prosperity. Thousands upon thousands migrated to the Las Vegas Valley, drawn by the resort boom and by Nevada's comparatively low rates of taxation. Throughout the postwar period the per capita personal income of Nevadans ranked among the highest in the nation. Newcomers discerned the opportunities most readily in Las Vegas, the fastest growing city in the state, where periodic shortages of labor and a relative immunity from recession kept the economy expanding at a rapid pace. Las Vegans enjoyed one of the highest average annual family incomes of any city in the country.[4]

The influx to southern Nevada included people from all walks of life. Construction workers employed on a never-ending series of projects, attorneys attracted by a lucrative trade in marriage and divorce, the elderly devoted to retiring in a warm climate, gamblers and dealers interested in practicing their professions legally, and service workers recruited for the opening of every major hotel, stood most noticeably among the crowds that flocked to the city during the 1940s and 1950s. In Las Vegas they found not only the "elbowroom and broadly tolerant freedom" that supposedly typified a last frontier town, but also the likely prospect of upward mobility.[5] In one sense, the new resident came for somewhat the same reason as the betting tourist. Like gambling, Las Vegas offered a chance to get ahead, if one did not mind taking a few risks.

Newcomers tended to come to the desert metropolis from the same places as tourists. As in other parts of the state, few Las Vegans, only 19 percent in 1960, had been born in Nevada. Most came from nearby states, particularly California, Utah, and Texas. Of the 42,000 migrants to Clark County between 1955 and 1960, a group that accounted for fully one third of the area's population, 12,000 came from the Golden State, and 8,600 hailed from the counties of Southern California.[6] These new arrivals strengthened the ties that held Las Vegas tightly in orbit around Los Angeles.

Many newcomers from Southern California, of course, had uprooted themselves at least once before prior to migrating to Southern Nevada.[7] For them and for many others, Las Vegas was but one of several way stations on the road to a permanent home amid the demographic upheavals shaping the twentieth-century Far West. Recreating the restlessness that typified earlier generations of westering Americans, many newcomers never considered Clark County a permanent residence. Perhaps they saw no future for the desert valley, or perhaps they intended to earn enough money in the resort to stake them to a future in places they preferred to regard as home. No matter what the case, they left in nearly as large numbers as they came; between 1955 and 1960 about forty-two thousand people moved into the Las Vegas metropolitan area while more than twenty-eight thousand departed.[8] A high rate of population turnover, typical of boom-town growth throughout the westward migration, continued to typify urban society on the twentieth-century Pacific slope.

Demographic transience translated into a social instability that became less tolerable as the numbers grew. Since 1930 southern Nevada had thrived on a fluid population and become accustomed to perpetual mobility. Large numbers of dam builders, war workers, and military personnel, not to mention divorcées and tourists, had all passed through the area by 1945, so the temporary residents of the postwar period were nothing new. Moreover, observers had long noted that the arid Southwest seemed utterly unsuited to permanent settlement. The land appeared not to accept inhabitants, J. B. Priestley commented in 1937, and inhabitants appeared not to accept the land. "It is all a *de luxe* camping," the Englishman decided. "Or the most expensive film set possible to be devised. The people were not here yesterday and will not be here tomorrow."[9]

As Las Vegas grew into a full-fledged city in spite of the arid climate, it acquired more citizens who intended to make the desert resort a long-term residence. Most Las Vegans had once welcomed the temporary inhabitant for his contribution to regional growth, but after 1945 they protested increasingly the transient's lack of commitment to their town. Editorials in local papers complained that too many people put personal fortune above all else and seldom reinvested earnings in southern Nevada's future. One columnist, capturing the common sentiment that likened uncommitted newcomers to visiting bettors, wrote that too many "citizens don't care about the future of the community and are marking time only until the golden flow of dollars, which lured them here in the first place, runs dry."[10]

Old-time Las Vegans no doubt felt outnumbered by the new arrival whose initial impulse, whether he intended to remain in the metropolis or not, was to confirm the expectation of gain that had guided him to Clark County in the first place. Although Las Vegans had thus identified one of the common problems with boom-town life, they tended to distinguish too finely between committed and uncommitted residents without considering the nature of society in the urban Far West. Almost all inhabitants of boom towns, including those who called themselves "natives," naturally have had as a first priority the continued priming of the economic pump. Old or new to the area, most Las Vegans considered the town's future primarily in terms of sustaining the economic boom, and only secondarily as a hometown. For newcomers hoping to reside there permanently, and for long-term townspeople suddenly caught up in growing prosperity, it took time to rediscover the importance of the community as home and to overcome indifference toward the town's tomorrow.

Boom-town priorities contributed to a shortage of the amenities that citizens require of a hometown, as did disconcertingly rapid growth. Las Vegans simply could not build the city fast enough to keep pace with the tremendous influx of people between 1940 and 1965. If migrants to southern Nevada had arrived more slowly, reconciliation to the gaming resort as hometown might have proceeded more smoothly. Instead, Las Vegans reshaped the resort into a livable residence only through a series of protracted crises. Public utilities were among the things acquired in a halting fashion. Water was essential to the continued growth of the city, but southern Nevadans only slowly secured the dependable supply that they needed after years of shortages. Similarly, they paid the most attention to the highways that brought tourists into town, while their own network of roads, sidewalks, streetlights, and crosswalks remained incomplete.[11]

The ordeals of building enough housing and acquiring adequate schools demonstrated more clearly the problems of domestic life in the gaming resort because both problems threatened more directly the cornerstone of traditional hometowns—the nuclear family. The perpetual undersupply of housing between 1940 and 1965 presented a major stumbling block for newcomers in southern Nevada. The crisis was worst during the 1940s because, while the population virtually tripled, the housing stock increased little more than two-fold. Workers recruited by wartime industry had to live in auto courts, trailers, cars, tents, and even remodeled packing crates. Conditions improved after the war, but the shortage of building supplies and the continuation of wartime controls inhibited residential construction. A 1947 housing survey estimated that the local vacancy rate stood at the tremendously low figure of 0.2 percent and reported that many people still lived in motels, mobile homes, or substandard structures.[12] Families hoping to build new homes must have found it difficult to lure construction labor away from the more profitable commercial projects under way in Glitter Gulch and on the Strip.

The crisis diminished during a housing boom in the 1950s as new residential construction kept pace, barely, with increases in population, but shortages remained. Approximately six thousand people yet lived in trailers at mid-decade, more than 13 percent of the city's inhabitants. Many homeowners built their houses themselves in order to circumvent the rising costs and the labor shortage. Property values generally soared throughout the 1950s as the demand for real estate grew unabated. Recently cut dirt roads led to raw new subdivisions that began to fill in patches of desert around downtown and the Strip. By 1960 the many recently completed residential units attested the sudden growth in southern Nevada. Almost two thirds of the housing stock of Clark County had been completed during the last ten years, and still more was needed to satisfy the continuing influx to the town.[13]

Las Vegans provided schools for their children in much the same manner that they acquired housing. From the early 1940s through the early 1960s, the town did not build schools quickly enough to accommodate ever-increasing enrollments. Sheer population growth, coupled with the postwar baby boom and boom-town thinking, made it virtually impossible to maintain adequate facilities. Between 1950 and 1955, the number of students expanded by an average of 21 percent annually, or 2½ times over the five-year span. Many students attended schools in double sessions for much of the postwar period, wearing out both their classrooms and their underpaid teachers. In Nevada a perennial lack of funds compounded the national shortage of educational facilities. Hoping to maintain its reputation as a tax haven, the state hesitated to raise enough revenue to finance substantial improvements in schools. Even after the legislature approved a sales tax with proceeds earmarked for education, children in the resort city continued to attend relatively overcrowded, obsolete, and understaffed schools.[14]

The development of a housing supply and a public school system typified Las Vegans' approach to the hometown. They tended to build the residential city in bursts that were inevitably begun long after needs became critical, leaving little time for coordinated planning. Uncontrolled growth certainly suited the individualism of Las Vegans, but they began to reconsider their priorities when their style of city building seemed to pose threats to the nuclear family.

Perhaps more than anything else, the plight of children prompted second thoughts about the quality of life in Las Vegas. Regretting increasingly the boom-town mentality, residents slowly began to realize that development of the city was keyed primarily to the interests of tourists and the resort industry rather than to the needs of permanent residents. Townspeople opened their eyes to see plenty of new hotel rooms and casinos but too few houses and apartments, a sparkling new airport and well-maintained highways but inadequate surface streets and poor public transit, abundant centers for adult entertainment but unsatisfactory facilities for children's education.[15] Such comparisons came naturally to a town dependent for its livelihood on tourism and gaming. Las Vegans faced a peculiar dilemma: on the one hand they promoted their city to pleasure-seekers hoping to indulge in "vices" that most hometowns prohibited, while on the other they preached conventional morality in order to protect their children. All the while, they wondered if they were gambling away domestic happiness as they pursued fortune in southern Nevada.

Las Vegans had particularly strong doubts about the casinos in their hometown during the latter 1950s. Like earlier western reformers, they focused resentment not so much on the activity of gambling as on the gamblers who controlled the business in their town. The elite of hotel and casino executives that had nurtured the postwar boom in southern Nevada now came increasingly under attack. Strip proprietors were portrayed as wealthy individuals who were reluctant to invest in the community that had suffered their industry. Townspeople often viewed the owners as opponents of both increased taxes for public schools and efforts to attract more manufacturing to the area. Las Vegas residents protested Strip hotels' use of city services, because the county township, run by major casino owners, refused annexation to the city proper. Any new project on the horizon, whether freeway exits or water system or convention center, rekindled taxpayers' suspicion that they were financing improvements that would benefit Strip establishments disproportionately. Moreover, some citizens took offense at the popular burlesque shows held in Strip showrooms, others alleged that major hotels recruited too many employees from outside Clark County instead of hiring locally, and still others complained that, unlike downtown casinos, roadtown establishments neglected local residents as customers and gave preference to tourists.[16] Few would have denied that casino gaming had been responsible for widespread prosperity, but Las Vegans gradually began to criticize gaming industrialists for paying too little attention to the future of the domestic community and too much attention to the interests and pleasures of outsiders.

Las Vegans' ambivalence toward the resort industry extended beyond casino proprietors to include visitors vacationing in southern Nevada. Residents worried that they had given too much of their community, or rather leased it out in perpetuity in packages of three days and two nights, to an erosive stream of travelers who cared little for Las Vegas as hometown. After promoting the resort so extensively, the city seemed more of a commodity for visitors than a home for inhabitants. The growing metropolis resembled nineteenth-century frontier towns which had been laid out as real-estate ventures. In both instances, residents toiled to sell the town to outsiders before they made it into their home. The existence of a speculative land boom and the transience of the population heightened the similarity. It consequently took time for newcomers to sell themselves as well as tourists on Las Vegas, to regard the city as both their community and their product. One by one, newly arrived residents began to consider themselves Las Vegans, and southern Nevada gradually became a hometown as well as a gambling capital. Only then could townspeople feel certain that they did not in fact live in the kind of place that visitors envisioned as the antithesis of home.

As much as they might resent adventuresome visitors, Las Vegans generally understood the vital role played by tourism in the local economy. During the 1950s between 30 and 40 percent of the labor force worked for such service industry employers as hotels, casinos, and restaurants. Additionally, for every one hundred people hired by the gaming industry and affiliated enterprises, local businesses and government agencies hired another one hundred thirty people. In short, most of the jobs in the metropolis depended ultimately on the business of gambling.[17] Furthermore, visitors paid many of the gambling, sales, and hotel taxes that funded city and county government. Tourists were the economic lifeblood of southern Nevada. As a result, townspeople turned much of their attention to publicizing the very style of fast living that visitors expected to find.

Tourists responded enthusiastically to the call of Las Vegas, more than keeping pace with population increases in Clark County. In 1960, while three million people visited Lake Mead and Hoover Dam, the attractions that had overshadowed the railroad town of the 1930s, fully ten million people vacationed in greater Las Vegas. Some residents must have wondered whether visitors were too plentiful, however. For each one of the 120,000 permanent residents of the metropolitan area, more than eighty-three tourists stopped in southern Nevada that year. Put another way, tourists on the average added almost sixty thousand to the permanent population of the place and amounted to between one-fourth and one-third of all people in Las Vegas Valley.[18] Residents who felt estranged from the resort city correctly figured that they had relinquished a major portion of the community to visitors.

Las Vegans coped with displacement from their hometown by drawing clear-cut distinctions between themselves and tourists. Southern Nevadans insisted that they remained comparatively immune to the pleasures marketed to outsiders, and local editors reminded residents to leave the casinos to the tourist and avoid the fast-paced life that the vacationer led. Although Las Vegans needed the visitor's money, they nonetheless looked upon him at times with disapproval. Like natives in any resort locale, southern Nevadans tended to view the tourist as a separate breed to be exploited and endured.[19]

Distaste for tourists may have resulted in part from Las Vegans' discomfort with their dependence on outsiders' good will, but it also stemmed from the problems actually encouraged by tourist perceptions of southern Nevada as an adult Disneyland. The visitor viewed the town as anything but home because he came to "sin" there. Like the transient population, he had no stake in the future of the city, no commitment to law and order, no interest in such amenities as housing and schools. Furthermore, tourists and tourism bred crime. Every time observers pointed out the relatively high crime rates of southern Nevada, defensive Las Vegans asserted that "people who come here from elsewhere" committed the majority of offenses.[20] The attitude that held outsiders responsible for most deviance actually suggested an accurate understanding of the nature of life in resort towns. But it also assigned blame too exclusively to the tourist, the favorite explanation for local troubles, without mentioning the contributions of the residents themselves.

Serious crime annoyed Las Vegans because it tarnished the luster of the resort and victimized residents as well as visitors. High rates of crime, however, could be accepted as inevitable for any tourist center, blamed on nonresidents, and countered by one of the largest police forces, per capita, in the country. More disturbing to southern Nevadans was the problem of juvenile delinquency, a mounting crisis between 1940 and 1965 that strengthened residents' doubts about whether the gambling capital could ever make a satisfactory hometown. The interests of tourists once again seemed arrayed against those of residents, but Las Vegans could not so easily blame outsiders for the troubles of their children. They had to hold themselves responsible for the juvenile problem and began to wonder if they had neglected domestic life while building the resort city. "[We have] the most diverse and most expensive array of entertainment and amusement imaginable for our adult population and the tourists," one local judge noted. "Why can't we do something to occupy the leisure hours of our boys and girls?"[21]

Suspicions about a problem with local youth had long circulated in the resort city, and national agencies confirmed the existence of trouble during the late 1950s and early 1960s by recognizing the high rate of delinquency in southern Nevada. Residents at first found it hard to believe that they had a real juvenile problem, and then regretted that they had not built facilities to occupy their children. Both the absolute number and the proportion of youths in the population had grown considerably over the 1950s, but expansion of facilities for juveniles—schools, parks, recreation centers, and social services—did not keep pace.[22] It occurred to Las Vegans once more that in paying so much attention to adult tourists they had perhaps neglected resident children.

Parents in Las Vegas Valley would have been pleased if solving the juvenile problem had simply been a matter of building more facilities, but in fact delinquency troubled them at a deeper level. It illuminated the shortcomings of the hometown by dramatizing the pitfalls faced by children. Las Vegans began to question whether the family could ever coexist healthfully with the resort city. The presence of casino gambling and its trappings—extensive drinking, burlesque shows, carefree tourists, prostitution—clearly contradicted people's notions of a proper childrearing environment. Residents also recognized that the round-the-clock schedule of the city, and the large percentage of one-parent households resulting from the high divorce rate, reduced adult supervision of young people. Parents concluded that family life was more difficult in southern Nevada and worried that raising children there was harder than elsewhere. Adults felt more powerless as parents. They held generally lower expectations for their offspring, according to one survey, and tended to raise children more permissively.[23]

At bottom, Las Vegans feared that they could not convey proper moral standards to youth and that their city had thus undermined one of the central functions of the family. One resident told of "the growing conviction that your children are going to be reared and reach maturity in an atmosphere of constant change and tinsel superlatives. More than anything, it is a question of values. You find yourself gradually ceasing to retain hardwon basic standards. It seems to me that Vegas has too much of a type of life which upsets one's values."[24] Whereas adults might survive and prosper in the permissive city, children seemed terribly vulnerable living in Las Vegas.

Although perceptions of family breakdown were perhaps exaggerated, wide-open gambling appeared to work against the interests of stable domestic society. It formed the basis of a tourist industry that catered to adults and gave Las Vegas an orientation that diverged from ideals that shaped most American communities during the postwar era. The suburban trend of the mid-twentieth century gave an unprecedented amount of attention to children as the principal focus of community organization.[25] Las Vegas parents felt the same impulse to build a hometown that would nurture and protect their children, but they also felt less optimistic about their chances for success. Gambling and tourism threatened family life, and therefore appeared as obstacles to the development of a satisfactory hometown.

Discontent with Las Vegas as a place of residence and the fragmentation of community were both heightened by the rapid rate of expansion. As the city grew and grew after 1940, long-term residents lamented the passing of the stable, cohesive, and friendly town they had once known. For each different observer, of course, decline from the good old days dated from the moment of his arrival in Las Vegas. Attorney Paul Ralli remembered the cordial, slow-paced railroad town into which he had first stepped during 1933, while publisher Hank Greenspun and gambler Benny Binion recalled the small, crime-free, old West town they came to in 1946.[26] Whatever the starting point, most residents found the new Las Vegas less satisfactory as a residence. California tourists and promoters, Florida hotel executives, crowds of footloose workers, and pragmatic management experts had seemingly converted the community into a commodity for vacationers and a way station for transients. When people began to discern in Las Vegas not the easy-going old West but some sort of makeshift combination of Hollywood and Miami Beach, those who regarded themselves as natives sensed that they had been overrun.[27] Often losing sight of their own contributions to the malaise that affected the city, Las Vegans wondered what had happened to their peaceful desert home.

Fast-paced urbanization was partly to blame for the social problems faced by southern Nevadans, but something even more insidious seemed to be at work. High rates of crime, youthful delinquency, drug and alcohol usage, suicide, juvenile venereal disease, divorce, and job absenteeism all pointed to deep-seated problems of "personal and social organization, alienation, and anomie," symptoms that would not disappear as growth slowed down.[28] As Las Vegas became a national case study of social dysfunction, residents' fears about the community seemed to be confirmed. The transiency and values generated by the resort industry appeared to be taking a toll on permanent citizens. Legal casino gambling provided a comfortable standard of living for most of the population, but it was undermining the residential city many inhabitants sought to build. Living with chance and change was perhaps the fate of far western cities like Las Vegas, but both natives and newcomers found it difficult to feel at ease in the desert town.

Las Vegans ultimately came to terms with their unusual city in a dualistic fashion. On the one hand they insulated themselves from the influence of gaming and tourism by turning inward and away from the problems of the gambling capital. They developed a culture of privacy by building residential subdivisions, traveling in automobiles, and espousing an individualistic credo. This response helped to distance residents from dangers perceived in the resort and permitted them to feel that they had more control over their fate, even as they dwelled in a place given over to tourists.

On the other hand, Las Vegans denied that their hometown was really abnormal and at the same time strove to redefine the city as something more than a gaming resort. Reacting in part to a need to conform to eastern standards, they defended their residence as a familiar kind of community. Then, as if to prove their point, they developed and boasted certain features other than gambling that seemed to make their community less singular. Las Vegans thus became committed builders and defenders of the town at the same time that they tried as private citizens to keep their distance from the resort city.

The atomistic kind of residential culture that southern Nevadans devised was nothing unique to the urban Far West, but it gained a certain significance as the obverse side of a gaming resort. Las Vegas was an exaggerated example of a new kind of society, neither urban nor suburban, that became increasingly prominent in the United States during the twentieth century. Defying customary measures of evaluation, this kind of metropolis appeared first in Southern California and spread quickly to such cities as Phoenix and Houston that shared characteristics of rapid growth, social division, and new ways of living. In Las Vegas, however, the presence of casino gaming cast the new patterns of urban life in bold outline, just as it dramatized the problems accompanying cultural change. Gambling tended to receive most of the blame for social problems in the resort city, but in fact the emergence of postindustrial ways of life also contributed to the symptoms experienced by Las Vegans.

Southern Nevada served as a glimpse of the future in part because it belonged to the Sunbelt. This urban region, defined by the demographic and economic expansion that had begun with increased federal expenditures in the South and West during World War II, was most receptive to the postindustrial culture appearing in the United States during the mid-twentieth century.[29] Its population consisted largely of newcomers whose expectations in migrating to the region encouraged acceptance of new technologies and new values. Compared to inhabitants of other parts of the country, growth-minded Sunbelt residents had less invested in the past and more invested in the future. As a result, they built societies that more readily pointed to the trend of tomorrow. Southern Nevada epitomized several of the tendencies that characterized the nation's shift to postindustrialism. Service occupations rather than industrial work dominated the economy, while new forms of leisure and affluent lifestyles demonstrated that consumer culture was supplanting the producer ethic. Even the increased drinking, delinquency, divorce, and other signs of "anomie" were conditions that the rest of the nation would soon face as well.[30] Las Vegas essentially summarized the Sunbelt's challenge to traditional ways of life in the United States.

During the postwar period, observers often examined the nature of society in Las Vegas and Los Angeles by comparing these new far western metropolises to old standards of urban life derived from the East. Not surprisingly, Southern California and southern Nevada, the leading edge of postindustrial culture, seldom measured up to traditional ideals. Residents of both places have been viewed as victims of their own fast society. They have been regarded as alienated, unhappy people who epitomized the flaws in modern American civilization. "Despiritualized, depersonalized, one-dimensional," one critic wrote of Las Vegas; "that is how life in any Disneyland must always be."[31]

Although the cultural styles of Sunbelt cities corresponded to no established ideal, they nonetheless became increasingly typical of American life during the postindustrial age as patterns of living first realized fully in the Far West spread eastward to the rest of the United States. And fortunately, despite the problems that troubled their innovative civilization, most Angelenos and Las Vegans never felt quite so maladjusted as critics alleged. Outsiders may have regarded residents of Los Angeles and Las Vegas as misguided, but both metropolitan areas grew so rapidly and prosperously that people living there generally looked past the malaise that preoccupied the outside observer and saw instead an enormous range of opportunities for personal fulfillment.[32] Some inhabitants recognized the division, restlessness, and aimlessness that characterized Southern California and its offshoots, but they also accepted the risks as inevitable in the special kind of city in which they chose to live.

The rapid growth and increasing mobility of the modern Far West profoundly shaped Los Angeles and Las Vegas. In a matter of only two or three decades, huge population increases, tremendous spatial expansion, and new technological orientations completely erased the likelihood that any conventional sense of community could survive in the urban culture of the Sunbelt. The migratory instincts of the modern Westerner further ensured the decentralization and rootlessness of the new societies. Such mobility resulted not only from the preeminence of the automobile, which recast both the geography and the lifestyle of metropolitan centers, but also from the waves of migrants beating ashore in the region. Cities such as Los Angeles and Las Vegas consisted for the most part of uprooted people, individuals who had already demonstrated their willingness to follow economic and cultural opportunity rather than remain in stable and familiar hometowns. Like the nineteenth-century frontier, the Sunbelt was peopled by Americans in the process of resettlement. The world of these urbanites, as a result, was naturally more restless, more individualistic, and more attuned to economic opportunity from the outset, and the residential cities that they built, sprawling and private and acquisitive, reflected the same westering orientations.

In Las Vegas the privacy offered by the residential culture of modern far western cities took on added importance. Southern Nevadans often felt that they had no city to call their own. Living in an unusual metropolis shared with tourists, Las Vegans felt they could lead ordinary lives only when they got away from Glitter Gulch and the Strip.[33] Townspeople who worked all day or all night in districts given over to the resort industry had to distance themselves from tourists during off hours. Because Las Vegans had no central district of their own, they flocked to the growing number of residential subdivisions where families could set themselves apart from visitors and gambling. The car played an important role in this flight from gaming districts to outlying homes.

Las Vegans' attachment to the automobile served as one expression of their heightened sense of mobility and privacy, and prompted planners to regard the town as "a city of two-car families." Between 1950 and 1960, while the population of Clark County grew 2½ times, auto registrations increased nearly four-fold. In 1960 there were two registered cars for every five Americans, but in Clark County the ratio was two to three. While 64 percent of the nation's labor force traveled to work by auto, almost 78 percent of working Las Vegans relied on such transport. In fact, southern Nevadans depended on private transportation so completely that they never expanded city bus service beyond the "woefully inadequate" system deplored by one editor in 1960.[34] There was no strong call for public transit because Las Vegas had converted to the auto quickly and thoroughly after the early years as a railroad town. Residents preferred the individualistic and flexible transport offered by cars and made the vehicle central to their way of life.

The auto shaped residential Las Vegas just as extensively as it had shaped the Strip. Its predominance on the local scene made downtown obsolete as a community center for local inhabitants. The central district, laid out in 1905 as a close-knit townsite, simply had too few parking spaces to continue to suffice as a major local shopping district. By the time that more parking lots were provided during the late 1950s and early 1960s, Las Vegans had already begun to patronize outlying shopping centers which were easily accessible to auto customers.[35] The city no longer had a central focus for residents. The conversion of downtown Las Vegas from townsite to tourist center symbolized the decentralization of residential society.

In addition to undermining the conventional downtown, the automobile enabled residents to migrate overland to the modern "frontier" known as the subdivision, "that new free land on which all settlers could recast their lives *tabula rasa*."[36] The new housing districts did not radiate out from the old city center, but rather appeared virtually full-blown during the 1950s as scattered, noncontiguous tracts. The wide-open desert spaces between each new addition demonstrated that the city had literally grown by leaps and bounds. As with the Strip, many of the subdivisions lay outside the city limits, and early developers tended to use the arid land inefficiently. Satellite neighborhoods of as few as eight blocks each emerged, isolated from one another save for raw roads connecting the sprawling residential patches.[37] Las Vegans only gradually began to fill in the gaps between neighborhoods, and even then they did it so sparsely that the city yet retained a low population density. Patterns of residential land use reiterated the atomistic society of southern Nevada.

Las Vegans pursued an individualistic and mobile style of living within each new subdivision. Construction trends showed a preference for single-family dwellings and owner-occupied housing over apartments. Between 1950 and 1960 the proportion of owner-occupied homes grew to 57 percent, despite the large number of temporary residents in the vicinity. More than 82 percent of all occupied dwellings were unattached units in 1960.[38] Even though multiple-family buildings would have solved the housing shortage more quickly and inexpensively, people preferred to purchase or rent autonomous homes, just as they chose private autos over public transportation.

The preference for single-family dwellings, however, did not imply that a house was necessarily a home. Many Las Vegans regarded real estate as both a speculation and a commodity for domestic consumption. Whenever boosters depicted the prosperity of southern Nevada, they inevitably cited increases in local property values as a sure sign of economic health.[39] Parcels of land in residential districts were in some cases regarded not as a site on which to maintain a home and raise a family, but as an investment and a stepping stone to some better place. Such a gambling attitude toward land inhibited the growth of stable neighborhoods and heightened the impermanent atmosphere of Las Vegas society.

Partly because of the constant influx of newcomers, and partly because residents so frequently relocated within the metropolitan area, many Las Vegans did not stay settled for very long. Whereas 50 percent of all Americans, and 40 percent of all Far Westerners, lived in the same house in 1960 that they had occupied in 1955, fewer than 25 percent of the people of Clark County had not changed residences during that five-year span. Census-takers found in 1960 that more than 60 percent of the people in greater Las Vegas had moved into their present dwellings since the beginning of 1957, slightly less than half of them from other addresses within the county.[40]

Residents of the burgeoning metropolis were likely to be either new to the town or else recently relocated Las Vegans. Such rootlessness, which was unusually high even for the modern Pacific slope, no doubt weakened the bonds that might naturally develop among long-term neighbors, and further detracted from residents' sense of community. Transiency was as integral to life in the forward-looking West during the twentieth century as it had been on nineteenth-century frontiers.

Living in Las Vegas generated residential patterns that paralleled the new patterns of leisure experienced by visitors on the Strip. Both tourists and townspeople depended on autos and aspired to stronger feelings of individual identity, and both relished the risk taking and speculation that the unique metropolis encouraged. Residential subdivisions, complete with local shopping centers, resembled in their independence from the rest of the city the island palaces along the Los Angeles highway where players did not need to leave the self-contained complex. Although Las Vegans often felt estranged from tourists, visitors derived from the culture of casino gambling a sense of self-determination that resembled the feeling of autonomy that local residents achieved in their subdivisions, autos, and unattached houses.

The resident and the tourist also experienced in common the relatively rapid unfolding of their destinies in Las Vegas. Both anticipated the future eagerly, and both accepted the risks that it implied. As bettors learned of their fates with a speedy flip of the card or a quick roll of the dice, and simultaneously proved something about their character, Las Vegans underwent a similar process of self-discovery in the face of the gambling resort.[41] The adopted city presented fateful choices through which residents established personal identity and learned of their destinies. Las Vegans liked to point out that if "something is going to happen to you, it happens quicker in Las Vegas." They regarded the hometown as a catalyst that accelerated the revelation of personal fate. Daily confronted with temptation and "vice," with crowds of visitors bent on behaving in a fashion unpermitted back home, Las Vegans learned rapidly about the mettle of which they were made. Those who overcame the resort city and stayed on despite its problems no doubt worried about how their children would survive the same test, but they themselves actually "felt stronger for the experience."[42]

Las Vegas challenged a resident's character in a way that few other cities could, and compelled him to prove himself, to learn quickly about his own strengths and weaknesses. This process reinforced the desire for autonomy and the capacity for privacy that Las Vegans derived from the hometown they were building. Moreover, southern Nevadans fashioned a style of individualism that was ideally suited to the dispersed and divided society of the residential city. Their hometown constituted a milieu that encouraged faith in the Silver State's ethos of personal freedom and toleration. The local credo stemmed in part from the open desert environment and "the real people that it breeds," according to one journalist: "Life is free in the state of Nevada. We are not bound around with confining laws and a man can live here in any manner he desires, provided he minds his own business."[43]

Although they had long abandoned the single promotional motif of the last frontier, Las Vegans still liked to think of themselves as pioneers. They had come to the West seeking a better opportunity or a new life, and they had generally thrived on the personal freedoms and plentiful choices that Nevada permitted. The prosperity of the area seemed to confirm Las Vegans' faith in frontier values, and the autonomy afforded by cars and new housing tracts strengthened residents' attachment to the ideal of individualism.

Southern Nevadans embraced a culture of privacy as a response to the effects of tourism and advocated individualism as the proper outlook for a prosperous boom town. These orientations, along with a preoccupation with growth for tomorrow, shaped the city's distinctive approach to politics. Las Vegans typified an attitude toward government that grew more widespread as Sunbelt cities expanded. Migrants to western and southern cities during the mid-twentieth century developed an outlook on public spending that contrasted sharply with the view of other regions. In the northeastern United States, as economic development became relatively sluggish, people generally looked to government for programs that would conserve past gains, provide economic security, and safeguard equality. Citizens in Sunbelt cities, on the other hand, did not reject government spending but rather eyed federal funds for different purposes. During and after the Second World War, the Sunbelt experienced rapid growth largely because of federal investment in new industries, especially those that contributed to national defense. Consequently, residents of the region expected government not to protect past gains, but rather to accelerate economic growth and enhance opportunities for individuals.[44] Federal funds represented venture capital for expanding communities.

People in the shipyards, aerospace factories, military installations, and high-technology plants of the West welcomed spending for warfare, but they often frowned upon spending for welfare. To Las Vegans, inhabitants of a city devoted to chance and speculation, government existed to encourage development rather than minimize social risk. The community welcomed federal defense spending, but it simultaneously developed a belief in minimal government. This attitude seemed natural in light of southern Nevadans' individualistic credo, but it tended to overlook the fact that the success of the community had been predicated on the helping hand of the public sector. During the 1930s the town had gained a new lease on life as enormous sums of federal money poured in to fund construction of Hoover Dam and finance New Deal programs. In the same decade, the state of Nevada provided another form of assistance when it legalized casino gaming. During the 1940s, Las Vegas benefited once again from federal largesse, this time in the form of military installations and wartime industry, and after the war continued to host an air force base while profiting from being the closest significant town to the Nevada nuclear test site.

Even as Las Vegans thrived on the public spending that underwrote postindustrial development in the Sunbelt, however, they developed an outlook on state and local government that encouraged them to overlook certain social needs. Southern Nevadans had generally found it difficult to accept city planning, provide sufficient schools, or improve local roads. By turning inward as private citizens and resisting expansion of the welfare state, they also grew less inclined to support social services or to employ the public sector to repair inequalities.

Nevada gained notoriety during the 1950s for its relatively incomplete system of social services. Priding themselves on low taxes and minimal government, Nevadans were reluctant to invest in welfare programs and the state did without services that many other Americans regarded as basic. During the 1950s Nevada was one of the very last states in the country to adopt either the Uniform Reciprocal Enforcement of Support Act, which reduced interstate barriers to tracking down deserting fathers, or the Aid to Dependent Children program, which provided federal funds and guidelines for the maintenance of families without breadwinners. In addition to featuring underfinanced schools that were incapable of growing apace with statewide population increases, Nevada in 1955 had no modern adoption program, no state-sponsored campaign against tuberculosis, no facilities for either delinquent girls or emotionally or mentally disturbed youth or the criminally insane, and comparatively meager monetary assistance to the poor and disabled. Female convicts and mentally diseased criminals were crowded into a men's state prison that was so outdated that it still used as cells some caves dug during the mid-nineteenth century.[45]

The city of Las Vegas did not add much to services offered by the state. Its postwar population grew too quickly to be covered by welfare programs as well as in other states, and even when government did render aid it gave relatively little. Before 1955 Clark County had no welfare department, and only one relief worker who operated out of a "drab" office on the outskirts of town. The county assisted the nonresident poor by doling out groceries and then sending them across the county line. If indigents had no means of travel, the welfare agent wired their "place of legal settlement" in order to get their fare home. Impoverished local residents hardly received more assistance. The county operated a camp of eleven trailers behind the relief office for fatherless families and the aged. Clark County afforded no other accommodations for the destitute, and doled out only a pittance—fifteen dollars a month in 1958—to those it had no room to house. Between 1950 and 1960 the population of the metropolitan area grew by 163 percent, but funds for poor relief grew by only 120 percent. By way of contrast, funding for police protection, a service regarded as more essential in a booming resort town, increased by more than 330 percent.[46]

The level of social services was raised after the mid-1950s, but southern Nevada still trailed most American cities in providing welfare assistance. This attitude toward the social services put residents both behind and ahead of their times. At one level Nevadans lagged behind other states in developing more extensive welfare programs. Long accustomed to paying first attention to providing lucrative services for visitors from out of state, and influenced by the state's reputation as tax haven and last frontier, Nevadans only slowly admitted the need for wider welfare coverage. On the other hand, Las Vegans presaged at the municipal level a broad movement throughout the Sunbelt to provide fewer government services and rely more on private enterprise to reduce social needs.[47] Like other western cities, mid-twentieth-century Las Vegas was youthful and prosperous, its population composed in large part of individualistic newcomers migrating toward economic opportunity. Residents were reluctant to share their newfound wealth in order to support welfare services at the level provided by older, less thriving cities in the United States.

That people needed social programs contradicted Las Vegans' expectations for the boom town to which they had come. Inhabitants saw the flush economy of the city and wondered why people needed public assistance. Economic and geographic mobility seemed so ubiquitous in Las Vegas that if an individual failed to support himself, he was doubtless expected to move on as quickly and easily as he had come. Because so many townspeople were new to the scene, citizens found it difficult to feel responsible for helping their fellow Las Vegans. Numerous residents planned not to stay in southern Nevada and had no apparent stake in any future that might be secured through welfare services; others simply did not conceive of the boom town and urban resort as a community that required the give-and-take of all its members. Programs of government assistance to the needy conflicted both with Las Vegans' view of the city as economic opportunity and with efforts to disconnect themselves from the social problems of the hometown.

The very patterns that limited commitment to welfare programs also reduced sympathy for the plight of local minorities. Since World War II, southern Nevada had a significant black population. In 1960 the minority accounted for 15 percent of the people inside the Las Vegas city limits. Virtually all blacks lived in an impoverished section of town known as Westside.[48] For them, there was little chance to escape to outlying subdivisions. During the 1940s and 1950s the segregation of blacks and their relatively low standard of living served as a counterpoint to the glitter and prosperity of the gambling capital.

Contemporary observers tended to explain local racism as an import from the Deep South.[49] Relations between blacks and whites in southern Nevada, however, actually followed the same cycle of accommodation and conflict that characterized earlier frontiers in the United States. Like professional gamblers, minorities had traditionally encountered less hostility on relatively new and open frontiers, but as each new West became more crowded, tensions between ethnic and racial groups increased. Whites were more likely to invoke prejudices as frontier societies grew more complex and competitive, thereby denying minority groups full access to opportunities and resources. All across the American West, blacks, Indians, Latinos, Asians, and other minority peoples had been relegated consistently to less rewarding jobs and less desirable lands once whites began to crowd into frontier regions. Blacks suffered something of the same fate in Las Vegas during the mid-twentieth century.

Blacks coexisted relatively easily with whites in southern Nevada from the founding of the railroad town in 1905 until whites began to throng to the boom town of the 1940s. A quite small percentage of the population before World War II, blacks resided not in a sharply defined district of their own but rather in close proximity to whites in downtown Las Vegas during the 1920s and 1930s.[50] The relative harmony broke down briefly in the early 1930s when blacks began to compete for jobs on Boulder Dam, but after completion of the project relations returned to normal until the tremendous influx of both whites and blacks during the Second World War. Blacks generally lost the ensuing competition for the best jobs and most comfortable housing. Whites, faced with more blacks than ever before, increasingly practiced policies of discrimination and segregation that cemented the plainly subordinate status of the minority. When blacks and whites kept arriving in southern Nevada after the war, amid fears of economic slump and housing shortages, whites continued to restrict the minority to the less rewarding jobs and the most run-down residential district.[51] By 1950 Las Vegas had become a tightly segregated city.

Throughout the 1940s and 1950s, Westside had poorer roads and fewer services than the rest of Las Vegas, but its vastly inferior housing attracted the most attention. Homes in the district were more crowded and dilapidated, and less valuable and secure, than other abodes in the metropolis. Unable to obtain loans from local banks until the mid-1950s, many blacks built what one survey called "sub-standard" houses out of cast-off lumber, without much heed to dangers posed by fire and poor sanitation. Even when blacks finally could borrow bank funds to improve the housing stock, they were generally prohibited from purchasing property outside of west Las Vegas. Whites living adjacent to the district in 1951 opposed the construction of a nearby public housing project because it would heighten "racial strife" and lower property values, echoing other Las Vegans' fears of blacks expanding into additional neighborhoods. Consequently, blacks remained concentrated in an area that was so impoverished that in 1965 it became one of the very first targets of VISTA, the Great Society's domestic Peace Corps program.[52]

At the same time that they confined the minority to Westside residences, whites closed off the resort city to blacks by erecting rigid racial barriers that earned the city comparison to the Deep South. Downtown and Strip establishments generally did not admit black patrons until the late 1950s and early 1960s, so black Las Vegans had to gamble at their own clubs in Westside. Black entertainers like Nat King Cole and Sammy Davis, Jr., when they were permitted to stay in Strip hotels at which they were performing, were sometimes discouraged from mingling with whites or having black friends accompany them on the grounds. Segregation was extended to other public places as well, including theaters, restaurants, swimming pools, and schools.

Many blacks had secure jobs with adequate pay in the booming resort, but they often could not advance beyond menial positions. Nevertheless, their steady employment seemed to assure whites that the minority was doing quite well in the sphere delimited for it. White Las Vegans assumed a complacency that gave tacit approval to conditions. When the mayor stated in 1954 that "Negroes seem to be doing all right in Las Vegas," he overlooked deplorable living conditions and minimal opportunities, and implied, in accordance with southern Nevadans' belief in minimal government and self-help, that the city bore little responsibility for improving blacks' standard of living.[53] The social milieu of the desert community generally discouraged recognition of the problems of minorities.

The prospects for black Las Vegans began to brighten during the late 1950s and early 1960s at the same time that conditions improved around the country. The quality of life in Westside started to change in 1955 as banks began to lend money to black homeowners and government agencies invested additional funds for rebuilding the run-down district. The coincidental opening of the first interracial hotel, the short-lived Moulin Rouge, indicated a growing interest in black tourists as well. Even greater strides were made, however, once Las Vegans realized that their racial policies tarnished the image of the city in the eyes of a country that was increasingly responsive to demands for civil rights. Exclusionary policies no longer seemed appropriate for a city hoping to be regarded as cosmopolitan. Las Vegans, who had previously been largely unmoved by protests organized by civil rights activists, were much more sensitive to the possible repercussions of a demonstration scheduled for March 1960, by the National Association for the Advancement of Colored People. Major hotels and casinos averted the protest, and the certain bad publicity, by agreeing to desegregate facilities quickly. Conditions for blacks did not improve overnight in Las Vegas, as evidenced by riots that rocked Westside in 1969, but positive changes had been started.[54] Racial barriers would not be permitted to stand in the way of the continuing boom in southern Nevada.

The treatment accorded to blacks and the needy dramatized the fragmented character of society in postwar Las Vegas. The loosely knit nature of the city permitted a great deal of privacy, mobility, and personal choice for most residents, but it also gave undue influence to prejudice and parsimony by allowing Las Vegans to restrict access to economic opportunities and community resources. As southern Nevada came into step with the rest of the nation in welfare programs and grew more sensitive to criticism of its racial policies, residents slowly dismantled the barriers erected to limit participation in their economic boom.

Las Vegans' need to conform to national civil rights standards demonstrated that, although they were not traditional or ideal citizens, they desired and sought approval for their town. Newcomers to southern Nevada needed reassurance that their community was not as abnormal as it appeared. Moreover, they needed to convince themselves that the deci-

sion to relocate in Las Vegas had been the right one. Like residents of earlier wests, they cared about the opinions of Easterners.

The nation did not always think highly of Las Vegas, however. Las Vegans
had seemingly insulated themselves as private citizens from the dangers of
their own city more effectively than from the sting of national reproach.
Outsiders' condemnation did not make Las Vegans less individualistic or
more traditional urbanites, but it did encourage them to identify more
closely with their adopted city. They responded to the nation's allegations
first by denying them altogether, and then by taking steps to prove them
untrue by trying to make their hometown conform more closely to American norms. A precarious sense of community came to be created, in part,
by the defensive reaction of residents to criticism of southern Nevada.

Las Vegas loomed so sensationally on the country's horizon that it
received considerable attention. Attitudes toward the town mirrored the
ambivalence that had long characterized American thinking about gambling. At the same time that millions visited the thriving city, others condemned it and its residents widely, which rankled Las Vegans. While
Nevada neglected "its poor, its sick, its socially misshapen," one reporter
wrote, it was also "coddling known racketeers." The charge that the desert
resort tolerated underworld figures made Las Vegans suspect around the
country. Ford Frick, the commissioner of professional baseball, preserved
the honor of the national pastime by vowing in 1955 to prohibit any team,
major-league or minor, from staying overnight in the gambling capital.[55]

Critics determined that the evils tolerated by Las Vegans, chiefly gambling and organized crime, corrupted residents. Some writers portrayed
southern Nevadans as avaricious exploiters of such human weaknesses as
the temptation to gamble, and suggested that, far from being fun, vacations
spent in casinos were nightmares that taxed visitors more than they could
afford. "Let's face it," one commentator summarized, "Las Vegas is a town
that capitalizes on greed. If it all sank back into the cauldron of a desert
from which it sprang, the world would be no poorer."[56]

In addition to corrupting the citizens exposed to it, casino gaming
reportedly inhibited the evolution of a typical, stable economy in Nevada.
The services orientation of the state's postindustrial economy lent some
truth to this charge, for between 1950 and 1960 the portion of civilian
workers engaged in manufacturing never topped 5 percent. Many industrialists preferred not to locate in Las Vegas because of the reputation of the
city. Howard Hughes's apocryphal response, when asked in 1954 if he
planned to move his aircraft company to southern Nevada, captured many
people's impression of the economic environment of the resort city: "The
gaming casinos and never-ending supply of free whiskey to the gamers
would make it highly impractical. Especially if those gamers were employees of mine. I'm not about to compete with blackjack, craps, and the slot
machines at their easy disposal."[57] The corruption supposedly generated
by gambling not only made Las Vegans suspect but also allegedly reduced

their fitness for the honest work that industry offered. An economy based on gambling seemed "completely unproductive" to many, good only for transferring money from tourists' pockets to mobsters' coffers.[58]

Criticism of Las Vegas was often based on assumptions that hardly recognized the new society of the postindustrial Sunbelt, but southern Nevadans were nonetheless sensitive to eastern attitudes. Much as they hoped to set themselves apart from the resort, Las Vegans felt troubled by depictions of their community as an American Gomorrah. Local columnists denied strenuously that the city differed from any typical American town, and advocated several measures that would prove the town's conformity to national standards. This defensiveness and quest for legitimacy in the eyes of others may have provided a sense of commitment to the desert town for a people who had almost purposely avoided such involvement in patterns of residential life.

Both by building a decentralized, privacy-seeking culture and by asserting the normality of the city, Las Vegans pursued the same end—denying the importance of gambling and its trappings to domestic life in southern Nevada. Sensitive to charges that they differed from other Americans, the people of Clark County publicized the conviction that they diverged not at all from national norms. In an almost ceaseless series of editorials addressed to tourists and other outsiders, local newspapers reminded the visitor of the normal hometown—the schools, churches, parks, and homes, fraternal orders, women's clubs, Boy Scouts, and cultural amenities—that he was likely to overlook in his preoccupation with casino betting. "We live normal lives" as "regular folks," Las Vegans typically pointed out, "just like those back in your home towns." And if the hometown did have its flaws, residents felt, the tourist was largely to blame.[59]

Residents of Las Vegas, in regarding themselves as indistinct from other Americans, refused to believe that they were susceptible to the same temptations as tourists. Of course, southern Nevadans as a whole tended to gamble more frequently than other Americans, but they held that constant exposure to gaming and associated "vices" had made them immune, and insisted that they could withstand the pressures of living in the resort. They tried to convince outsiders that gaming was not very important to townspeople, and sometimes even denied that casinos provided the primary resort attraction to vacationers, too. This argument doubtless sprang from residents' appreciation of the diverse features of Las Vegas Valley, but it simply proved inaccurate. When resort hotels appeared without casinos, such as the Talleyho which opened for eight months in 1963 because its owner believed that tourists would visit Las Vegas solely for its outdoor recreation, they inevitably folded quickly.[60]

As much as residents might deny the fact, gambling was plainly the primary attraction of the resort, and that made Las Vegans uncomfortable. Try as they might to convince outsiders that they were truly normal citizens in an average town, they could not overcome the primacy of gambling in the reputation and the economy of the metropolis. Consequently, residents undertook several campaigns to reshape the city, all the while insisting that it was not really any different. Southern Nevadans could afford neither to outlaw the economic staple of gaming nor to chase gamblers out of town, but they did try to enhance their reputation by attracting additional economic activities that might help reduce the primacy of gaming and tourism. None of the efforts actually succeeded in reducing the significance of gambling, either to outsiders or to the local economy, but Las Vegans gained from each campaign a greater sense of legitimacy.

Southern Nevadans' acceptance and promotion of the testing of atomic weapons typified the quest for respectability. Still smarting from the negative publicity that accompanied the hearings of the Kefauver committee in late 1950, Las Vegans readily adopted the nuclear weapons experiments beginning in early 1951 as their own. Anxious to show that their community was more than a playground for adults, they quickly came to regard the detonations as the town's contribution to the Cold War advance of military science and national defense. One local newspaper editor explained the significance of the blasts to a citizenry eager to have higher purpose thrust upon it: "Las Vegas has spent hundreds of thousands of dollars upon questionable publicity to exploit our area. We have glorified gambling, divorces and doubtful pleasures to get our name before the rest of the country. Now we can become a part of the most important work carried on by our country today. We have found a reason for our existence as a community."[61]

Happy to accept such a noble mission, residents soon became knowledgeable about the blasts and disputed any criticism of the testing program. When the people of southern Utah wondered, with good reason, about the harmful effects of radioactive fallout from the above-ground explosions, Las Vegans generally discounted such fears and admonished critics to accept the detonations willingly. Of course, southern Nevadans did not live downwind from the test site, but they nonetheless took pride in the "sacrifices" they had made for national defense by surviving the blasts. After nicknaming the town "Atomic City," an appropriate label for that midcentury vision of tomorrow, residents congratulated themselves for their courage and asked who else "could have endured experiments of the world's most horrible weapons."[62]

Las Vegans parlayed their proximity to nuclear weapons tests into a tough patriotism that was not uncommon in the Sunbelt. They welcomed atomic blasts as well as the nearby air force base because defense projects, by identifying the city with the global struggle against communism, erased some of the stigma attached to a gambling capital. Eager to overcome a reputation for cynicism and greed, southern Nevadans posed as among the fiercest Cold Warriors in the nation. Typical of the sentiment was one paper's editorial of 1954, at the height of McCarthysim, that was headlined, "Outlawing Communist Party Will Not Affect Civil Rights." Six years later, on the eve of an international training meet of fighter jets, another paper ran an article with the presumptuous title "Vegas May Hold Key to Free World Fate." Both columns exemplified southern Nevadans' attachment to Cold War assumptions. By 1961 townspeople could look back upon a decade of defense projects that put the city "in the enviable position of making perhaps the most telling contributions to this high priority national effort."[63] Las Vegans felt that involvement in defense programs dispelled any doubt that they were respectable citizens.

In addition to a sense of direction, southern Nevada, like the rest of the Sunbelt, gained an economic windfall from federal military spending, as well as from other public employment. In a town that questioned the premises of the welfare state, government provided the second highest number of jobs to the local work force in 1960. Industrial employment, on the other hand, remained quite limited throughout the postwar period. Many Nevadans did not want the pollution, unions, and taxes that factories would supposedly bring. Casino owners in particular long resisted efforts to attract more manufacturing to the area. They worried that industrial labor, which might not be able to afford to gamble very much, might provide the nucleus of an attempt to do away with legal gaming. Two hotel publicists explained that "gamblers had seen many other towns lose their freedom when factory labor came in and union leaders combined with groups of wives to demand that the temptations be removed. There is no doubt that industry will hurt gaming."[64]

Sensitive to the charge that legal gambling inhibited the evolution of a more traditional industrial economy, and eager to declare independence from the elite of the gambling business, Las Vegans grew more interested in diversifying their economic base after the 1955 crisis in the resort trade. By attracting more manufacturing, residents hoped to reduce their reliance on tourists and to limit the impact of slumps in the gaming business. They also hoped to overcome the bad publicity earned by the problems of several new hotels. The Southern Nevada Industrial Foundation, launched in early 1956 by civic leaders and local businesspeople, worked to encourage outside investors to take a chance on Las Vegas. The promotion had little success in recruiting new industrial employers, perhaps because it could not overcome the reputation of the resort city or the resistance of local gamblers.[65] Nevertheless, the foundation helped to restore confidence in the town, not only within the national business community but, more importantly, among Las Vegans themselves, who appreciated the steps taken toward development of a more traditional and respectable type of hometown.

Whereas the prospect of new factories promised to normalize Las Vegas by diversifying the economy, conventions held out hope of making tourism itself more respectable by giving visitors a more serious purpose for coming to the resort. Residents would feel better about their town if tourists

had more legitimate reasons for traveling there. Once again, the fiscal crisis
of 1955 stimulated the development of this alternative industry.

Las Vegas had hosted conventions since its days as western sideshow to
Boulder Dam in the 1930s, but most meetings had been small, regional
conferences. In August 1947, the town hosted its first "national convention," the Disabled American Veterans, but such affairs remained a tiny offshoot of the main business of gambling. The six thousand people who
attended conventions in 1951 made up but a tiny fraction of the millions
who visited southern Nevada that year.[66]

Over the course of the 1950s, the seasonal nature of tourism and the
disrepute of casino gambling increasingly encouraged Las Vegans to view
large conventions as an essential addition to the local economy. One far-
sighted county commissioner even threatened in 1954 to restrict the reckless construction of more and more hotels if the town did not start to build
meeting facilities that could draw enough new business to fill the additional hotel rooms. The serious slump of the next year finally prompted
the town to approve funding for a convention complex. By 1959 the hall,
as futuristic in design as "Atomic City" itself, opened to host the World
Congress of Flight, a meeting of 6,500 delegates that was ideal for Cold
War Las Vegas. Hundreds of national conferences quickly booked the convention center, and individual resort hotels began adding their own meeting facilities. Las Vegas had gained a respectable "new career." The number of meeting delegates and the money they spent yet amounted to a quite
small percentage of the receipts from tourism in 1960, and many conven-
tioneers no doubt appreciated Las Vegas casinos more than the town's new
meeting facilities, but the significance of the new hall was disproportionately larger for residents.[67] They had once again heightened their sense of
purpose.

Like the atomic tests and the industrial foundation, and like the sprawling subdivisions and the pervasive automobile, national conventions
helped Las Vegans to insulate themselves from the gambling that identified
the community to other Americans. Each additional "career" for the city
seemed to dilute the importance of casino gaming and to make the resort
a more average hometown. By normalizing their adopted metropolis, newcomers found it easier to call Las Vegas home.

The modification of the gambling capital, of course, was more perceived
than real. None of the new missions for the town, nor even the desperate
assertion of normality, actually changed the nature of the resort metropolis, and Las Vegans never truly became committed citizens in any traditional sense. They preferred to isolate themselves in a residential culture
from the central city and the Strip, and gambling remained the predominant force in the local economy as well as, in many regards, the entire
society. But like the outlying subdivisions and the individualistic outlook
that set inhabitants apart from the resort districts, the atomic tests, the campaign for industry, and the national conventions all made residents feel

more at home in the unusual metropolis, making the town more legitimate by ostensibly reducing the significance of casino gaming.

Once Las Vegans decided that gambling amounted to something less than their reason for existence as a community, once they felt more certain that they remained within the boundaries of respectable society, they accepted the resort industry more willingly. Even while worrying about the influence of gaming on the moral fiber of the community and experiencing the disorientation that accompanied rapid change, southern Nevadans seldom lost sight of the positive role played by gambling in their lives. By reducing its significance in their own minds, residents were able to embrace more openly the advantages that the industry afforded the hometown. The same hotels and casinos that accommodated and entertained tourists, and repelled eastern moralists, also provided Las Vegas with distinctive architecture, historic landmarks, a prosperous and rewarding economy, and cultural attractions. Southern Nevadans resisted the domination of their lives by casino gaming, but as the resort industry seemed less threatening, they enjoyed its amenities increasingly and incorporated them more easily into their picture of a respectable and livable hometown.

Las Vegans redefined the resort city in their own minds by striving to dilute the importance of gambling, and reshaped it into a suitable place of residence by building a domestic culture that protected families from tourist activities. Both practices were responses to an uncomfortable environment, reactions that, like maintaining well-watered lawns in the middle of the desert, seemed to make the metropolis more acceptable by making it conform more closely to familiar models. This process, by which newcomers became Las Vegans, took place more in the minds of individual residents, one at a time over the entire postwar period, than throughout the whole city at any single time. As townspeople grew accustomed to the city, they adopted the boosterism that characterized promotional efforts on behalf of southern Nevada. They demonstrated an attachment to their chosen city like converts to a new faith, deriving vindication for the decision to settle in such a questionable hometown.[68] Even if they were not the best of citizens, they accepted Las Vegas as hometown—a large enough task in itself—and took pride in the city's progress.

Las Vegans were often justified in their pride. They had helped to build a vital metropolis at an inhospitable site selling the unlikely commodity of casino gaming. The conditions of a boom town and the priorities of an atomistic culture often placed the dependent and the disadvantaged at risk in Las Vegas, demonstrating that not everyone shared in the blessings of rapid growth and good times. Nonetheless, residents perceived success as justification for relocating in southern Nevada and as evidence of overcoming the problems presented by the unusual setting. Prosperity reassured inhabitants that their way of living and their community were respectable and legitimate.

In settling southern Nevada, Las Vegans both followed in the footsteps of Americans who had settled previous gamblers' frontiers and represented a culmination of the westering experience. In earlier Wests, between 1607 and 1890, the rootlessness of new regions had contributed to the inclination to gamble, and the forms that gaming assumed on every frontier mirrored the changing culture of each new country. Early American horse racing and lotteries distinguished colonists as adventurers who had broken away from aristocratic England. Gamblers in the Southwest flourished without much interference so long as society remained as fluid as the Mississippi River itself, but when the civilization of the Slave South began to make inroads into that frontier, gamblers became more respectable, or else paid a price for their livelihood. Californians had accepted gambling almost as a way of life during the last half of the nineteenth century, but they slowly yielded to eastern conventions and eliminated gaming from the state.

Frontier rootlessness reappeared in mid-twentieth-century Las Vegas and no doubt contributed to the tolerance for gambling. But whereas the changes inherent in any new country encouraged gaming on American frontiers, gambling itself heightened the transiency and prolonged the process of resettlement in Las Vegas. As the core of the local economy and the centerpiece of the city's image across the country, casino gaming ensured that the westering process, and the speculative state of mind intrinsic to the experience of the frontier, persisted in modern southern Nevada. It sparked the turbulent growth of a boom town and made the city a precarious residence by threatening families, attracting an endless stream of transients, and fragmenting the community both spatially and socially. Gambling helped to recreate conditions of frontier life in the desert metropolis.

If Las Vegas resembled the old West, however, it also represented tomorrow's West, for gambling evoked both the last frontier and the frontier as future. Las Vegas thus highlighted the continuity between yesterday and tomorrow on the Pacific slope. Casino gaming exaggerated cultural trends that had originated in California and were beginning to spread through the Sunbelt to other parts of the country. Reacting in part to legal betting, Las Vegans wholeheartedly adopted a lifestyle characterized by mobility, restlessness, and speculation. They cherished the opportunities that casino gaming provided in Nevada, but they also paid a price for them in social and psychological terms.

Las Vegans lived in a city that seemed to threaten traditional domestic values, and often found it difficult to feel at home with the future that the resort represented. They ultimately came to terms with the unusual city by insulating themselves from resort activities and dispelling their own doubts about life in southern Nevada. Insisting that they dwelled not on the fringes but in the mainstream of American life, they found great satisfaction in relatively unsuccessful attempts to normalize Las Vegas.

Even as they resisted the influence of casino gaming or worked to dilute its significance, Las Vegans built a hometown in patterns that paralleled the culture of gambling. They were directed by the same futuristic orientations that guided the Californians who proved so instrumental in shaping both the recreational styles and the residential ways of Las Vegas. Residents felt uneasy with the Strip, but they shared its sprawl and mobility and decentralization. They lived in houses and subdivisions as autonomous as its self-contained palaces. They relished in their lives the very fatefulness and individualism that bettors derived from casino games, and they found a kind of transiency in the urban setting that resembled the tourist experience in the resort.

Like other Westerners, Las Vegans came to grips with the gambling that, more than on previous frontiers, remained a central fixture in their lives. Partly by tolerating casino gaming and partly by sheltering themselves from its impact, they built a thriving city against all odds, at an unlikely site, with an unprecedented reason for existence. Parlaying so little into so much, Las Vegans perpetuated the affinity between gambling and the societies of the American West.

Epilogue

The mid-1960s marked a turning point in the history of modern Las Vegas. For two decades following the Second World War, life in southern Nevada had reflected the abundance and optimism of American society. In visits to the resort, players had tasted the fuller, easier, more stimulating future that seemed to await a confident and prosperous people. Analogously, in choosing the gambling capital as a hometown, Las Vegans had staked their claim to the blessings that belonged to the Sunbelt. By the mid-1970s, however, both groups were encountering the end of yet another frontier as American society and its gambling culture entered a new phase. The desert resort continued to expand, attesting even greater popularity, but, like the rest of the country, its future grew less certain.

Once a sure thing, the bright tomorrow of the postwar period faced increasingly forbidding odds as Americans encountered limitations that forced them to reconsider the future. Near the epicenter of Southern California culture, the eruption of the Watts riots of 1965 and the heightened awareness of air pollution in Los Angeles constituted the first shocks that threatened the foundations of an affluent society. These coincided with tremors across the country that by 1975 had undermined Americans' view of the future as nothing other than a richer version of the present. A divisive war and a reckless executive shook the nation's faith in its place in the world as well as its leadership, while the social, economic, and environmental costs of Cold War consensus and prosperity exacted an ever more painful toll from the country's well-being.

200

Las Vegas survived the changes of the late sixties and early seventies in better shape than the rest of the nation by continuing to grow and prosper. Even a town based upon fantasy, however, could not help but feel the reality of each of the risks that loomed in the years ahead. Threatened natural resources and increasing fuel prices brought environmental dilemmas home to a city that had long denied the constraints of its desert climate and remote location. Once reputedly impervious to hard times, Las Vegas appeared more vulnerable to strikes and recessions. Furthermore, as other states turned to gambling as a source of revenue during economic straits, Nevada lost its monopoly on legalized casino gaming in the United States. During the late 1970s, the rise of gambling in Atlantic City, New Jersey, served to punctuate the end of an era in American betting culture. The historical significance of this eastern resort lay not so much in the competition that it represented for Las Vegas, but rather in the perspective that it lent to those styles of gambling that had developed in successive American Wests. Atlantic City helped to usher in a different approach to public and commercial gambling, a style that had little to do with western society.

The rise of casino gaming on the East Coast seemed to shorten the horizons of Las Vegas, but the resort's prospects remained solid. By the time the first casino opened its doors in Atlantic City in 1978, the business of gambling in Las Vegas had undergone dramatic changes for more than a decade. During the late 1960s and the 1970s new investors placed the Nevada industry upon a firmer financial footing. In a span of little more than twelve months in 1966 and 1967, Howard Hughes spent approximately $70 million on four Strip hotel-casinos, including the recently remodeled and renamed Frontier, and by 1970 Hughes owned six gaming establishments in Las Vegas and another in Reno.[1] The investments of the eccentric millionaire, along with those of tycoon Kirk Kerkorian, lent greater respectability to an industry plagued continually in these years by highly publicized charges of corruption and the involvement of organized crime. Another more legitimate source of financing came to be tapped when the state agreed to permit publicly traded companies to own hotel-casinos in 1969. Throughout the 1970s large corporations gained still more control of the resort industry in southern Nevada. Such companies as Hilton Hotels and Metro-Goldwyn-Mayer soon discovered that their Las Vegas establishments brought in gross revenues that far exceeded the income from any of their other holdings.[2] Casino gaming in Las Vegas continued to offer enormous potential for profit.

To players and to local residents who liked to remember the "hoodlum" era of more personal casino management, the new corporate ownership seemed faceless.[3] Complaints about fewer complimentary goods and services, stricter cost-accounting, more impersonal treatment, and declining sensitivity to the surrounding community were hardly new in southern Nevada. On the other hand, a walkout by culinary and bartenders' unions in March 1970, which closed casinos and darkened the Strip for four days, was unprecedented. Daily losses of $600,000 in casino profits, $500,000 in workers' wages and tips, and $33,000 in tax revenue did not prevent the recurrence of serious breakdowns in industrial negotiations in 1976 and 1984.[4] New tensions between management and labor dramatized the heightened importance of corporate ownership of casinos and hotels.

The larger units of ownership may have created additional difficulties, and they never truly overcame such problems as organized crime and corruption, but growth nonetheless continued to characterize Las Vegas. The belief that more meant better still held sway in the development of new hotel-casinos. Caesars Palace, which opened along the Los Angeles highway in 1966, topped its predecessors in opulence, and the MGM Grand Hotel, opened in 1973, outsized everything along the Strip.[5] The new structures stood decidedly more upright. By surpassing the electric signs that had dominated the skyline during the mid-1960s, casino and hotel buildings downtown and on the Strip came to dominate the cityscape.[6] Meanwhile, Las Vegas spread horizontally at the same time that it climbed vertically. The population of the metropolitan area grew from 273,288 in 1970 to 461,816 in 1980, sprawling throughout the desert valley.[7]

Continued prosperity in the gambling industry sustained expansion in southern Nevada. In the years following the mid-1960s, numbers of visitors increased significantly, while gross income grew even more quickly. Inflation accounted for part of the multiplying total revenues, but even more important was the lengthening amount of time spent in the resort. The average visitor, who had stayed 2.3 nights in Las Vegas in 1970, spent 4.3 nights there by 1980. Because it now cost more to get to the resort, visitors seemed determined to get the most for their travel money. The bulk of tourists, especially Southern Californians, continued to arrive by car, but they found fuel costs rising rapidly after 1970. Meanwhile, the rising number of visitors traveling by plane also generally paid more to get to Las Vegas and stayed longer as a result. The growth in total revenues, from $1.9 billion in 1974 to $4.8 billion in 1980, suggested that Las Vegas tourism could survive higher transportation costs.[8] Las Vegas remained a boom town through the 1970s.

The success of Las Vegas indicated that Nevada casinos continued to suit the orientations of American society. As the postwar vision of a boundless future grew more obsolete, the appeal of a gambling resort that made anything seem possible was strengthened. Moreover, as postindustrial patterns of work and leisure became more prevalent, and as individuals heightened their efforts to establish identity in a mass society, gambling in Las Vegas retained its appeal to tourists. In fact, as other states came to consider gaming as a source of tax revenue, Las Vegas became more tolerable to Americans. By the late 1970s it stood as an accepted feature of the cultural landscape, a place that no longer attracted much scorn and suspicion.

Las Vegas remained unique but seemed more accessible. More women, blacks, and foreigners played in the casinos, adding to the growing numbers of tourists. Increasingly diverse crowds and relaxed dress codes permitted observers to see more clearly than before that the gambling resort catered to the broad middle strata of American society. Las Vegas seemed to be a "monument to American classlessness and—if the truth be told—tastelessness too."[9]

The Reverend Billy Graham consecrated Las Vegas's place in the American cultural mainstream by taking his "crusade for Christ" to southern Nevada in early 1978. The resort greeted the evangelist as it might have welcomed any headliner, and Graham, who for the first time on this occasion allowed his picture to be advertised on billboards, played his audience quite skillfully. Although he indicated that a "spiritual awakening in this state could do more to touch America than any other state," Graham carefully avoided criticism of Las Vegas. He found the resort "a nice place to visit," and ranked Wall Street ahead of southern Nevada as "the greatest center of gambling in the United States." He pointed out that, while he did not gamble himself, the Bible said nothing definitive against the practice.[10] Billy Graham made it clear that he worried primarily about those who gambled their souls, not tourists playing in casinos or employees in the resort industry.

Residents of Las Vegas no doubt appreciated the growing acceptance of their town. The city itself, once without a secure future, now seemed a more permanent fixture in the desert terrain. Rapid population growth helped to expand the settlement, but it simultaneously perpetuated the fluid character of Las Vegas society. Newcomers still perceived the community as a place "to strike it rich," and the residents of Las Vegas still worried about the fate of their children, the influence of the fast life, and the social problems associated with rapid expansion.[11]

Economic and ecological concerns combined during the 1970s to reduce confidence that Las Vegas could continue to grow as it long had. Increases in the resident population placed a heavy strain on natural resources. Pollution tainted the atmosphere of Las Vegas Valley and prospective shortages of water and electrical energy worried a population that was devoted to modifying the desert climate through sprinklers and air conditioners. A tourist-based economy made conservation difficult. The town needed to present itself as an oasis in order to attract customers to the desert of southern Nevada, and could hardly expect visitors to sympathize with the environmental plight of permanent residents.[12] Perhaps more than other people in the arid West, Las Vegans found the future of their hometown thrown into question by threats to natural resources.

Local risks were compounded by the nation's new attitudes toward energy which increased the costs of travel. The gambling resort had succeeded in part because it stood at a distance from large population centers. In years of inexpensive gasoline and airfare, Las Vegas could afford to be remote. During the 1970s, on the other hand, the rising price of fuel cast doubt on sustained rapid expansion. During the energy crisis of late 1973, major casinos turned off many exterior lights as a gesture toward saving energy. Darkened casinos raised the question of how long Las Vegas could continue to attract enough customers to keep growing, and conditions deteriorated as the decade progressed. By 1980 rising fuel prices had altered Las Vegas tourist profiles substantially. A larger number of Westerners visited Las Vegas, perhaps because it now cost them too much to travel outside the region. At the same time, however, even more Easterners stopped going to southern Nevada. The cost of transportation to Las Vegas from outside the West proved increasingly prohibitive, especially after the opening of casinos in Atlantic City during the late 1970s and early 1980s made that gambling resort a more convenient destination from East Coast population centers.[13]

Changing patterns of travel and new ecological constraints created weaknesses in the Las Vegas economy that could not be masked by rising total revenues. During the slumps of the mid-1970s and early 1980s, support industries suffered more than the tourist trade, accounting in large part for unemployment rates that climbed above 10 percent. The resort's reputation as a boom town suffered accordingly. Tourist volume grew steadily from 1974 through 1980, but then fell off slightly in 1981 and 1982. The addition of new hotel and motel rooms demonstrated businessmen's faith in continued growth, but occupancy rates peaked during the late 1970s and then started to decline sharply, too. The town appeared to have overexpanded once more, and the financial troubles faced by several hotels and casinos suggested that Las Vegans needed to come to terms with the reality of slower growth. Attempts to broaden the appeal of the resort by diversifying its attractions—adding sporting and musical events as well as stressing family-oriented themes—and by promoting and packaging gambling more aggressively indicated that the community was responding to the new conditions.[14]

In reevaluating old formulas for prosperity, Las Vegas could gain perspective by reexamining its history. Western styles of gaming had long been incorporated into mainstream culture, and the rise of Atlantic City, a resort that imitated the ways of Las Vegas, in fact attested the importance and success of casino gambling in southern Nevada. Moreover, the regional setting of Las Vegas suggested that it would remain resourceful enough to overcome the obstacles placed in its path by economic change and ecological challenge. Western societies in American history continually demonstrated an ability to prosper while embracing the risks presented by growth. Continued expansion seemed more precarious in southern Nevada after the mid-1960s, but the record showed that the metropolis had adjusted to previous crises.

With fewer tourists arriving from the East, Las Vegas found itself thrown back increasingly upon the very Far West that had proven so fruitful and innovative in previous decades. As tourists' lengthening visits suggested, Westerners still derived satisfaction from vacations in Las Vegas, where they could reenact the gamble of their lives. Moreover, the doubts engendered by political, economic, and ecological crises after the mid-1960s must have made the range of possibilities available in Las Vegas even more attractive, as choices in other dimensions of life declined. On balance, location still appeared to favor the desert gambling capital.

The meteoric rise of Atlantic City as a rival of Las Vegas raised doubts about the future of gaming in southern Nevada, but in light of its past Las Vegas seemed to have the odds on its side as it looked to the future. The rapid growth of Atlantic City after 1978 seemed to suggest that it, too, could regard success as a sure thing, but in fact the New Jersey resort was moving with an uncertain new current in the American culture of gambling. It appealed explicitly to Easterners, rather than Westerners, and instead of shaping a new frontier, gambling was reshaping an old, rather run-down city. Moreover, Atlantic City typified Americans' new perception that gambling had some redeeming social value, not because it might prove therapeutic for society but rather because it might provide a more painless form of taxation. Eastern populations had often been reluctant to accept public, commercial gambling as a respectable activity, but now New Jersey residents decided that casinos had a mission to serve in society. After expecting so little from gambling for so long, people began to ask a lot from the practice—perhaps too much.

Atlantic City casinos embodied the newfound belief that gaming had a more legitimate place in American life. Throughout the country, revenue shortfalls, tax revolts, interest in economic revitalization, and greater tolerance for betting encouraged a number of states to reconsider restrictions against gambling. A new role for gaming appeared first not in the Far West, where cities were still booming, but rather in the fragile Northeast where New Hampshire, Massachusetts, New York, New Jersey, and Pennsylvania authorized lotteries and New York inaugurated off-track betting.[15] These states regarded legalized gambling as an expedient capable of generating something for nothing—new government revenues for little political cost.

In New Jersey casino gaming, portrayed as an alternative to a state income tax, was viewed as an integral source of funds for subsidies to the aged and handicapped. Moreover, it was seen as the key to recovery for moribund Atlantic City. Once a thriving vacation spot tied by rail to East Coast population centers, the resort had long been declining as tourists selected other destinations. Now, legalized and regulated gambling would help to solve the problems of poverty, urban decay, and economic stagnation. In contrast to restless western societies, where chance taking was an end in itself, gambling was a means to an end in New Jersey, as one state senator explained: "the end is not the casino industry. The end is the tourism, resort and convention industry of Atlantic City in particular, and the State of New Jersey."[16]

In putting gambling at the service of the welfare state, New Jersey hoped to duplicate in Atlantic City the financial success of Las Vegas, but simultaneously tried to ensure that gaming remained less influential than it had become in Nevada. Lawmakers authorized casinos solely in Atlantic City, the town that stood to profit most from legalization, and sought to regulate betting in order to safeguard the respectability of the "wholesome family resort" that had inspired street names for the board game of "Monopoly" and since 1921 hosted the annual Miss America beauty pageant. Advocates of legal gaming presented local citizens with a vision of fathers placing harmless bets in casinos, mothers shopping along the Boardwalk, and children playing on the beaches. To this end, controls placed upon the casino industry aimed to exclude undesirable patrons and unreliable businesses, attract the family and convention trade, and protect the tourist from himself. Contrary to the relatively permissive policies of Nevada, New Jersey casinos were initially required to have an accompanying hotel of at least five hundred rooms; limit daily operation to eighteen hours on weekdays and twenty hours on weekends; forbid tipping by players; restrict the amount of credit; prohibit service of alcohol at playing tables; accept nickel wagers in at least 5 percent of their slot machines; and minimize the amount of nudity in floor shows.[17] Such restrictions seemed to promise to keep Atlantic City life from being dominated by the atmosphere of gambling that prevailed in Las Vegas.

Experience dashed the high expectations of those who intended to reduce the risks associated with casinos at the same time that they harnessed gaming to the needs of social programs. In the early going gambling could not bear the burden thrust upon it by the citizens of New Jersey. Casinos found it difficult to start up profitably, organized crime seemed even more deeply rooted on the East Coast than it had in the Far West, and the payoff in revenue and welfare services materialized but slowly. Hopes for urban renewal had to be postponed as Atlantic City seemed to take one step backward for each that it moved forward. While critics concluded that "the costs of New Jersey's style of casino gambling as a means of revitalization far outweigh its virtues," New Jersey pushed on with its quest to raise more revenue and resuscitate Atlantic City. Like a number of other states that had failed to realize all the promised benefits of legal gambling, it quietly lowered expectations and reduced restrictions in an effort to make the industry more profitable for both private and public interests.[18]

The casinos of Atlantic City soon began to imitate the rapid success that had characterized southern Nevada establishments during the postwar period. By 1981 the New Jersey city, with 19 million visitors, became the leading resort attraction in the nation, drawing more tourists than either New York City or Disney World. In 1982 it attracted more than 23 million visitors, almost twice the number that traveled to Las Vegas, and earned about the same gross revenues from gaming, $1.5 billion.

The tourist industry as a whole was still more lucrative in southern Nevada, where casino operators paid lower overhead, visitors stayed about four times longer, and players spent more money on goods and services besides gambling. Some of the controlling corporations in Las Vegas participated in the new growth by investing in establishments in New Jersey, while others remained confident about their future. Nonetheless, the trend in American gambling at long last favored East over West. Because growth in the Las Vegas industry seemed to be leveling off during the early 1980s, while New Jersey casinos expanded their patronage by 2 to 4 million annually, observers predicted that Atlantic City would soon become the nation's gaming capital.[19]

The bright prospects of the New Jersey resort seemed to suggest that Las Vegas might be beaten at its own game, but the nature of East Coast casino operation indicated that Atlantic City gambling had developed a distinctive style. New Jersey casinos relied upon different markets and a separate economic structure. Its eastern orientation and its proximity to such metropolitan centers as Philadelphia, Baltimore, New York, and Washington, D.C., which accounted for the tremendous volume, made it more suitable for tourists interested in shorter visits. In contrast to the experience of southern Nevada, where most players made their own way to the resort, New Jersey casinos played a bigger role in bringing customers to the tables by chartering bus trips. Whereas travelers to Las Vegas, having come a longer distance, stayed for an average of four days, those who went to Atlantic City seldom remained for longer than one day. Thus, while southern Nevada had about 50,000 hotel rooms in early 1983, a relatively high occupancy rate, and a substantial convention business, Atlantic City had but 8,000 hotel rooms, many fewer overnight tourists, and inadequate as well as underutilized convention facilities. The New Jersey resort earned far fewer revenues from such support businesses as restaurants, bars, and motels. Its visitors also had a reputation as less sophisticated bettors, perhaps because few stayed long enough to learn how to gamble at games other than the slot machines.[20]

In part because of newness and location, but also because of its isolation from frontier traditions, Atlantic City was slow to parlay gambling into the lodestone that it had become in Nevada. In fact, as attempts to regulate the industry illustrated, the eastern state hesitated to embrace casino gaming fully. Although New Jersey expected great benefits from gambling, it only accepted the practice conditionally, as a tool for expediting urban redevelopment and enlarging state revenues in a politically popular fashion. Moreover, visitors who came from nearby urban areas were also less than wholehearted in their acceptance of legal casino gaming. Their short visits suggested that they regarded gambling neither as an integral part of their life nor as a means of recreating the adventure of westering, but rather as a way to amuse themselves for a day. For eastern players and for eastern lawmakers, gambling was a means to an end rather than an end in itself.

Gaming in southern Nevada had developed along a somewhat different path. Both more dependent upon casinos as an economic staple and more tolerant of gambling as a way of life, Las Vegans appreciated casino gambling not only as a means to an end but also as an end in itself. They did not lose sight of the benefits to both public and private sectors that were financed by revenues from gambling and related business, but neither did they toil so laboriously to keep the risks at arm's length. Similarly, like earlier generations of frontiersmen, the Westerners who traveled to wager in downtown and Strip casinos accepted gambling as a fact of life in a restless society. Since 1931, Las Vegans and Westerners had parlayed an appreciation of chance into a prosperous and precarious resort city, and sustained the West's role as source of new styles of American gambling.

The desert resort represented not only a culmination of the development of indigenous styles of casino gambling, but also a continuation of the westering process. Its gambling summarized the cultural significance of successive Wests in American history, for the games played by visitors reflected centuries of shaping by a series of frontiers. Although each generation of players had naturally derived different meanings from betting, most Westerners shared the sense that gambling paralleled the risk and change that had characterized their way of living. Tourists and residents in southern Nevada were no different. Las Vegas stood out during the mid-twentieth century as another far western frontier, a monument to risk taking in a society that increasingly seemed more concerned with achieving security than with testing its fortune. However, the popularity of the gambling resort also suggested that, in meeting the future as the perpetual frontier, Americans still aspired to be a people of chance.

Bibliographical Essay

Like the study of leisure in general, the serious study of the history of gambling is gaining momentum in the United States, but the subject has not been thoroughly explored. Americans have had to look overseas for this scholarship in the same fashion that colonists looked to Britain for proper fashions of play. The serious study of the relationship between gambling and society among English-speaking people seems to have begun in 1674 when Charles Cotton published *The Compleat Gamester*, more recently reprinted in Cyril Hughes Hartmann (ed.), *Games and Gamesters of the Restoration; The Compleat Gamester By Charles Cotton, 1674 and Lives of the Gamesters By Theophilus Lucas, 1714* (London, 1930). Cotton's treatise initiated a series of commentaries on English gaming during the late seventeenth and early eighteenth centuries. Historical perspective on the role of recreation and leisure in people's lives was broadened substantially by Europeans during the twentieth century. A pioneering work by Johan Huizinga, *Homo Ludens: A Study of the Play-Element in Culture* (Boston, 1955; orig. pub. 1938), inspired additional investigations of play, of which one of the most useful is Meyer Barash (trans.), *Man, Play, and Games, by Roger Caillois* (New York, 1979; orig. pub. 1958).

Because Americans' scholarly interest in gambling has been largely problem- or policy-oriented, the recent study of gaming and play in the United States has been dominated by social scientists and not by historians. Many scholars have been responding, in one way or another, to psychologists' dialogue about gambling that resulted from Sigmund Freud's analysis of Fyodor Dostoyevski's gaming habits, while others have been commissioned to probe the effects of gambling on society by governments considering legalization of betting as a means of increasing revenues. The resulting studies have tended to regard gaming as a problem or a potential problem, although a few scholars have written about gambling as a normal fact of daily life. Among works that have helped to direct attention away from such concerns as organized crime and gaming as an addiction, Erving Goffman, "Where the Action Is," *Interaction Ritual: Essays in Face-to-Face Behavior* (Chicago, 1967), 149-270, and Robert D. Herman, *Gamblers and Gambling: Motives, Institutions, and Controls* (Lexington, Mass., 1976), provide valuable insights into the significance of gambling for American culture. D. M. Downes, B. P. Davies, M. E. David, and P. Stone, *Gambling, Work and Leisure: A Study Across Three Areas* (London, 1976), helpfully summarizes the sociological literature.

The U. S. Commission on the Review of the National Policy Toward Gambling, *Gambling in America: Final Report* and *Gambling in America: Appendix I* (Washington, D.C., 1976), the products of numerous scholars' contributions, approach the topic from many angles. Entries in the bibliography included in the appendix to the Commission's report, along with two other thorough bibliographies—Susan Anderl (comp.), *A Gambling Catalog: a list of monographs from the research collection at the University of Nevada, Las Vegas* (Las Vegas, 1978), and Jack Gardner (comp.), *Gambling: A Guide to Information Sources* (Detroit, 1979)—indicate how much attention has recently been devoted to the topic by American and English social scientists.

In contrast to sociologists' and psychologists' analysis, historians have tended to bring a descriptive approach to the subject. Indeed, much betting has been too amorphous and too private to encourage extensive historical interpretation. Perhaps reflecting the breadth of the topic, most histories of American gambling have been mainly anecdotal in nature. Some such works that contribute to a large fund of information include: Herbert Asbury, *Sucker's Progress: An Informal History of Gambling in America from the Colonies to Canfield* (New York, 1938); Henry Chafetz, *Play the Devil: A History of Gambling in the United States from 1492 to 1955* (New York, 1960); and Stephen Longstreet, *Win or Lose: A Social History of Gambling in America* (Indianapolis, 1977). The importance of the frontier to the culture of gaming has not received much attention from these or most other students of betting in the United States.

The lottery was the first aspect of American gambling to receive scholarly historical treatment in recent years, no doubt because it played an important role as a business institution and political issue. John Samuel Ezell, *Fortune's Merry Wheel: The Lottery in America* (Cambridge, Mass., 1960), offered a new deal upon publication by taking much more than an antiquarian interest in gambling. It has since been supplemented by G. Robert Blakey, "State Conducted Lotteries: History, Problems, and Promises," *Journal of Social Issues*, 35 (Summer 1979), 62-86. For a discussion of early laws regarding gambling, consult Philip D. Jordan, "Lady Luck and Her Knights of the Royal Flush," *Southwestern Historical Quarterly*, 72 (Jan. 1979), 295-312.

Several recent scholarly works contribute further to a historical understanding of gambling. T. H. Breen, "Horses and Gentlemen: The Cultural Significance of Gambling Among the Gentry of Virginia," *William and Mary Quarterly*, 3rd ser., 34 (April 1977), 239-57, demonstrates how gambling might be analyzed in order to yield insights about society. David R. Johnson, "A Sinful Business: The Origins of Gambling Syndicates in the United States, 1840-1887," David H. Bayley (ed.), *Police and Society* (Beverly Hills, Calif., 1977), 17-47, explains the beginnings of organized crime's involvement in betting, and Mark Haller probes the relationship between "Bootleggers and American Gambling, 1920-1950" in U. S. Commission on the Review of the National Policy Toward Gambling, *Gambling in America: Appendix 1*, pp. 102-43. The U. S. Department of Justice, Law Enforcement Assistance Administration, National Institute of Law Enforcement and Criminal Justice, *The Development of the Law of Gambling: 1776-1976* (Washington, D.C., 1977), surveys two centuries of legislation and court decisions concerning betting in America. A fresh perspective on gambling has been provided by John Dizikes, *Sportsmen and Gamesmen* (Boston, 1981), a fruitful discussion of American styles of play. Anne Vincent Fabian, "Rascals and Gentlemen: The Meaning of American Gambling, 1820-1890" (Ph.D. diss., Yale University, 1982), examines betting as a cultural problem for the nineteenth-century United States.

American styles of gambling derived in part from English practices. For the colonial period, the shapes of these patterns have been depicted by: Hartmann (ed.), *Games and Gamesters of the Restoration*; Dennis Brailsford, *Sport and Society: Elizabeth to Anne* (London, 1969); Robert W. Malcolmson, *Popular Recreations in English Society 1700-1850* (Cambridge, 1973); and J. H. Plumb, *The Commercialisation of Leisure in Eighteenth-century England* (Reading, Eng., 1973). These works represent just a small portion of a rapidly growing number of studies of leisure. John Ashton, *A History of English Lotteries Now for the First Time Written* (London, 1893), provides an overview of early British schemes, and Robert C. Johnson, "The Lotteries of the Virginia Company, 1612-1621," *Virginia Magazine of History and Biography*, 74 (July 1966), 259-92, depicts the short but eventful career of the contests that helped to finance the Jamestown plantation.

Details about the early development of American gambling can be found in a wide variety of sources. Religious authorities were largely responsible for guiding colonists' attitudes toward gaming. Two tracts, one from New England and the other from Virginia, demonstrate the range of ecclesiastical thinking about gambling in the colonies: William Peden (ed.), *Testimony against prophane customs namely health drinking, dicing, cards, Christmas-keeping, New Year's gifts, cock-scaling, Saints' Days, etc. by Increase Mather* (1687) (Charlottesville, Va., 1953), and William Stith, *The Sinfulness and pernicious Nature of Gaming. A Sermon Preached before the General Assembly of Virginia: At Williamsburg, March 1st 1752* (Williamsburg, Va., 1752).

Of the diaries and journals examined for Chapter 1, Jack P. Greene (ed.), *The Diary of Landon Carter of Sabine Hall, 1752-1778* (Charlottesville, Va., 1965), and Richard J. Hooker (ed.), *The Carolina Backcountry on the Eve of the Revolution: The Journal and Other Writings of Charles Woodmason, Anglican Itinerant* (Chapel Hill, N.C., 1953), proved most rewarding. Accounts by William Byrd, Timothy Dwight, Philip Vickers Fithian, Samuel Sewall, and Elkanah Watson were also helpful in contributing bits and pieces of information about early American practices. General histories of the colonial period that have collected and interpreted these fragments on gambling include Carl Bridenbaugh, *Cities in the Wilderness: The First Century of Urban Life in America, 1625-1742* (New York, rev. ed., 1971) and *Cities in Revolt: Urban Life in America, 1743-1776* (New York, rev. ed., 1971); Perry Miller, *The New England Mind: The Seventeenth Century* (Cambridge, Mass., 1954); and Jane Carson, *Colonial Virginians at Play* (Williamsburg, Va., 1965). Studies that deal specifically with gambling in the colonial period include: Ezell, *Fortune's Merry Wheel*; Breen, "Horses and Gentlemen"; and J. T. Sable, "Pennsylvania's Blue Laws: A Quaker Experiment in the

Suppression of Sport and Amusements, 1682-1740,'' *Journal of Sport History*, 1 (Spring 1974), 107-21.

In trying to view the American colonies as an English frontier, I have construed several studies of the era as works in western history, a perspective that is of course easier to gain when dealing with John Smith's Jamestown than when discussing Benjamin Franklin's Philadelphia. Materials on early Virginia are especially plentiful, and I have benefited from Philip L. Barbour (ed.), *The Jamestown Voyages Under the First Charter 1606-1609* (Cambridge, 1969), Susan Myra Kingsbury (ed.), *The Records of the Virginia Company of London* (Washington, D.C., 1906-1935), and Johnson, "Lotteries of the Virginia Company, 1612-1621."

Insightful analysis of the Mississippi River Valley as another far West has been provided by Malcolm J. Rohrbough, *The Trans-Appalachian Frontier; People, Societies, and Institutions 1775-1850* (New York, 1978). Gerald M. Capers, Jr., *The Biography of a River Town; Memphis: Its Heroic Age* (Chapel Hill, N.C., 1939), now somewhat dated, performs a similar service by focusing on the early development of Memphis; Dickson D. Bruce, Jr., *Violence and Culture in the Antebellum South* (Austin, Tex., 1979), includes an excellent chapter on frontier and plain-folk violence; and Philip D. Jordan, "The Mississippi—Spillway of Sin," *Frontier Law and Order: Ten Essays* (Lincoln, Neb., 1970), 23-37, portrays the diverse underworld of the old Southwest. Flatboat and steamboat days in the great midwestern valley have been helpfully recalled by: T. B. Thorpe, "Remembrances of the Mississippi," *Harper's New Monthly Magazine*, 12 (Dec. 1855), 25-41; [Samuel Clemens], *Life on the Mississippi, By Mark Twain* (New York, 1979; orig. pub. 1883); John Habermehl, *Life on the Western Rivers* (Pittsburgh, 1901); and Louis C. Hunter, *Steamboats on the Western Rivers: An Economic and Technological History* (Cambridge, Mass., 1949).

Fortunately for historians, the lower Mississippi Valley in its frontier phase was described frequently and ably by numerous contemporary Americans. C. Hartley Grattan (ed.), *Recollections of the Last Ten Years, By Timothy Flint* (New York, 1932; orig. pub. 1826), and Joseph Holt Ingraham, *The South-West. By a Yankee* (New York, 1835), are classic travelers' accounts. Robert Baird, *View of the Valley of the Mississippi, or the Emigrant's and Traveller's Guide to the West . . .* (Philadelphia, 1834), is as useful a guidebook for researchers today as it must have been for migrants in the antebellum years, and [Johnson Jones Hooper], *Some Adventures of Captain Simon Suggs, Late of the Tallapoosa Volunteers; Together with "Taking the Census" and Other Alabama Sketches. By a Country Editor* (Philadelphia, 1845), contains incomparable tales that offer a vivid sense of the southern backcountry. Many valuable accounts have been included in three anthologies: John Francis McDermott (ed.), *Before Mark Twain: A Sampler of Old, Old Times on the Mississippi* (Carbondale, Ill., 1968); Wright Morris (ed.), *Mississippi River Reader* (Garden City, N.Y., 1962); and B. A. Botkin (ed.), *A Treasury of Mississippi River Folklore* (New York, 1955).

The Europeans who inundated America during the antebellum period saw the scene with different eyes. Their perspective captured people and events that American observers no longer noticed. Many of these visitors traveled through the old Southwest and described both the social conditions and the gambling that they witnessed there. I have relied especially upon John William Ward (ed.), *Society, Manners, and Politics in the United States: Letters on North America by Michel Chevalier* (Gloucester, Mass., 1967; orig. written 1835), Harriett Martineau, *Retrospect of Western Travel* (London, 1838), Frederick Marryatt, *A Diary in America, with Remarks on its Institutions* (Philadelphia, 1839) and *Second Series of a Diary in America, with Remarks on its Institutions* (Philadelphia, 1840), G. W. Featherstonhaugh, *Excursion Through the Slave States, from Washington on the Potomac to the Frontier of Mexico, with Sketches of Popular Manners and Geological Notices* (London, 1844), and Arnold Schrier and Joyce Story (trans. and eds.), *A Russian Looks at America: The Journey of Aleksandr Borisovich Lakier in 1857* (Chicago, 1979).

Alexis de Tocqueville, the European who commented most insightful on the society he toured, also explained better than other visitors those aspects of the national character that made Americans a people of chance. Even though *Democracy in America* included no substantial discussion of gaming or frontier social conditions, it provided an acute understanding of the forces that encouraged men and women to embrace chance and change in the antebellum United States.

In addition to producing the country's first clear-cut class of sharpers, the frontier of the lower Mississippi Valley was in large part the point of origin for a sizable body of literature devoted to the topic of gambling. First-hand accounts of betting as practiced by professionals were published regularly during the nineteenth century. Often presented as exposés of the sharps' underworld, these books ranged from Atlantic to Pacific in following gamblers' exploits, but they gave special attention to activities in the Southwest. Works that have been particularly useful include: Robert Bailey, *The Life and Adventures of Robert Bailey, from His Infancy up to December, 1821. Interspersed with Anecdotes, and Religious and Moral Admonitions. Written by Himself* (Richmond, Va., 1822); Jonathan Green, *Gambling Unmasked! or the Personal Experience of the Reformed Gambler, J. H. Green; Designed as a Warning to the Young Men of This Country; Written By Himself* (New York, 1844) and *An Exposure of the Arts and Miseries of Gambling; Designed Especially as A Warning to the Youthful and Inexperienced Against the Evils of that Odious and Destructive Vice* (Philadelphia, 5th rev. ed., 1847); [John O'Connor], *Wanderings of a Vagabond. An Autobiography. Edited By John Morris* (New York, 1873); George H. Devol, *Forty Years a Gambler on the Mississippi* (Austin, Tex., 1967; orig. pub. 1887); and John Philip Quinn, *Fools of Fortune or Gambling and Gamblers, Comprehending a History of the Vice in Ancient and Modern Times, and in Both Hemispheres . . .* (Chicago, 1892). In part because these works were written by retired or reformed gamblers whose perspectives had been altered by age or by change of heart, they are neither wholly reliable nor mutually consistent. They should be sifted with care, as Fabian, "Rascals and Gentlemen," has attempted. Nonetheless, they constitute invaluable sources for a social history of gambling in the United States. The works by Quinn and O'Connor cover not only the old southwestern frontier but also the California Gold Rush and gaming in early San Francisco.

Historians who have dealt at length with gambling in frontier settings have mostly focused on the trans-Mississippi West of the last fifty years of the nineteenth century. Recent studies of gambling in this region have included: a popular work by the Editors of Time-Life Books, *The Old West: The Gamblers* (Alexandria, Va., 1978); an essay by George H. Blackburn and Sherman L. Ricards, "The Prostitutes and Gamblers of Virginia City, Nevada: 1860," *Pacific Historical Review*, 48 (May 1979), 239-58; Robert K. DeArment, *Knights of the Green Cloth: The Saga of the Frontier Gamblers* (Norman, Okla., 1982), which concentrates extensively on personalities and legends in early far western gambling; and Gary L. Cunningham, "Chance, Culture, and Compulsion: The Gambling Games of the Kansas Cattle Towns," *Nevada Historical Society Quarterly*, 26 (Winter 1983), 255-71, a suggestive piece that recommends its author's forthcoming book on frontier morals.

The Far West, which has attracted the most attention from students of the history of frontier gambling, has also been a focus for some of the most penetrating discussion of the westering process. My understanding of the frontier has benefited greatly from the works of Earl Pomeroy—including "Toward a Reorientation of Western History: Continuity and Environment," *Mississippi Valley Historical Review*, 41 (March 1955), 579-99, and *In Search of the Golden West: The Tourist in Western America* (New York, 1957)—and the writings of Ray Allen Billington, especially *America's Frontier Culture: Three Essays* (College Station, Tex., 1977) and *Westward Expansion: A History of the American Frontier* (New York, 4th ed., 1974). Gunther Barth, *Instant Cities: Urbanization and the Rise of San Francisco and Denver* (New York, 1975), is particularly helpful on city life in the early Far West and on attitudes toward chance and change. J. S. Holliday, in *The World Rushed In: The California Gold Rush Experience* (New York, 1981), and Rodman Wilson Paul, in *Mining Frontiers of the Far West 1848-1880* (New York, 1963) and *California Gold: The Beginnings of Mining in the Far West* (Lincoln, Neb., 1965; orig. pub. 1947), have staked out the miners' frontiers. Finally, the works of Hubert Howe Bancroft continue to serve as valuable references for the early history of the American Far West. Bancroft's chapter on gambling in *California Inter Pocula* (San Francisco, 1888), contains many useful observations by a historian who was practically a contemporary commentator.

My discussion of gambling in nineteenth-century California is based largely on the accounts of migrants and visitors to the Pacific slope. These letters, journals, guides, and narratives were penned both by foreign-born and native-born newcomers. Of especial value from the former group were: Friedrich Wilhelm Christian Gerstaecker, *Narrative of a Journey Round the World . . .* (London, 1853); George Cosgrave (trans.), *Scenes of Life in California by Friedrich Gerstäcker* (San Francisco, 1942; orig. pub. 1856); James Bryce, *The American Commonwealth* (London, 2nd rev. ed., 1889); Abraham P. Nasatir (ed.), *A French Journalist in the California Gold Rush: The Letters of Etienne Derbec* (Georgetown, Calif., 1964); and Clarkson Crane (trans.), *Last Adventure: San Francisco in 1851, Translated from the original journal of Albert Benard de Russailh* (San Francisco, 1931). Among the more detailed descriptions by American observers were: Walter Van Tilburg Clark (ed.), *The Journals of Alfred Doten 1849-1903* (Reno, 1973); Bayard Taylor, *El Dorado, or Adventures in the Path of Empire . . .* (New York, 1949; orig. pub. 1850); Louise Amelia Knapp Smith Clappe, *The Shirley Letters, Being Letters written in 1851-1852 from the California Mines by "Dame Shirley"* (Santa Barbara, 1970; orig. pub. 1854-1855); Franklin Langworthy, *Scenery of the Plains, Mountains and Mines: or a Diary Kept Upon the Overland Route to California . . .* (Ogdensburgh, N.Y., 1855); J. D. Borthwick, *Three Years in California* (Oakland, Calif., 1948; orig. pub. 1857); George R. Stewart and Edwin S. Fussell (eds.), *San Francisco in 1866 by Bret Harte, Being Letters to the* Springfield Republican (San Francisco, 1951). The early years of San Francisco are covered in detail by Frank Soulé, John H. Gihon, and James Nisbet, *The Annals of San Francisco . . .* (New York, 1855), and the heyday of Virginia City,

Nevada, was captured by [William Wright], *The Big Bonanza; An Authentic Account of the Discovery, History, and Working of the World-Renowned Comstock Lode of Nevada . . . by Dan De Quille* (New York, 1967; orig. pub. 1876).

The story of frontier vigilantism, like that of American gambling, has generally been told more through anecdote than through analysis. Because primary accounts of lynchings almost invariably disagree among themselves, it is difficult merely to depict the events accurately. In dealing with popular justice in Vicksburg and San Francisco, I have viewed vigilante incidents as indications of sudden and forceful changes in public opinion regarding not only gamblers but also the nature of new societies. Two newspapers that were sympathetic to the vigilantes' cause, the *Vicksburg Register*, July-August, 1835, and the San Francisco *Daily Evening Bulletin*, November, 1855–April, 1856, have been particularly helpful for understanding shifting attitudes in Mississippi and California. In addition, I have profited from the insights of Earl Pomeroy (ed.), *California, From the Conquest in 1846 to the Second Vigilance Committee in San Francisco; A Study of the American Character, by Josiah Royce* (Santa Barbara, 1970; orig. pub. 1886); Bruce, *Violence and Culture in the Antebellum South*; and Richard Maxwell Brown, *Strain of Violence: Historical Studies of American Violence and Vigilantism* (New York, 1975).

While vigilantism and other aspects of nineteenth-century frontiers have received a great deal of attention, the twentieth-century Far West has not been so thoroughly treated by historians. Studies on the development of Las Vegas are increasing slowly in number, but they are few at present and, except for John Cawelti, "God's Country, Las Vegas and the Gunfighter: Differing Versions of the West," *Western American Literature*, 9 (Winter 1975), 273-83, they do not much address the significance of Las Vegas for the region and the nation. Stanley M. Paher, *Las Vegas: As It Began—As It Grew* (Las Vegas, 1971), and Perry Bruce Kaufman, "The Best City of Them All: A History of Las Vegas, 1930-1960" (Ph.D. diss., University of California, Santa Barbara, 1974), are detailed narratives that offer few interpretive conclusions. Oral history interviews on blacks in Las Vegas have been distilled by Elizabeth Nelson Patrick (ed.), "The Black Experience in Southern Nevada," *Nevada Historical Society Quarterly*, 22 (Summer and Fall 1979), 128-40, 209-20, and a series of articles titled "The Great Resorts of Las Vegas: How They Began," written by George Stamos, Jr., and published biweekly throughout 1979 in Sunday editions of the *Las Vegas Sun*, portrays the development of major hotel-casinos in southern Nevada.

The backbone for any history of Las Vegas since the 1920s is the city's pair of surviving daily newspapers, the *Review-Journal* and the *Sun*. I have looked repeatedly to the columns and editorials of the two papers in order to get a sense of how Las Vegans shaped and responded to the town's development. Herman M. "Hank" Greenspun, publisher of the *Sun*, made quite a splash when his paper came upon the Las Vegas scene in the early 1950s. Greenspun's daily columns during that decade in many ways embodied the impressions of a newcomer who was gradually adjusting to Las Vegas at the same time that he tried to make the city a more livable hometown. On the other hand, the columns of A. E. Cahlan, longtime publisher of the more established *Review-Journal*, tended to mirror the reactions of earlier-day residents who experienced both the joys and the pains of rapid growth from desert way station to modern resort. While Greenspun frequently challenged the established order in Las Vegas, Cahlan was inclined to defend the status quo. Both men, in their own ways, were tireless advocates of the city.

Several autobiographical and promotional accounts by local residents have helped to illuminate the nature of life in southern Nevada during the middle third of the twentieth century. Paul Ralli, who arrived in the area in 1933, authored two volumes on the urban resort—*Nevada Lawyer, A Story of Life and Love in Las Vegas* (Culver City, Calif., 1949), and *Viva Vegas* (Hollywood, Calif., 1953). Susan Berman, daughter of a prominent figure in organized crime, recalls her Las Vegas childhood in *Easy Street* (New York, 1981), and Lester Ben "Benny" Binion, maverick owner of a downtown casino, recounts his past in "Some Recollections of a Texas and Las Vegas Gambling Operator" (MS of oral history interview, University of Nevada, Reno, Special Collections, 1975). Two accounts by newspapermen are Hank Greenspun and Alex Pelle, *Where I Stand; The Record of a Reckless Man* (New York, 1966), and John F. Cahlan, "Reminiscences of a Reno and Las Vegas, Nevada Newspaperman, University Regent, and Public Spirited Citizen" (MS of oral history interview, University of Nevada, Reno, Special Collections, 1968). Publicity efforts generally spared few words in praise of Las Vegas but still managed to say very little. One exception was Katharine Best and Katharine Hillyer, *Las Vegas, Playtown U.S.A.* (New York, 1955).

During the mid-twentieth century, sensational Las Vegas quickly became a regular beat for many reporters and critics. The first national commentary appeared in the early 1940s, and by the time Las Vegas hit its stride in the 1950s, some of the very best writers in American journalism had begun to cover the town and examine its importance for the rest of the country. To be sure, a few reporters focused on specific important problems—James Goodrich, "Negroes Can't Win in Las Vegas," *Ebony*, 9 (March 1954), 44-53, for example, and Albert Deutsch, "The Sorry State of Nevada," *Collier's*, 135 (March 18, 1955), 74-88—but most national correspondents pondered the implications of the gambling capital. Among the best accounts of Las Vegas between 1950 and 1960 were articles by five journalists: A. J. Liebling, "Our Footloose Correspondents: Action in the Desert," *New Yorker*, 26 (May 13, 1950), 106-13, and "Our Far-flung Correspondents: Out Among the Lamisters," *New Yorker*, 30 (March 27, 1954), 71-86; Gladwin Hill, "Atomic Boom Town in the Desert," *New York Times Magazine*, Feb. 11, 1951, p. 14, "Klondike in the Desert," *New York Times Magazine*, June 7, 1953, pp. 14-15, 65-67, and "Why They Gamble: A Las Vegas Survey," *New York Times Magazine*, Aug. 25, 1957, pp. 27, 60; Daniel Lang, "Our Far-flung Correspondents: Blackjack and Flashes," *New Yorker*, 28 (Sept. 20, 1952), 90-99; William S. Fairfield, "Las Vegas: The Sucker and the Almost-even Break," *Reporter*, 8 (June 9, 1953), 15-21; and Horace Sutton, "Old Gamblers Fade Away," *Saturday Review*, 38 (Feb. 5, 1955), 28-30, and "Cowboys and Croupiers," *Saturday Review*, 43 (March 5, 1960), 32-33. More recently, the tradition of insightful reporting has been sustained by A. Alvarez, "A Reporter at Large; The Biggest Game in Town—I," *New Yorker*, 59 (March 7, 1983), 53-109, and "A Reporter at Large; The Biggest Game in Town—II," *New Yorker*, 59 (March 14, 1983), 55-133.

To gain additional perspective on the importance of Las Vegas gambling, I have relied upon the works of David Riesman, which are studded with astute observations about American society as it entered the postindustrializing age. *The Lonely Crowd: A Study of the Changing American Character* (New Haven, Conn., 1969; orig. pub. 1950) and many of Riesman's essays, including those compiled in *Abun-*

dance for What? And Other Essays (Garden City, N.Y., 1964) as well as *Individualism Reconsidered and Other Essays* (Glencoe, Ill., 1954), help substantially in understanding the changes affecting American life in the decades after World War II.

The chapter on Las Vegas in Tom Wolfe, *The Kandy-Kolored Tangerine-Flake Streamline Baby* (New York, 1966; orig. pub. 1965) relies upon a different angle to provide penetrating discussion of southern Nevada. An example of a new generation of reporting, Wolfe's comments were some of the first widely read remarks on the unique skyline of the gambling resort. The discussion of architectural styles was sustained fruitfully by Reyner Banham, "Q: What is the Main Drag of the American Fantasy? A: The Vegas Strip, in Case You Hadn't Heard," *Los Angeles Times' West Magazine*, Nov. 8, 1970, pp. 36-41, and John Pastier, "The Architecture of Escapism: Disney World and Las Vegas," *American Institute of Architects Journal*, 67 (Dec. 1978), 26-37. A more technical understanding of local design has been developed in a path-breaking study by Robert Venturi, Denise Scott Brown, and Steven Izenour, *Learning from Las Vegas* (Cambridge, Mass., 1977).

While architectural critics evaluated the exteriors of the city that gambling built, other observers sought to explain the inner workings of casinos. Jerome Skolnick, *House of Cards: Legalization and Control of Casino Gambling* (Boston, 1978), and William R. Eadington, "The Evolution of Corporate Gambling in Nevada," William R. Eadington (ed.), *The Gambling Papers; Proceedings of the Fifth National Conference on Gambling and Risk Taking* (Reno, 1982), VII: 88-126, provide a thorough discussion of the regulations governing Nevada's gaming industry. The geography and economics of the business have been covered by Don Robinson Murphy, "The Role of Changing External Relations in the Growth of Las Vegas, Nevada" (Ph.D. diss., University of Nebraska, 1969); Robert L. Decker, "The Economics of the Legalized Gambling Industry in Nevada" (Ph.D. diss., University of Colorado, 1961); and Robert E. Willard, "The Quantitative Significance of the Gaming Industry in the Greater Las Vegas Area" (Ph.D. diss., University of Arizona, 1968).

After surveying the *Review-Journal* and *Sun*, a good deal of fundamental data about Las Vegans can be found in federal census figures for 1940, 1950, and 1960. In addition to performing basic demographic tabulations, the U. S. Bureau of the Census sampled a large portion of the population of greater Las Vegas in order to derive statistics that described significant trends in housing, migration, mobility, segregation, and auto usage. Government figures have been supplemented by the findings of commissioned studies, like C. B. McClelland Co., *Report of a Las Vegas, Nevada, Housing Survey, December, 1947* (Riverside, Calif., 1948), and Duff, Anderson and Clark, *Las Vegas and Clark County, Nevada: A Summary of an Economic and Industrial Analysis* (Chicago, 1956), as well as by such publications of the Research and Statistical Bureau of the Las Vegas Chamber of Commerce as *Las Vegas Report 1961* (Las Vegas, 1961), and *Las Vegas Report: A Decade of Progress* (Las Vegas, 1966).

As residents of America's gambling capital, Las Vegans have naturally been the subject of many investigations into the consequences of extended exposure to life in the fast lane. These efforts have concentrated on the social problems that result from boom-town growth as well as from the predominance of a tourist economy based upon gaming, and have devoted little attention to residents' success in adjusting to the unusual hometown environment. Useful examinations of Las Vegas society include: Charles W. Fisher and Raymond J. Wells, *Living in Las Vegas; Some*

Social Characteristics, Behavior Patterns and Values of Local Residents (Las Vegas?, 1967); Philip Richardson, "Effects of Legalized Gambling on Community Stability in the Las Vegas Area" (MS on file in University of Nevada, Las Vegas, Special Collections, 1974); William T. White, Bernard Malamud, and John E. Nixon, *Socioeconomic Characteristics of Las Vegas, Nevada* (Las Vegas, 1975); and Betty Yantis, William J. Corney, John E. Nixon, and Jeffrey Baxter, "The Participation of Locals in the Resort Industry" (MS on file in University of Nevada, Las Vegas, Special Collections, 1978). Charles L. Adams, "Las Vegas as Border Town: An Interpretive Essay," *Nevada Historical Society Quarterly*, 21 (Spring 1978), 51-55, offers notable insights into the transitory quality of life in southern Nevada.

In discussing the relationship between Las Vegas and Los Angeles, I have begun to tap a reservoir of materials on Southern California that overwhelms in mass the literature on southern Nevada. Among the more suggestive works, Robert M. Fogelson, *The Fragmented Metropolis: Los Angeles 1850-1930* (Cambridge, Mass., 1967), is an exhaustively researched history that provides a great deal of information. Reyner Banham, *Los Angeles: The Architecture of Four Ecologies* (New York, 1973; orig. pub. 1971), and David Brodsly, *L. A. Freeway: An Appreciative Essay* (Berkeley, 1983; orig. pub. 1981), are more sympathetic to the city, and provide both more impressionistic and more balanced discussion. Hortense Powdermaker, *Hollywood, The Dream Factory* (Boston, 1950), offers an anthropologist's look at the movie industry at midcentury; Christopher Rand, *Los Angeles: The Ultimate City* (New York, 1967), captured the metropolis near the height of its fortunes; Jan Morris, "Los Angeles: The Know-How City" (1976), in Morris, *Destinations: Essays from* Rolling Stone (New York, 1980), 81-100, discusses Southern California's shifting status after the mid-1960s; and James Q. Wilson offers "A Guide to Reagan Country: The Political Culture of Southern California," *Commentary*, 43 (May 1967), 37-45. The role of California and the Far West as cultural pacesetters is discussed by Ted K. Bradshaw, "Trying Out the Future," *The Wilson Quarterly*, 4 (Summer 1980), 66-82, and Gerald D. Nash, *The American West in the Twentieth Century: A Short History of an Urban Oasis* (Albuquerque, 1977).

Notes

Introduction

1. Phillips Bradley (ed.), *Democracy in America By Alexis de Tocqueville* (New York, Vintage Books ed., orig. pub. 1945), II: 165. Unless otherwise noted, all quotations are as found in the sources. Very long titles have been shortened below through the use of ellipses, and long titles cited fully in the bibliographical essay have also been condensed.

2. In analyzing the cultural influence of the frontier, I have benefited from the comments of Earl Pomeroy, "Toward a Reorientation of Western History: Continuity and Environment," *Mississippi Valley Historical Review*, 41 (March 1955), esp. 581-82, and Ray Allen Billington, *America's Frontier Culture: Three Essays* (College Station, Tex., 1977), esp. 56, 67-68.

3. Theodore S. Hittell, *History of California* (San Francisco, 1897), II: 764.

4. The distinction was suggested by Jerome O. Steffen, "Insular *v.* Cosmopolitan Frontiers: A Proposal for the Comparative Study of American Frontiers," Jerome O. Steffen (ed.), *The American West, New Perspectives, New Dimensions* (Norman, Okla., 1979), 94-123, and developed further in Jerome O. Steffen, *Comparative Frontiers: A Proposal for Studying the American West* (Norman, Okla., 1980).

Chapter 1

1. The crisis of the Virginia Company in 1612 is discussed by Robert C. Johnson, "The Lotteries of the Virginia Company, 1612-1621," *Virginia Magazine of History and Biography*, 74 (July 1966), 259-60. On the character of early settlers and the circumstances contributing to idleness, turn to: Charles M. Andrews, *The Colo-*

nial Period of American History (New Haven, Conn., 1964), I: 88, 93; Karen Ordahl Kupperman, "Apathy and Death in Early Jamestown," *Journal of American History*, 66 (June 1979), 24-40. The observations of John Smith and Gabriel Archer are reprinted in Philip L. Barbour (ed.), *The Jamestown Voyages Under the First Charter 1606-1609* (Cambridge, 1969), II: 282, 374, 440.

2. For accounts of gaming in early Jamestown, see Carl Bridenbaugh, *Jamestown 1544-1699* (New York, 1980), 123; [Ralph Hamor], *A True Discourse of the Present Estate of Virginia, and the successe of the affaires there till the 18 of June 1614* . . . (London, 1615), 26; Henry C. Murphy (trans.), "Voyages from Holland to America, A.D. 1632 to 1644. By David Peterson de Vries," in New-York Historical Society, *Collections*, 2nd ser., 3 (1857), 36, 125. For evidence of efforts to suppress gambling, turn to [William Strachey (ed.)], *For the Colony in Virginia Britannia. Lawes Divine, Morall and Martiall, &c.* (London, 1612), 4, 27, 29, 44; Jane Carson, *Colonial Virginians at Play* (Williamsburg, Va., 1965), 54; Philip D. Jordan, "Lady Luck and Her Knights of the Royal Flush," *Southwestern Historical Quarterly*, 72 (January 1969), 296.

3. Andrews, *Colonial Period of American History*, I: 103, 116-17; John Ashton, *A History of English Lotteries Now for the First Time Written* (London, 1893), 28-29; Johnson, "Lotteries," 267, 274; Barbour (ed.), *Jamestown Voyages*, II: 377.

4. Johnson, "Lotteries," 261, 265-68, 270-71, 282-87; Alexander Brown (ed.), *The Genesis of the United States* . . . (Boston, 1890), II: 570-71; John Samuel Ezell, *Fortune's Merry Wheel: The Lottery in America* (Cambridge, Mass., 1960), 6-7. Lottery projects were commonly referred to as "schemes."

5. Johnson, "Lotteries," 262-81.

6. Theodore K. Rabb, *Enterprise & Empire: Merchant and Gentry Investment in the Expansion of England, 1575-1630* (Cambridge, Mass., 1967), 37-41, 100.

7. Johnson, "Lotteries," 262, 266-68.

8. Johnson, "Lotteries," 274.

9. The importance of lotteries to the company was manifest in its records: Susan Myra Kingsbury (ed.), *The Records of the Virginia Company of London* (Washington, D.C., 1906-1935), I: 93, 94, 358, 373, 379, 411, 412, 492, 556; IV: 524. Smith's quotation is found at I: 451.

10. Wesley Frank Craven, *Dissolution of the Virginia Company; The Failure of a Colonial Experiment* (Gloucester, Mass., 1964; orig. pub. 1932), 149-50, 183-84.

11. Kingsbury (ed.), *Records*, I: 279; III: 49-56; IV: 184; Brown (ed.), *Genesis*, II: 575, 594, 633-34; Johnson, "Lotteries," 266, 270-71, 275, 287-88, 290.

12. Johnson, "Lotteries," 289-90; Kingsbury (ed.), *Records*, IV: 215, 294; Louis B. Wright (ed.), *A Plain Pathway to Plantations (1624) by Richard Eburne* (Ithaca, N.Y., 1962), 79.

13. Andrews, *Colonial Period of American History*, I: 137-38; Johnson, "Lotteries," 290; Ezell, *Fortune's Merry Wheel*, 8; Kingsbury (ed.), *Records*, III: 434-35.

14. Kingsbury (ed.), *Records*, I: 470.

15. Andrews, *Colonial Period of American History*, I: 168-69; Kingsbury (ed.), *Records*, IV: 153-54; Johnson, "Lotteries," 291-92.

16. Robert W. Malcolmson, *Popular Recreations in English Society 1700-1850* (Cambridge, 1973), ch. 2; Cyril Hughes Hartmann (ed.), *Games and Gamesters*

of the Restoration (London, 1930), 11; Marcia Vale, *The Gentleman's Recreations; Accomplishments and Pastimes of the English Gentleman 1580-1630* (Cambridge, 1977), 4, 135; U. S. Department of Justice, Law Enforcement Assistance Administration, National Institute of Law Enforcement and Criminal Justice (hereafter abbreviated as NILECJ), *The Development of the Law of Gambling: 1776-1976* (Washington, D.C., 1977), 5-8. The quotations come from Joseph Strutt, *Glig-Gamena Angel-Deod. Or the Sports and Pastimes of the People in England* . . . (London, 2nd ed., 1810), xxxvi-xxxix.

17. Carl Bridenbaugh, *Vexed and Troubled Englishmen 1590-1642* (New York, 1968), 112-14. The quotation comes from Dennis Brailsford, *Sport and Society: Elizabeth to Anne* (London, 1969), 120.

18. Lawrence Stone, *The Crisis of the Aristocracy 1558-1641* (Oxford, 1965), 567-69, 570.

19. Brailsford, *Sport and Society*, 204, 199; NILECJ, *Development of the Law of Gambling*, 11-13; Hartmann (ed.), *Games and Gamesters*, x-xii, xvii-xviii, ix.

20. See the comments of Edward Waterhouse, *The Gentleman's Monitor* (1665), reprinted in Lawrence Stone (ed.), *Social Change and Revolution in England 1540-1640* (New York, 1965), 137; Hartmann (ed.), *Games and Gamesters*, x-xi, xiii-xiv, xv, xvi-xvii, xxi, 100-101. The verse comes from the play *The Gamester* (1705), cited by Jay Barrett Botsford, *English Society in the Eighteenth Century As Influenced from Oversea* (London, 1924), 246.

21. Hartmann (ed.), *Games and Gamesters*, xxv-xxvii, 1-11, 119-22.

22. Brailsford, *Sport and Society*, 213-15.

23. J. H. Plumb, *The Commercialisation of Leisure in Eighteenth-century England* (Reading, Eng., 1973), 9, 16-17; J. H. Plumb, "The Public, Literature, and the Arts in the Eighteenth Century," Michael Robert Marrus (ed.), *The Emergence of Leisure* (New York, 1974), 16-17, 34-35.

24. See the comments made in 1579 by John Northbrooke, cited by Vale, *Gentleman's Recreations*, 140, and Malcolmson, *Popular Recreations*, 9.

25. Stone, *Crisis of the Aristocracy*, 567-69; Christopher Hill, *Society and Puritanism in Pre-Revolutionary England* (New York, 2nd ed., 1967), ch. 5.

26. Malcolmson, *Popular Recreations*, ch. 1; Hill, *Society and Puritanism*, ch. 5; Derek Jarrett, *England in the Age of Hogarth* (London, 1974), 180-81.

27. William Bradford exemplified puritan attitudes toward Christmas. See his account of the first Yuletide in Plymouth colony in Samuel Eliot Morison (ed.), *Of Plymouth Plantation 1620-1647 by William Bradford, Sometime Governor Thereof* (New York, 1966), 97.

28. The site commonly referred to as Merry Mount was actually christened "Mare Mount" by Thomas Morton, and his usage is followed here.

29. Primary sources on the career of Ma-re Mount include: Thomas Morton, *New English Canaan; or, New Canaan, containing An Abstract of New England. Composed in Three Books* (1637), reprinted in Peter Force (comp.), *Tracts and Other Papers, relating principally to the Origin, Settlement, and Progress of the Colonies in North America from the Discovery of the Country to the Year 1776* (Washington, D.C., 1838), II; and Morison (ed.), *Of Plymouth Plantation*, 204-10, 216-17. For a discussion of Puritan and Pilgrim views of Indian gambling, turn to George Eisen, "Voyageurs, Black-Robes, Saints, and Indians," *Ethnohistory*, 24 (Summer 1977), 195-97, 200. The term "grizzly saints" was coined by Nathaniel Hawthorne in his short story "The May-pole of Merry Mount" (1835) published in

Twice-Told Tales. History has not treated Morton and Ma-re Mount very judiciously. Charles Francis Adams, *Three Episodes of Massachusetts History* (New York, rev. ed., 1965), I: chs. 11-15, relies too heavily and uncritically on saints' accounts, while Richard Drinnon, *Facing West: The Metaphysics of Indian Hating and Empire-Building* (Minneapolis, 1980), chs. 1-3, takes Morton's account too much at face value and does not convincingly explain Puritans' and Pilgrims' motives.

30. NILECJ, *Development of the Law of Gambling*, 38-39; Edwin Powers, *Crime and Punishment in Early Massachusetts 1620-1692: A Documentary History* (Boston, 1966), 63, 170-71, 205-6, 427; Carl Bridenbaugh, *Cities in the Wilderness* (New York, 1971), 78.

31. William Peden (ed.), *Testimony against prophane customs* (1687) (Charlottesville, Va., 1953), 30-35.

32. Massachusetts Bay Colony, "At a Council Held at Boston the 9th. of April, 1677" (Cambridge, Mass., broadside, 1677); NILECJ, *Development of the Law of Gambling*, 39-49.

33. Peden (ed.), *Testimony*, 4-5, 30-35, 47-48; *A Letter to a Gentleman on the Sin and Danger of Playing at Cards and other Games* (Boston, 1755), 5-7; Perry Miller, *The New England Mind: The Seventeenth Century* (Cambridge, Mass., 1954), 15-16.

34. Powers, *Crime and Punishment*, 170; Eisen, "Voyageurs, Black-Robes, Saints, and Indians," 196-97; T. H. Breen, "Horses and Gentlemen: The Cultural Significance of Gambling among the Gentry of Virginia," *William and Mary Quarterly*, 3rd. ser., 34 (April 1977), 242n.

35. J. T. Sable, "Pennsylvania's Blue Laws: A Quaker Experiment in the Suppression of Sport and Amusements, 1682-1740," *Journal of Sport History*, 1 (Spring 1974), 107-21; G. Robert Blakey, "State Conducted Lotteries: History, Problems, and Promises," *Journal of Social Issues*, 35 (Summer 1979), 63-64; Eisen, "Voyageurs, Black-Robes, Saints, and Indians," 198.

36. The contrast between colonies has been mentioned by Philip Alexander Bruce, *Social Life of Virginia in the Seventeenth Century* . . . (Richmond, Va., 1907), 177; John Hervey, *Racing and Breeding in America and the Colonies* (London, 1931), 1-2, 4-6, 11; Breen, "Horses and Gentlemen," 242n.

37. Carson, *Colonial Virginians at Play*, 53, 78n; Louis B. Wright, *The First Gentlemen of Virginia; Intellectual Qualities of the Early Colonial Ruling Class* (San Marino, Calif., 1940), 88.

38. Carson, *Colonial Virginians at Play*, 108-11; William G. Stanard, "Racing in Colonial Virginia," *Virginia Magazine of History and Biography*, 2 (Jan. 1895), 293.

39. Bruce, *Social Life*, 190; Charles M. Andrews, *Colonial Folkways; A Chronicle of American Life in the Reign of the Georges* (New Haven, Conn., 1921), 106-20; Hervey, *Racing and Breeding*, 4; Carson, *Colonial Virginians at Play*, 106-7.

40. Stanard, "Racing in Colonial Virginia," 294; Wright, *First Gentlemen of Virginia*, 88.

41. Bernard Bailyn, "Politics and Social Structure in Virginia," Stanley N. Katz (ed.), *Colonial America: Essays in Politics and Social Development* (Boston, 2nd ed., 1976), 119-43, describes the emergence of an insecure gentry in late seventeenth-century Virginia.

42. Breen, "Horses and Gentlemen," 243-45, 247, 256-57.

43. Bruce, *Social Life*, 209-10; Carson, *Colonial Virginians at Play*, 151-52.

44. Pepys quoted by William Biggs Boulton, *The Amusements of Old London* . . . (London, 1901), II: 173-75, 178. A similarly diverse crowd was depicted by William Hogarth in his mid-eighteenth-century print "The Cockpit," reproduced in Jarrett, *England in the Age of Hogarth*, 175.

45. Andrews, *Colonial Folkways*, 115-16; Carson, *Colonial Virginians at Play*, 152-64; Hunter Dickinson Farish (ed.), *Journal & Letters of Philip Vickers Fithian 1773-1774: A Plantation Tutor of the Old Dominion* (Williamsburg, Va., 1965), 91, 96, 121, 161-62, 186, 190, 200, 201-2, 241; Richard R. Beeman, "Social Change and Cultural Conflict in Virginia; Lunenburg County, 1746 to 1774," *William and Mary Quarterly*, 3rd ser., 35 (July 1978), 458, 466; Richard R. Beeman and Rhys Isaac, "Cultural Conflict and Social Change in the Revolutionary South: Lunenburg County, Virginia," *Journal of Southern History*, 46 (Nov. 1980), 529-30; Winslow C. Watson (ed.), *Men and Times of the Revolution; or, Memoirs of Elkanah Watson* . . . (New York, 1856), 300. Landon Carter also commented on gambling by Anglican pastors; see Jack P. Greene (ed.), *The Diary of Landon Carter of Sabine Hall, 1752-1778* (Charlottesville, Va., 1965), II: 820, 998.

46. Fairfax Harrison, "The Equine F.F.V.'s," *Virginia Magazine of History and Biography*, 35 (Oct. 1927), 334; John Dizikes, *Sportsmen and Gamesmen* (Boston, 1981), 15-21; Stanard, "Racing in Colonial Virginia," 301; Carson, *Colonial Virginians at Play*, 49-53; Breen, "Horses and Gentlemen," 248, 248n. See William Byrd's complaints about the vulgarity of racing in 1709, in Louis B. Wright and Marian Tinling (eds.), *The Secret Diary of William Byrd of Westover 1709-1712* (Richmond, Va., 1941), 75.

47. Hennig Cohen, *The South Carolina Gazette 1732-1775* (Columbia, S.C., 1953), 71-72, 74-75; E. D. Cuming, "Sports and Games," A. S. Turberville (ed.), *Johnson's England: An Account of the Life & Manners of his Age* (Oxford, 1933), I: 373.

48. NILECJ, *Development of the Law of Gambling*, 127-30; Bridenbaugh, *Cities in the Wilderness*, 120; Carl Bridenbaugh, *Cities in Revolt* (New York, 1971), 166-67, 364-65.

49. Stella Margetson, *Leisure and Pleasure in the Eighteenth Century* (London, 1970), 68; Cuming, "Sports and Games," I: 365; Dorothy Marshall, "Manners, Meals, and Domestic Pastimes," Turberville (ed.), *Johnson's England*, I: 354-55.

50. Margetson, *Leisure and Pleasure*, 69-70; James Spershott, *Memoirs of Chichester* (1783), and William Guthrie, *A New Geographical, Historical, and Commercial Grammar* (1787), both cited by M. D. George, *English Social Life in the Eighteenth Century Illustrated from Contemporary Sources* (London, 1923), 110, 115-17; Cuming, "Sports and Games," I: 372; Jarrett, *England in the Age of Hogarth*, 172-76.

51. Jarrett, *England in the Age of Hogarth*, 176, 205; Hartmann (ed.), *Games and Gamesters*, xviii; T. S. Ashton, *An Economic History of England: The 18th Century* (London, 1955), 24-26; John Ashton, *The History of Gambling in England* (London, 1898), 83.

52. Johan Huizinga, *Homo Ludens; A Study of the Play-Element in Culture* (Boston, 1955; orig. pub. 1938), 64-65.

53. Stone, *Crisis of the Aristocracy*, 568, 571.

54. Richard Seymour, *The Court-Gamester: or Full and Easy Instructions for Playing the Games Now in Vogue* . . . (London, 3rd ed., 1722), iii.

55. Daniel Defoe, *A Tour Thro' the whole Island of Great Britain* . . . (London, 1927), I: 75-76.

56. Marshall, "Manners, Meals, and Domestic Pastimes," I: 355; William Biggs Boulton, *In the Days of the Georges* (London, 1909), 237; Robert J. Allen, *The Clubs of Augustan London* (Cambridge, Mass., 1933), 146-47; William Biggs Boulton, *The History of White's* (London, 1892), I: chs. 1-10; Norman Pearsons, *Society Sketches in the Eighteenth Century* (London, 1911), 242, 250-52; Madame van Muyden (trans. and ed.), *A Foreign View of England in the Reigns of George I and George II. The Letters of Monsieur César de Saussure to his Family* (London, 1902), 161-65. Bridenbaugh, *Vexed and Troubled Englishmen*, 362, points to seventeenth-century precedents for gaming in taverns.

57. Dizikes, *Sportsmen and Gamesmen*, 14.

58. NILECJ, *Development of the Law of Gambling*, 15-16, 236-40.

59. Greene (ed.), *Diary of Landon Carter*, I: 320, 352, 522, 580; II: 630, 640, 674, 677, 755-56, 795, 830, 850, 870; Jack P. Greene, *Landon Carter: An Inquiry into the Personal Values and Social Imperatives of the Eighteenth-Century Virginia Gentry* (Charlottesville, Va., 1965), 18-26, 76-77. See also the discussion of William Byrd's half-hearted struggle to gamble more moderately, dramatized in Wright and Tinling (eds.), *Secret Diary of William Byrd*, 442, 516.

60. William Stith, *The Sinfulness and pernicious Nature of Gaming* (Williamsburg, Va., 1752), esp. 20-23.

61. NILECJ, *Development of the Law of Gambling*, 240; Carson, *Colonial Virginians at Play*, 53.

62. Vale, *Gentleman's Recreation*, 136; Ashton, *History of Gambling in England*, 21-22.

63. Ashton, *History of Gambling in England*, 21-22; van Muyden (trans. and ed.), *Foreign View of England*, 161-65; Botsford, *English Society in the Eighteenth Century*, 208-12.

64. Farish (ed.), *Journal & Letters of Philip Fithian*, 108-9; Albert Bushnell Hart (ed.), *Hamilton's Itinerarium; Being a Narrative of a Journey* . . . *from May to September, 1744 By Doctor Alexander Hamilton* (St. Louis, 1907), xvii, xix, 55, 57-58, 218; Bridenbaugh, *Cities in the Wilderness*, 265-74, 426-34; John Ferdinand Dalziel Smyth, *A Tour in the United States of America: Containing An Account of the Present Situation of that Country* . . . (New York, 1968; orig. pub. 1784), I: 49-50. On colonial taverns, consult W. J. Rorabaugh, *The Alcoholic Republic: An American Tradition* (New York, 1979), 27-29, 32-35.

65. Carson, *Colonial Virginians at Play*, 70-71; Herbert Asbury, *Sucker's Progress* (New York, 1938), 155-56.

66. Ezell, *Fortune's Merry Wheel*, 9-11; NILECJ, *Development of the Law of Gambling*, 25-26, 27-28; Ashton, *History of English Lotteries*, chs. 1-5, esp. 49-54, 58-66, 75, 90. The importance of the South Sea Bubble in inhibiting the development of English finance is discussed by John Carswell, *The South-Sea Bubble* (Stanford, Calif., 1960), 270-72.

67. Ezell, *Fortune's Merry Wheel*, 12-14; NILECJ, *Development of the Law of Gambling*, 135-39; Bridenbaugh, *Cities in the Wilderness*, 147, 149, 310, 348-49. See also the following broadsides depicting various kinds of lottery schemes: "Biles-Island Lottery. 1771. The Scheme" (New York, 1771); "Jonas Seely's Christiana-Bridge Land & Cash Lottery . . ." (Wilmington, Del., 1771); William Masters, "Pettie's Island Land and Cash Lottery, To be Drawn on the said Island . . ." (Phil-

adelphia, 1771); "Pettie's-Island Land and Cash Lottery, For Disposing of Sundry Houses and Lots . . ." (Philadelphia, 1772); "Pettie's-Island Lottery, For disposing of a great Variety of curious pictures, Jewellry, &c. &c." (Philadelphia, 1772); "Scheme of a Lottery, For disposing of the following Houses . . ." (New York, 1773).

68. NILECJ, *Development of the Law of Gambling*, 52-54, 241; Ezell, *Fortune's Merry Wheel*, 29.

69. Gary B. Nash, *The Urban Crucible: Social Change, Political Consciousness, and the Origins of the American Revolution* (Cambridge, Mass., 1979), 65, 173, 176, 403; Bridenbaugh, *Cities in Revolt*, 9, 11, 219-21, 252; Russel B. Nye (ed.), *Autobiography and Other Writings by Benjamin Franklin* (Boston, 1958), 102, 104-5.

70. Ezell, *Fortune's Merry Wheel*, 17-18, 19-28.

71. "Pettie's Island Cash Lottery . . . to be applied to . . . a Presbyterian Church . . . , a German Lutheran Church . . . , the Newark Academy . . . " (Philadelphia, broadside, 1772).

72. [David James Dove], *The Lottery. A Dialogue Between Mr. Thomas Trueman and Mr. Humphrey Dupe* (Germantown, Pa., 1758); Ezell, *Fortune's Merry Wheel*, 16-17, 32-36, 53, 55-59; A. Franklin Ross, "The History of Lotteries in New York," *Magazine of History with Notes and Queries*, 5 (Feb.-June 1907), 98-100. See the following broadsides announcing lotteries to benefit such local improvements as churches, schools, docks, new industries, and German immigrants: "A Scheme of a Lottery, For raising the Sum of Three Hundred and Seventy-five Pounds, in order to discharge a debt upon the Methodist PREACHING-HOUSE, in Philadelphia; . . . " (Philadelphia, 1771); New York Christ Church, "The Scheme of Christ-Church Lottery" (New York, 1771); "The Reformed German Church Lottery . . . " (New York, 1772); "Scheme of a Lottery . . . for the Benefit of the Presbyterian C——h . . . " (New York, 1773); [Providence Baptist Society], "Scheme of a Lottery, Granted by the Honourable General Assembly of . . . Rhode Island . . . " (Providence, R.I., 1774); "The Managers of the Delaware Lottery, for the College of New Jersey, &c." (Philadelphia, 1774); "Wind Mill Island Cash Lottery . . . " (Philadelphia, 1774); "Newcastle Lottery, Instituted by the Friends of the American China Manufactory . . . " (Philadelphia, 1771); "Pettie's Island Cash Lottery . . . for . . . improving, planting, inlarging, and properly fencing and securing A Public Vineyard" (Philadelphia, 1773); Pettie's Island Cash Lottery . . . towards the Support of the American Glass Manufactory . . . and the following Charitable Societies . . . " (Philadelphia, 1773); "The German Charitable Society's Lottery . . . " (Philadelphia, 1773).

73. Andrew Skinner (ed.), *The Wealth of Nations, [by] Adam Smith* (Middlesex, Eng., 1980; orig. pub. 1776), 210.

74. Ezell, *Fortune's Merry Wheel*, 37-40, 44-50; NILECJ, *Development of the Law of Gambling*, 665-66.

75. Peter Force (ed.), *American Archives: Fourth Series. Containing a Documentary History of the English Colonies . . . from March 7, 1774, to the Declaration of Independence by the United States* (Washington, D.C., 1837-1846), III: 150; VI: 1463, 1590; Stanard, "Racing in Colonial Virginia," 305; Hervey, *Racing and Breeding*, 14-15. The extensive gaming of Americans during the early Revolutionary era has been noted by Oscar Handlin and Lillian Handlin, *A Restless People: Americans in Rebellion 1770-1787* (Garden City, N.Y., 1982), 99.

76. Ezell, *Fortune's Merry Wheel*, 60-62.

77. Ezell, *Fortune's Merry Wheel*, 62-63; Stephen Longstreet, *Win or Lose: A Social History of Gambling in America* (Indianapolis, 1977), 35-36. The terms of the United States Lottery are described in Peter Force (ed.), *American Archives: Fifth Series. Containing a Documentary History of the United States . . . from . . . July 4, 1776, to . . . September 3, 1783* (Washington, D.C., 1848-1853), III: 1557, 1573-75, 1599; "United States Lottery; 1776" (Philadelphia, broadside, 1776); "U. S. Continental Congress, In Congress, May 2, 1778. Resolved, That the Managers of the Lottery . . . " (Philadelphia?, broadside, 1778); "United States Lottery; The Scheme is, That this Lottery consist of Four Classes . . . " (Philadelphia, broadside, 1778); *A List of the Fortunate Numbers in the First Class of the United States Lottery* (Yorktown, Va., 1778); *A List of the Fortunate Numbers in the Second Class of the United States Lottery* (Philadelphia, 1779); "United States Lottery. The Scheme Is, That this Lottery consist of Four Classes . . . " (Philadelphia, broadside, 1779); *A List of the Fortunate Numbers in the Third Class of the United States Lottery* (Philadelphia, 1780); *A List of the Fortunate Numbers in the Fourth Class of the United States Lottery* (Philadelphia, 1782).

78. Miller, *New England Mind*, 15-16; NILECJ, *Development of the Law of Gambling*, 60-63.

79. Bridenbaugh, *Cities in the Wilderness*, 276; Bridenbaugh, *Cities in Revolt*, 166-67, 364-65. Samuel Sewall remarked that Governor Samuel Shute of Massachusetts attended an organized "Horse-Race" in 1718; M. Halsey Thomas (ed.), *The Diary of Samuel Sewall 1674-1749* (New York, 1973), II: 901. The Virginia scene has been depicted by: Farish (ed.), *Journal and Letters of Philip Fithian*, 72; Beeman, "Social Change and Cultural Conflict in Virginia," 470; Beeman and Isaac, "Cultural Conflict and Social Change in the Revolutionary South," 527, 531, 533.

80. Rhys Isaac, "Evangelical Revolt: The Nature of the Baptists' Challenge to the Traditional Order in Virginia, 1765 to 1775," *William and Mary Quarterly*, 3rd ser., 31 (July 1974), 367-68.

81. Richard J. Hooker (ed.), *The Carolina Backcountry on the Eve of the Revolution: The Journal and Other Writings of Charles Woodmason, Anglican Itinerant* (Chapel Hill, N.C., 1953), 52, 56, 80-81, 98-101, 225-26, 281.

82. Robert Greenhalgh Albion and Leonidas Dodson (eds.), *Philip Vickers Fithian: Journal, 1775-1776 Written on the Virginia-Pennsylvania Frontier and in the Army Around New York* (Princeton, N.J., 1934), 158, 110.

83. Barbara Miller Solomon (ed.), *Travels in New England and New York, By Timothy Dwight* (Cambridge, Mass., 1969), III: 118-19; Thomas Ashe, *Travels in America, Performed in the Year 1806 . . .* (London, 1809), 84-87, 171. Ray Allen Billington, *Land of Savagery/Land of Promise: The European Image of the American Frontier* (New York, 1981), 76, 271, warns against accepting accounts of "eye-gouging" fights at face value.

84. Mrs. William Bayle Bernard, Laurance Hutton, and Brander Matthews (eds.), *Retrospections of America, 1797-1811, by John Bernard* (New York, 1887), 155. I have been unable to locate Mrs. Bernard's given name; she was John Bernard's daughter-in-law.

85. Wayne Gard, "Racing on the Frontier," *Quarter Horse Journal*, 7 (April 1955), 62.

86. Robert Moorman Denhardt (comp.), *The Quarter Horse . . .* (Fort Worth, 1941), 119, 143-44, 160-63.

87. Bernard, Hutton, and Matthews (eds.), *Retrospections of America,* 155-56; Thomas Anburey, *Travels Through the Interior Parts of America* (Boston, 1923; orig. pub. 1789), II: 227-28; Smyth, *Tour in the United States of America,* I: 22-23; John Spencer Bassett and J. Franklin Jameson (eds.), *Correspondence of Andrew Jackson* (Washington, D.C., 1926-1935), I: 111n; Harrison, "Equine F.F.V.'s," 367n.

88. Bernard, Hutton, and Matthews (eds.), *Retrospections of America,* 155-56.

89. Longstreet, *Win or Lose,* 31-32.

90. James Parton, *Life of Andrew Jackson* (Boston, 1886), III: 695; Robert V. Remini, *Andrew Jackson and the Course of American Empire, 1767-1821* (New York, 1977), 9.

91. Bassett and Jameson (eds.), *Correspondence,* I: vi, viii, 111-12, 112n; Marquis James, *The Life of Andrew Jackson, Complete in One Volume* (Indianapolis, 1938), *passim,* esp. 18, 33-34, 98, 100, 597; Barbara Stern Kupfer, "A Presidential Patron of the Sport of Kings: Andrew Jackson," *Tennessee Historical Quarterly,* 29 (Fall 1970), 246, 247-54; Remini, *Jackson and the Course of American Empire,* 12-13, 27-30, 37-38, 134; Harriet Chappell Owsley, "Discoveries Made in Editing The Papers of Andrew Jackson," *Manuscripts,* 27 (Fall 1975), 278-79. On the lottery Jackson proposed in 1826 for Cumberland College, turn to Bassett and Jameson (eds.), *Correspondence,* III: 303-4.

92. The duel is covered by Remini, *Jackson and the Course of American Empire,* 136-43.

93. The citation from the General's letter to his nephew can be found in Bassett and Jameson (eds.), *Correspondence,* IV: 475.

94. Bassett and Jameson (eds.), *Correspondence,* III: 267; James, *Life of Jackson,* 469; John William Ward, *Andrew Jackson: Symbol for an Age* (New York, 1974; orig. pub. 1955), 175-77; Dizikes, *Sportsmen and Gamesmen,* 28.

95. The shifting nature of lotteries is described by Ezell, *Fortune's Merry Wheel,* ch. 5; NILECJ, *Development of the Law of Gambling,* 74-88. The role played by lotteries in the United States economy before the Civil War has been taken up by Ezell, *Fortune's Merry Wheel,* 69, ch. 7; George Rogers Taylor, *The Transportation Revolution 1815-1860* (New York, 1951), 51-52, 89-90; Asbury, *Sucker's Progress,* 76-77; Stuart Bruchey, *The Roots of American Economic Growth 1607-1861; An Essay in Social Causation* (New York, 1968), 144-45. Barnum's career can be traced in George S. Bryan (ed.), *Struggles and Triumphs: or, The Life of P. T. Barnum, Written by Himself* (New York, 1927; orig. pub. 1855, 1869, 1889), I: 44-48, 52-54, 84-85, 87.

96. *Report of a Committee Appointed to Investigate the Evils of Lotteries, in the Commonwealth of Pennsylvania, and to suggest a Remedy for the Same* (Philadelphia, 1831).

97. [Thomas Man], *Picture of a Factory Village, to which are annexed, remarks on Lotteries. By Sui Generis: alias Thomas Man* (Providence, R.I., 1833), 134-35; Thomas Doyle, *Five Years in a Lottery Office; or an Exposition of the Lottery System in the United States* (Boston, 1841), 16; John H. Stiness, *A Century of Lotteries in Rhode Island. 1744-1844* (Providence, R.I., 1896), vii-ix.

98. Henrietta M. Larson, "S. & M. Allen—Lottery, Exchange, and Stock Brokerage," *Journal of Economic and Business History,* 3 (May 1931), 424-25; Taylor, *Transportation Revolution,* 320-21.

99. Doyle, *Five Years in a Lottery Office*, 9-11, 35, 51-52; Ezell, *Fortune's Merry Wheel*, chs. 10, 11.

100. [Man], *Picture of a Factory Village*, 119, 136-37, 127, 129.

101. Bassett and Jameson (eds.), *Correspondence*, V: 430.

102. NILECJ, *Development of the Law of Gambling*, 259-61; [Job R. Tyson], *A Brief Survey of the Great Extent and Evil Tendencies of the Lottery System* . . . (Philadelphia, 1833), 8-9, 16-25, 28; Taylor, *Transportation Revolution*, 263; Marvin Meyers, *The Jacksonian Persuasion: Politics and Belief* (Stanford, Calif., 1960; orig. pub. 1957), 22, 30, 173-76. In his *Brief Survey*, 7-8, Tyson made the typical comment that the lottery derived from aristocratic England, not American "soil."

Chapter 2

1. William C. Hall's story was related under the pseudonym of "Yazoo" as "Reminiscences of Natchez 'Under-the-Hill.' 'My Grandmother's Trick,'" *The Spirit of the Times; A Chronicle of the Turf, Agriculture, Field Sports, Literature and the Stage*, 13 (Dec. 11, 1843), 523, and conveniently reprinted in John Francis McDermott (ed.), *Before Mark Twain: A Sampler of Old, Old Times on the Mississippi* (Carbondale, Ill., 1968), 196-99. My recapitulation of the incident relies upon additional contemporary remarks on Natchez-under-the-Hill, taken from: the 1820 account of John James Audubon, reprinted in Wright Morris (ed.), *Mississippi River Reader* (Garden City, N.Y., 1962), 51; C. Hartley Grattan (ed.), *Recollections of the Last Ten Years, By Timothy Flint* (New York, 1932; orig. pub. 1826), 284-85; [Charles Sealsfield], *The Americans as They Are; Described in a Tour Through the Valley of the Mississippi* . . . (London, 1828), 121-22; James Edward Alexander, *Transatlantic Sketches, Comprising Visits to the Most Interesting Scenes in North and South America* . . . (London, 1833), II: 61-62; [Joseph Holt Ingraham], *The South-West. By a Yankee* (New York, 1835), II: 19-20, 54. For a glimpse of the landing in 1817, turn to the sketch by Edouard de Montulé, reprinted in D. Clayton James, *Antebellum Natchez* (Baton Rouge, La., 1968), 178-79.

2. [Robert Baird], *View of the Valley of the Mississippi* . . . (Philadelphia, 1834), 103.

3. Cyril Hughes Hartmann (ed.), *Games and Gamesters of the Restoration* (London, 1930), 4.

4. This picture of gambling comes from accounts written by retired or reformed gamblers, including Robert Bailey, *The Life and Adventures of Robert Bailey* (Richmond, Va., 1822); Jonathan Green, *Gambling Unmasked!* (New York, 1844); Jonathan H. Green, *An Exposure of the Arts and Miseries of Gambling* (Philadelphia, 5th rev. ed., 1847); [John O'Connor], *Wanderings of a Vagabond. An Autobiography. Edited by John Morris* (New York, 1873); George H. Devol, *Forty Years a Gambler on the Mississippi* (Austin, Tex., 1967; orig. pub. 1887); John Philip Quinn, *Fools of Fortune* (Chicago, 1892).

5. [O'Connor], *Wanderings of a Vagabond*, 430; John Dizikes, *Sportsmen and Gamesmen* (Boston, 1981), 294-97.

6. Bailey, *Life and Adventures*, 66-67; Edwin Adams Davis and William Ransom Hogan, *The Barber of Natchez: Wherein a Slave is Freed and Rises to a very High Standing* . . . (Baton Rouge, La., 1954), 206; U. S. Department of Justice, Law

Enforcement Assistance Administration, National Institute of Law Enforcement and Criminal Justice (hereafter cited as NILECJ), *The Development of the Law of Gambling: 1776-1976* (Washington, D.C., 1977), 255-56.

7. Dizikes, *Sportsmen and Gamesmen*, 60-61. The popular literature depicting the southwestern trickster or river confidence man included [Johnson Jones Hooper], *Some Adventures of Captain Simon Suggs* (Philadelphia, 1845), and a variety of short stories published in the *Spirit of the Times*, the paper that printed William C. Hall's vignette. For a sample, see William T. Porter (comp.), *Major Thorpe's Scenes in Arkansaw . . .* (Philadelphia, 1858).

8. Marvin Meyers, *The Jacksonian Persuasion: Politics and Belief* (Stanford, Calif., 1960; orig. pub. 1957), 12.

9. Meyers, *Jacksonian Persuasion*, 173-75.

10. Charles Caldwell, *An Address on the Vice of Gambling; Delivered to the Medical Pupils of Transylvania University; November 4, 1834* (Lexington, Ky., 1834).

11. Frederick Marryat, *Second Series of a Diary in America* (Philadelphia, 1840), 88, 142; *Niles' Weekly Register*, 48 (Aug. 8, 1835), 401.

12. [Thomas Hamilton], *Men and Manners in America. By the Author of* Cyril Thornton (Edinburgh, 1833), II: 189-90; Marryat, *Second Series of a Diary in America*, 141. Ray Allen Billington, *Land of Savagery/Land of Promise; The European Image of the American Frontier in the Nineteenth Century* (New York, 1981), 269-72, advises one to discount European evaluations of frontier life.

13. Phillips Bradley (ed.), *Democracy in America By Alexis de Tocqueville* (New York, Vintage Books ed., orig. pub. 1945), I: 305; II: 165, 248-49.

14. Meyer Barash (trans.), *Man, Play, and Games by Roger Caillois* (New York, 1979; orig. pub. 1958), 19, 74-75.

15. Barbara Miller Solomon (ed.), *Travels in New England and New York, By Timothy Dwight* (Cambridge, Mass., 1969), IV: 186; Marryat, *Second Series of a Diary in America*, 141-42.

16. On Southerners' and Westerners' love for gambling, turn to Grattan (ed.), *Recollections*, 62, 324; Frederick Law Olmsted, *A Journey Through Texas; or, a Saddle-Trip on the Southwestern Frontier . . .* (New York, 1857), 39. For a discussion of New Orleans as the "fountain-head" of American gambling, see Herbert Asbury, *Sucker's Progress* (New York, 1938), 109-17. David R. Johnson, "A Sinful Business: The Origins of Gambling Syndicates in the United States, 1840-1887," David H. Bayley (ed.), *Police and Society* (Beverly Hills, Calif., 1977), 18-19, discusses the impact of European traditions.

17. Southerners' identification with English gentlemen is discussed by William J. Cooper, Jr. (ed.), *Social Relations in Our Southern States, by Daniel R. Hundley* (Baton Rouge, La., 1979; orig. pub. 1860), 27; Clement Eaton, *A History of the Old South* (New York, 2nd ed., 1966), 68, 82-83, 389.

18. See the examination of horse racing in Edwin A. Davis (ed.), *Plantation Life in the Florida Parishes of Louisiana, 1836-1846 as Reflected in the Diary of Bennet H. Barrow* (New York, 1967), 57-60.

19. Dizikes, *Sportsmen and Gamesmen*, 123-29.

20. On Southerners' "pessimism" and the duel, turn to Dickson D. Bruce, Jr., *Violence and Culture in the Antebellum South* (Austin, Tex., 1979), intro., ch. 1.

21. Frank Lawrence Owsley, "Patterns of Migration and Settlement on the Southern Frontier" (1945), in Harriet Chappell Owsley (ed.), *The South: Old and New*

Frontiers; Selected Essays of Frank Lawrence Owsley (Athens, Ga., 1969), 9. W. J. Cash, *The Mind of the South* (New York, 1941), argued that frontier conditions characterized much of the South. The issue of the South as perpetual frontier has been clarified by James Oakes, *The Ruling Race, A History of American Slaveholders* (New York, 1982), ch. 3.

22. The stories of [Hooper], *Simon Suggs*, and the reminiscences of Joseph Glover Baldwin, *The Flush Times of Alabama and Mississippi. A Series of Sketches* (New York, 1835), suggest that the "inner frontier" had its own abundant western gambling.

23. Gerald M. Capers, Jr., *The Biography of a River Town; Memphis: Its Heroic Age* (Chapel Hill, N.C., 1939), uses the dialectic of West and South in explaining the development of antebellum Memphis. My understanding of the development of southwestern towns has been informed by Richard Wade, *The Urban Frontier; The Rise of Western Cities, 1790-1830* (Cambridge, Mass., 1959).

24. Thomas P. Abernethy, *The South in the New Nation 1789-1819* (Baton Rouge, La., 1961), chs. 4, 6.

25. James, *Antebellum Natchez*, 43-44; Abernethy, *South in the New Nation*, 150-51.

26. Leland D. Baldwin, *The Keelboat Age on Western Waters* (Pittsburgh, 1941), 102; Louis C. Hunter, *Steamboats on the Western Rivers: An Economic and Technological History* (Cambridge, Mass., 1949), 420-21; Richard A. Bartlett, *The New Country: A Social History of the American Frontier, 1776-1890* (New York, 1974), 308; Capers, *Biography of a River Town*, 95; Grattan (ed.), *Recollections*, 89-90.

27. On the myth and the reality of boatmen's lives, see T. B. Thorpe, "Remembrances of the Mississippi," *Harper's New Monthly Magazine*, 12 (Dec. 1855), 29-31; [Samuel Clemens], *Life on the Mississippi, By Mark Twain* (New York, 1979; orig. pub. 1883), 10-21; John Habermehl, *Life on the Western Rivers* (Pittsburgh, 1901), 11-13.

28. Grattan (ed.), *Recollections*, 16-18, 100-102.

29. Perry T. Rathbone (ed.), *Mississippi Panorama* (St. Louis, 1950), frontispiece, 60; Thorpe, "Remembrances," 38; Virginia Park Matthias, "Natchez-Under-the-Hill as It Developed Under the Influence of the Mississippi River and the Natchez Trace," *Journal of Mississippi History*, 7 (Oct. 1945), 203.

30. See: the 1810 account of Christian Schultz, reprinted in McDermott (ed.), *Before Mark Twain*, 13-19; John Bradbury, *Travels in the Interior of America, in the Years 1809, 1810, and 1811 . . .* (Liverpool, 1817), 208; the 1847 account of Charles Ross, reprinted in B. A. Botkin (ed.), *A Treasury of Mississippi River Folklore* (New York, 1955), 218-21; Thorpe, "Remembrances," 30-31.

31. Robert V. Remini, *Andrew Jackson and the Course of American Empire, 1767-1821* (New York, 1977), 396, ch. 19.

32. The Great Migration is discussed by Malcolm J. Rohrbough, *The Trans-Appalachian Frontier; People, Societies, and Institutions 1775-1850* (New York, 1978), 192-97, 207, 301, 310; Abernethy, *South in the New Nation*, ch. 16; Owsley, "Patterns of Migration and Settlement," 4, 6-7, 16-19; [Baird], *View of the Valley*, 100-101; Ray Allen Billington, *Westward Expansion: A History of the American Frontier* (New York, 4th ed., 1974), 393. Travelers who noted the lack of

settlement adjacent to the rivers included Donald McDonald and Thomas Hamilton in McDermott (ed.), *Before Mark Twain*, 42, 49, 51, 54, 57; and Herbert Van Thal (ed.), *Domestic Manners of the Americans by Frances Trollope* (London, 1974; orig. pub. 1832), 38, 47.

33. Grattan (ed.), *Recollections*, 259-60; G. W. Featherstonhaugh, *Excursion Through the Slave States* (London, 1844), II: 42-43, 60; Rohrbough, *Trans-Appalachian Frontier*, ch. 11.

34. Rohrbough, *Trans-Appalachian Frontier*, 198, 403.

35. Rohrbough, *Trans-Appalachian Frontier*, 107, 118-19; Rathbone (ed.), *Mississippi Panorama*, 120-21.

36. Davis and Hogan, *Barber of Natchez*, 11; James, *Antebellum Natchez*, 34-37, 137, 169, 194; Eaton, *History of the Old South*, 129.

37. Harriet Martineau, *Retrospect of Western Travel* (London, 1838), II: 20, 23; Grattan (ed.), *Recollections*, 96, 171-73.

38. John William Ward (ed.), *Society, Manners, and Politics in the United States: Letters on North America by Michel Chevalier* (Gloucester, Mass., 1967; orig. written 1835), 217; [Baird], *View of the Valley*, 342-43; Charles Augustus Murray, *Travels in North America, including a Summer Residence with the Pawnee Tribe of Indians* . . . (London, 1854), II: 114. See also the essay by Philip D. Jordan, "The Mississippi—Spillway of Sin," in Jordan, *Frontier Law and Order: Ten Essays* (Lincoln, Neb., 1970), 23-37.

39. Ward (ed.), *Society, Manners, and Politics*, 216.

40. The quotation comes from Grattan (ed.), *Recollections*, 62, 71.

41. Johnson, "Sinful Business," 19. See also the 1832 account of Englishman Charles Joseph Latrobe, a steamboat passenger, in McDermott (ed.), *Before Mark Twain*, 35, which documents river travelers' preoccupation with money.

42. [Baird], *View of the Valley*, 345n; Green, *Exposure*, 65.

43. McDermott (ed.), *Before Mark Twain*, 60-61, 68-69. Cowell witnessed "a trip down the river" in 1829.

44. Grattan (ed.), *Recollections*, 297-98; Lester B. Shippee (ed.), *Bishop Whipple's Southern Diary 1843-1844* (Minneapolis, 1937), 101; W. Adolphe Roberts, *Lake Pontchartrain* (Indianapolis, 1946), 141-42.

45. J. S. Buckingham, *The Slave States of America* (London, 1842), I: 350. John Harkins, city archivist of Memphis, suggested to me the importance of the pestilential conditions along the river in the early nineteenth century.

46. John Davis (trans.), *Travels in Louisiana and The Floridas, in the Year 1802, Giving a Correct Picture of Those Countries* [By Berquin-Duvallon] (New York, 1806), 53-54; Christian Schultz, *Travels on an Inland Voyage* . . . *in the Years 1807 and 1808* . . . (New York, 1810), II: 196-97; Shippee (ed.), *Bishop Whipple's Southern Diary*, 100; W. Aitken, *A Journey up the Mississippi River, From Its Mouth to Nauvoo, the City of the Latter Day Saints* (Ashton-Under-Lyne, Eng., 1845), 7.

47. *Louisiana Gazette*, Jan. 22, 1805, June 10, 1806, Oct. 19, 1815; Asbury, *Sucker's Progress*, 109-10.

48. Antebellum observers of New Orleans gambling included Bailey, *Life and Adventures*, 192-211; Alexander, *Transatlantic Sketches*, II: 31; Buckingham, *Slave States*, I: 351. For historical accounts, turn to the New Orleans *Daily Picayune*, Aug. 20, 1882; Quinn, *Fools of Fortune*, 458-59; Asbury, *Sucker's Progress*,

110-13, 115-19; Lura Robinson, *It's an Old New Orleans Custom* (New York, 1948), 104-5, 111.

49. Asbury, *Sucker's Progress*, 20, 44-47, 51, 55, 109; Johnson, "Sinful Business," 19; Dizikes, *Sportsmen and Gamesmen*, 294; New Orleans *Times Picayune*, Sept. 22, 1957; R. E. Banta, "Gambling on the River," *American Heritage*, 2nd ser., 4 (Summer 1953), 22. Timothy Flint termed New Orleans "the modern Sodom" in 1826; see Grattan (ed.), *Recollections*, 297.

50. New Orleans *Daily Picayune*, Aug. 20, 1882; Johnson, "Sinful Business," 21, 23, 24; Asbury, *Sucker's Progress*, 112-14. In the mid-1830s Joseph Holt Ingraham visited in New Orleans "one of the far-famed temples which the goddess of fortune has erected in this, her favourite city." His description makes the hall sound like John Davis's club. See [Ingraham], *South-West*, I: 126-35.

51. [Ingraham], *South-West*, I: 129-30.

52. Quinn, *Fools of Fortune*, 455-56.

53. The term comes from [Clemens], *Life on the Mississippi*, 191.

54. Asbury, *Sucker's Progress*, 213-14. For a description of the prevalence of gamblers in Louisville, Kentucky, turn to Green, *Gambling Unmasked*, 33-35.

55. The "civilizing" process was discussed by Frederick Marryat, *A Diary in America, with Remarks on its Institutions* (Philadelphia, 1839), II: 196-201; James Hall, *The Romance of Western History: or, Sketches of History, Life, and Manners, in the West* (Cincinnati, 1857), 242-44; Rohrbough, *Trans-Appalachian Frontier*, 398-99.

56. [Ingraham], *South-West*, II: 20; Capers, *Biography of a River Town*, 50, 69-70; article in the *Natchez Courier*, reprinted in the *Vicksburg Register*, July 30, 1835.

57. Bruce, *Violence and Culture*, 12, 17.

58. J. S. Buckingham, *The Eastern and Western States of America* (London, 1842), III: 10; Marryat, *Second Series of a Diary in America*, 88n; account by (?) Falconbridge, *Dan. Marble; A Biographical Sketch of that Famous and Diverting Humorist, with Reminiscences, Comicalities, Anecdotes, Etc., Etc.* (New York, 1851), reprinted in Botkin (ed.), *Treasury of Mississippi River Folklore*, 222; Capers, *Biography of a River Town*, 50.

59. Marryat, *Second Series of a Diary in America*, 97-98; Rohrbough, *Trans-Appalachian Frontier*, 289-90; Asbury, *Sucker's Progress*, 226-27; *Niles' Weekly Register*, 48 (Aug. 8, 22, 1835), 401, 440.

60. On changing attitudes toward slavery in Memphis, see Capers, *Biography of a River Town*, 52-53, 56, 68, 80, 102, 110.

61. For a discussion of different outlooks on violence among planters and frontier townspeople, consult Bruce, *Violence and Culture*, 89-94, 98, 102, 109-12.

62. Preston E. James, "Vicksburg: A Study in Urban Geography" (1931), George A. Theodorson (ed.), *Urban Patterns: Studies in Human Ecology* (University Park, Pa., rev. ed., 1982), 62; Herbert A. Kellar (ed.), "A Journey Through the South in 1836: Diary of James D. Davidson," *Journal of Southern History*, 1 (Aug. 1935), 356; Martineau, *Retrospect*, II: 17.

63. Letter from Reverend Richard Wynkoop, Vicksburg, Miss., Oct. 1, 1836, reprinted in Vicksburg *Daily Herald*, Dec. 27, 1912, cited hereafter as Wynkoop letter, Oct. 1, 1836.

64. Kellar (ed.), "Journey Through the South," 355.

65. [O'Connor], *Wanderings of a Vagabond*, 340-41; James, *Antebellum Natchez*, 190; John F. Stover, *History of the Illinois Central Railroad* (New York, 1975), 294.

66. [O'Connor], *Wanderings of a Vagabond*, 248, 341; James, "Vicksburg," 61; Falconbridge, *Dan. Marble*, reprinted in Botkin (ed.), *Treasury of Mississippi River Folklore*, 222; H. S. Fulkerson, *Random Recollections of Early Days in Mississippi* (Baton Rouge, La., 1937), 95; Henry S. Foote, *Casket of Reminiscences* (Washington, D.C., 1874), 252.

67. Fulkerson, *Random Recollections*, 95; Featherstonhaugh, *Excursion*, II: 247; Asbury, *Sucker's Progress*, 218-19. For an example of leading citizens consorting with professional gamblers in Arkansas Territory during 1829, turn to Philip D. Jordan, "Lady Luck and Her Knights of the Royal Flush," *Southwestern Historical Quarterly*, 72 (Jan. 1969), 299.

68. L. S. Houghton to Henry Bosworth, Vicksburg, Miss., July 10, 1835 (transcribed copy of letter in Old Courthouse Museum, Vicksburg, Miss.).

69. James Lal Penick, Jr., *The Great Western Land Pirate: John A. Murrell in Legend and History* (Columbia, Mo., 1981), the best discussion of Murrell and the Clan, explains how a petty outlaw was inflated into a fictional monster. Some authors, including Robert M. Coates, *The Outlaw Years: The History of the Land Pirates of the Natchez Trace* (Detroit, 1974; orig. pub. 1930), 276-78; Asbury, *Sucker's Progress*, 214-19; and Matthias, "Natchez-Under-the Hill," 218-20, take the Murrell conspiracy at face value and view it as the cause of all vigilantism in Mississippi in 1835. More persuasive writers, including Martineau, *Retrospect*, II: 17-18; Capers, *Biography of a River Town*, 68; Foote, *Casket of Reminiscences*, 250-51; and Edwin A. Miles, "The Mississippi Slave Insurrection Scare of 1835," *Journal of Negro History*, 42 (Jan. 1957), 55-56, discount reports of the conspiracy scheme but admit that it provoked Southerners to react violently. Articles in Dixie newspapers demonstrated that Southerners believed that abolitionist mailings fueled slave rebellion. See: *Niles' Weekly Register*, 48 (Aug. 8, 22, 1835), 402-4, 439-44; and Miles, "Mississippi Slave Insurrection Scare," 48, 56. The abolitionists' campaign and Southerners' violent response have been discussed by Leonard L. Richards, *"Gentlemen of Property and Standing": Anti-Abolition Mobs in Jacksonian America* (New York, 1970), 51-62, 71-74; John Hope Franklin, *The Militant South* (Cambridge, Mass., 1956), 87-88; Clement Eaton, *The Freedom-of-Thought Struggle in the Old South* (New York, 1964), 197-99; Richard Maxwell Brown, *Strain of Violence: Historical Studies of American Violence and Vigilantism* (New York, 1975), 99-100, 305, 306, 312.

70. On the lynchings in central Mississippi during the summer of 1835, consult Penick, *Great Western Land Pirate*, ch. 5; Miles, "Mississippi Slave Insurrection Scare," 49-54; Franklin, *Militant South*, 88. Bruce, *Violence and Culture*, 15, 131, analyzes southern responses to suspected slave revolts.

71. This portrayal of events in Vicksburg, including the direct quotations, comes from the *Vicksburg Register*, July 9, 1835, an account that was reprinted in *Niles' Weekly Register*, 48 (Aug. 1, 1835), 381-82, as well as in abridged form in Richard Hofstadter and Michael Wallace (eds.), *American Violence: A Documentary History* (New York, 1971), 450-53. Another important and accurate source was Houghton to Bosworth, July 10, 1835. L. S. Houghton believed that the gamblers' defiance was related to the slave conspiracy, while the *Vicksburg Register* did not mention the slave insurrection and focused solely on the problem of the gamblers.

Asbury, *Sucker's Progress*, esp. 212-29, contains much color but is less reliable. Ann Vincent Fabian, "Rascals and Gentlemen: The Meaning of American Gambling, 1820-1890" (Ph.D. diss., Yale University, 1982), 281-300, reviews various responses to the lynchings in Vicksburg.

72. *Vicksburg Register,* July 9, 1835; Bruce, *Violence and Culture,* 82-83.

73. Foote, *Casket of Reminiscences,* 252-53; *Vicksburg Register,* July 9, 1835.

74. *Vicksburg Register,* July 9, 1835. The haste with which the mob dispatched its captives obscured the identities of the victims. Featherstonhaugh, *Excursion,* II: 143-45, 237-55, claimed that one of the doomed gamblers was a New Englander named Smith, a man recognizable by his "pale dough face, every feature of which was a proclamation of bully, sneak, and scoundrel." Other sources suspected that the vigilantes hanged the wrong men; see Wynkoop letter, Oct. 1, 1836; Martineau, *Retrospect,* II: 17-18; [O'Connor], *Wanderings of a Vagabond,* 340-45.

75. *Vicksburg Register,* July 9, 1835; Houghton to Bosworth, July 10, 1835; *Vicksburg Evening Post,* Nov. 4, 1979. The passage from Houghton's letter has been improved from a rough transcription of the original document.

76. *Vicksburg Register,* July 9, 1835. See also: Foote, *Casket of Reminiscences,* 252-53; Falconbridge, *Dan. Marble,* reprinted in Botkin (ed.), *Treasury of Mississippi River Folklore,* 222-23.

77. *Niles' Weekly Register,* 48 (Aug. 1, 22, 1835), 377, 440; Charles Augustus Murray, *Travels in North America During the Years 1834, 1835, & 1836* . . . (London, 1839), II: 107-109; Martineau, *Retrospect,* II: 17-18. On lynching as a "confession" of a community's "past sin," see Earl Pomeroy (ed.), *California . . . by Joisah Royce* (Santa Barbara, 1970; orig. pub. 1886), 332.

78. Marryat, *Second Series of a Diary in America,* 97-98; *Niles' Weekly Register,* 48 (Aug. 1, 22, 1835), 401, 440; Asbury, *Sucker's Progress,* 117, 225-26; Jordan, "Lady Luck," 307-310; Rohrbough, *Trans-Appalachian Frontier,* 289-90. On reforms in Natchez, consult Davis and Hogan, *Barber of Natchez,* 10, 148-49; Murray, *Travels in North America During the Years 1834* . . ., II: 176-77; the account of J. H. Freligh, reprinted in McDermott (ed.), *Before Mark Twain,* 159-60; Matthias, "Natchez-Under-the-Hill," 220-21. On Memphians' actions, turn to Capers, *Biography of a River Town,* 50, 62-64, 69, 72-74; James Phelan, *History of Tennessee: The Making of a State* (Boston, 1888), 354-55. Vicksburg had its "flatboat war," too, according to Fulkerson, *Random Recollections,* 97-99.

79. City records suggest that Memphians worried about gambling among slaves, primarily, during the 1850s, and seemed not to enforce antigambling statutes against whites unless those whites played with blacks. See the Minutes of the Memphis Mayor and Board of Aldermen, City Hall, March 27, 1850 (MS, Memphis/Shelby County Archives, Memphis, Tenn.); Memphis Recorder's Docket, 1857-1858 (MS, Memphis/Shelby County Archives, Memphis, Tenn.). For further discussion of laws against gambling by slaves, see NILECJ, *Development of the Law of Gambling,* 257-58; Roger A. Fischer, "Racial Segregation in Ante Bellum New Orleans," *American Historical Review,* 74 (Feb. 1969), 934-36.

80. Foote, *Casket of Reminiscences,* 186; Bruce, *Violence and Culture,* 70, ch. 1.

81. On the permissive and lawless atmosphere on board steamboats, see Habermehl, *Life on the Western Rivers,* 45; Herbert Quick and Edward Quick, *Mississippi Steamboatin'; A History of Steamboating on the Mississippi and its Tribu-*

taries (New York, 1926), 240; Editors of Time-Life Books, *The Old West: The Gamblers* (Alexandria, Va., 1978), 55.

82. *Niles' Weekly Register*, 48 (Aug. 8, 1835), 401.

83. Ward (ed.), *Society, Manners, and Politics*, 206, 212-13; Timothy Flint, *A Condensed Geography and History of the Western States, or the Mississippi Valley* (Cincinnati, 1828), excerpted in McDermott (ed.), *Before Mark Twain*, 9-11; [Baird], *View of the Valley*, 342-43; Van Thal (ed.), *Domestic Manners*, 35-36; Martineau, *Retrospect*, II: 7, 10-11.

84. On the dull scenery, see W. Robert Nitske and Savoie Lottinville (trans. and eds.), *Travels in North America 1822-1824, by Paul Wilhelm, Duke of Wurttemberg* (Norman, Okla., 1973), 86, 88; Van Thal (ed.), *Domestic Manners*, 37, 38, 40, 47; Ward (ed.), *Society, Manners, and Politics*, 212-13; [O'Connor], *Wanderings of a Vagabond*, 413. The phrase "floating palaces" comes from Thorpe, "Remembrances," 33, although it was surely used before then.

85. Hunter, *Steamboats on the Western Rivers*, 69, 390-97; Lyle Saxon, Edward Dreyer, and Robert Tallant (comps.), *Gumbo Ya-Ya: A Collection of Louisiana Folk Tales* (Boston, 1945), 379.

86. Hunter, *Steamboats on the Western Rivers*, 390-91.

87. Hunter, *Steamboats on the Western Rivers*, 409-410; [O'Connor], *Wanderings of a Vagabond*, 433-34; and James Stuart, *Three Years in North America* (Edinburgh, 1833), II: 295, suggest that gambling was more modest aboard riverboats than legends claim. Works such as Devol, *Forty Years a Gambler*, have exaggerated the size and extent of betting.

88. Arnold Schrier and Joyce Story (trans. and eds.), *A Russian Looks at America: The Journey of Aleksandr Borisovich Lakier in 1857* (Chicago, 1979), 191-92, 222, 226. Other observers who corroborated Lakier's general view of riverboat gambling included Charles Joseph Latrobe, Joseph L. Cowell, and Donald McDonald, excerpted in McDermott (ed.), *Before Mark Twain*, 34, 44, 65; [Baird], *View of the Valley*, 343-45; Thomas Hamilton, *Men and Manners in America [1833] With additions from the edition of 1843* (New York, 1968), 174-75; Murray, *Travels in North America, including a Summer Residence with the Pawnee*, II: 114-15; Featherstonhaugh, *Excursion*, II: 239-45; Robert A. Hereford, *Old Man River. The Memories of Captain Louis Rosché, Pioneer Steamboatman* (Caldwell, Ida., 1943), 119; Quinn, *Fools of Fortune*, 461.

89. Asbury, *Sucker's Progress*, 203, 229-30; Neill O'Rourke, "Mississippi River Gambler," *New Orleans Post Record*, 2 (May 1944), 25; William Gilmore Simms, "The Last Wager, or the Gamester of the Mississippi," *The Wigwam and the Cabin* (Chicago, 1890; orig. pub. 1846), 71-119; Rathbone (ed.), *Mississippi Panorama*, 24; Memphis *Commercial Appeal*, Feb. 18, March 10, June 9, 16, 1940. In 1873 John O'Connor warned against romanticizing gamblers in *Wanderings of a Vagabond*, 432-33.

90. Louis Fitzgerald Tasistro, *Random Shots and Southern Breezes . . .* (New York, 1842), II: 29-30, and Simms, "Last Wager," 93, discussed gamblers' jewelry. On their politeness, see the vignette of Jonathan H. Green, *Exposure*, 65-68.

91. George Byron Merrick, *Old Times on the Upper Mississippi; The Recollections of a Steamboat Pilot from 1854 to 1863* (Cleveland, 1909), 139; Irvin Anthony, *Paddle Wheels and Pistols* (Philadelphia, 1929), 261-62; [O'Connor], *Wanderings of a Vagabond*, 430-31.

92. Cowell's story was reprinted in McDermott (ed.), *Before Mark Twain*, 66-68. Other incidents of teamwork were mentioned by Green, *Exposure*, 68; [O'Connor], *Wanderings of a Vagabond*, 423; Merrick, *Old Times*, 139; Anthony, *Paddle Wheels*, 261-62; Asbury, *Sucker's Progress*, 205; Hunter, *Steamboats on the Western Rivers*, 409; Devol, *Forty Years a Gambler, passim*.

93. Asbury, *Sucker's Progress*, 205; Johnson, "Sinful Business," 19; [O'Connor], *Wanderings of a Vagabond*, 430-31.

94. [O'Connor], *Wanderings of a Vagabond*, 423; Hunter, *Steamboats on the Western Rivers*, 408-9.

95. [O'Connor], *Wanderings of a Vagabond*, 434; Hunter, *Steamboats on the Western Rivers*, chs. 12, 14; Asbury, *Sucker's Progress*, 123, 159, 185.

96. Johnson, "Sinful Business," 18-19; Asbury, *Sucker's Progress*, 123, 159, 185.

97. J. S. Holliday, *The World Rushed In: The California Gold Rush Experience* (New York, 1981), 76, 89, 96; Editors of Time-Life Books, *The Old West: The Gamblers*, 74-75; Dale L. Morgan and James R. Scobie (eds.), *Three Years in California: William Perkins' Journal of Life at Sonora, 1849-1852* (Berkeley, 1964), 3-4. Robert K. DeArment, *Knights of the Green Cloth: The Saga of the Frontier Gamblers* (Norman, Okla., 1982), 14, 17, 18, gives some examples of prominent gamblers in Gold Rush San Francisco who came from careers as sharpers aboard Mississippi Valley riverboats.

Chapter 3

1. George Cosgrave (trans.), *Scenes of Life in California by Friedrich Gerstäcker* (San Francisco, 1942; orig. pub. 1856), viii, ix, xi-xii, 67-105, esp. 69-73, 75-77, 80-86, 103; Friedrich Wilhelm Christian Gerstaecker, *Narrative of a Journey Round the World* (London, 1853), I: 221-22, 332-33.

2. Charles Loring Brace, *The New West: or, California in 1867-1868* (New York, 1869), 68.

3. Gerstaecker, *Narrative*, II: 56.

4. The phrase derives from depictions of restless, speculative Californians. See: John S. Hittell, *Mining in the Pacific States of North America* (San Francisco, 1861), 35; B. E. Lloyd, *Lights and Shades in San Francisco* (San Francisco, 1876), 203.

5. Theodore H. Hittell, *History of California* (San Francisco, 1897), II: 764.

6. Hubert Howe Bancroft, *California Inter Pocula* (San Francisco, 1888), 702; Walter Van Tilburg Clark (ed.), *The Journals of Alfred Doten 1849-1903* (Reno, 1973), I: 321; Hittell, *Mining in the Pacific States*, 34-35.

7. Earl Pomeroy, "California, 1846-1860: Politics of a Representative Frontier State," *California Historical Society Quarterly*, 32 (Dec. 1953), 292.

8. Hittell, *Mining in the Pacific States*, 35.

9. Brace, *New West*, 66-67. See also the comments of James Bryce, *The American Commonwealth* (London, 2nd rev. ed., 1889), II: 698. Gunther Barth, *Instant Cities: Urbanization and the Rise of San Francisco and Denver* (New York, 1975), 138-39, stresses the role of chance in the nineteenth-century Far West.

10. Bryce, *American Commonwealth*, II: 385, 697.

11. Rodman Wilson Paul, *Mining Frontiers of the Far West, 1848-1880* (New York, 1963), 39-40, 42, 43, 49-51.

12. Earl Pomeroy (ed.), *California . . . By Josiah Royce* (Santa Barbara, 1970; orig. pub. 1886).

13. Franklin Langworthy, *Scenery of the Plains, Mountains and Mines* (Ogdensburgh, N.Y., 1855), 185; Patrice Dillon, "La Californie dans les Derniers Mois de 1849," *Revue des Deux Mondes* (Jan. 15, 1850), reprinted in Abraham P. Nasatir (trans. and comp.), *French Activities in California: An Archival Calendar-Guide* (Stanford, Calif., 1945), 545; Barth, *Instant Cities*, 129.

14. Gerald D. Nash, "Stages of California's Economic Growth, 1870-1970: An Interpretation," George H. Knoles (ed.), *Essays and Assays: California History Reappraised* (San Francisco, 1973), 39-53.

15. Gunther Barth, *Bitter Strength: A History of the Chinese in the United States 1850-1870* (Cambridge, Mass., 1964), 34, 38-40, discusses the doomed efforts of Americans in Gold Rush California to build a more perfect version of United States civilization. See also: Louis B. Wright, *Culture on the Moving Frontier* (Bloomington, Ind., 1955), 142-43; "Current Comment," *Overland Monthly*, 2nd ser., 2 (Dec. 1883), 657-58.

16. For typical Yankee characterizations of Mexicans in California, see Zenas Leonard, *Narrative of the Adventures of Zenas Leonard, Written by Himself* (Lincoln, Neb., 1978; orig. pub. 1839), 166-74, 184; Richard Henry Dana, Jr., *Two Years Before the Mast: A Personal Narrative* (New York, 1964; orig. pub. 1840 and 1869), 75-78, 81. Depictions of bull-and-bear fights can be found in Timothy Flint (ed.), *The Personal Narrative of James O. Pattie of Kentucky* (Chicago, 1930; orig. pub. 1831), 384-86; Leonard, *Narrative*, 178-83; Thomas C. Russell (ed.), *Narrative of a Voyage to California Ports in 1841-1842 . . . by Sir George Simpson* (San Francisco, 1930), 137; Frederic Hall, *The History of San Jose and Surroundings with Biographical Sketches of Early Settlers* (San Francisco, 1871), 228-31; Maurice H. Newmark and Marco R. Newmark (eds.), *Sixty Years in Southern California 1853-1913, Containing the Reminiscences of Harris Newmark* (Los Angeles, 4th ed., 1970), 161-62. On American efforts to regulate Californio gaming and bloodsports, turn to Leonard Pitt, *The Decline of the Californios; A Social History of the Spanish-Speaking Californians* (Berkeley, 1970), 196-97; Joseph S. O'Flaherty, *An End and a Beginning: The South Coast and Los Angeles 1850-1887* (New York, 1972), 64-65.

17. On Chinese gambling in California, consult Barth, *Bitter Strength*, 126-27, 153; Steward Culin, *The Gambling Games of the Chinese in America* (Las Vegas, 1972; orig. pub. 1891).

18. Bancroft, *California Inter Pocula*, 720.

19. Frank Soulé, John H. Gihon, and James Nisbet, *The Annals of San Francisco* (New York, 1855), 223-24, 248.

20. Louise Amelia Knapp Smith Clappe, *The Shirley Letters, Being Letters written in 1851-1852 from the California Mines by "Dame Shirley"* (Santa Barbara, 1970; orig. pub. 1854-1855), 123; George P. Hammond (ed.), *Digging for Gold—Without a Shovel; The Letters of Daniel Wadsworth Coit From Mexico City to San Francisco 1848-1851* (San Francisco, 1967), 77; Langworthy, *Scenery*, 208; Samuel Williams, *The City of the Golden Gate; A Description of San Francisco in 1875* (San Francisco, 1921), 12; J. S. Holliday, *The World Rushed In: The California Gold Rush Experience* (New York, 1981), 353.

21. Cited in Holliday, *World Rushed In*, 376.

22. Frank Merriam Stanger (ed.), "Letters of an Artist in the Gold Rush," *California Historical Society Quarterly*, 22 (Sept. 1943), 243.

23. Hubert Howe Bancroft, *Essays and Miscellany* (San Francisco, 1890), 420; Bayard Taylor, *El Dorado, or Adventures in the Path of Empire* . . . (New York, 1949; orig. pub. 1850), 233; Albert D. Richardson, *Beyond the Mississippi* . . . (Hartford, Conn., 1867), 443-44.

24. L. M. Schaeffer, *Sketches of Travel in South America, Mexico and California* (New York, 1860), 27. See also F. P. Wierzbicki, *California As It Is, And As It May Be, or, A Guide To The Gold Region* (San Francisco, 1849), 49; Frank Marryat, *Mountains and Molehills; or Recollections of A Burnt Journal* (Philadelphia, 1962; orig. pub. 1855), 14-15.

25. Bancroft, *California Inter Pocula*, 694; see also Holliday, *World Rushed In*, 355.

26. Marryat, *Mountains and Molehills*, 15; Gerstaecker, *Narrative*, I: 217.

27. John S. Hittell, "The Mining Excitements of California," *Overland Monthly*, 1st ser., 2 (May 1869), 415; Bryce, *American Commonwealth*, II: 385-90.

28. Holliday, *World Rushed In*, 297, 300; Wierzbicki, *California As It Is*, 50; Marryat, *Mountains and Molehills*, 15.

29. Francis P. Farquhar (ed.), *Up and Down California in 1860-1864; The Journal of William H. Brewer* (Berkeley, 1966), 104; Abraham P. Nasatir (ed.), *A French Journalist in the California Gold Rush: The Letters of Etienne Derbec* (Georgetown, Calif., 1964), 127, 166-67; Holliday, *World Rushed In*, 321-22, 336; Hubert Howe Bancroft, *History of California* (San Francisco, 1884-90), VI: 238, 607; Hall, *History of San Jose*, 256; Newmark and Newmark (eds.), *Sixty Years*, 131; Clark (ed.), *Journals of Alfred Doten*, I: 321.

30. Frank Heywood Hodder (ed.), *Audubon's Western Journal: 1849-1850, Being the MS. record of a trip from New York . . . to the gold-fields of California, by John W. Audubon* (Cleveland, 1906), 193, 196; Union City, Calif., *Times*, Dec. 10, 1874.

31. J. A. Benton, *The California Pilgrim: A Series of Lectures* (Sacramento, 1853), 48; John Philip Quinn, *Fools of Fortune* (Chicago, 1892), 447.

32. Soulé, Gihon, and Nisbet, *Annals*, 231; Bancroft, *California Inter Pocula*, 698, 710. San Jose licensed gambling in 1853; see Eugene T. Sawyer, *History of Santa Clara County, California* (Los Angeles, 1922), 162. For remarks regarding an 1849 lottery scheme in San Francisco, consult the *Daily Alta California*, Sept. 22, 1849.

33. Perspective on gambling as a profession in the Far West has been provided by Robert K. DeArment, *Knights of the Green Cloth: The Saga of the Frontier Gamblers* (Norman, Okla., 1982), and George M. Blackburn and Sherman L. Ricards, "The Prostitutes and Gamblers of Virginia City, Nevada: 1870," *Pacific Historical Review*, 48 (May 1979), 239-58. Blackburn and Ricards suggest that the business of gambling did not serve dealers in Virginia City as a reliable means of upward social mobility. Conditions may have been different in Gold Rush San Francisco.

34. Clark (ed.), *Journals of Alfred Doten*, I: 322.

35. Clarkson Crane (trans.), *Last Adventure; San Francisco in 1851, Translated from the original journal of Albert Benard de Russailh* (San Francisco, 1931), 16-17; Cosgrave (trans.), *Scenes of Life*, 69-70.

36. Soulé, Gihon, and Nisbet, *Annals*, 249; Bancroft, *California Inter Pocula*, 700-702; Bancroft, *Essays and Miscellany*, 421; [John O'Connor], *Wanderings of a Vagabond. An Autobiography. Edited by John Morris* (New York, 1873), 219; Quinn, *Fools of Fortune*, 439; Herbert Asbury, *The Barbary Coast; An Informal History of the San Francisco Underworld* (New York, 1933), 20.

37. Soulé, Gihon, and Nisbet, *Annals*, 250; Bancroft, *California Inter Pocula*, 705-9; J. D. Borthwick, *Three Years in California* (Oakland, Calif., 1948; orig. pub. 1857), 51.

38. Bancroft, *History of California*, VI: 240-41; William Kelly, *An Excursion to California over the Prairie, Rocky Mountains, and Great Sierra Nevada* (London, 1851), II: 246-47.

39. Duncan Emrich, *It's an Old Wild West Custom* (New York, 1949), 81-82; Taylor, *El Dorado*, 90-92; Gerstaecker, *Narrative*, II: 48.

40. Borthwick, *Three Years*, 46; Newmark and Newmark (eds.), *Sixty Years*, 21-22; Schaeffer, *Sketches of Travel*, 27-28.

41. Dillon, "La Californie dans les Derniers Mois de 1849," Nasatir (trans. and comp.), *French Activities*, 545; Taylor, *El Dorado*, 44; Holliday, *World Rushed In*, 301; Soulé, Gihon, and Nisbet, *Annals*, 254; Stanger (ed.), "Letters of an Artist," 244.

42. Gerstaecker, *Narrative*, I: 336-37; II: 45; Cosgrave (trans.), *Scenes of Life*, 71; Nasatir (ed.), *French Journalist*, 166.

43. Crane (trans.), *Last Adventure*, 4; Dale L. Morgan (ed.), *In Pursuit of the Golden Dream: Reminiscences of San Francisco and the Northern and Southern Mines, 1849-1857 By Howard C. Gardiner* (Stoughton, Mass., 1970), 324; Marryat, *Mountains and Molehills*, 13.

44. *Daily Alta California*, May 27, 1850.

45. Nasatir (ed.), *French Journalist*, 165-66; Soulé, Gihon, and Nisbet, *Annals*, 216.

46. Taylor, *El Dorado*, 227-28; Kelly, *Excursion to California*, 245-46. For other depictions of gaming halls at the plaza, consult Hammond (ed.), *Digging for Gold*, 78-79, 84; Marguerite Eyer Wilbur (trans.), *A Frenchman in the Gold Rush: The Journal of Ernest de Massey, Argonaut of 1849* (San Francisco, 1927), 16, 29; Dale L. Morgan and James R. Scobie (eds.), *Three Years in California: William Perkins' Journal of Life at Sonora, 1849-1852* (Berkeley, 1964), 341; Marryat, *Mountains and Molehills*, 18-19; Lucius Beebe and Charles M. Clegg (eds.), *Dreadful California . . . by Hinton Helper* (Indianapolis, 1948; orig. pub. 1855), 56; Soulé, Gihon, and Nisbet, *Annals*, 501; Borthwick, *Three Years*, 37, 46-48; Bancroft, *California Inter Pocula*, 709.

47. Nasatir (ed.), *French Journalist*, 166-67. See also Crane (trans.), *Last Adventure*, 17; Borthwick, *Three Years*, 93.

48. Marguerite Eyer Wilbur (trans.), *A Gil Blas in California, by Alexandre Dumas* (Los Angeles, 1933; orig. pub. 1852), 55; Marryat, *Mountains and Molehills*, 19; Morgan and Scobie (eds.), *Three Years*, 341-42; Crane (trans.), *Last Adventure*, 12-13.

49. On private gaming rooms, see Bancroft, *California Inter Pocula*, 709-10; Morgan and Scobie (eds.), *Three Years*, 343.

50. Borthwick, *Three Years*, 48-49.

51. Langworthy, *Scenery*, 222; Taylor, *El Dorado*, 91; Morgan (ed.), *In Pursuit of the Golden Dream*, 118; Bancroft, *History of California*, VI: 239-40.

52. Bancroft, *History of California*, VI: 240; Crane (trans.), *Last Adventure*, 13-14; Morgan and Scobie (eds.), *Three Years*, 342.

53. Crane (trans.), *Last Adventure*, 14-16.

54. Bancroft, *California Inter Pocula*, 702-3, 704, 711. See also Morgan (ed.), *In Pursuit of the Golden Dream*, 131.

55. Barth, *Instant Cities*, 144-45.

56. Schaeffer, *Sketches of Travel*, 27-28, 49, 53; Bancroft, *California Inter Pocula*, 698-99; DeArment, *Knights of the Green Cloth*, 14; G. R. Fardon, *San Francisco in the 1850s: 33 Photographic Views* (New York, 1977; orig. pub. 1856), 7; Asbury, *Barbary Coast*, 20-22, 25-26.

57. Marryat, *Mountains and Molehills*, 182; Soulé, Gihon, and Nisbet, *Annals*, 252, 368; Pomeroy (ed.), *California*, 178-79, 334-35n; Mary Floyd Williams (ed.), "Papers of the San Francisco Vigilance Committee of 1851. III. Minutes and Miscellaneous Papers, Financial Accounts and Vouchers," *Publications of the Academy of Pacific Coast History*, IV (1919), 46n; Bancroft, *History of California*, VI: 241; Asbury, *Barbary Coast*, 18-19; Morgan (ed.), *In Pursuit of the Golden Dream*, 324.

58. Richard H. Dillon (ed.), "'Rejoice Ye Thieves and Harlots!' The Vigilance Editorials of the San Francisco Journalist James King of William," *California Historical Society Quarterly*, 37 (June 1958), 141; Pomeroy (ed.), *California*, 343.

59. San Francisco *Daily Evening Bulletin* (hereafter cited as *Bulletin*), Nov. 19, 22, Dec. 12, 1855. [O'Connor], *Wanderings of a Vagabond*, 248, asserted that Charles Cora had operated out of Vicksburg, Mississippi, during the early 1830s. See also the comments of DeArment, *Knights of the Green Cloth*, 18-20.

60. [James O'Meara], *The Vigilance Committee of 1856. By a Pioneer California Journalist* (San Francisco, 1857), 11-14, 16; *Bulletin*, Jan. 17, 1856.

61. *Bulletin*, Feb. 12, 13, 14, March 20, April 14, 15, 30, 1856; Hubert Howe Bancroft, *Popular Tribunals* (San Francisco, 1887), II: 33.

62. *Bulletin*, March 8, April 15, 30, 1856.

63. *Bulletin*, April 16, 18, 1856.

64. *Bulletin*, April 9, 11, 16, 18, 21, 1856.

65. Robert Glass Cleland (ed.), "The San Francisco Committee of Vigilance of 1856: An Estimate of a Private Citizen," *Historical Society of Southern California, Quarterly*, 31 (Dec. 1949), 293.

66. Richard Maxwell Brown, "Pivot of American Vigilantism: The San Francisco Vigilance Committee of 1856," John A. Carroll (ed.), *Reflections of Western Historians* (Tucson, 1969), 111; Williams (ed.), "Papers of the San Francisco Vigilance Committee of 1851. III," 1, 1n.

67. See the summary of legislation in Deering's California Codes, *Penal Code, Annotated, of the State of California, sec. 207 to sec. 443* (San Francisco, 1971), 774-75.

68. Quinn, *Fools of Fortune*, 441; Farquhar (ed.), *Up and Down California*, 486-87.

69. Lloyd, *Lights and Shades*, 205. See also the 1876 cartoon mocking police enforcement of antigambling laws in San Francisco in Editors of Time-Life Books, *The Old West: The Gamblers* (Alexandria, Va., 1978), 102-3.

70. Roger W. Lotchin, *San Francisco 1846-1856; From Hamlet to City* (New York, 1974), 298.

71. Soulé, Gihon, and Nisbet, *Annals*, 250, 502; Lloyd, *Lights and Shades*, 205, 483-84; [Ben Goodkind], *An American Hobo in Europe, By Windy Bill* (San Francisco, 1907), 42; Editors of Time-Life Books, *The Old West: The Gamblers*, 102, 104.

72. Clark (ed.), *Journals of Alfred Doten*, I: 323; George R. Stewart and Edwin S. Fussell (eds.), *San Francisco in 1866 by Bret Harte, Being Letters to the* Springfield Republican (San Francisco, 1951), 63; Farquhar (ed.), *Up and Down California*, 189, 198.

73. Quinn, *Fools of Fortune*, 441-44; Bancroft, *California Inter Pocula*, 719.

74. Letter from John W. Jones to *Missouri Republican*, Feb. 23, 1859, reprinted in LeRoy R. Hafen (ed.), *Colorado Gold Rush: Contemporary Letters and Reports 1858-1859* (Glendale, Calif., 1941), 207-8; Farquhar (ed.), *Up and Down California*, 421. Thomas J. Dimsdale, *The Vigilantes of Montana, or Popular Justice in the Rocky Mountains . . .* (Norman, Okla., 1953; orig. pub. 1866), 6, 8-9, provided a like view of gambling in Montana Territory during the mining rush of the early 1860s. Editors of Time-Life Books, *The Old West: The Gamblers*, 95, 99, and Duane A. Smith, *Rocky Mountain Mining Camps; The Urban Frontier* (Bloomington, Ind., 1967), 226, trace the careers of two professional gamblers from Gold Rush California to other mineral strikes in the Far West. On the cattle frontier of the later nineteenth century, consult Gary L. Cunningham, "Chance, Culture, and Compulsion: The Gambling Games of the Kansas Cattle Towns," *Nevada Historical Society Quarterly*, 26 (Winter 1983), 255-71.

75. Bancroft, *California Inter Pocula*, 695.

76. Brace, *New West*, 48. See also Bryce, *American Commonwealth*, II: 704; Barth, *Instant Cities*, 131-33.

77. Barth, *Instant Cities*, 146-47; William Laird MacGregor, *San Francisco California in 1876* (Edinburgh, 1876), 25; Henry George, "What the Railroad Will Bring Us," *Overland Monthly*, 1st ser., 1 (Oct. 1868), 298.

78. Ralph Mann, "The Decade After the Gold Rush: Social Structure in Grass Valley and Nevada City, California, 1850-1860," *Pacific Historical Review*, 41 (Nov. 1972), 484-504, analyzes the changes accompanying the industrialization of mining.

79. Dillon, "La Californie dans les Derniers Mois de 1849," Nasatir (ed.), *French Activities*, 545; *Bulletin*, April 24, 1856.

80. Lloyd, *Lights and Shades*, 204; MacGregor, *San Francisco in 1876*, 29-32.

81. Williams, *City of the Golden Gate*, 12.

82. MacGregor, *San Francisco in 1876*, 34.

83. [William Wright], *The Big Bonanza; An Authentic Account of the Discovery, History, and Working of the World-Renowned Comstock Lode of Nevada . . . by Dan De Quille* (New York, 1967; orig. pub. 1876), 115-16, 301-15, 366-68. See also the comments of [Samuel Clemens], *Roughing It, by Mark Twain* (New York, 1963; orig. pub. 1872), chs. 44, 58.

84. Bancroft, *California Inter Pocula*, 686, 692-94; Bancroft, *Essays and Miscellany*, 421; Stewart and Fussell (eds.), *San Francisco in 1866*, 56-59. As Bret Harte indicated, some people viewed their investment as "feet" in a mine shaft rather than shares of a mining firm.

85. MacGregor, *San Francisco in 1876*, 19, 32.

86. Quinn, *Fools of Fortune*, 448; Thomas W. Knox, *The Underground World: A Mirror of Life Below the Surface . . .* (Hartford, Conn., 1878), 115-16; [Squire

Pierce Dewey], *The Bonanza Mines of Nevada. Gross Fraud in the Management Exposed* . . . (New York, 1974; orig. pub. 1878), 60-61.

87. Bancroft, *History of California*, VII: 711-12; Bancroft, *Essays and Miscellany*, 421.

88. Robert M. Fogelson, *The Fragmented Metropolis: Los Angeles, 1850-1930* (Cambridge, Mass., 1967), 78-79, 85.

89. W. H. Hutchinson, "The Genie of Yang-Na," *California History*, 60 (Spring 1981), 46-47; Ashleigh E. Brilliant, "Some Aspects of Mass Motorization in Southern California, 1919-1929," *Southern California Quarterly*, 47 (June 1965), 191-208.

90. Sarah Comstock, "The Great American Mirror; Reflections from Los Angeles," *Harper's Monthly Magazine*, 156 (May 1928), 715, 723.

91. Louis Adamic, *The Truth About Los Angeles* (Girard, Kan., 1927), 15.

92. Bertram Wallace Korn (ed.), *Incidents of Travel and Adventure in the Far West, by Solomon Nunes Carvalho* (Philadelphia, 1954; orig. pub. 1857), 310-11; Newmark and Newmark (eds.), *Sixty Years*, 29-32. On conditions in Los Angeles in the 1850s, turn to John W. Caughey (ed.), *The Indians of Southern California in 1852: The B. D. Wilson Report and a Selection of Contemporary Comment* (San Marino, Calif., 1952), xvii-xviii.

93. William A. Spalding (comp.), *History and Reminiscences of Los Angeles City and County, California* (Los Angeles, 1931), 283; Joseph S. O'Flaherty, *Those Powerful Years: The South Coast and Los Angeles 1887-1917* (Hicksville, N.Y., 1978), 280-82.

94. Oscar Osburn Winther, "The Rise of Metropolitan Los Angeles, 1870-1900," *Huntington Library Quarterly*, 10 (Aug. 1947), 393-94; Fogelson, *Fragmented Metropolis*, 67; Newmark and Newmark (eds.), *Sixty Years*, 569-74; T. S. Van Dyke, *Millionaires of a Day: An Inside History of the Great Southern California "Boom"* (New York, 1890), 206.

95. U. S. Department of Justice, Law Enforcement Assistance Administration, National Institute of Law Enforcement and Criminal Justice, *The Development of the Law of Gambling: 1776-1976* (Washington, D.C., 1977), 410-15; Ralph J. Roske, "Nevada Gambling, First Phase, 1861-1931" (paper delivered at meeting of Western Historical Association, Oct., 1977), 6-7.

96. Earl Pomeroy, *In Search of the Golden West: The Tourist in Western America* (New York, 1957), 185.

Chapter 4

1. Las Vegas, Nevada, Chamber of Commerce, "Las Vegas and Boulder Dam Nevada," promotional brochure (Las Vegas, 1939; on file in Bancroft Library, Berkeley); Stanley M. Paher, *Las Vegas: As It Began—As It Grew* (Las Vegas, 1971), 146.

2. LeRoy R. Hafen and Ann W. Hafen, *Old Spanish Trail; Santa Fe to Los Angeles* . . . (Glendale, Calif., 1954), 19, 22, 80-81, 355; LeRoy R. Hafen and Ann W. Hafen (eds.), *Central Route to the Pacific, by Gwin Harris Heap* . . . (Glendale, Calif., 1957), 240; Jules Remy and Julius Brenchley, *A Journey to Great-Salt-Lake City* . . . (London, 1861), II: 411-13. The early history of Las Vegas has been surveyed by Glenn S. Dumke, "Mission Station to Mining Town; Early Las Vegas," *Pacific Historical Review*, 22 (Aug. 1953), 257-70.

3. Dumke, "Mission Station to Mining Town," 259-66.

4. Charles Hall Page & Associates, *City of Las Vegas: Historic Preservation Inventory and Planning Guidelines* (San Francisco, 1978), 16, 18; Florence Lee Jones Cahlan and John F. Cahlan, *Water: A History of Las Vegas* (Las Vegas, 1975), I: 57-62.

5. Charles Hall Page & Associates, *City of Las Vegas*, 16, 18, 36, 48-53; Cahlan and Cahlan, *Water*, I: 57. For an illustration of architectural uniformity, turn to the title page of Charles Hall Page & Associates, *City of Las Vegas*.

6. The dam, called both Boulder Dam and Hoover Dam in this work, was actually located in Black Canyon on the Colorado River. It anchored the far-reaching Boulder Canyon Project.

7. U. S. Department of Interior, Bureau of Reclamation, *Boulder Canyon Project Final Reports. Part I—Introductory. Bulletin I. General History and Description of Project* (Boulder City, Nev., 1948), ch. VI (hereafter cited as: Bureau of Reclamation, *Boulder Canyon Project General History*); C. Gregory Crampton, *The Complete Las Vegas* (Salt Lake City, 1976), 49; Katharine Best and Katharine Hillyer, *Las Vegas, Playtown U.S.A.* (New York, 1955), 157-58; Perry Bruce Kaufman, "The Best City of Them All: A History of Las Vegas, 1930-1960" (Ph.D. diss., University of California, Santa Barbara, 1974), 28, 44; Cahlan and Cahlan, *Water*, I: 56, 86-88, 92-93; Eugene P. Moehring, "Public Works and the New Deal in Las Vegas, 1933-1940," *Nevada Historical Society Quarterly*, 24 (Summer 1981), 106-29; Richard Lowitt and Maurine Beasley (eds.), *One Third of a Nation; Lorena Hickok Reports on the Great Depression* (Urbana, Ill., 1981), 317.

8. Best and Hillyer, *Las Vegas, Playtown U.S.A.*, 53; Paul Ralli, *Nevada Lawyer, A Story of Life and Love in Las Vegas* (Culver City, Calif., 1949), 3; *New York Times*, Aug. 23, 1936.

9. Russell R. Elliott, *History of Nevada* (Lincoln, Neb., 1973), 283-84; Don Robinson Murphy, "The Role of Changing External Relations in the Growth of Las Vegas, Nevada" (Ph.D. diss., University of Nebraska, 1969), 48. "The Meadows" is a translation of the Spanish term Las Vegas.

10. Kaufman, "Best City," 45-47; Cahlan and Cahlan, *Water*, I: 59, 61, 97; Crampton, *Complete Las Vegas*, 50-51; Las Vegas *Review-Journal*, July 6, 1937 (hereafter referred to as *Review-Journal*). Westerners' changing attitudes toward tourists are covered by Earl Pomeroy, *In Search of the Golden West: The Tourist in Western America* (New York, 1957), 132-33.

11. Crampton, *Complete Las Vegas*, 50-51; Elliott, *History of Nevada*, 279-80, 283; Ralli, *Nevada Lawyer*, 1-2, 5-6; Pomeroy, *In Search of the Golden West*, 187-88; *Review-Journal*, Jan. 19, 20, 21, 23, March 3, 7, 1939.

12. *New York Times*, March 11, 1940; *Review-Journal*, Nov. 7, 1940.

13. Pomeroy, *In Search of the Golden West*, 185.

14. Crampton, *Complete Las Vegas*, 54; "Wild, Woolly and Wide-Open," *Look*, 4 (Aug. 13, 1940), 24; Paher, *Las Vegas*, 146, 158-63; J. B. Priestley, *Midnight on the Desert; A Chapter of Autobiography* (London, 1937), 109-11; *Review-Journal*, March 5, 1937, April 2, 8, 1938.

15. Priestley, *Midnight on the Desert*, 109. Similar ideas were presented by Max Miller, *Reno* (New York, 1941), 257 and *passim*.

16. Local publicists were most likely largely responsible for the contents of the *Look* magazine article that described the town just as they wished: "Wild, Woolly and Wide-Open," 21-25. See also: Las Vegas, Nevada, Chamber of Commerce, "Las

Vegas and Boulder Dam Nevada''; Bureau of Reclamation, *Boulder Canyon Project General History*, 150; reprint of article by Ely Sims from *The Reclamation Era* in the *Review-Journal*, Oct. 28, 1938.

17. Crampton, *Complete Las Vegas*, 51; Kaufman, "Best City," 46; *Review-Journal*, Dec. 31, 1937, Feb. 9, 1938.

18. Harold L. Ickes, *The Secret Diary of Harold L. Ickes* (New York, 1954), II: 581.

19. *Review-Journal*, March 5, 1937.

20. On the changing law of gambling in Nevada, see: Ralph J. Roske, "Nevada Gambling, First Phase, 1861-1931" (paper delivered at meeting of Western Historical Association, 1977); U. S. Department of Justice, Law Enforcement Assistance Administration, National Institute of Law Enforcement and Criminal Justice (hereafter cited as NILECJ), *The Development of the Law of Gambling: 1776-1976* (Washington, D.C., 1977), 427-32; Robert L. Decker, "The Economics of the Legalized Gambling Industry in Nevada" (Ph.D. diss., University of Colorado, 1961), 13-18. On prizefighting, consult: Pomeroy, *In Search of the Golden West*, 186; NILECJ, *Development of the Law of Gambling*, 425-25; Oscar Lewis, *Sagebrush Casinos; The Story of Legal Gambling in Nevada* (Garden City, N.Y., 1953), 41-49.

21. NILECJ, *Development of the Law of Gambling*, 286-88, 290-91, 297-99, 398-99; "Nevada: 'One Sound State,'" *Time*, 29 (March 8, 1937), 16-17. Complaints about "wide-open" Nevada and the legalization of gambling were voiced by Anne Martin, "Nevada: Beautiful Desert of Buried Hopes," *Nation*, 115 (July 26, 1922), 89-92; and Paul Hutchinson, "Nevada, a Prostitute State," "Reno—A Wide-Open Town," "Reno's Divorce Mill," and "Can Reno Be Cured?" *Christian Century*, 48 (Nov. 26, Dec. 2, 9, 16, 1931), 1488-90, 1519-20, 1557-59, 1592-94. Anthony M. Turano, "Nevada's Trial of Licensed Gambling," *American Mercury*, 28 (Feb. 1933), 190-92, defended the experiment by arguing that Nevada was the most logical site for an inevitable activity.

22. Daniel Boorstin, *The Americans: The Democratic Experience* (New York, 1974; orig. pub. 1973), 64-77.

23. Boorstin, *The Americans: The Democratic Experience*, 64-77; *Review-Journal*, Feb. 14, 18, 1939.

24. On Reno attitudes and practices, turn to: Miller, *Reno*, esp. 256-58; Walter Van Tilburg Clark, "Reno: The State City," Ray B. West, Jr. (ed.), *Rocky Mountain Cities* (New York, 1949), 50; Pomeroy, *In Search of the Golden West*, 185. Figures come from the *Review-Journal*, Jan. 5, 6, 1939.

25. *Review-Journal*, July 9, 1937, April 8, 1938.

26. *Review-Journal*, Aug. 5, 13, 22, Oct. 14, 1938, Jan. 2, March 1, 1939, Sept. 6, Oct. 16, 17, 25, 1941, May 27, June 5, 17, 1942.

27. Kaufman, "Best City," 168; NILECJ, *Development of the Law of Gambling*, 436-37; Turano, "Nevada's Trial of Licensed Gambling," 192; "Wild, Woolly and Wide-Open," 23. Besides Ickes, other commentators on the nature of Las Vegas gambling included author Mildred Seydell and nationally syndicated sportswriter Henry McLemore, whose observations were reprinted in the *Review-Journal*, Dec. 8, 1937, Jan. 13, 1938.

28. Mark Haller, "Bootleggers and American Gambling, 1920-1950," U. S. Commission on the Review of the National Policy Toward Gambling, *Gambling in America: Appendix I* (Washington, D.C., 1976), 102-43, analyzes the relationship

between Prohibition-era bootleggers and mid-twentieth-century gamblers. On a later influx of Texan gamblers after World War II, see Lester Ben "Benny" Binion, "Some Recollections of a Texas and Las Vegas Gambling Operator" (MS of oral history interview, University of Nevada, Reno, Special Collections, 1975), 6, 18.

29. Kaufman, "Best City," 168-70; Dick Pearce, "Pleasure Palaces," *Harper's Magazine*, 210 (Feb. 1955), 80; Lewis, *Sagebrush Casinos*, 195. The activities of Los Angeles gamblers were reported by Guy W. Finney, *Angel City in Turmoil* (Los Angeles, 1945), 99, 130-31, 169; *Los Angeles Times*, June 1, 1939; Susan Berman, *Easy Street* (New York, 1981), 20.

30. *Review-Journal*, July 22, 24, 27, 31, Aug. 31, Sept. 1, Oct. 26, Nov. 20, 1937, Jan. 5, April 28, May 25, 1938, May 3, 24, June 1, 24, 1939, June 25, 29, July 24, 1942.

31. *Review-Journal*, Feb. 15, June 1, 1937, Oct. 28, 1938, March 7, 1939; Las Vegas, Nevada, Chamber of Commerce, "Las Vegas and Boulder Dam Nevada"; Wesley Stout, "Nevada's New Reno," *Saturday Evening Post*, 215 (Oct. 31, 1942), 68-69; Paher, *Las Vegas*, 166.

32. See, for example, the figures provided by the *Review-Journal*, June 1, 1937.

33. *Los Angeles Times*, May 23, 24, 1939, reprinted on same days in the *Review-Journal*. Guy McAfee appreciated Las Vegas as well; see his comments in the *Review-Journal*, May 31, 1939, reprinted from the *Los Angeles Examiner*.

34. The film was covered by the *Review-Journal*, Sept. 4, Nov. 4, 13, 1940, Jan. 10, April 7, 1941. Publisher A. E. Cahlan captured Las Vegans' growing awareness of the importance of Los Angeles to their future in the *Review-Journal*, Aug. 15, 1941.

35. Kaufman, "Best City," 49-51, 54-56; *Review-Journal*, Jan. 23, 1941; Elliott, *History of Nevada*, 312, 313; Cahlan and Cahlan, *Water*, I: 97; U. S. Commission on the Review of the National Policy Toward Gambling, "Survey of American Gambling Attitudes and Behavior," *Gambling in America: Final Report* (Washington, D.C., 1976), supplement: 230-31.

36. Kaufman, "Best City," 58-64; Richard English, "The Boom Came Back," *Collier's*, 110 (Aug. 22, 1942), 36, 48; Elliott, *History of Nevada*, 310, 346; *Review-Journal*, Jan. 27, Aug. 13, 1941. Employment figures for Basic Magnesium, Inc., ranged widely because the size of the labor force changed markedly during its two years of production. Estimates for construction workers on the plant ranged from 11,000 to 16,000, and for production workers from 3,600 to 6,500.

37. Stout, "Nevada's New Reno," 12-13; Best and Hillyer, *Las Vegas, Playtown U.S.A.*, 54-57; Cahlan and Cahlan, *Water*, I: 99. Population figures do not include personnel stationed at the air base and the defense plant townsite, but encompass only the city proper.

38. Crampton, *Complete Las Vegas*, 53; *Review-Journal*, March 19, 23, April 6, 7, May 20, 1942; English, "Boom Came Back," 48-49; Ralli, *Nevada Lawyer*, 38-39. Figures on marriages and divorces are available from the *Las Vegas Sun* (hereafter cited as *Sun*), Sept. 3, 1961. The number of marriages in Las Vegas rose to around 20,000 in 1941 and 1942, fell to about 10,000 in 1944 and 1945, and rose dramatically again in 1946. The number of divorces hovered between 2,000 and 3,000 in 1941 and 1942, climbed to 3,600 in 1945, and topped 6,000 in 1946.

39. Ralli, *Nevada Lawyer*, 38-39; Best and Hillyer, *Las Vegas, Playtown U.S.A.*, 57; *Review-Journal*, Aug. 8, Nov. 1, 4, 1941, March 19, 23, April 6, 7, 24, May 20,

Nov. 20, 26, 28, Dec. 1, 7, 1942; Kaufman, "Best City," 173-74; "Las Vegas Gambling," *Life*, 13 (Dec. 21, 1942), 91; English, "Boom Came Back," 36.

40. "Nevada: Gambler's Luck," *Time*, 45 (April 9, 1945), 20; Kaufman, "Best City," 173. The quickening pace of change and growth was depicted by: Ralli, *Nevada Lawyer*, 249-50; *Review-Journal*, Nov. 1, 1941, April 24, 1942.

41. Tom Wolfe, *The Kandy-Kolored Tangerine-Flake Streamline Baby* (New York, 1966; orig. pub. 1965), 9; Perry Bruce Kaufman, "City Boosters, Las Vegas Style," *Journal of the West*, 13 (July 1974), 55; *Sun*, Sept. 3, 1961. The suggested ordinance regarding architecture was rejected, but last-frontier design nonetheless naturally became prevalent downtown. The newly opened El Cortez Hotel exemplified use of the old West theme, as reflected by coverage in the *Review-Journal*, Nov. 7, 1941.

42. Stout, "Nevada's New Reno," 68; Paher, *Las Vegas*, 157; Murphy, "Changing External Relations," 48; Crampton, *Complete Las Vegas*, 53; Charles Hall Page & Associates, *City of Las Vegas*, 18; *Review-Journal*, June 12, 1941; [Erle Stanley Gardner], *Spill the Jackpot, by A. A. Fair* (New York, 1941), 24.

43. English, "Boom Came Back," 36, 48-49; Paher, *Las Vegas*, 157; *Review-Journal*, May 21, 1940, June 13, 1941; *Sun*, Jan. 27, 1951, Sept. 11, 12, 1952, Dec. 17, 1954.

44. *Review-Journal*, June 24, 1940, March 6, 1942.

45. The term "roadtown" comes from Lewis Mumford, "Megalopolis as Anti-City," *Architectural Record*, 132 (Dec. 1962), 101-8.

46. Ralli, *Nevada Lawyer*, 298-99; Paul Ralli, *Viva Vegas* (Hollywood, Calif., 1953), photos; Paher, *Las Vegas*, 168; Best and Hillyer, *Las Vegas, Playtown U.S.A.*, 60-61; *Review-Journal*, Dec. 13, 29, 1939, Oct. 25, 1940, April 2, 4, 19, 1941, Oct. 29, 31, 1942; *Sun*, April 1, 1979.

47. These interiors, and the Last Frontier western museum, were illustrated in the photographs accompanying Ralli, *Viva Vegas*, and depicted in the *Review-Journal*, Oct. 10, 1949.

48. Horace Sutton, "Old Gamblers Fade Away," *Saturday Review*, 38 (Feb. 5, 1955), 28-29; Ralli, *Viva Vegas*, 32-33; *Review-Journal*, April 9, 1942.

49. Sutton, "Old Gamblers Fade Away," 28; Horace Sutton, "Cowboys and Croupiers," *Saturday Review*, 43 (March 5, 1960), 32; A. J. Liebling, "Our Footloose Correspondents: Action in the Desert," *New Yorker*, 26 (May 13, 1950), 108; Lucius Beebe, "Las Vegas," *Holiday*, 12 (Dec. 1952), 135.

50. *Review-Journal*, Dec. 30, 1946; Hank Greenspun and Alex Pelle, *Where I Stand; The Record of a Reckless Man* (New York, 1966), 68. See also Berman, *Easy Street*, 43. Nationwide attention derived from: A. J. Liebling, "Our Far-flung Correspondents: Out Among the Lamisters," *New Yorker*, 30 (March 27, 1954), 74; "Why the Big Boom in the Desert States," *U. S. News and World Report*, 43 (Oct. 11, 1957), 83. Promotions and descriptions by Nevadans included: "Annual Rodeos and Parades Are Part of Nevada Life," *Nevada Highways and Parks*, 7 (Spring 1947), 23; Best and Hillyer, *Las Vegas, Playtown U.S.A.*, 3, 54; "Las Vegas, Nevada; Fun in the Sun, The Last Frontier," *Nevada Parks and Highways*, 14 (Jan.-April 1954), 21; *Review-Journal*, May 31, 1959; Jonreed Lauritzen, *Las Vegas, Nevada for Fun and Sun* (Las Vegas, 1947), 13; Robert Laxalt, "What Has Wide-open Gambling Done to Nevada?" *Saturday Evening Post*, 225 (Sept. 20, 1952), 44; Ralli, *Viva Vegas*, 12.

51. Best and Hillyer, *Las Vegas, Playtown U.S.A.*, 177-78; "Las Vegas: 'It Just Couldn't Happen,'" *Time*, 62 (Nov. 23, 1953), 30; Kaufman, "City Boosters," 53; Ed Reid, *Las Vegas: City Without Clocks* (Englewood Cliffs, N.J., 1961), 18; *Sun*, July 21, 1959.

52. Best and Hillyer, *Las Vegas, Playtown U.S.A.*, 24-25; Kaufman, "City Boosters," 48-49; "Las Vegas: 'It Just Couldn't Happen,'" 30.

53. *Review-Journal*, March 21, 1947; Aben Kandel, *The Strip* (New York, 1961), 17; Liebling, "Our Footloose Correspondents," 108; Jerome Skolnick, *House of Cards: Legalization and Control of Casino Gambling* (Boston, 1978), 41.

54. *Review-Journal*, March 31, 1954; Jack Richardson, *Memoir of a Gambler* (London, 1980), 153-54; A. Alvarez, "A Reporter at Large; The Biggest Game in Town—I," *New Yorker*, 59 (March 7, 1983), 63, 64; Liebling, "Our Footloose Correspondents," 108; *Sun*, July 29, 1979.

55. Robert D. Herman, *Gamblers and Gambling: Motives, Institutions, and Controls* (Lexington, Mass., 1976), 84-85, 86-88.

56. On the idea of the West as liberation from constraints, see John Cawelti, "God's Country, Las Vegas and the Gunfighter: Differing Versions of the West," *Western American Literature*, 9 (Winter 1975), 276-79.

57. Richardson, *Memoir of a Gambler*, 154.

Chapter 5

1. The opening of the New Frontier was described by the *Las Vegas Sun*, April 4, 5, 6, 1955, April 8, 1979; Katharine Best and Katharine Hillyer, *Las Vegas, Playtown U.S.A.* (New York, 1955), 58-59, 96, 100-101. The original hotel was depicted by the *Las Vegas Sun*, Sept. 3, 1961; A. J. Liebling, "Our Footloose Correspondents: Action in the Desert," *New Yorker*, 26 (May 13, 1950), 109; Stanley W. Paher, *Las Vegas: As It Began—As It Grew* (Las Vegas, 1971), 169; Las Vegas *Review-Journal*, Oct. 29, 31, 1942. The Las Vegas papers will hereafter be referred to as the *Sun* and *Review-Journal*.

2. The figures come from the *New York Times*, June 9, 1957; C. Gregory Crampton, *The Complete Las Vegas* (Salt Lake City, 1976), 58.

3. Liebling, "Our Footloose Correspondents," 106; Earl Pomeroy, *In Search of the Golden West: The Tourist in Western America* (New York, 1957), 188; Neil Bowen Morgan, *Westward Tilt, The American West Today* (New York, 1963), 310; Ross Macdonald, *The Barbarous Coast* (New York, 1966; orig. pub. 1956), 140.

4. Cynthia Hobart Lindsay, *The Natives Are Restless* (Philadelphia, 1960), 190.

5. The tourist figures come from Gladwin Hill, "Klondike in the Desert," *New York Times Magazine*, June 7, 1953, p. 67; Don Robinson Murphy, "The Role of Changing External Relations in the Growth of Las Vegas, Nevada" (Ph.D. diss., University of Nebraska, 1969), 106-7. For statewide figures on Nevada and California that parallel statistics for Las Vegas and Los Angeles, turn to Robert L. Decker, "The Economics of the Legalized Gambling Industry in Nevada" (Ph.D. diss., University of Colorado, 1961), 131.

6. Richard Gilbert, *City of the Angels* (London, 1964), 31, discusses fantasy in Los Angeles, and John Pastier, "The Architecture of Escapism: Disney World and Las Vegas," *American Institute of Architects Journal*, 67 (Dec. 1978), 27-28, notes that Las Vegas styles derived in large part from Hollywood themes.

7. Hortense Powdermaker, *Hollywood, The Dream Factory* (Boston, 1950), 24, 37, 289-90; Joan Didion, *The White Album* (New York, 1980; orig. pub. 1979), 158-59.

8. The connection was made by Julian Halevy, "Disneyland and Las Vegas," *Nation*, 186 (June 7, 1958), 510-13; Pastier, "Architecture of Escapism," 26-37; Perry Bruce Kaufman, "The Best City of Them All: A History of Las Vegas, 1930-1960" (Ph.D. diss., University of California, Santa Barbara, 1974), ch. 4.

9. The importance of auto travel to Las Vegas was recognized by the Las Vegas, Nevada, Chamber of Commerce, Research and Statistical Bureau, *Las Vegas Report 1961* (Las Vegas, 1961), 12-13; Liebling, "Our Footloose Correspondents," 108-9; Ward Herman Gubler, "Las Vegas: An International Recreation Center" (M.S. thesis, University of Utah, 1967), 56; Murphy, "Changing External Relations," 104; Kaufman, "Best City," 165. On national trends, turn to Pomeroy, *In Search of the Golden West*, 127-30, 145-47; James J. Flink, *The Car Culture* (Cambridge, Mass., 1975), 189-90; John B. Rae, *The Road and Car in American Life* (Cambridge, Mass., 1971), 104-5, 138-39, 142.

10. Rae, *Road and Car*, 145.

11. Crampton, *Complete Las Vegas*, 56.

12. Reyner Banham, "Q: What is the Main Drag of the American Fantasy? A: The Vegas Strip, in Case You Hadn't Heard," *Los Angeles Times' West Magazine*, Nov. 8, 1970, pp. 37, 39, 41; Reyner Banham, *Los Angeles: The Architecture of Four Ecologies* (New York, 1973; orig. pub. 1971), 84-87.

13. Ted K. Bradshaw, "Trying Out the Future," *The Wilson Quarterly*, 4 (Summer 1980), 66-70.

14. Christopher Rand, *Los Angeles: The Ultimate City* (New York, 1967), 3; James Q. Wilson, "A Guide to Reagan Country: The Political Culture of Southern California," *Commentary*, 43 (May 1967), 43.

15. Rand, *Los Angeles, passim*; Jan Morris, *Destinations: Essays from* Rolling Stone (New York, 1980), 83-85.

16. The role of Southern California as "the cultural hearth for a new American 'lifestyle,'" beginning in the 1920s, is discussed by D. W. Meinig in "The Continuous Shaping of America: A Prospectus for Geographers and Historians," *American Historical Review*, 83 (Dec. 1978), 1200, and "Symbolic Landscapes: Some Idealizations of American Communities," in D. W. Meinig (ed.), *The Interpretation of Ordinary Landscapes; Geographical Essays* (New York, 1979), 169-72. Gerald D. Nash, *The American West in the Twentieth Century: A Short History of an Urban Oasis* (Albuquerque, 1977), 1-2, 6-7, 291-99, deals in a Turnerlike fashion with the West as a "pacesetting society" for the United States.

17. Best and Hillyer, *Las Vegas, Playtown U.S.A.*, 145.

18. Edmund Wilson, *The Boys in the Back Room: Notes on California Novelists* (San Francisco, 1941), 59; Rand, *Los Angeles*, 142.

19. Meyer Barash (trans.), *Man, Play, and Games, by Roger Caillois* (New York, 1979; orig. pub. 1958), 117; Pastier, "Architecture of Escapism," 26-27; Kaufman, "Best City," 544.

20. Tom Wolfe, *The Kandy-Kolored Tangerine-Flake Streamline Baby* (New York, 1966; orig. pub. 1965), xvi.

21. Students of leisure have not been able to chart the growth of leisure time very conclusively, in part because they have not agreed upon criteria for measurement. Compare, for example, Staffan Burenstam Linder, *The Harried Leisure Class*

(New York, 1970), 135-37, with Max Kaplan, *Leisure in America: A Social Inquiry* (New York, 1960), 35-40.

22. David Riesman, Nathan Glazer, and Reuel Denny, *The Lonely Crowd, A Study of the Changing American Character* (New Haven, Conn., rev. ed., 1969; orig. pub. 1950), 141, 146, 157.

23. Robert W. Malcolmson, *Popular Recreations in English Society, 1700–1850* (Cambridge, 1973); Riesman, Glazer, and Denny, *Lonely Crowd*, 116–17, 136, 141; David Riesman and Walter Bloomberg, Jr., "Work and Leisure: Fusion or Polarity?" (1957), in David Riesman, *Abundance for What? And Other Essays* (Garden City, N.Y., 1964), 148.

24. David Riesman, "The Suburban Dislocation," *Annals of the American Academy of Political and Social Science*, 314 (Nov. 1957), 143; Riesman, Glazer, and Denny, *Lonely Crowd*, 141; David Riesman, "Some Observations on Changes in Leisure Attitudes" (1952), in Riesman, *Individualism Reconsidered and Other Essays* (Glencoe, Ill., 1954), 211-12; David Riesman, "Leisure and Work in Postindustrial Society" (1958), in Riesman, *Abundance for What?*, 166.

25. Nathanael West, *Miss Lonelyhearts & The Day of the Locust* (New York, 1969; orig. pub. 1933 and 1937), 178.

26. Gilbert, *City of the Angels*, 34; Morris, *Destinations*, 87-88.

27. Barash (trans.), *Man, Play, and Games*, 44-45.

28. Murphy, "Changing External Relations," 154-55.

29. See Riesman and Bloomberg, "Work and Leisure," 160.

30. Phillip H. Ault, *How to Live in California: A Guide to Work, Leisure, and Retirement There and in the Southwest* (New York, 1961), 288; A. Alvarez, "A Reporter at Large: The Biggest Game in Town—I," *New Yorker*, 59 (March 7, 1983), 80, 81; Pastier, "Architecture of Escapism," 29. Noel Coward described how casinos were arranged to provide effortless leisure; see Gilbert Millstein, "Mr. Coward Dissects Las Vegas," *New York Times Magazine*, June 26, 1955, p. 41.

31. Wilson, "Guide to Reagan Country," 40-41; Robert M. Fogelson, *The Fragmented Metropolis: Los Angeles, 1850-1930* (Cambridge, Mass., 1967), 198.

32. Erving Goffman, "Where the Action Is," *Interaction Ritual: Essays in Face-to-Face Behavior* (Chicago, 1967), 149-270, esp. 184-85, 216-17, 237, 260-61; D. M. Downes, B. P. Davies, M. E. David, and P. Stone, *Gambling, Work and Leisure: A Study Across Three Areas* (London, 1976), 16-17.

33. William S. Fairfield, "Las Vegas: The Sucker and the Almost-even Break," *Reporter*, 8 (June 9, 1953), 17; Best and Hillyer, *Las Vegas, Playtown U.S.A.*, 17, 25-26. On the increasingly "social" or "other-directed" nature of play in postindustrial society, turn to Riesman, Glazer, and Denny, *Lonely Crowd*, 287.

34. Hill, "Klondike in the Desert," 65; Horace Sutton, "Old Gamblers Fade Away," *Saturday Review*, 38 (Feb. 5, 1955), 28; Best and Hillyer, *Las Vegas, Playtown U.S.A.*, 76. On the sense of autonomy inherent in betting, see Robert D. Herman, *Gamblers and Gambling: Motives, Institutions, and Controls* (Lexington, Mass., 1976), 53; Darrell W. Bolen, "Sexual and Non-Sexual Factors in Gambling," *Sexual Behavior*, 1 (Oct. 1971), 82. The phrase "lonely crowd" of course stems from Riesman, Glazer, and Denny, *Lonely Crowd*.

35. Oscar Lewis, *Sagebrush Casinos; The Story of Legalized Gambling in Nevada* (Garden City, N.Y., 1953), 171, mentions the absence of women dealers in Las Vegas. Among those who noted women's "preference" for slot machines were: Jack Goodman, "Jackpot Jamboree," *New York Times Magazine*, Aug. 15,

1948, p. 30; Liebling, "Our Footloose Correspondents," 112; Paul Ralli, *Viva Vegas* (Hollywood, Calif., 1953), 56-57; Best and Hillyer, *Las Vegas, Playtown U.S.A.*, 17. Goffman, "Where the Action Is," 209, suggests that the pursuit of such "action" as gambling, and the related quest to define character, have largely been the province of men.

36. Wilson, "Guide to Reagan Country," 42-43; Downes, et al., *Gambling, Work and Leisure*, 24-26; Edward C. Devereux, Jr., "Gambling," in David L. Sills (ed.), *International Encyclopedia of the Social Sciences* (New York, 1968), VI: 58; Halevy, "Disneyland and Las Vegas," 512. In a 1949 dissertation directed by Talcott Parsons at Harvard University, "Gambling and the Social Structure: A Sociological Study of Lotteries and Horse Racing in Contemporary America," Edward C. Devereux, Jr., suggested that "the acquisitive materialism of full-blown consumer capitalism" was modifying American attitudes toward risk taking, and that in gambling people still aspired in some sense to behave as independent entrepreneurs had during the age of industrialization. See Devereux, "Gambling," VI: 58, for a summary.

37. Automobility in Los Angeles has been dissected by Banham, *Los Angeles*, ch. 11, and David Brodsly, *L. A. Freeway: An Appreciative Essay* (Berkeley, 1981).

38. Cited in Kaufman, "Best City," 206-7. See also Halevy, "Disneyland and Las Vegas," 513.

39. Herman, *Gamblers and Gambling*, 73, 74.

40. Goffman, "Where the Action Is," 198-99; *Review-Journal*, Feb. 25, 1954.

41. Wolfe, *Kandy-Kolored Tangerine-Flake Streamline Baby*, xvi; Aben Kandel, *The Strip* (New York, 1961), 17; Gladwin Hill, "Why They Gamble: A Las Vegas Survey," *New York Times Magazine*, Aug. 25, 1957, p. 27; Millstein, "Mr. Coward Dissects Las Vegas," 411.

42. Wolfe, *Kandy-Kolored Tangerine-Flake Streamline Baby*, 14; Best and Hillyer, *Las Vegas, Playtown U.S.A.*, 94; Alan Wykes, *Gambling* (London, 1964), 286.

43. Hill, "Klondike in the Desert," 65; Hill, "Why They Gamble: A Las Vegas Survey," 60; Sean O'Faolain, "The Coarse and Lovely Illusions of Las Vegas," *Holiday*, 20 (Sept. 1956), 58; *New York Times*, June 9, 1957. Las Vegas businessmen distinguished between a "non-producer," or professional gambler who contributed little to casino income, and a "producer," whose primary vocation was something besides gambling, and who promised the most profits for casinos, in Fairfield, "Las Vegas," 16.

44. Both players and operators were reluctant to admit how much money changed hands in casinos, so financial estimates were often likely to be lower than actual figures. See: "Las Vegas Strikes It Rich," *Life*, 22 (May 26, 1947), 99-105; Liebling, "Our Footloose Correspondents," 110; Robert Laxalt, "What Has Wide-open Gambling Done to Nevada?" *Saturday Evening Post*, 225 (Sept. 20, 1952), 45; Lucius Beebe, "Las Vegas," *Holiday*, 12 (Dec. 1952), 137; Leonard Slater, "Las Vegas: Nice People Live on Divorce, Gambling," *Newsweek*, 41 (April 20, 1953), 32; "Las Vegas: 'It Just Couldn't Happen,'" *Time*, 62 (Nov. 23, 1953), 30; Best and Hillyer, *Las Vegas, Playtown U.S.A.*, 7, 31; Gilbert Millstein, "Cloud on Las Vegas' Silver Lining," *New York Times Magazine*, March 18, 1956, pp. 63-64; *New York Times*, Oct. 19, 1958; Nevada Department of Highways, *Nevada Out-of-State Visitor Survey 1958* (n.p., 1959), table 8; Ed Reid, *Las Vegas: City Without Clocks* (Englewood Cliffs, N.J., 1961), 17; Peter Wyden, "How Wicked is Vegas?" in Richard Blackburn Taylor and Patricia Howell, *Las Vegas, City of Sin? The Inside Story*

From "Behind the Scenes" (San Antonio, 1963), 20; Ed Reid and Ovid Demaris, The Green Felt Jungle (New York, 1963), 95; Murphy, "Changing External Relations," 72-73.

45. Fairfield, "Las Vegas," 18; Murphy, "Changing External Relations," 96; Nevada Department of Highways, Out-of-State Visitor Survey 1958, p. 31.

46. Alarmed accounts of organized crime in Las Vegas included: Sidney Shallet (ed.), Crime in America, By Estes Kefauver (Garden City, N.Y., 1951), 233, and passim; Mary K. Hammond, "Legalized Gambling in Nevada," Current History, 21 (Sept. 1951), 177-79; New York Times, Dec. 6, 1951; Reid and Demaris, Green Felt Jungle, 6, and passim; Donald R. Cressey, Theft of a Nation: The Structure and Operations of Organized Crime in America (New York, 1969), 99-101, 294. Calmer accounts have been rendered by: Kaufman, "Best City," 190, 312-14; Mark Haller, "Bootleggers and American Gambling, 1920-1950," U. S. Commission on the Review of the National Policy Toward Gambling, Gambling in America: Appendix I (Washington, D.C., 1976), 131-32; Daniel Bell, "Crime as an American Way of Life," Antioch Review, 13 (June 1953), 136, 142; Steven Brill, The Teamsters (New York, 1978), 209-11; "Las Vegas: 'It Just Couldn't Happen,'" 30. Susan Berman, Easy Street (New York, 1981), esp. 18-19, provides a view from a daughter of one of the kingpins of organized crime in Las Vegas. A column in the Sun, May 2, 1951, typified the community's ambivalence toward experienced operators. Jerome Skolnick, House of Cards: Legalization and Control of Casino Gambling (Boston, 1978), explains the development of Nevada's system of taxation, licensing, and regulation, and furnishes the term "pariah industry," while William R. Eadington, "The Evolution of Corporate Gambling in Nevada," in William R. Eadington (ed.), The Gambling Papers . . . (Reno, 1982), VII:94-105, reviews the beginning years of taxation and regulation by the state.

47. Perry Bruce Kaufman, "City Boosters, Las Vegas Style," Journal of the American West, 13 (July 1974), 54, 57; Best and Hillyer, Las Vegas, Playtown U.S.A., ch. 11; Hill, "Klondike in the Desert," 67; Crampton, Complete Las Vegas, 57; Review-Journal, Jan. 28, 31, 1951; Daniel Lang, "Our Far-flung Correspondents: Blackjack and Flashes," New Yorker, 28 (Sept. 20, 1952), 103-4; Elizabeth Nelson Patrick (ed.), "Oral Interview of Cora Williams," in Elizabeth Nelson Patrick and Rita O'Brien, The Black Experience in Southern Nevada (Las Vegas, 1978), 8-9. The latter is a collection of transcripts of oral histories conducted during the late 1970s, available in Special Collections at the University of Nevada, Las Vegas.

48. Lang, "Our Far-flung Correspondents," 100, 105; Gladwin Hill, "Atomic Boom Town in the Desert," New York Times Magazine, Feb. 11, 1951, p. 14; O'Faolain, "Coarse and Lovely Illusions," 58; Best and Hillyer, Las Vegas, Playtown U.S.A., 103-4, 106; New York Times, June 9, 1957. Novelist Frank Waters gave more philosophical consideration to the juxtaposition of gambling resort and atomic test site in The Woman at Otowi Crossing (Denver, 1966), 244-51.

49. Kaufman, "City Boosters," 46-60; Maxwell Kelch, "Does Las Vegas Like Advertising?" Western Advertising, 49 (May 1947), 48; "Reno Challenged," Business Week, July 14, 1945, pp. 24, 26; Fairfield, "Las Vegas," 20-21.

50. Kaufman, "City Boosters," 57-58.

51. "Las Vegas' Industrial Hope," Business Week, Oct. 25, 1947, p. 28; Goodman, "Jackpot Jamboree," 30; Fairfield, "Las Vegas," 18, 20; Decker, "Economics of Legalized Gambling Industry," 53, 54; Review-Journal, Sept. 8, 1947.

52. Fairfield, "Las Vegas," 17, 19, 20; Lester Ben "Benny" Binion, "Some Recollections of a Texas and Las Vegas Gambling Operator" (MS of oral history interview, University of Nevada, Reno, Special Collections, 1975), 22, 78-79.

53. Beebe, "Las Vegas," 135; "Las Vegas: 'It Just Couldn't Happen,'" 30; Fairfield, "Las Vegas," 17, 20; *Sun*, Jan. 13, 1951. See also the account of casino owners conspiring, at the behest of United States Senator Patrick A. McCarran, to boycott an upstart newspaper, in Jerome E. Edwards, "The *Sun* and the Senator," *Nevada Historical Society Quarterly*, 24 (Spring 1981), 3-16.

54. Good accounts of the difficulties can be found in: David Kenyon Webster, "Las Vegas Bust? Slim Spending, Tough Competition Make Gambling City Fret," *Wall Street Journal*, 53 (Aug. 2, 1955), 1, 15; Kaufman, "Best City," 202-6; Duff, Anderson and Clark, *Las Vegas and Clark County, Nevada: A Summary of an Economic and Industrial Analysis* (Chicago, 1956), 4-5, 8, 13; "Las Vegas Hedges Its Bets," *Business Week*, Aug. 11, 1956, p. 157; *Sun*, July 14, Aug. 11, 1955; Millstein, "Cloud on Las Vegas' Silver Lining," 17, 63, 64; "Hotels: Snake Eyes in Las Vegas," *Time*, 66 (Sept. 19, 1955), 98; "Gambling Town Pushes Its Luck," *Life*, 38 (June 20, 1955), 25.

55. "Hotels: Snake Eyes in Las Vegas," 97; Millstein, "Cloud on Las Vegas' Silver Lining," 63-64; Charles N. Stabler, "Fades and Factories: Las Vegas and Reno Want More Industry to Back Dice Tables," *Wall Street Journal*, 56 (Jan. 22, 1957), 1; "Why the Big Boom in the Desert States?" *U. S. News and World Report*, 43 (Oct. 11, 1957), 84; *Sun*, July 15, Sept. 9, 1979.

56. The story of the Moulin Rouge has been told by: Kaufman, "Best City," 202; Elizabeth Nelson Patrick (ed.), "Oral Interview of William H. (Bob) Bailey," in Patrick and O'Brien (eds.), *Black Experience in Southern Nevada*, 5-8; Elizabeth Nelson Patrick (ed.), "The Black Experience in Southern Nevada," *Nevada Historical Society Quarterly*, 22 (Summer and Fall 1979), 209n., 212-15; "Gambling Town Pushes Its Luck," cover, 22, 23, 27; *New York Times*, May 22, Oct. 12, 1955.

57. Bob Bailey heard that other hotel owners in Las Vegas pressured lenders to foreclose on notes against the Moulin Rouge; Patrick (ed.), "Oral Interview of William H. (Bob) Bailey," 5-8. The watering of the company's stock is mentioned by Patrick (ed.), "Black Experience in Southern Nevada," 214-15. The reluctance of established owners to accept nonwhite patrons was discussed by Kaufman, "Best City," 364-70; Patrick, "Black Experience in Southern Nevada," *passim*; James Goodrich, "Negroes Can't Win in Las Vegas," *Ebony*, 9 (March 1954), 44-53. See the *Sun*, June 1, July 2, 1955, for mention of the interracial hotel's comparatively small debts and a warning that other owners would try to ensure its failure.

58. Paul Ralli, *Nevada Lawyer, A Story of Life and Love in Las Vegas* (Culver City, Calif., 1949), 297-98; Best and Hillyer, *Las Vegas, Playtown U.S.A.*, 85; Webster, "Las Vegas Bust?" 15; *New York Times*, June 9, 1957; "Las Vegas Hedges Its Bets," 158; *Sun*, July 3, 1955, Jan. 1-5, 1956; Binion, "Some Recollections," 22.

59. Webster, "Las Vegas Bust?" 1, 15; "Whose Glitter Gulch?" *Newsweek*, 52 (Sept. 29, 1958), 72; Kaufman, "Best City," 206. The euphemism comes from Fairfield, "Las Vegas," 20. For a recommendation that future expansion be regulated in Las Vegas, see Duff, Anderson and Clark, *Las Vegas and Clark County, Nevada*, 4, 5, 8, 13. On the startup methods used by the Hacienda Hotel, turn to Taylor and Howell, *Las Vegas, City of Sin?*, 58-68. Decker, "Economics of Legalized Gambling Industry," esp. 99, helpfully explains the nature of "industrial integration" among casinos.

60. Powdermaker, *Hollywood*, ch. 2.

61. The orientation of the Strip and its signs to cars has been discussed by Beebe, "Las Vegas," 137; Sid W. Meyers, *The Great Las Vegas Fraud* (Chicago, 1958), 28; Wolfe, *Kandy-Kolored Tangerine-Flake Streamline Baby*, 7; J. Meredith Neil, "Las Vegas on My Mind," *Journal of Popular Culture*, 7 (Fall 1973), 382; Crampton, *Complete Las Vegas*, 8-10. On the problems faced by pedestrians on the Strip, see the *Review-Journal*, May 21, 1957, and the *Sun*, March 12, 1961.

62. Banham, "Main Drag," 41.

63. Ian Fleming, *Diamonds Are Forever* (New York, 1956), 96; O'Faolain, "Coarse and Lovely Illusions," 58; Reid, *Las Vegas: City Without Clocks*, 20.

64. On restaurants, see Best and Hillyer, *Las Vegas, Playtown U.S.A.*, 112-14. On the Desert Inn, turn to Kaufman, "Best City," 218, and "Las Vegas: Sin and Sun Pay Off," *Business Week*, June 17, 1950, p. 23. The pool wars were covered by. Dick Pearce, "Pleasure Palaces," *Harper's Magazine*, 210 (Feb. 1955), 81; Horace Sutton, "Cowboys and Croupiers," *Saturday Review*, 43 (March 5, 1960), 32; Reid, *Las Vegas: City Without Clocks*, 26-27. The AAU or Amateur Athletic Union, an American sports organization, had substantial standards for the size of pools used for competitive swimming.

65. Lewis, *Sagebrush Casinos*, 207-8; A. J. Liebling, "Our Far-flung Correspondents: Out Among the Lamisters," *New Yorker*, 30 (March 27, 1954), 85; *New York Times*, June 9, 1957, May 28, 1961; Kaufman, "Best City," 214-16; Wolfe, *Kandy-Kolored Tangerine-Flake Streamline Baby*, 14-15.

66. Halevy, "Disneyland and Las Vegas," 511.

67. Pastier, "Architecture of Escapism," 27, 33-34, speaks to the importance of these borrowed cultural forms.

68. Banham, *Los Angeles*, 124.

69. Cited in Pomeroy, *In Search of the Golden West*, 16-17.

70. Figures on the location of motels and hotels come from the Las Vegas, Nevada, Chamber of Commerce, Research and Statistical Bureau, *Las Vegas Report 1961*, 14. Photographs of auto courts can be found in the *Review-Journal*, April 19, 1941, and Charles Hall Page & Associates, *City of Las Vegas: Historic Preservation Inventory and Planning Guidelines* (San Francisco, 1978), 65, 78, 79, 84.

71. Kaufman, "Best City," 170-73; Lewis, *Sagebrush Casinos*, 194-95; Reid, *Las Vegas: City Without Clocks*, 60-61; John F. Cahlan, "Reminiscences of a Reno and Las Vegas, Nevada Newspaperman, University Regent, and Public Spirited Citizen" (MS of oral history interview, University of Nevada, Reno, Special Collections, 1968), 121.

72. The adventures of Benjamin Siegel have been covered by Wolfe, *Kandy-Kolored Tangerine-Flake Streamline Baby*, 9-10; Berman, *Easy Street*, 19-23; Skolnick, *House of Cards*, 111-13. On plans for postwar construction, consult "Resort Hotel for Postwar Travelers," *Architectural Record*, 96 (Aug. 1944), 74-76; "Desert Hotel," *Architectural Forum*, 83 (Nov. 1945), 142-43; Kaufman, "Best City," 175-76.

73. Ralli, *Nevada Lawyer*, 281-82; Ralli, *Viva Vegas*, photographs; *Sun*, April 22, 1979; Best and Hillyer, *Las Vegas, Playtown U.S.A.*, 62-63; Wolfe, *Kandy-Kolored Tangerine-Flake Streamline Baby*, 9-10. Banham, *Los Angeles*, 124, notes that Siegel employed Douglas Honnold on the Flamingo project, an architect who later became a prominent figure in the Los Angeles profession.

74. *Review-Journal*, Dec. 27, 28, 30, 1946.

75. *Review-Journal*, March 1, 5, 1947; Cahlan, "Reminiscences of a Reno and Las Vegas, Nevada Newspaperman," 124-25.

76. *Review-Journal*, April 23, 1950; Slater, "Las Vegas: Nice People Live on Divorce, Gambling," 32; Lewis, *Sagebrush Casinos*, 200-201; Beebe, "Las Vegas," 108; "Gambling: Wilbur's Dream Joint," *Time*, 55 (May 8, 1950), 16-17; Ralli, *Viva Vegas*, photographs; Liebling, "Our Far-flung Correspondents," 82-84; Best and Hillyer, *Las Vegas, Playtown U.S.A.*, 64-67. The major hotels of Las Vegas have been discussed by George Stamos, Jr., in a 1979 series of articles titled "The Great Resorts of Las Vegas: How They Began," in Sunday issues of the *Sun*. On the Desert Inn, Sands, Sahara, and Thunderbird, see the *Sun*, May 6, 20, June 3, 17, 1979.

77. On the Tropicana and Stardust, consult the *Sun*, Sept. 3, 1961, Aug. 26, Sept. 9, 1979; *New York Times*, June 9, 1957; Reid, *Las Vegas: City Without Clocks*, 22-24, 26-27; Sutton, "Cowboys and Croupiers," 32; *Review-Journal*, April 4, 5, 1957.

78. Best and Hillyer, *Las Vegas, Playtown, U.S.A.*, 10; "Hotels: Snake Eyes in Las Vegas," 97; *New York Times*, May 19, 1963; Kaufman, "Best City," 201; *Sun*, Jan. 4, April 25, 1955, July 1, 1979.

79. *Sun*, Sept. 23, 1979; Skolnick, *House of Cards*, ch. 10.

80. *New York Times*, July 16, 1962; Allen Freeman, "Atlantic City Warily Welcomes a New Industry," *American Institute of Architects Journal*, 67 (Dec. 1978), 38.

81. Gubler, "Las Vegas: An International Recreation Center," 152-53.

82. "Las Vegas Hedges Its Bets," 157; Kaufman, "Best City," 207-9; Gubler, "Las Vegas: An International Recreation Center," 157-59; Reid, *Las Vegas: City Without Clocks*, 18-19; *Review-Journal*, May 31, 1959; *Sun*, June 12, 1959, July 29, 1979.

83. Waters, *Woman at Otowi Crossing*, 244.

84. Beebe, "Las Vegas," 107.

85. See the discussion of "the additive principle" in American life during the 1950s in Riesman, "The Suburban Dislocation," 127.

86. Morris, *Destinations*, 100, discusses changing Los Angeles.

Chapter 6

1. U. S. Senate Special Committee to Investigate Organized Crime in Interstate Commerce, *The Kefauver Committee Report on Organized Crime* (New York, 1951), 71-75; Sidney Shalett (ed.), *Crime in America, By Estes Kefauver* (Garden City, N.J., 1951), 232. See one local newspaperman's hostile reaction to the local committee hearing in the Las Vegas *Review-Journal*, Nov. 17, 1950, hereafter referred to as *Review-Journal*.

2. Joan Didion, *Slouching Towards Bethlehem* (New York, 1979; orig. pub. 1968), 90.

3. U. S. Bureau of the Census, *U. S. Census of Population: 1950*, v. II, *Characteristics of the Population*, Part 28, *Nevada* (Washington, D.C., 1952), 5; U. S. Bureau of the Census, *U. S. Census of Population: 1960*, v. I, *Characteristics of the Population*, Part 30, *Nevada* (Washington, D.C., 1963), 7, 9; Don Robinson Murphy, "The Role of Changing External Relations in the Growth of Las Vegas, Nevada" (Ph.D. diss., University of Nebraska, 1969), 51, 163; William T. White, Bernard Malamud, and John E. Nixon, *Socioeconomic Characteristics of Las Vegas, Nevada* (Las Vegas, 1975), 5.

4. Las Vegas, Nevada, Chamber of Commerce, Research and Statistical Bureau, *Las Vegas Report 1961* (Las Vegas, 1961), 5; "Why the Big Boom in the Desert States?" *U. S. News and World Report*, 43 (Oct. 11, 1957), 83; U. S. Bureau of the Census, *Statistical Abstract of the United States: 1955* (Washington, D.C., 1955), 295; U. S. Bureau of the Census, *Statistical Abstract of the United States: 1965* (Washington, D.C., 1965), 334, 343, 344; C. B. McClelland Co., *Report of Las Vegas, Nevada, Housing Survey, December, 1947* (Riverside, Calif., 1948), 5; Katharine Best and Katharine Hillyer, *Las Vegas, Playtown U.S.A.* (New York, 1955), 165-67; White, Malamud, and Nixon, *Socioeconomic Characteristics of Las Vegas*, 56; U. S. Bureau of the Census, *U. S. Census of the Population: 1950*, v. II, *Characteristics of the Population*, Part 28, *Nevada*, 29; U. S. Bureau of the Census, *U. S. Census of Population and Housing: 1960, Census Tracts: Las Vegas, Nev., SMSA* (Washington, D.C., 1961), 13; *Las Vegas Sun*, Jan. 11, 1955, hereafter referred to as *Sun*.

5. A. J. Liebling, "Our Far-flung Correspondents: Out Among the Lamisters," *New Yorker*, 30 (March 27, 1954), 78, 81; Paul Ralli, *Nevada Lawyer, A Story of Life and Love in Las Vegas* (Culver City, Calif., 1949), 285; William S. Fairfield, "Las Vegas: The Sucker and the Almost-even Break," *Reporter*, 8 (June 9, 1953), 16, 19; Best and Hillyer, *Las Vegas, Playtown U.S.A.*, 65; Hank Greenspun and Alex Pelle, *Where I Stand; The Record of a Reckless Man* (New York, 1966), 69.

6. Charles W. Fisher and Raymond J. Wells, *Living in Las Vegas, Some Social Characteristics, Behavior Patterns and Values of Local Residents* (Las Vegas?, 1967), 20; U. S. Bureau of the Census, *U. S. Census of Population: 1960*, v. I, *Characteristics of the Population*, Part 30, *Nevada*, 51, 88; U. S. Bureau of the Census, *U. S. Census of Population: 1960, Subject Reports, Mobility for States and State Economic Areas*, Final Report PC (2)-2B (Washington, D.C., 1963), 240-45, 275-79; U. S. Bureau of the Census, *U. S. Census of Population: 1960, Subject Reports, Migration Between State Economic Areas*, Final Report PC (2)-2E (Washington, D.C., 1967), 320; Liebling, "Our Far-flung Correspondents," 78, 81. For parallel statewide patterns, see U. S. Bureau of the Census, *U. S. Census of Population: 1950*, v. IV, *Special Reports*, Part 4, Chapter A, *State of Birth* (Washington, D.C., 1953), 14, 15, 19, 20-23; U. S. Bureau of the Census, *U. S. Census of the Population: 1950*, v. IV, *Special Reports*, Part 4, Chapter B, *Population Mobility—States and State Economic Areas* (Washington, D.C., 1956), 37.

7. Two-thirds of the people living in California during 1950 had not been born in the state. See James J. Parsons, "The Uniqueness of California," *American Quarterly*, 7 (Spring 1955), 53.

8. C. B. McClelland Co., *Report of Las Vegas Housing Survey*, 1; Lester Ben "Benny" Binion, "Some Recollections of a Texas and Las Vegas Gambling Operator" (MS of oral history interview, University of Nevada, Reno, Special Collections, 1975), 18; Fisher and Wells, *Living in Las Vegas*, 97; U. S. Bureau of the Census, *U. S. Census of Population: 1960, Subject Reports, Mobility for States and State Economic Areas*, 184. Statewide figures for 1949-1950 corroborated those for Clark County between 1955 and 1960. See U. S. Bureau of the Census, *U. S. Census of the Population: 1950*, v. IV, *Special Reports*, Part 4, Chapter B, *Population Mobility—States and State Economic Areas*, 31-32.

9. J. B. Priestley, *Midnight on the Desert; A Chapter of Autobiography* (London, 1937), 174-75.

10. *Review-Journal*, Nov. 24, 1949, June 30, 1943, April 24, 1947, Feb. 1, 1954; *Sun*, Feb. 16, 1961.

11. On water shortages and the slow process of acquiring an adequate supply, turn to Florence Lee Jones Cahlan and John F. Cahlan, *Water: A History of Las Vegas* (Las Vegas, 1975), I: 86, 135, 137, 144; II: 1; *Review-Journal*, June 30, 1943, Aug. 19, 1947, Oct. 11, 12, 1949; *Sun*, March 30, Oct. 25, 1955; Gloria Lewis, *Las Vegas . . . The Way It Was; Diary of a Pioneer Las Vegas Woman* (Las Vegas, 1979), 146, 154, 191 (a fictional diary grounded in real events); Charles N. Stabler, "Fades and Factories: Las Vegas and Reno Want More Industry to Back Dice Tables," *Wall Street Journal*, 56 (Jan. 22, 1957), 12. On city services, public facilities, and urban planning, consult the *Sun*, Jan. 1, 1961, May 15, 1959, March 15, Oct. 24, 1955, Jan. 23, 1956, March 18, 1959, April 12, 1960, March 12, 1961; *Review-Journal*, May 21, July 24, 1957; Best and Hillyer, *Las Vegas, Playtown U.S.A.*, 167-68; Elizabeth Nelson Patrick and Rita O'Brien (eds.), "Oral Interview of Ruth Sweet," in Elizabeth Nelson Patrick and Rita O'Brien (eds.), *The Black Experience in Southern Nevada* (Las Vegas, 1978), 15-16.

12. U. S. Bureau of the Census, *U. S. Census of the Population: 1950*, v. II, *Characteristics of the Population*, Part 28, *Nevada*, 5; U. S. Bureau of the Census, *U. S. Census of Housing: 1950*, v. I, *General Characteristics*, Part 4: Michigan–New York (Washington, D.C., 1953), 28-14, 28-15, 28-16; Richard English, "The Boom Came Back," *Collier's*, 110 (Aug. 22, 1942), 36-37, 48-49; *Review-Journal*, June 10, 1943; C. B. McClelland Co., *Report of Las Vegas Housing Survey*, 4-6.

13. U. S. Bureau of the Census, *U. S. Census of Population: 1960*, v. I, *Characteristics of the Population*, Part 30, *Nevada*, 7, 9; U. S. Bureau of the Census, *U. S. Census of Housing: 1960*, v. I, *States and Small Areas*, Part 5: Michigan–New Hampshire (Washington, D.C., 1963), 30-3, 30-11, 30-14, 30-17, 30-38; U. S. Bureau of the Census, *U. S. Census of Housing: 1960*, v. III, *City Blocks*, Series HC (3), No. 238, *Las Vegas, Nev.* (Washington, D.C., 1961), 1, 3; *Sun*, March 20, 1955, March 7, 1956; *Review-Journal*, Dec. 9, July 12, 1953, Jan. 13, March 7, 1960; Best and Hillyer, *Las Vegas, Playtown U.S.A.*, 169; Neil Bowen Morgan, *Westward Tilt, the American West Today* (New York, 1963), 312; Ward Herman Gubler, "Las Vegas: An International Recreation Center" (M.S. thesis, University of Utah, 1967), 140; Las Vegas, Nev., City Planning Commission (hereafter cited as LVCPC), *General Master Plan for the City of Las Vegas, Nevada* (Las Vegas, 1959), 22; Las Vegas, Nevada, Chamber of Commerce, Research and Statistical Bureau, *Las Vegas Report 1961*, 10; Las Vegas, Nevada, Chamber of Commerce, Research and Statistical Bureau, *Las Vegas Report: A Decade of Progress* (Las Vegas, 1966), 23.

14. English, "Boom Came Back," 49; Mary B. Kieser, *A History of Las Vegas Schools* (Las Vegas, 1977), 50, 52-53; *Review-Journal*, Oct. 5, 1949, April 27, 1954, Feb. 28, 1955; *Sun*, Sept. 15, 1951, Jan. 16, Sept. 23, 1955, Oct. 2, 1960, May 10, Sept. 3, 1961; Morgan, *Westward Tilt*, 312-13.

15. Two representative editorials can be located in the *Review-Journal*, June 10, 1947, and *Sun*, Sept. 12, 1955.

16. *Review-Journal*, April 29, 1954, April 24, July 4, 7, 1957; *Sun*, April 15, May 4, Sept. 25, Oct. 22, 1955, Feb. 5, March 4, April 29, 30, June 25, 1959, Jan. 8, 1961. Some Nevadans held big casino owners responsible for obstructing political channels. See the *Sun*, June 19, 1952; Edward F. Sherman, "Nevada: The End of the Casino Era," *Atlantic Monthly*, 218 (Oct. 1966), 112-16.

17. Perry Bruce Kaufman, "The Best City of Them All: A History of Las Vegas, 1930-1960" (Ph.D. diss., University of California, Santa Barbara, 1974), 541; Las Vegas, Nevada, Chamber of Commerce, Research and Statistical Bureau, *Las Vegas Report 1961*, 32; Robert E. Willard, "The Quantitative Significance of the Gaming Industry in the Greater Las Vegas Area" (Ph.D. diss., University of Arizona, 1968), vii-viii; *Sun*, Aug. 17, 1951; Morgan, *Westward Tilt*, 310.

18. Calculations to estimate the average percentage of tourists among the total population of greater Las Vegas are based on the following 1960 figures: 10 million tourists for the year (2 million stopping for the day only, or 0.5 days, and 8 million stopping for the average visit of 3 days and 2 nights, or 2.5 days), staying a mean of 2.1 days each, or 21 million tourist days annually, divided by 366 days for the leap year, amounting to just over 57,000 "tourist years," roughly half the resident population in Las Vegas Valley of approximately 120,000. Las Vegas, Nevada, Chamber of Commerce, Research and Statistical Bureau, *Las Vegas Report 1961*, 6, 7, 14; Gladwin Hill, "Klondike in the Desert," *New York Times Magazine*, June 7, 1953, p. 65; Sean O'Faolain, "The Coarse and Lovely Illusions of Las Vegas," *Holiday*, 20 (Sept. 1956), 58; White, Malamud, and Nixon, *Socioeconomic Characteristics of Las Vegas*, 5. Robert L. Decker, "The Economics of the Legalized Gambling Industry in Nevada" (Ph.D. diss., University of Colorado, 1961), 128, arrives at a slightly lower figure using 1958 data, and the *New York Times*, June 9, 1957, focusing solely on the population of the city proper of Las Vegas, calculated a higher figure for 1956.

19. *Sun*, Nov. 23, 24, 1955, Jan. 14, 1959; Paul Ralli, *Viva Vegas* (Hollywood, Calif., 1953), 35-36; Earl Pomeroy, *In Search of the Golden West: The Tourist in Western America* (New York, 1957), v-vi; Polly Redford, *Billion-Dollar Sandbar: A Biography of Miami Beach* (New York, 1970), 225.

20. On high crime rates in southern Nevada, consult Wesley Stout, "Nevada's New Reno," *Saturday Evening Post*, 215 (Oct. 31, 1942), 69; Albert Deutsch, "The Sorry State of Nevada," *Collier's*, 135 (March 18, 1955), 74; *Sun*, Dec. 1, 1955, Jan. 4, 1956; Richard Blackburn Taylor and Patricia Howell, *Las Vegas, City of Sin? The Inside Story From "Behind the Scenes"* (San Antonio, 1963), 7; Philip Richardson, "Effects of Legalized Gambling on Community Stability in the Las Vegas Area" (MS prepared for Twentieth Century Fund, on file at University of Nevada, Las Vegas, Special Collections, 1974), 17. The U. S. Commission on the Review of the National Policy Toward Gambling, *Gambling in America: Final Report* (Washington, D.C., 1976), 86-87, discussed the problem of crime in such resort cities as Las Vegas, Nevada, and Miami Beach and Daytona Beach, Florida. For a sampling of Las Vegans' defensive reactions, turn to the *Sun*, Oct. 10, 1955, Sept. 28, 1960; *Review-Journal*, Feb. 12, 1943; Taylor and Howell, *Las Vegas, City of Sin?*, 27. Charles L. Adams, "Las Vegas as Border Town: An Interpretive Essay," *Nevada Historical Society Quarterly*, 21 (Spring 1978), 51-55, explores the "shady" character of the resort by comparing it to disreputable border towns like El Paso, Texas, and Tijuana and Juarez in Mexico.

21. *Sun*, Jan. 18, 1951. See also the *Sun* editorial of June 11, 1960.

22. *Review-Journal*, Feb. 5, June 7, 9, July 3, 1943; "Las Vegas Twilight?" *Newsweek*, 35 (June 5, 1950), 24-25; *Sun*, May 8, June 7, 9, 1959, Jan. 28, March 12, May 12, 13, 14, 16, 1961; Peter Wyden, "How Wicked is Vegas?" in Taylor and Howell, *Las Vegas, City of Sin?* 27; Tom Wolfe, *The Kandy-Kolored Tangerine-Flake Streamline Baby* (New York, 1966; orig. pub. 1965), 11; U. S. Bureau of the

Census, *U. S. Census of Population: 1960*, v. I, *Characteristics of the Population*, Part 30, *Nevada*, 27-28.

23. *Sun*, May 29, 1955, April 14, 1960; Fisher and Wells, *Living in Las Vegas*, 56, 97-100.

24. Ralli, *Viva Vegas*, 38-39.

25. On the importance of children to 1950s suburban life, consult John R. Seeley, R. Alexander Sim, and Elizabeth W. Loosley, *Crestwood Heights: A Study of the Culture of Suburban Life* (New York, 1956).

26. Ralli, *Nevada Lawyer*, 3; *Review-Journal*, Nov. 1, 4, 1941; Greenspun and Pelle, *Where I Stand*, 68; Binion, "Some Recollections," 19; Susan Berman, *Easy Street* (New York, 1981), 42-43.

27. *Review-Journal*, Feb. 20, 1943, May 3, 1957; Ralli, *Nevada Lawyer*, 319; Kaufman, "Best City," 532-33.

28. Wyden, "How Wicked is Vegas?" 27; Fisher and Wells, *Living in Las Vegas*, 62-103; Richardson, "Effects of Legalized Gambling," ch. 9; Wolfe, *Kandy-Kolored Tangerine-Flake Streamline Baby*, 11.

29. Carl Abbott, *The New Urban America; Growth and Politics in Sunbelt Cities* (Chapel Hill, N.C., 1981), and Richard H. Bernard and Bradley R. Rice (eds.), *Sunbelt Cities: Politics and Growth Since World War II* (Austin, Tex., 1983), esp. 1-30, have staked out the Sunbelt, and Daniel Bell, *The Coming of Post-Industrial Society; A Venture in Social Forecasting* (New York, 1976), has speculated most systematically about postindustrialism, following in the footsteps of David Riesman. Abbott points out that the Sunbelt includes fast-growing southern as well as western cities, but discussion here is limited to urban areas of the Far West and Southwest.

30. See the provocative comments by Gerald D. Nash, "Stages of California's Economic Growth, 1870-1970: An Interpretation," in George H. Knoles (ed.), *Essays and Assays: California History Reappraised* (San Francisco, 1973), 52.

31. See depictions of "misguided" Southern Californians by Robert M. Fogelson, *The Fragmented Metropolis: Los Angeles, 1850-1930* (Cambridge, Mass., 1967), 195-98, 276; Michael Paul Rogin, "Southern California's Right-Wing Behavior and Political Symbols," in Michael Paul Rogin and John L. Shover, *Political Change in California: Critical Elections and Social Movements, 1890-1966* (Westport, Conn., 1970), ch. 6. The quotation regarding Las Vegas comes from A. Alvarez, "A Reporter at Large; The Biggest Game in Town—I," *New Yorker*, 59 (March 7, 1983), 109.

32. Students of society in Los Angeles and its suburbs may benefit from the approach of Robert Venturi, Denise Scott Brown, and Steven Izenour, *Learning from Las Vegas* (Cambridge, Mass., rev. ed., 1977), 3, 161-62, who suggest that critics of Las Vegas architecture should approach their subject "nonjudgmentally," that is without being "dissatisfied with existing conditions" at the outset, in order to come to a better understanding of "people's architecture as the people want it."

33. *Sun*, May 29, 1955.

34. LVCPC, *General Master Plan*, 71; U. S. Bureau of the Census, *Statistical Abstract of the United States: 1962* (Washington, D.C., 1962), 5, 562-64; Las Vegas, Nevada, Chamber of Commerce, Research and Statistical Bureau, *Las Vegas Report 1961*, 18; U. S. Bureau of the Census, *U. S. Census of Population: 1960*, v. I, *Characteristics of the Population*, Part 30, *Nevada*, 88; U. S. Bureau of the Census, *U. S. Census of Population and Housing: 1960, Census Tracts: Las Vegas,*

Nev., SMSA, 23; *Review-Journal*, Jan. 3, 1960. In 1960, according to *Las Vegas Report 1961*, 16, about one-quarter of all retail sales in Las Vegas were related to cars.

35. *Sun*, Aug. 8, 1952, May 28, 1961; Gubler, "Las Vegas: An International Recreation Center," 158. Maps published in Venturi, Brown, and Izenour, *Learning from Las Vegas*, 28-29, compare the dispersal of residents' markets and churches to the concentration of such tourist facilities as car rental agencies and wedding chapels.

36. Joan Didion, *The White Album* (New York, 1980; orig. pub. 1979), 180.

37. LVCPC, *General Master Plan*, 21, plate 6; Gubler, "Las Vegas: An International Recreation Center," 142-48; Murphy, "Changing External Relations," 122; *Sun*, May 5, 1959; John Gregory Dunne, *Vegas: A Memoir of a Dark Season* (New York, 1974), 20. One can trace the addition of subdivisions through the following maps: C. D. Baker (comp.), *Map of the City of Las Vegas Nevada* (n.p., 1940), Travel-Aid Distributors, *Map of Las Vegas, Nevada* (Las Vegas, 1947), *Welcome Map, Greater Las Vegas Area and Scenic Routes To and From There, Christmas Edition* (n.p., 1956), and Thomas Bros., *Las Vegas and Vicinity Street Map* (Los Angeles, 1961), all on file at the Map Room, Doe Library, University of California, Berkeley; and Redwood Publishing Company (comp.), *Map of the City of Las Vegas, North Las Vegas, the "Strip"* (Las Vegas, 1956), and Campbell Realty Company (comp.), *A General Map of Las Vegas* (Las Vegas, 1969), on file at University of Nevada, Las Vegas, Special Collections.

38. U. S. Bureau of the Census, *U. S. Census of Population and Housing: 1960, Census Tracts: Las Vegas, Nev., SMSA*, 21, 23; C. B. McClelland Co., *Report of Las Vegas Housing Survey*, 4; U. S. Bureau of the Census, *U. S. Census of Housing: 1950*, v. I, *General Characteristics*, Part 4: Michigan–New York, 28-14, 28-15, 28-16; U. S. Bureau of the Census, *U. S. Census of Housing: 1960*, v. I, *States and Small Areas*, Part 5: Michigan–New Hampshire, 30-3, 30-11, 30-14, 30-17, 30-18. By way of contrast, three-quarters of all new housing in Los Angeles during the early 1960s consisted of "multiple family structures," according to Christopher Rand, *Los Angeles: The Ultimate City* (New York, 1967), 30. On the cultural importance of private property and individual homes in Southern California, see James Q. Wilson, "A Guide to Reagan Country: The Political Culture of Southern California," *Commentary*, 43 (May 1967), 38, 40-41.

39. See the columns of A. E. Cahlan in the *Review-Journal*, May 14, 1953, Nov. 5, 1956, Jan. 15, 1960; *Sun*, Sept. 4, 1955.

40. U. S. Bureau of the Census, *U. S. Census of Population: 1960*, v. I, *Characteristics of the Population*, Part 1, *United States Summary* (Washington, D.C., 1964), 204, 205, 257, 258; U. S. Bureau of the Census, *U. S. Census of Population: 1960*, v. I, *Characteristics of the Population*, Part 30, *Nevada*, 51, 88; U. S. Bureau of the Census, *U. S. Census of Population: 1960, Subject Reports, Mobility for States and State Economic Areas*, 166; U. S. Commission on the Review of the National Policy Toward Gambling, "Survey of American Gambling Attitudes and Behavior," *Gambling in America: Final Report*, supplement: 381, 383.

41. On the gambler's confrontation with fate, see Erving Goffman, "Where the Action Is," *Interaction Ritual: Essays in Face-to-Face Behavior* (Chicago, 1967), 184-85, 216-17, 237, 260-62; D. M. Downes, B. P. Davies, M. E. David, and P. Stone, *Gambling, Work and Leisure: A Study Across Three Areas* (London, 1976), 16-17. For an example of the future-minded nature of Las Vegans, see: *Sun*, Jan. 6,

1951, Sept. 3, 1961; Jack Murray, *Las Vegas, Zoomtown U.S.A.* (Las Vegas, 1961), 162, 164.

42. Jude Wanniski, "Why Live in Las Vegas," *Review-Journal*, April 28, 1965; Adams, "Las Vegas as Border Town," 52, 55.

43. *Review-Journal*, March 19, 1943, Feb. 21, 1960; *Sun*, Jan. 17, 1951. See also Goffman's discussion of the individualism and toleration of Nevada in "Where the Action Is," 194.

44. The Sunbelt's attitude toward federal funds as venture capital for economic growth rather than money to conserve past gains was early recognized in Southern California by Wilson, "A Guide to Reagan Country," 43-45.

45. *Review-Journal*, Feb. 24, 1954; Deutsch, "Sorry State of Nevada," 75, 78, 81-82, 85; Kaufman, "Best City," 468-69; Morgan, *Westward Tilt*, 312; Ed Reid, *Las Vegas: City Without Clocks* (Englewood Cliffs, N.J., 1961), 135; Ed Reid and Ovid Demaris, *The Green Felt Jungle* (New York, 1963), 11.

46. Deutsch, "Sorry State of Nevada," 78, 80; Steve Fisher, *No House Limit* (New York, 1958), 163; *Sun*, Dec. 1, 1955; Kaufman, "Best City," 467. The importance of the police force to Las Vegans was discussed by A. J. Liebling, "Our Footloose Correspondents: Action in the Desert," *New Yorker*, 26 (May 13, 1950), 109; Best and Hillyer, *Las Vegas, Playtown U.S.A.*, 87.

47. Sherman, "Nevada: The End of the Casino Era," 112, 116, depicts some improvement in social welfare programs since the late 1950s, and Mary Ellen Glass, "Nevada Turning Points: The State Legislature of 1955," *Nevada Historical Society Quarterly*, 23 (Winter 1980), 223-35, pinpoints the beginnings of political reform during the mid-1950s. Peter A. Lupsha and William J. Siembieda, "The Poverty of Public Services in the Land of Plenty: An Analysis and Interpretation," in David C. Perry and Alfred J. Watkins (eds.), *The Rise of the Sunbelt Cities* (Beverly Hills, Calif., 1977), 169-90, discuss welfare trends in the urban Southwest during the mid-twentieth century.

48. Eight percent of the people in Clark County were black. See U. S. Bureau of the Census, *U. S. Census of Population and Housing: 1960, Census Tracts: Las Vegas, Nev., SMSA*, 13.

49. Best and Hillyer, *Las Vegas, Playtown U.S.A.*, 135, 137; James Goodrich, "Negroes Can't Win in Las Vegas," *Ebony*, 9 (March 1954), 47-49; Kaufman, "Best City," 369-70. The Mormon community may have contributed to hostility toward blacks in this era; see Elizabeth Nelson Patrick (ed.), "Oral Interview of William H. (Bob) Bailey," in Patrick and O'Brien (eds.), *Black Experience in Southern Nevada*, iii.

50. Elizabeth Nelson Patrick (ed.), "The Black Experience in Southern Nevada," *Nevada Historical Society Quarterly*, 22 (Summer and Fall 1979), 128, 132; Elizabeth Nelson Patrick and Rita O'Brien (eds.), "Oral Interview of Rev. Prentiss Walker," in Patrick and O'Brien (eds.), *Black Experience in Southern Nevada*, 1; Goodrich, "Negroes Can't Win in Las Vegas," 51-53; Kaufman, "Best City," 326-27, 334. Two early photographs appear to show blacks in local gaming halls with whites around 1910 and 1940; see Stanley W. Paher, *Las Vegas: As It Began—As It Grew* (Las Vegas, 1971), 127; "Wild, Woolly, and Wide-Open," *Look*, 4 (Aug. 13, 1940), 22.

51. Kaufman, "Best City," 327-31, 336, 340, 346-47, 350; Stout, "Nevada's New Reno," 71; Elizabeth Nelson Patrick (ed.), "Oral Interview of Lubertha Johnson," in Patrick and O'Brien (eds.), *Black Experience in Southern Nevada*, 2; Elizabeth

Nelson Patrick and Rita O'Brien (eds.), "Oral Interview of Lee Henry Lisby," in Patrick and O'Brien (eds.), *Black Experience in Southern Nevada*, 1-2, 10; Patrick and O'Brien (eds.), "Oral Interview of Rev. Prentiss Walker," 2-10; Patrick (ed.), "Black Experience in Southern Nevada," 128.

52. Patrick (ed.), "Black Experience in Southern Nevada," 136-38, 217; Patrick (ed.), "Oral Interview of William H. (Bob) Bailey," 12-13; Elizabeth Nelson Patrick (ed.), "Oral Interview of Cora Williams," in Patrick and O'Brien (eds.), *Black Experience in Southern Nevada*, 2-3; C. B. McClelland Co., *Report of Las Vegas Housing Survey*, 11; Goodrich, "Negroes Can't Win in Las Vegas," 52; U. S. Bureau of the Census, *U. S. Census of Housing: 1960*, v. III, *City Blocks*, Series HC (3), No. 238, *Las Vegas, Nev.*, 1, 3; Elizabeth Nelson Patrick (ed.), "Oral Interviews of Stella Parson and Rev. Claude H. Parson," in Patrick and O'Brien (eds.), *Black Experience in Southern Nevada*, 7, 10; Elizabeth Nelson Patrick and Rita O'Brien (eds.), "Oral Interview of Sarah Ann Knight," in Patrick and O'Brien (eds.), *Black Experience in Southern Nevada*, 18; Patrick (ed.), "Oral Interview of Lubertha Johnson," 8-9; *Sun*, April 13, 1951; *New York Times*, Jan. 11, 1965. The acronym VISTA stood for Volunteers in Service to America.

53. Goodrich, "Negroes Can't Win in Las Vegas," 45-47, 49-50, 53; Patrick (ed.), "Black Experience in Southern Nevada," 134, 138-39, 140; *New York Times*, Oct. 19, 1958; Patrick (ed.), "Oral Interview of William H. (Bob) Bailey," 1-2, 14-15, 25; Rita O'Brien (ed.), *West Las Vegas at the Crossroads: A Forum* (Las Vegas, 1977), 21; Elizabeth Nelson Patrick and Rita O'Brien (eds.), "Oral Interview of Arlone Scott," in Patrick and O'Brien (eds.), *Black Experience in Southern Nevada*, 5.

54. Best and Hillyer, *Las Vegas, Playtown U.S.A.*, 137-38; *Sun*, March 18, 24, 26, 27, 1960; *Review-Journal*, March 15, 1954, March 17, 25, 1960; Patrick (ed.), "Black Experience in Southern Nevada," 217, 217n., 218; *New York Times*, March 12, 1960, July 16, 1961, Oct. 7, 11, 1969.

55. Deutsch, "Sorry State of Nevada," 85; *New York Times*, Nov. 18-22, Dec. 1, 1963; *Sun*, March 20, 1955.

56. Morris Ploscowe and Edwin J. Lukas (eds.), "Gambling," *Annals of the American Academy of Political and Social Science*, 269 (May 1950), 17-19; Sid W. Meyers, *The Great Las Vegas Fraud* (Chicago, 1958), 19-21, 34; *Review-Journal*, Feb. 12, 1943 (reprint of opinion voiced by Los Angeles judge); Reid and Demaris, *Green Felt Jungle*, 1; Morgan, *Westward Tilt*, 318. The quotation comes from John Haase, "Las Vegas, Our Home Town," *Los Angeles Times' West Magazine*, Oct. 8, 1967, p. 29. Local papers naturally publicized more positive evaluations, too; see the *Sun*, Sept. 23, 1955.

57. U. S. Bureau of the Census, *U. S. Census of the Population: 1950*, v. II, *Characteristics of the Population*, Part 28, *Nevada*, 11; U. S. Bureau of the Census, *U. S. Census of Population: 1960*, v. I, *Characteristics of the Population*, Part 30, *Nevada*, 51; Wyden, "How Wicked is Vegas?" 27; Carey McWilliams, "Legalized Gambling Doesn't Pay," *Nation*, 171 (Nov. 25, 1950), 483. The Hughes comment is cited by Ralph Pearl, *Las Vegas Is My Beat* (Seacaucus, N.J., rev. ed., 1978), 145. Stabler, "Fades and Factories," 12, discussed the precautions taken by local employers to limit gaming among their workers.

58. Mary K. Hammond, "Legalized Gambling in Nevada," *Current History*, 21 (Sept. 1951), 179.

59. The quotations come from the *Sun*, Feb. 14, April 25, 1955. See also: *Sun*, Oct. 10, 1955, Sept. 3, 1961; *Review-Journal*, May 11, 1938, July 31, Oct. 2, 1940, Nov. 3, 1953; Alvarez, "Reporter at Large—I," 77; Haase, "Our Home Town," 21; "Wild, Woolly, and Wide-Open," 21; *New York Times*, March 24, 1946; "Las Vegas Twilight?" 24; Hill, "Klondike in the Desert," 67; Best and Hillyer, *Las Vegas, Playtown U.S.A.*, 78; Horace Sutton, "Cowboys and Croupiers," *Saturday Review*, 43 (March 5, 1960), 32; Grant Sawyer, "Remarks of Governor Grant Sawyer, State of Nevada," in *An Inter-Agency and Community Approach to Youth Problems; Papers presented at the Second Annual Institute, Nevada Council on Crime and Delinquency* (Boulder, Colo., 1964), 53; Fisher and Wells, *Living in Las Vegas*, 19; C. Gregory Crampton, *The Complete Las Vegas* (Salt Lake City, 1976), 60.

60. Robert Laxalt, "What Has Wide-open Gambling Done to Nevada," *Saturday Evening Post*, 225 (Sept. 20, 1952), 129; *Sun*, Nov. 23, 1955; Stabler, "Fades and Factories," 12; Fisher and Wells, *Living in Las Vegas*, 5; Liebling, "Our Footloose Correspondents," 107; *New York Times*, Nov. 6, 1960; *Los Angeles Times*, May 24, 1939. Las Vegans typically gambled more than other Americans, according to the U. S. Commission on the Review of the National Policy Toward Gambling, *Gambling in America: Final Report*, 58, 60, 61, 74; Betty Yantis, William J. Corney, John E. Nixon, and Jeffrey Baxter, "The Participation of Locals in the Resort Industry" (paper presented at Annual Conference on Gambling, Reno, 1978; on file at University of Nevada, Las Vegas, Special Collections), 2, 4. The information on the Talleyho and other casino-less hotels comes from the *Sun*, Sept. 23, 1979; *New York Times*, May 13, 1962, Nov. 18, 1963; Gubler, "Las Vegas: An International Recreation Center," 151n.

61. *Sun*, Jan. 30, 1951; Gladwin Hill, "Atomic Boom Town in the Desert," *New York Times Magazine*, Feb. 11, 1951, p. 14; *Review-Journal*, Jan. 12, 1951. The atomic testing episode has been reviewed by A. Costandina Titus, "A-Bombs in the Backyard: Southern Nevada Adapts to the Nuclear Age, 1951-1963," *Nevada Historical Society Quarterly*, 26 (Winter 1983), 235-54.

62. Daniel Lang, "Our Far-flung Correspondents: Blackjack and Flashes," *New Yorker*, 28 (Sept. 20, 1952), 100, 109-10; *Review-Journal*, Jan. 16, 31, 1951, May 24, 1953, May 12, 1957; Edgerton, Germeshansen, and Grier, Inc., *The Nevada Test Site and Southern Nevada* (Las Vegas, 1961), 12-13; *Sun*, Dec. 16, 1955, April 12, 1959.

63. *Sun*, Jan. 31, 1951, Sept. 3, 1961, Oct. 6, 1960; *Review-Journal*, March 1, 1954.

64. Las Vegas, Nevada, Chamber of Commerce, Research and Statistical Bureau, *Las Vegas Report 1961*, 32; *Sun*, Sept. 3, 1961, March 12, 1959; "Las Vegas Hedges Its Bets," *Business Week,* Aug. 11, 1956, p. 157; Morgan, *Westward Tilt*, 314-15; Sherman, "Nevada: The End of the Casino Era," 113; Taylor and Howell, *Las Vegas, City of Sin?* 113. The nearby town of Henderson was reluctant, on the other hand, to accept wide-open gaming because it might threaten its industrial economic base; see the *Review-Journal*, Feb. 28, 1954.

65. *Sun*, Jan. 24, 1956, May 24, 1961; John F. Cahlan, "Reminiscences of a Reno and Las Vegas, Nevada Newspaperman, University Regent, and Public Spirited Citizen" (MS of oral history interview, University of Nevada, Reno, Special Collections, 1968), 215-16; Stabler, "Fades and Factories," 1, 12; "Las Vegas Hedges Its

Bets," 157-58; *Review-Journal*, Oct. 29, Dec. 6, 1956; LVCPC, *General Master Plan*, 9-10.

66. *Review-Journal*, Aug. 18, 1947; Laxalt, "What Has Wide-open Gambling Done to Nevada," 45.

67. *Sun*, Aug. 11, 1951, Dec. 1, 16, 1954, April 29, 1959, Jan. 7, 1961; Las Vegas, Nevada, Chamber of Commerce, Research and Statistical Bureau, *Las Vegas Report 1961*, 15; Richard P. Cooke, "Las Vegas Making Pitch for Conventions At New Center to Fill Monday-Friday Lull, *Wall Street Journal*, 60 (April 20, 1959), 6; "Las Vegas Goes Respectable," *Economist*, 194 (Feb. 13, 1960), 627; *Review-Journal*, April 1-5, 10, 16, 20, 21, 1959, March 8, 1960; Murphy, "Changing External Relations," 62-66. LVCPC, *General Master Plan*, 16, advocated in 1959 more conventions, along with more diverse types of recreational facilities, as means to achieve greater "balance" within the tourist trade.

68. In this regard, Las Vegans imitated the "steadfast dedication" of early Southern Californians to their similarly divided city, an attachment that made average citizens "unparalleled boosters" of Los Angeles according to Fogelson, *Fragmented Metropolis*, 189-90.

Epilogue

1. *New York Times*, Nov. 29, 1967, May 17, 1970; Jerome Skolnick, *House of Cards: Legalization and Control of Casino Gambling* (Boston, 1978), 134-40; William R. Eadington, "The Evolution of Corporate Gambling in Nevada," in William R. Eadington (ed.), *The Gambling Papers . . .* (Reno, 1982), VII: 106-7.

2. *New York Times*, Nov. 22, 1980; Peter Wiley and Robert Gottlieb, *Empires in the Sun: The Rise of the New American West* (New York, 1982), 207-8; Skolnick, *House of Cards*, 142-45; Eadington, "Evolution of Corporate Gambling," VII: 107-9.

3. *New York Times*, April 17, June 26, 1972; Robert Alan Aurthur, "Hanging Out," *Esquire*, 81 (Feb. 1974), 30.

4. *New York Times*, Feb. 16, 1984, March 16, 1970, March 12, 16, 1976.

5. "Notes and Comment," *New Yorker*, 42 (Aug. 20, 1966), 25-26; *New York Times*, Nov. 22, 1980.

6. John Pastier, "The Architecture of Escapism: Disney World and Las Vegas," *American Institute of Architects Journal*, 67 (Dec. 1978), 32.

7. *1981 Las Vegas Perspective* (Las Vegas, 1981), 3.

8. Greater Las Vegas Chamber of Commerce, *Greater Las Vegas 1976* (Las Vegas, 1976), 12, 13, 15; Greater Las Vegas Chamber of Commerce, *Greater Las Vegas 1981* (Las Vegas, 1981), 27; Greater Las Vegas Chamber of Commerce, *Greater Las Vegas 1983* (Las Vegas, 1983), 7; *1981 Las Vegas Perspective*, 52; Henry A. Sciullo and Lawrence Dandurand, "A Strategic Profile of the Los Angeles Market" (paper submitted to the 10th Anniversary Conference of the Travel Research Association, June 3-6, 1979, San Antonio, Texas, and on file at University of Nevada, Las Vegas, Special Collections).

9. *New York Times*, Sept. 26, 1973, Feb. 16, 1984; A. Alvarez, "A Reporter at Large; The Biggest Game in Town—I," *New Yorker*, 59 (March 7, 1983), 60. The quotation comes from Robert G. Kaiser and Jon Lowell, *Great American Dreams: A Portrait of the Way We Are* (New York, 1979), 173, 253.

10. *New York Times*, Feb. 2, 3, 1978.

11. *1981 Las Vegas Perspective*, 3-5; Kaiser and Lowell, *Great American Dreams*, 68; *New York Times*, April 17, 1982.

12. Wiley and Gottlieb, *Empires in the Sun*, 211-12.

13. *New York Times*, Dec. 12, 1973; Paula Rene Adamo, "The Effects of the 1979 Gasoline Shortage on the Las Vegas Resort Economy" (M.A. thesis, University of Nevada, Las Vegas, 1983), 47, 50-52.

14. Duane James Rosa, "Differential Impacts of Recent National Recessions on a City's Closely Related Base and Support Sectors" (M.A. thesis, University of Nevada, Las Vegas, 1981), 77-78; *New York Times*, Dec. 15, 1982. Figures describing economic trends can be found in the annual reports of the Greater Las Vegas Chamber of Commerce, entitled *Greater Las Vegas 1976* through *Greater Las Vegas 1983* (Las Vegas, 1976-83).

15. Gilbert Geis, *Not the Law's Business: An Examination of Homosexuality, Abortion, Prostitution, Narcotics, and Gambling in the United States* (New York, 1979; orig. pub. 1972), 224.

16. George Sternlieb and James W. Hughes, *The Atlantic City Gamble, A Twentieth Century Fund Report* (Cambridge, Mass., 1983), 2-6, 43, 59; Charles Stansfield, "Atlantic City and Casinos: Gambling as Rescuer of a Foundering Resort" (paper on file at University of Nevada, Las Vegas, Special Collections, 1979), 5, 6, 10, 14.

17. Allen Freeman, "Atlantic City Warily Welcomes a New Industry," *American Institutue of Architects Journal*, 67 (Dec. 1978), 38, 40, 44; Sternlieb and Hughes, *Atlantic City Gamble*, 60-61; Ian Walker, "City of the Giant Vultures," *New Society*, 49 (Aug. 16, 1979), 359; E. J. Kahn, Jr., "Our Far-flung Correspondents: The Only Game in Town," *New Yorker*, 54 (Dec. 18, 1978), 124, 126, 127.

18. *San Francisco Chronicle*, March 17, April 19, 1981; *New York Times*, June 23, 1981; David May and Mark Hosenball, "Atlantic City Goldrush," *Sunday Times Magazine*, Sept. 28, 1980, pp. 62-77; Sternlieb and Hughes, *Atlantic City Gamble*, 18-25, 172, 177, chs. 5-8.

19. *New York Times*, June 23, 1981, Aug. 29, 30, Dec. 15, 1982, Feb. 20, 1983.

20. *New York Times*, Aug. 30, 31, 1982, Feb. 20, 1983; Sternlieb and Hughes, *Atlantic City Gamble*, 92-93, 164-66.

Index

265